Defense in Depth

IEEE Press
445 Hoes Lane
Piscataway, NJ 08854

Defense in Depth

Modern Cybersecurity Strategies and Evolving Threats

Edited by

Hewa Majeed Zangana
Duhok Polytechnic University
Iraq

IEEE Press
WILEY

Published by John Wiley & Sons, Inc., Hoboken, New Jersey.
Published simultaneously in Canada.

Library of Congress Cataloging-in-Publication Data applied for

Hardback ISBN: 9781394340729

Cover Design: Wiley
Cover Image: © Xuanyu Han/Getty Images

Set in 9.5/12.5pt STIXTwoText by Straive, Chennai, India
Printed and bound by CPI Group (UK) Ltd, Croydon, CR0 4YY

C9781394340729_250925

Contents

Editor Biography

Hewa Majeed Zangana is an Assistant Professor at Duhok Polytechnic University (DPU), Iraq, and a PhD candidate in Information Technology Management. He has over 15 years of academic and administrative experience and served in key roles such as Acting Dean of the College of Computer and IT at Nawroz University, Head of the Computer Science Department, Director of the Curriculum Division at DPU, and Manager of the Information Unit at DPU's Research Center.

His research expertise spans network systems, cybersecurity, computer vision, intelligent systems, and Information Technology, with a strong focus on integrating classical methods and advanced AI-driven approaches. Dr. Zangana has authored and co-authored numerous peer-reviewed journal articles, conference papers, and more than ten academic books with IGI Global, of which several are indexed in Scopus and Web of Science (Clarivate). His work appears in respected outlets such as *IEEE, EAI Endorsed Transactions on AI and Robotics, Sistemasi, BAMJ,* and others.

In addition to his prolific research output, he actively contributes to the academic community as a reviewer, editorial board member, and scientific committee member. He currently serves on the Editorial Board of *EAI Endorsed Transactions on AI and Robotics* (Scopus Q2), alongside roles with other international journals and organizations. Dr. Zangana is also an active member of several professional associations, including the European Alliance for Innovation (EAI), International Association of Engineers (IAENG), and the Computer Science Teachers Association (CSTA).

Fluent in Kurdish, Arabic, and English, Dr. Zangana continues to contribute to advancing knowledge in AI, cybersecurity, and IT management while mentoring future generations of scholars and practitioners in Iraq and beyond.

List of Contributors

Luay Albtosh
Capitol Technology University
Laurel
MD
USA

Sia Gholami
The Institute of Electrical and Electronics Engineers
San Francisco
CA
USA

Rebet Keith Jones
Cyber and Information Security Department
Capitol Technology University
Laurel
Maryland
USA

Jamal N. Al-Karaki
College of Interdisciplinary Studies (CIS)
Zayed University Abu Dhabi
UAE

Derek Mohammed
College of CARDS
Saint Leo University
FL
USA

Marwan Omar
Information Technology and Management
Illinois Institute of Technology
Chicago
USA

Hewa Majeed Zangana
IT Department
Duhok Technical College
Duhok Polytechnic University
Duhok
Iraq

Preface

The advances in cyber technology have evolved quickly and are now altering the security horizons for organizations and users. With threats evolving in terms of both scale and frequency, it becomes unlikely that a competent and efficient defense strategy will suffice. This book, Defense in Depth: Modern Cybersecurity in its Spectrum: Threats and Innovative Approaches, spells out the complexities of modern cybersecurity and proffers a solid ground on how to combat current threats and prepare for future ones. In this volume, scholars from academia, industry, and research organizations offer their work on defense-in-depth strategies and tools. Since this approach is based on an overlapping paradigm, an attacker who has penetrated one layer is still locked out of the rest of the layers. Recognizing that the "what" can just as readily be applied as the "why," the book aims to provide its readers with direct utility and a more profound perspective on contemporary cybersecurity.

The objectives of this book are as follows:

1) **Enhance Awareness of Evolving Threats**: Acquaint the participants with current threats that exist in organizations and societies, and their effects on important systems.
2) **Promote Advanced Defense Strategies**: Emphasize contemporary techniques, including artificial intelligence, decentralized databases in a blockchain format, and human-centered approaches to strengthening security.
3) **Bridge Theory and Practice**: Discuss examples and case studies to illustrate specific defense strategies in practice.
4) **Chart the Path for Future Innovation**: Discuss new technologies and future anticipations that will shape the future of cybersecurity.

The book is intended for such readers as professionals and academicians in cybersecurity, researchers, students, and decision-makers who wish to advance their knowledge of modern and sophisticated defense strategies. All in all, readers, whether beginners or professionals in the field, will learn something from the different angles that were considered.

Organization of the Book

The chapters are arranged to guide readers from foundational concepts to advanced applications and forward-thinking perspectives:

1) **Introduction to Modern Cybersecurity**
   A brief insight into present-day security threats and the importance of cybersecurity.
2) **Evolving Cyber Threats: Understanding the New Battlefield**
   Information on emerging new-generation threats in cyberspace and their repercussions.

3) **Defense in Depth: A Multilayered Approach**
   A brief analysis of the layered security model, focusing on its significance for building resilient systems.
4) **The Role of Artificial Intelligence in Cybersecurity**
   How AI technologies are changing threat detection and response at the C-Suite level.
5) **Blockchain Technology: Enhancing Security in a Decentralized World**
   The importance of blockchain in checking data accuracy and enhancing security in transactions.
6) **Human Factors in Cybersecurity: The Weakest Link**
   Introducing the role of the human factor in cybersecurity, the place of training, and understanding human behavior.
7) **Advanced Defense Techniques: Beyond Traditional Security Measures**
   Discussions on new-generation security technologies to reduce the chances of such attacks.
8) **Practical Applications and Case Studies**
   Practical instances describing how and when defense strategies are utilized.
9) **Future Directions in Cybersecurity**
   New directions, new technologies, and the future of cybersecurity.
10) **Conclusion: Building a Resilient Cyber Defense Framework**
    Integration of lessons learnt from the preceding chapters for the building of both **a** robust and flexible security framework.

In Conclusion

With the ever-growing globalization, the risks associated with cybersecurity have never been higher in today's world. "Defense in Depth: Modern Cybersecurity Strategies and Evolving Threats" offers readers the means for an objective analysis of modern cybersecurity solutions, alongside viable models for facing future threats. It is our desire to see this book help engage in innovation, collaboration, and determination in creating organizational systems that can sustain the threat of a constantly shifting cyber environment.

Editor

Hewa Majeed Zangana
Duhok Polytechnic University—Iraq

1

Introduction to Modern Cybersecurity

Hewa Majeed Zangana

IT Department, Duhok Technical College, Duhok Polytechnic University, Duhok, Iraq

1.1 Overview of Cybersecurity Evolution

This shows that the field of cybersecurity has gone through several changes in the last few decades, starting with technical barriers to developing a powerful mechanism that represents a defense against numerous threats. Cryptography earlier was aimed at ensuring that data and systems were protected from access by any unauthorized individuals' rudimentary concept of firewalls and antivirus programs [1]. However, with the advancement of digital disruption, intent became to establish complex cyber threats, which, in turn, called for further enhanced strategies and measures [2, 3].

In the early 2000s, cybersecurity advanced to reacting to the more emergence of network systems as the technological world extended a broader phase of the digitalization of facilities. In this period, new ideas appeared, for instance, the defense in depth (DiD) idea that promoted protection in layers, protecting data, networks, and systems [4]. This strategy became particularly valuable in an era where an isolated defensive element posed is not enough to address better and synchronized attacks [5]. The measures taken in further reach of the first decade of the twenty-first century became concerned with early threat recognition and prevention as new forms of threats—advanced persistent threats, as well as more evolved forms of malicious software began to appear [6, 7]. It also witnessed the development of the cryptographic processes for communicating sensitive information securely in complicated networks and on an international level [8]. Today, cybersecurity is facing new challenges resulting from technologies such as artificial intelligence (AI), cloud computing, and Internet of Things (IoT). These innovations have developed new risks, solidifying the need to consider security that is enriched as a constituent part of the ongoing growth of technology [9, 10]. Furthermore, even the frameworks and industry standard like NIST cybersecurity framework is vital in leading organization's toward practices that are both relevant to current and new threats [11, 12].

Cybersecurity is expected to remain an evolving field in the foreseeable future as new technologies are developed and new forms of attacks appear. The call for the collaborative and cross-sectoral approaches, along with the integration of AI in threat analysis, are some of the strategic imperatives that could be seen as defining the further development of the field [13, 14]. Such evolution emphasizes the need not only for sound and effective technical countermeasures but also for proactive and innovative approaches able to contain and prevent the rather fluid and ever-changing nature of cyber threats [15]. Successful cybersecurity transition from first-level technical solutions

Defense in Depth: Modern Cybersecurity Strategies and Evolving Threats, First Edition. Edited by Hewa Majeed Zangana.

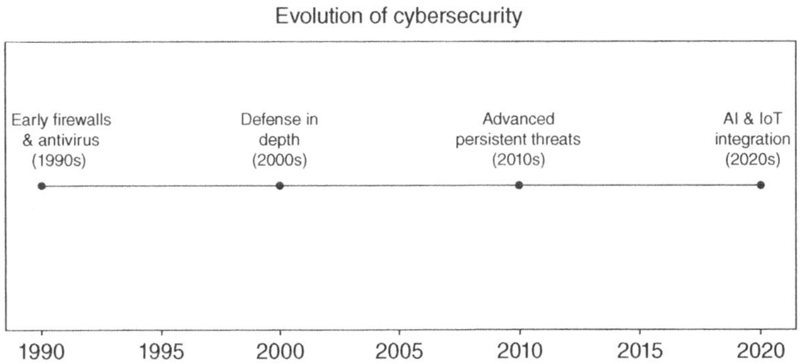

Figure 1.1 Evolution of cybersecurity. Source: Hewa Majeed Zangana.

to complex approaches is crucial for comprehending present threat environment. The following timeline highlights the latter distilling cybersecurity throughout the important phases discovered and the primary milestones that led to the evolution of the present-day cybersecurity technology (Figure 1.1).

1.2 Current Cyber Threat Landscape

The contemporary cyberspace threat environment is complex and constantly evolving in response to innovation in technologies, the evolving character of threat actors, and the escalating complexity and proliferation of attack methods. Advanced threats aims to attack personal and corporate networks in different fields such as banking, medical, infrastructure, and agricultural, hence the need to implement cybersecurity solutions across the board [6, 16]. The aimed threat actors are manifold and so are the sectors they are going after. The bar chart in Figure 1.2 below provides the analysis of the most-hit sectors depicting the proportional risk of an attack on sectors like finance, health, and other sensitive sectors.

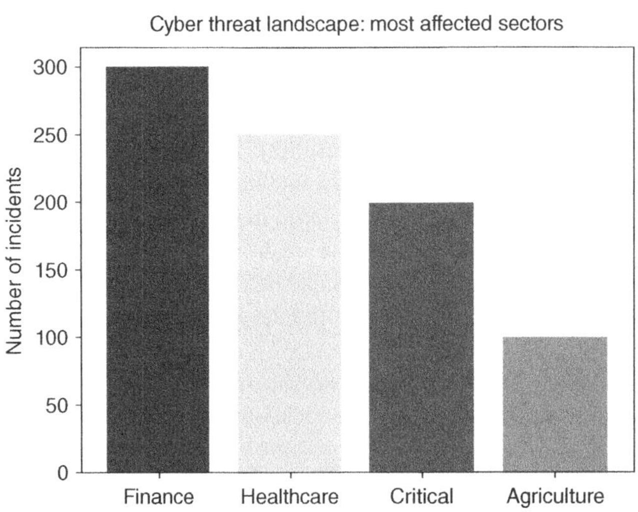

Figure 1.2 Modern cyber threat landscape. Source: Hewa Majeed Zangana.

In this section, basic information about the main cyber threat actors, familiar types of attacks, and general consequences of threats in societies are mentioned.

1.2.1 Threat Actors: Evolving Motives and Techniques

The world of cyber threats is full of different actors: cybercriminals, state actors, hacktivists, and insiders. Hackers are normally, largely motivated by funds and consequently exploit cracks in an organization's security layout, embracing, for instance, ransomware and phishing [4, 17].

There are the nation-states that act for purely political, economic, or military benefits and gains; they hack and steal; they propagate malware; they attack infrastructures. The last few years have witnessed a rise in professionalized nation-state actions, indicating the new trend toward using cyberspace as a cyber weapon in world affairs [15, 18]. Quite peculiar are insider risks; it is one thing to have an employee payday and another to watch as insiders exploit their privileged status, either intentionally or through sheer ignorance, causing great harm to organizations [2]. The ability of external actors to get insider access due to utilizing social engineering as a tool has led to the development of frequent insider attacks, whereby the employees are forced to relinquish sensitive information [3, 7].

1.2.2 Common Types of Cyberattacks

The threats have advanced from simple penetration to methods that can bypass usual security measures. Some of the most prevalent attack types include:

- **Malware and Ransomware**: Computer viruses such as viruses and worms, and ransomware are still one of the most widespread threats. Ransomware, in specific, has gained meaning as aggressors go after firms and authorities, locking files and seeking an exchange for the unlock. The particular technique is rather invasive and expensive, with some substantive services being stopped in the course of incidents [10, 19].
- **Phishing and Social Engineering**: A common evidence of cyberspace attacks is phishing which is useful for creating an entry point and can compromise individuals into discharging private or sensitive data or installing malicious software. Social engineering, which is a form of advanced phishing, rely on manipulation of the target; it's risky given that it targets weaknesses in people as opposed to the technical [17, 20].
- **Distributed Denial of Service (DDoS) Attacks**: These involve overloading the network resources with traffic that results in services being unavailable for a while. These attacks are usually carried out by hacktivists or nation states for the purpose of causing havoc toward economic loss, apposite in attacks on financial and government websites as pointed out in Refs. [21, 22].
- **Advanced Persistent Threats (APTs)**: APTs are long-term system attacks that are often implemented by advanced threat agents to gain access to systems and neighbor undisturbed. Such attacks are aimed at extorting personal data or obtaining persistent access, and such attacks are prevalently used by nation-states in cyber spying [11, 14].

It is very important to learn about various forms of cyber threats to be able to effectively identify suitable measures to protect an organization. The following piece of the pie chart in Figure 1.3 shows the distribution of frequency of common cyber threats such as malware, phishing, ransomware, etc.

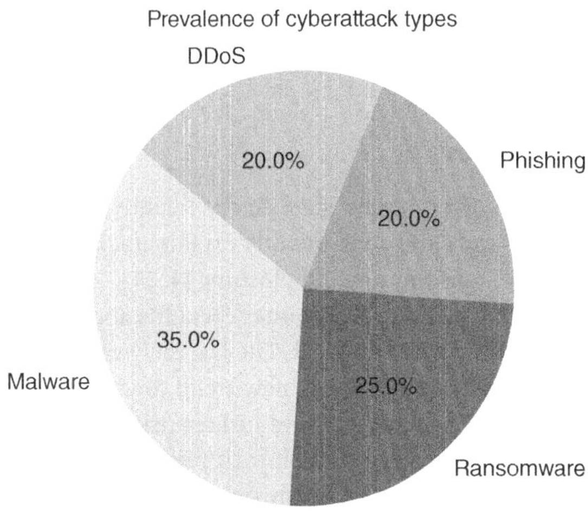

Figure 1.3 Types of cyberattacks. Source: Hewa Majeed Zangana.

1.2.3 Impact on Various Sectors

Cyber threats cut across all industry segments because each segment comes with its challenges. For instance, in smart agriculture, IoT appliances that are used on the farm level and in the supply, chain is often under threats of attacks [6]. In finance, identity theft of financial data has made finance organizations protect consumer data through encryption and anonymization [8]. Likewise, health care threat as records, which have high values on the dark web, are attacked by hackers [23, 24].

Critical infrastructures such as the power and water sectors are an interest of nation-state actors because a successful attack could cause widespread disruption in national critical infrastructures [10]. These threats have been countered by employing AI and machine learning (ML) to reinforce credible security in real-time cybersecurity solutions across since sectors, aiming to ensure untainted detection and response systems [9, 13].

1.2.4 Emerging Threats and Challenges

In today's society, new technologies have created new threats that require new methods of protection. Incorporation of AI in cyber operations has triggered the rise of smart cyberattacks which are proficient in learning from their targets which makes it even harder to defend against. The use of IoT has also increased the vector length because millions of interconnected devices are potential targets for attackers [25]. Moreover, with a proliferation of data, big data offer some specific issues, and cybercriminals primarily attack databases with the intention of stealing information [16]. While cloud computing has brought increased flexibility and scalability, the environment has posed new and unique security issues such as data privacy, compliance, and multi-tenant issues [2, 26]. Such changes suggest the emergence of a world where complacent security measures are no longer the solution to new risks [15, 21].

1.3 Core Principles of Cybersecurity

The fundamental concepts of cybersecurity define the baseline approach to stemming the tide of threats within cyberspace and preserving the confidentiality, integrity, and accessibility of vehicle information and the supporting systems. These principles, collectively known as the

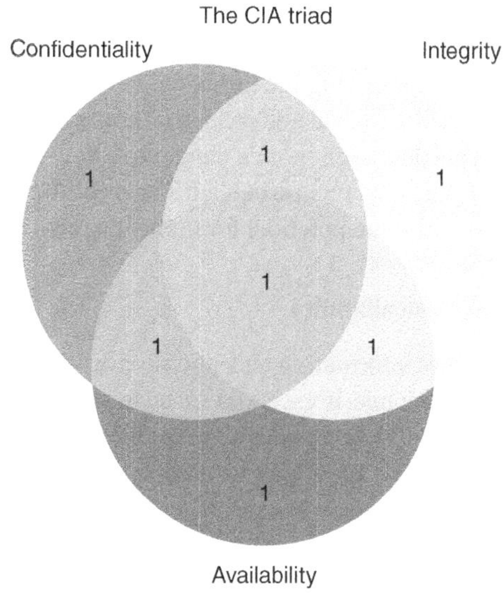

Figure 1.4 The CIA triad in cybersecurity. Source: Hewa Majeed Zangana.

CIA triad are the principles of confidentiality, integrity, and availability that have become the foundational principles used in designing effective cybersecurity models across the fields [1, 4]. Apart from the CIA triad, other principles such as, authentication, authorization, accountability, and non-repudiation are also important factors improving the cybersecurity measures. CIA triad means Confidentiality, Integrity, and Availability are acronym and basic pillars of cybersecurity. The below Venn diagram in Figure 1.4 shows how these components intertwine and interact to enhance the institute's cybersecurity.

These principles are described in this section, and the report also explores how they apply to today's principal cybersecurity concerns.

1.3.1 Confidentiality

Confidentiality is the idea that only the right people should be able to see information, people with the necessary permissions [8]. Confidentiality controls ensure that information is not conveyed to the wrong people and are a key control in the area of privacy and data protection which includes General Data Protection and Regulation (GDPR). To protect the confidentiality, some measures include cryptography, security zip codes, and security passwords [20]. To simplify it, organizations can set up their security perimeter so that even if the attacker is able to intercept the data or gain access to the disk or other storage medium, the data cannot be understood without decryption keys [15]. It is more important to have confidentiality measures where there is sensitivity such as in the health and treasury sectors. Companies employ encapsulation, personal controls, and identity verification to restrict data accessibility to only the required individuals, reducing the chances of leakage to those who are not authorized [6]. Furthermore, insiders are very dangerous as they pose a major threat to the confidentiality area, hence the reinforcement of monitoring and controlling access in an organization [17].

1.3.2 Integrity

The integrity principle makes certain data within a database is unadulterated and can only be written to with authorization to prevent deletion [2]. Data consistency is indeed relevant and especially required in areas where data reliability is critical such as health care, accounting, economics, and protection of the physical infrastructure [16]. Checksums, hash, and digital signatures are routine instruments which led to check the integrity of messages, documents, or other information by comparing the initial data with the data received or stored. For instance, application areas such as smart grid and industrial control systems employ integrity for indication of cyber-physical threats that might pose a danger to safety [10]. Reliability of information in industries that require real-time data processing helps prevent the occurrence of operational blockages or other scenarios that create the potential for ineffectiveness and even safety concerns [18, 22].

1.3.3 Availability

It makes information and systems available to those who are permitted to use them when required. This principle is essential in business continuity, more so to the companies that offer services that need to be up all the time, for instance, emergency response systems and financial organizations [21]. To reduce availability insecurity, organizations use backup, distribution of loads, and cleaning services in case of a disruption. In cybersecurity, availability is compromised by DDos attacks, where network traffic is flooded in an effort to make it unavailable to those that need to use it [4, 27]. The preventive measures include network monitoring and the use of firewall and intrusion prevention systems to check the availability threats. Moreover, incident response and disaster recovery solutions are critical to guaranteeing that availability is rather restored quickly after the attack or a natural disaster to help organizations decrease interruptions to operations [3].

1.3.4 Authentication and Authorization

Authentication and authorization are basic when it comes to confirming user identity and providing him or her with a certain level of access to certain resources. Passwords, fingerprint scanning, and multifactor authentication reveal the identity of the user, whereas authorization defines actions an authorized user is permitted to take within a system [9]. Proper methods of authentication and authorization decrease the tendencies of unauthorized access and containment of risky insiders, which, in turn, improves confidentiality and integrity of organizational systems [28]. Since cloud services and IoT devices are increasingly being used in modern digital networks, it is important that a good authentication and authorization method of a digital system is even more stringent than in the past. Such controls enable or deny users from using the system and retrieving or inputting information or performing other functions that may be destructive to the system or the user and, thus, play significant roles for networks to control access in various environments [25, 26].

1.3.5 Accountability and Non-Repudiation

Accountability allows the linking of activity or an action performed in a system and its cause to a specific person; it is a record that can be audited, used to comply, or analyzed with forensic intent [5]. This principle is used when analyzing security threats and, in particular, when analyzing data leakage or investigation of an insider attack. The utilization of logs, audit trails, and real-time monitoring enables organizations to monitor and analyze users' actions, thus enhancing an organization's transparency and accountability in the cybersecurity process [11]. It rejects users from denying the transaction occurred by using technological features such as digital signatures and cryptographic hashings. Something as important as this principle is vital to guarantee that you would be able to blame users; hence, it is a component of the law and regulation [14]. Self-attributes of non-repudiation in sectors like e-commerce and banking, protect against fake transactions making digital operations more secure and dependable [12].

1.3.6 Resilience and Adaptive Security

As such, it is imperative that cybersecurity principles also put lot of emphasis on the concepts of agility as the threat landscape continues to worsen in the modern world. Cyber resilience is the ability of an organization to prevent, contain, and recover from cyber threats which are complex in the contemporary world [19]. The use of adaptive security principles allows the organizations to counter threats flexibly, relying on the real-time data to change the defensive approaches where necessary [23, 29]. AI and ML entry is enhancing efficient adaptive security solutions by promoting threat prevention, automatic incident handling, and risk estimation. This approach is particularly helpful when there is severe interdependency that exists in some systems, for instance, smart grid systems and the IoT ecosystems to where an attack usually has the potential to spread with further related attacks necessitating prompt containment [7, 13]. In other words, by preparing oneself as a periodically disrupted adaptive system, one can be more resistant to the complex assaults and reduce the possible harm done to the organization [9, 21].

1.4 DiD as a Cybersecurity Strategy

DiD is a robust security model that acts on various levels of an organization to prevent cyberattackers from accessing an organization's system and data. The principle behind DiD is simple: This means that even if one measure would be compromised, there are still other layers to protect you. This is a multiple DiD concept that aims to provide fuller protection provided that the technologies, processes, and policies are associated with it [4, 17]. DiD strategy involves a number of layers of protection in order to safeguard an organization's resources. Figure 1.5 shows how the main components of this strategy fit together, which layers align with which, etc.

As the threats hit the virtual world more complex and frequent, some measures such as DiD are vital.

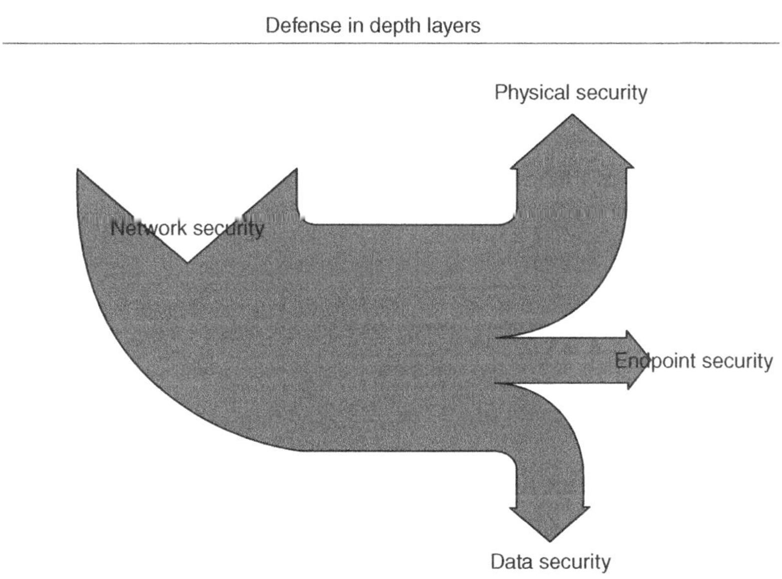

Figure 1.5 Defense in depth layers. Source: Hewa Majeed Zangana.

1.4.1 Overview of DiD

The concept of DiD has been derived from the military where adversaries are forced to undergo tiers of protection before they could have access to the sensitive information or resource they would wish to attack [8]. DiD in cybersecurity consists of using a set of interrelated security measures that respond to threats at several levels within an organization's information technology environment. The first level of defense in DiD strategy mainly are physical, network, end point, application, and data security [29]. Consequently, it is possible to use a variety of protection methods that allow organizations to protect against malware threats, phishing, ransomware, and internal threats [26]. Such an approach to security also creates an overall awareness of security responsibility, involving all the people in the organization.

1.4.2 Key Components of a DiD Strategy

A successful DiD strategy encompasses several key components:

- **Physical Security**: This is the first line of protection, including limited access to facilities, security systems, and climate preservation of tangible resources [15]. If there is no strong physical control, all other layers are easily penetrated.
- **Network Security**: This layer uses firewalls, intrusion detection system (IDS), and virtual private networks (VPNs) to defend the organization's internal networks against threats from outside the organization. It can also reduce the spread of nefarious operations by segmenting a firm's network.
- **Endpoint Security**: Due to the growing adoption of mobile devices and distributed work environments, endpoint security has become relevant. Tools like antivirus, Endpoint Detection and Response (EDR), mobile device management (MDM) guard endpoints against malware and other unauthorized access attempts [2, 27].
- **Application Security**: Security at the application layer safeguards software and applications from meant to be built and implemented incorrectly. This involves professional code writing, periodic scanning for risks, and employing tools known as web application firewalls (WAFs) to defend against threats such as Structured Query Language injection (SQLi), cross-site scripting (XSS), among others [16].
- **Data Security**: Measures of securing data include the use of code in concealing information, hiding in invoices and other places, scrambling or dividing the information into segments. Data loss prevention (DLP) technologies provide control/monitor information leakage or access for unauthorized users [9, 14].
- **User Awareness and Training**: One of the most essential features of DiD is to explain to users about the implemented security policies and measures. There are trainings that employees can attend to differentiate between phishing schemes as well as lessons regarding how to properly handle passwords within the organizational culture [19, 24].

1.4.3 Implementing DiD

To effectively implement a DiD strategy, organizations should consider the following steps:

- **Risk Assessment**: This should be done by organizing a risk assessment to discover possible risks and hazards, the weaknesses a business has, and the valuable things that need protection against the risks. This will help in choosing the most appropriate security measures to be taken [5].

- **Layered Security Design**: Design a framework which will bring together all the components that has been discussed above. It is important that each layer should mitigate certain risks and vulnerabilities; thus, each is adequate in its coverage [29].
- **Regular Testing and Updates**: In order to assess the strength of the security measures implemented, constant assessments, such as penetration testing and vulnerability assessment, should be performed. One of the more important security best practices is to keep software code updated and patched, whether for systems and/or applications [10, 15].
- **Incident Response Plan**: Develop an action plan which states what should be done in case of a security breach incident. They should identify specific tasks, people to assign the tasks, the way information will flow, and the mitigation strategies that the firm should employ if it suffers from a cyberelite security breach as well as how it will regain normalcy [13].
- **Continuous Monitoring**: On this basis, various methods of continuous monitoring, including detection of anomalies and possible threats, should be considered as the most suitable measures. Security Information and Event Management (SIEM) systems can collect and process security data in order to highlight the state of the organization's security [25].

An improvement in risk management is a prerequisite to the success of cybersecurity measures. The following plan is a checklist of activities that are encompassed in a general risk assessment process (Figure 1.6).

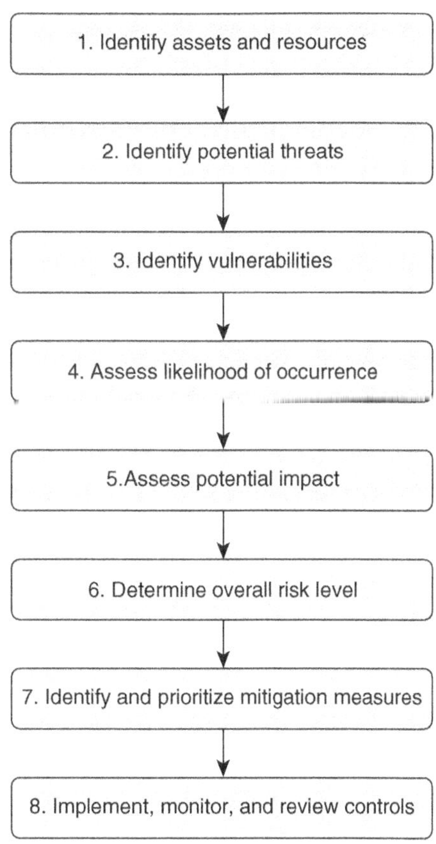

Figure 1.6 Risk assessment process. Source: Hewa Majeed Zangana.

1.4.4 Challenges and Considerations

Despite the fact that DiD has a number of advantages, it is also effective for organizations from the following points of view. These include:

- **Complexity**: Applying numerous severities can cause problems with administration and the combination of the measures. It remains the organization's responsibility to guarantee that the various security applications can interconnect and work in harmony [22].
- **Resource Allocation**: It can be concluded that a DiD approach implies vast efforts needed for its implementation in terms of funding as well as specific staff education. Hence, resources must be properly distributed to all the layers and formats to support their continued functioning effectively [18].
- **Evolving Threat Landscape**: These risks and threats are not new; however, their form and proclivity for creation keep adapting, and the same can be said for organizations. Reviewing and updating the DiD strategy periodically is quite relevant because of new threats and risks appearance [4].

1.4.5 Summary

DiD is a powerful concept of cybersecurity which provides protection at multiple layers. If and only if diverse security measures are incorporated and the security awareness is promoted, an organization can become prepared for the whole scope of cyber threats. Due to the ever-changing threats operating in the cyber environment, it is crucial to evaluate and analyze the DiD approach to stay protected and keep businesses going.

1.5 Cybersecurity Frameworks and Standards

In understanding the system security, frameworks and standards are of great importance within the global landscape of securing corporations' networks and preventing cyber threats. These frameworks give organizations a guide on how they can design, implement, and monitor strong cybersecurity practices that can meet the organizational and legal needs of an organization. Cybersecurity models adopted vary across organizations, based on the industrial and regulatory requirements. Below is a bar chart showing the various adopted frameworks grouped by the number of adoptions: National Institute of Standards and Technology (NIST), International Organization for Standardization (ISO), and Payment Card Industry Data Security Standard (PCI DSS) (Figure 1.7).

These frameworks need to be grasped and implemented by any organization that seeks to improve its security against a changing and complex set of cyber threats.

1.5.1 Importance of Cybersecurity Frameworks

CSFs are structured elements that define the critical challenges an organization faces when protecting its assets, and it's used to analyze threats and choose adequate protection measures. When applied, these frameworks help organizations to be in compliance with legal and regulatory rules, diminish risks of a leakage of sensitive data, and enhance handling of such situations [2, 5]. Moreover, they encourage a standard approach used by the concerned stakeholders for discussing cybersecurity issues so that they have ways of effectively communicating.

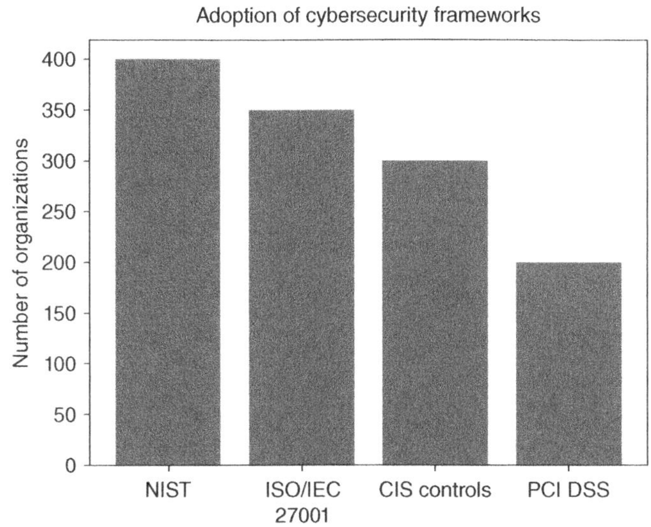

Figure 1.7 Cybersecurity frameworks overview. Source: Hewa Majeed Zangana.

1.5.2 Popular Cybersecurity Frameworks

There are some relatively recent cybersecurity frameworks, which have risen in popularity due to implementing distinct methodologies and approaches. Some of the most widely recognized frameworks include:

- **NIST Cybersecurity Framework (NIST CSF)**: The NIST CSF is a coordinated, proactive framework for managing cybersecurity risks that is completely voluntary and was created by the NIST. It consists of five core functions: The five strategies are: identification, protection, monitoring, reaction, and restoration. This framework is most helpful to organizations that are planning to build a sound cybersecurity program that suits the environment it operates in [21].
- **ISO/IEC 27001**: This international standard provides guidance on what needs to be done in order to design, implement, operate, monitor, and review an information security management system (ISMS). ISO/IEC 27001 covers methods by managing information security for all forms of business organizations, focusing on utility, confidentiality, and integrity. Adherence to this standard may thus contribute to an improvement in the reputation and reliability of an organization in the market [19].
- **CIS Controls**: The specific detailing was brought out by the Center for Internet Security, also known as CIS control, which designs a high-priority level of security measures in compliance with the most frequent threats. The controls are divided into three categories: three categories of measures: basic, foundational, and organizational measures to ensure it is easy for an organization to adopt measures based on their available resources [29].
- **COBIT**: COBIT acronym for control objectives for information and related technologies is a framework mainly used to address governance and management of enterprise IT. It assists corporate institutions to adopt the IT plans in adherence to the business strategies within the context of risk management. In particular, COBIT is considered a rich source of tools, information, and recommendations to manage and sufficiently regulate information security, or IS [18].

1.5.3 Standards and Best Practices

Besides, various standards and their best practices are enriched as of security to develop cybersecurity to the required level. These standards often complement existing frameworks and provide additional guidance on specific areas of cybersecurity:

- **Payment Card Industry Data Security Standard**: Known more formally as the PCI DSS, it is a series of security requirements that apply to the completed or incomplete process of obtaining and processing card information. Card payment processing organizations have to adhere to PCI DSS to avoid leakage of essential data and to prevent hacks [26].
- **NIST Special Publications**: The NIST Special Publications (SP) include SP 800-53 that contains a catalog of security and privacy controls for federal information systems (ISs) and organizations. These publications provide direction on how to choose and apply security controls from risk analysis [4].
- **Federal Information Processing Standard**: Federal Information Processing Standard (FIPS) publication defined the security specifications for federal agencies and their contractors. FIPS prescribes certain requirements on a cryptographic module which guarantees that the sensitive data is adequately safeguarded [22].

1.5.4 Challenges in Implementing Frameworks and Standards

While the benefits of adopting cybersecurity frameworks and standards are substantial, organizations may encounter several challenges during implementation.

- **Resource Constraints**: The smaller organizations can only afford to implement some aspects of the frameworks since they have restricted funding and human resources [17]. That is why some organizations may pay much attention to basic controls while overlooking other essential aspects in security.
- **Complexity of Compliance**: The existence of more than one framework and standard is likely to cause confusion and compliance issues. It is therefore important for organizations to unravel whatever requirements are incumbent on each framework and how the different frameworks correlate so as to avoid repetition of efforts and consequent wastes.
- **Evolving Threat Landscape**: Because the threat landscape is constantly changing, so too are frameworks and standards that are required in order to meet the specifics of an organization's environment. Enterprises must subjectively update themselves about the threats that are unfolding and adjust the security measures they have in their practices [14].

1.5.5 Future Directions in Cybersecurity Frameworks

There will be changes in cybersecurity frameworks over time due to the dynamic nature of the ever-changing digital environment. Considering the further enhancement of employing emerging technologies in cybersecurity, for instance, AI and ML, it can be expected that the new concepts of frameworks with automatic procedures and early threat recognition will appear [9, 10]. Moreover, social functionalities between organizations shall emerge as important as frameworks that enable information sharing, and defense shall become compulsory.

1.5.6 Summary

Cybersecurity frameworks and standards offer crucial are used to establish key requirements that organizations can use to build their effective cybersecurity solutions. Actually, by adopting well-recognized models, such as the NIST CSF and ISO/IEC 27001, different organizations can improve their security situation, obey the rules, and allow people become conscious of security. Of course, there are always barriers to implementing these frameworks, but if the work is done actively, adverse effects and cyber threats can be minimized as a part of organism's interaction with the digital world.

1.6 Emerging Technologies and Their Security Implications

In the modern world, where organizations pursue more and more the adoption of novel technologies, cybersecurity equally grows as a field of possibilities and threats. Contemporary technologies including AI, the IoT, cloud, and blockchain are changing operations while providing novel risks. The constant advances of new technologies like AI or IoT have brought change in the cybersecurity world. From the line graph below, you can understand the relationship between the implementation of new age technologies and the subsequent rise in cyber threats (Figure 1.8).

Knowledge of such consequences is therefore significant for organizations to endeavor at implementing sound cybersecurity measures that would address the challenges from the adoption of such technologies.

1.6.1 Artificial Intelligence

As it has already been realized, AI is now playing the role of a catalyst in the improvement of cybersecurity. Friends, ML algorithms can work with large data sets to look for signals of system deviation or of a threat. For instance, AI can enhance threat prediction since a particular protocol in the network may be indicative of the presence of threats [9]. In addition, AI raises the concern in security acceptance or security vulnerabilities of systems that require AI. Terrorists use AI technology to advance attack methods, for example, attacking through a phishing campaign or creating malware and Wi-Fi exploits that typical security cannot overcome [19]. Since AI is used both transparently and in malicious ways, the same problem applies with the requirement that organizations must utilize AI while at the same time develop ways to resist potential AI-based attacks [15].

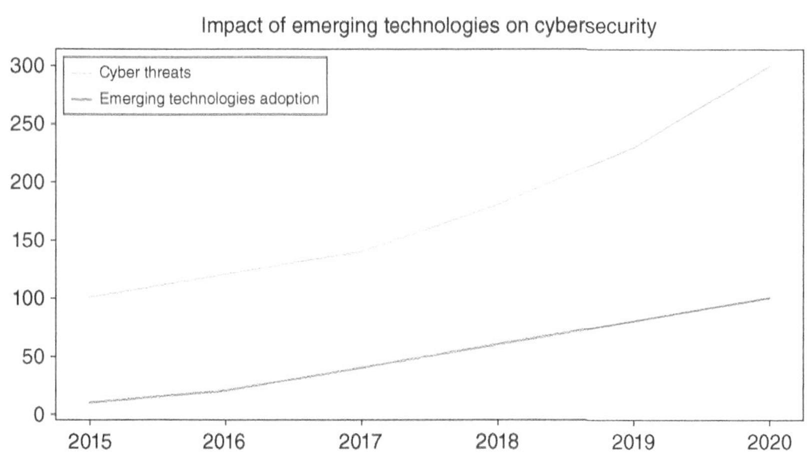

Figure 1.8 Impact of emerging technologies on cybersecurity. Source: Hewa Majeed Zangana.

1.6.2 Internet of Things

The use of IoT devices has transformed many industries by enhancing connectivity and enabling the collection of more data. However, many of these devices lack adequate security measures, making them vulnerable to hacking. Additionally, some IoT devices are inherently insecure, allowing intruders to exploit them and gain unauthorized access to other connected systems [2]. For instance, IoT devices inspect environmental conditions in the farming industry under farms, monitoring soil quality and crop health, but due to poor security, they can cause havoc or consume resources or possibly harvest information [6]. Consequently, it is high time organizations received significant recognition in the battle against these risks through the integration of concepts such as updating firmware, network segmentation, and encryption.

1.6.3 Cloud Computing

Cloud computing has become popular as organizations have outsourced the management of their data by providing space for their data. But this gives rise to challenges to security in different ways and extents. Unauthorized access to and leakage of data and loss of control over it are some of the common risks faced in cloud computing [26]. It is crucial for organizations to perform due diligence and ensure that the CSPs employ compliance with high standards of security, together with the usage of encryption and access control mechanisms of data in transit and data in use [16].

Besides that, it is possible to understand another theoretic basis of security—the shared responsibility model, in which the cloud provider and an organization are twin sisters of protection responsibilities.

1.6.4 Blockchain Technology

The major application of blockchain is cryptocurrencies, and this brings unmatched security due to its decentralized and indelible character. This can help improve data quality and ensure secure transactions can be made without the use of middlemen [20]. Nevertheless, there are still fairly significant risks including those associated with smart contracts and decentralized applications, which an attacker can use for their purposes [8]. With blockchain implementations, security is an even more significant concern, so testing and auditing have to be uncompromising while working to build best practices to deal with these threats [4].

1.6.5 Cybersecurity Training and Awareness

Thanks to these emerging technologies, consistent and efficient cybersecurity training and awareness has become unavoidable. Such technologies pose a challenge to organizations since employees need to be informed on the threats inherent in these technologies and need to obey security guidelines [24]. This paper has identified several factors that can impact posture in the face of ceaseless advancing threats: As threats change, the need to train can help foster security mindedness in the organization.

1.6.6 Challenges in Adapting to New Technologies

Mainly, there are countless opportunities in using emerging technologies, which from the same point simultaneously puts organizations before some peculiar challenges related to the need to integrate these technologies into the existing cybersecurity-oriented frameworks. This is due to the fact that due to the increasing rate of technological growth, there always tends to be a mismatch of the available security techniques [14]. Additionally, the case may be a challenge to achieve the innovation of the organization's services while at the same time maintaining its security from the cyber threats that may be prevalent in the environment.

1.6.7 Future Directions and Recommendations

To effectively address the security implications of emerging technologies, organizations should consider the following strategies:

- **Risk Assessment**: Spearhead risk assessment frequently in order to determine the risks that may relate to new technologies and mitigate them [5].
- **Collaborative Approaches**: Encourage cooperation between cybersecurity specialists and other teams, as well as between IT and organizational divisions, to provide a centralized view on security that would apply to technology utilization across the board [13].
- **Adaptability**: Be updated on new threats that are usually on the prowl, and prior to this, ensure key measures have been adapted to counter these risks [21]. That may include using threat intelligence in order to prevent attacks before they may happen.

1.6.8 Summary

The development of IT offers the joy of gaining some reward in cybersecurity. On the other hand, AI, IoT, cloud computing, and blockchain are opportunities that can improve organizational capability, but where these opportunities exist, threats such as those that are explored below have to be considered. In getting to the security risks of these technologies, security personnel and organizations can be in a good position to protect their databases and infrastructures from new and emerging threats.

1.7 Cybersecurity Skills and Workforce Development

Furthermore, as more and more organizations are faced with advanced cyber threats, there is increased need for more professionals in this field. Making it a priority for an organization's employees to raise their levels of cyber literacy concerning cyberspace and its security threats becomes of paramount importance in this growing era of cyberspace exploitation. The cybersecurity skills gap, which continues to widen, is one of the biggest challenges organizations face today. The chart below shows the existing supply of cybersecurity workforce and the demand across different regions. (Figure 1.9).

In this section, the critical elements in the cybersecurity skills and workforce components of the current situation, education, and development are discussed.

1.7.1 Current Challenges in Cybersecurity Workforce Development

As cybersecurity becomes increasingly critical, many organizations fail to find experts who meet their requirements. A significant skills gap exists, driven by several factors.

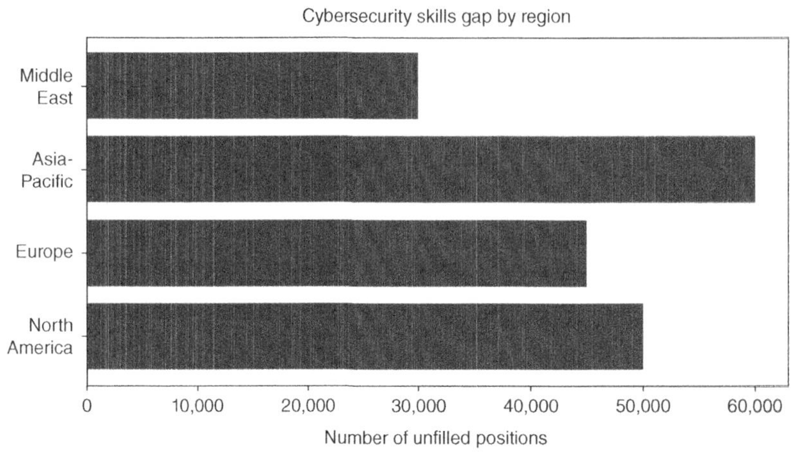

Figure 1.9 Cybersecurity skills gap. Source: Hewa Majeed Zangana.

- **Rapid Technological Advancements**: Cyber threats and technologies are advancing constantly, and the complexity of those threats push educational institutions, as well as training programs, into the constant race to catch up with changing threats and technologies.
- **Diverse Skill Requirements**: Cybersecurity positions cut across all the disciplines of computer engineering and even those of soft skills such as communication and critical thinking. This diversity makes it difficult when it comes to skilled training and staffing of the workforce [29].
- **Inadequate Awareness and Training**: Most aspiring cybersecurity professionals are unknown to employment options in the cybersecurity industry. In addition, the current training services may not develop realistic services that can solve problems; this is because they may not synchronize with the current market challenges [24].

1.7.2 Educational Initiatives and Training Programs

In order to fill the skills gap, institutions of learning and other organizations have begun to focus on efficient skills training for cybersecurity. Some effective initiatives include:

- **Formal Education**: A large number of universities and colleges have introduced the degree programs in cybersecurity, which basically encompasses the information security management, ethical hacking, and digital forensics [20]. Basically, these programs are critical for offering fundamental information and professional competencies.
- **Certification Programs**: Certification in the IT industry would provide added value and credibility for one's field knowledge, and that covers certifications like Certified Information Systems Security Professional (CISSP) and Certified Ethical Hacker (CEH) [3]. They can also offer specialized knowledge reliable in an industry as required by the market.
- **Workshops and Bootcamps**: Other short courses, like a coding boot camp, or even practical sessions tend to offer a shorter time to skill. Many of these programs may be centered on particular cornerstones of cybersecurity, for example, penetration testing or incident handling [12].
- **Online Learning Platforms**: Thanks to new technologies predominating in the form of online learning platforms, cybersecurity training is now easier to implement. Some of the companies that provide cybersecurity courses include Coursera and Udemy, which proffer courses on diverse cybersecurity themes to support credential learners develop skills at flexible progression [19].

1.7.3 Promoting Diversity in the Cybersecurity Workforce

It has been discovered that having a diverse workforce can improve creativity and innovation in decision-making in the field of cybersecurity. But the industry is still struggling with diversity issues such as gender and minority groups. Initiatives aimed at promoting diversity include:

- **Outreach Programs**: Issues that can be addressed in targeted programs in an effort to increase the interest of the underrepresented groups include awareness of careers in the field of cybersecurity and mentorship. For example, activities like "Girls Who Code" are taking efforts to attract young women to the technology and cybersecurity domain [21].
- **Internships and Apprenticeships**: Internships and apprenticeships can be useful to help people from different backgrounds test drive a cybersecurity career [25]. This may be useful in creating desire for the work and creating a more diverse skilled workforce.

1.7.4 Continuous Learning and Professional Development

Cybersecurity as a practice is not stagnant, rather a rapidly evolving and always demanding call for enhanced knowledge and expertise. Organizations must foster a culture of ongoing education by:

- **Offering Training Programs**: Employers should promote or offer to train their staff so that more enhanced skills are acquired. This may comprise local and online training, seminars, and conferences that give information on the current trends and practices in cyberspace [17].
- **Encouraging Knowledge Sharing**: Development of measures that seek to ensure that employees share ideas that can help in skill development and cooperation among the employees. This can encompass daily team briefs, co-implementation of projects, and organizational cross-training programs [15].
- **Recognizing Achievements**: Encouragement to take more training and get more certifications is indicated by the acknowledgment of the accomplishment of such formal learning by the employee [4].

1.7.5 Future Directions for Cybersecurity Workforce Development

In order to tackle the increasing requirements of cybersecurity, organizations and higher learning institutions need to collaborate to develop courses that will suit the ever-changing market forces. Future directions include:

- **Integrating Cybersecurity into science, technology, engineering, and mathematics (STEM) Education**: Introducing cybersecurity concepts in STEM education necessarily promotes the learners' learning interest in the cybersecurity field at a tender age [14].
- **Adapting to Emerging Technologies**: The training programs need to change and extend to skills needed for future technologies like AI and ML [9].
- **Building Partnerships**: The works have demonstrated that collaboration between academics and employers can take measures to make changes to the programs so that the trained workforce is prepared for the current and forthcoming cybersecurity threats [10].

1.7.6 Summary

Building up a cybersecurity personnel talent pool is a necessity in view of the increasing and continued threat existence. It means for an organization to build an effective approach to the modern cybersecurity threats; it is mandatory to focus only on the educational initiatives with the diversity promotion and the culture of the constant development. Workforce development is not only contingent upon the stability of the organization but also an important process in the continual development of our digital security.

1.8 Conclusion and Road Ahead

They form the backbone of modern cybersecurity as we try to decipher various factors that inform the general public regarding matters of cybersecurity. Cyber threats are always emerging, and global powers require a complex solution set that involves a sophisticated technological, human, and legal solution set. This chapter has sought to map out broad themes in current cybersecurity, discussing those crucial elements required to enhance security against ever escalating threats.

1.8.1 Recap of Key Themes

Throughout this chapter, several central themes emerged that underscore the imperative for a comprehensive approach to cybersecurity:

- **Emerging Technologies**: That is why more and more often when organizations are using new technologies such as AI, blockchain, and the IoT, potential threats are increasing as well. However, every innovation is attached to specific risks should be recognized and eradicated [16]. Measures and tactics must be adjusted progressively to address these developments, distinctly targeting preventive approaches over repairs.
- **Workforce Development**: When looking at the issue of cybersecurity, it becomes really critical to understand that there is a serious skills shortage around the globe. Alternative 3 consists in guaranteeing that specialists are ready for the greatest challenge, they know the necessary things, and have all the necessary knowledge. Education in general, training and development, increasing diversity in hiring practices of health care organizations, and collaboration in between academia and industry can support in development of a more competent health care labor force [20].
- **Policy and Governance**: Cyber security policies play an integral part in the provision of culture security within organizations. This includes a framework that looks into data protection, data breach preparedness, and adhering to data privacy laws. To meet this need, organizations need to make changes to these policies from time to time in order to address new challenges and new technologies [13].

1.8.2 Looking Ahead

The future of cybersecurity, therefore, holds gains as well as risks for a company. As we progress, organizations must adopt a proactive and adaptive approach to cybersecurity that incorporates the following elements:

- **Adopting a Zero Trust Model**: In particular, the main reason that perimeter-based security is no longer viable is that the environment has become highly interconnected. It is recommended that organizations secure their systems using a zero trust model which posits that threats can be internal or external. This approach involves constant procedures of authenticating the users and their authorizations [26].

- **Leveraging Automation and AI**: First, the application of automation and AI in cybersecurity can improve threat identification, analysis, and mitigation of security breaches and overall risk assessment. Though AI technology can function automatically and analyze a large amount of data to explore odd behavior and likely threat situations for security teams, those members can dedicate more time to strategic decisions [9].
- **Enhancing Collaboration**: Cybersecurity is a teamwork task, and it cannot be addressed by an individual organization but rather by collective efforts. Stakeholders such as governments, private sectors, and academia should come in close collaboration in order to share threat intelligence and ideas on best practices. Thus, achieving a more resilient cybersecurity ecosystem presents the opportunity for public/private partnerships to effectively advance in their areas of interest [15].
- **Investing in Research and Development**: Companies must remain in a constant development of the tools that it employs to fight cyber threats. Senior management in organizations should encourage creative strategies and research novel approaches to tackling the ever-emerging security threats [4]. This includes supporting the studying of novel encryption algorithms, detection of intrusion, and analysis of behavior.
- **Promoting Cybersecurity Awareness**: However, going a step further to imply organizational culture change and increase the employees' awareness of the issue is important. So, training should be motivated to familiarize the organizational members with how to identify phishing scams, how to protect data, and what procedures to follow when ensuring security [29]. Cybersecurity expert personnel are all important since they make up the first line of defense against cyber threats.

Discussing the future developments of the cybersecurity, it is possible to identify several main trends. The radar chart below shows how specific areas of cybersecurity will be affected by new trends such as Zero Trust, AI, and automation in the future years (Figure 1.10).

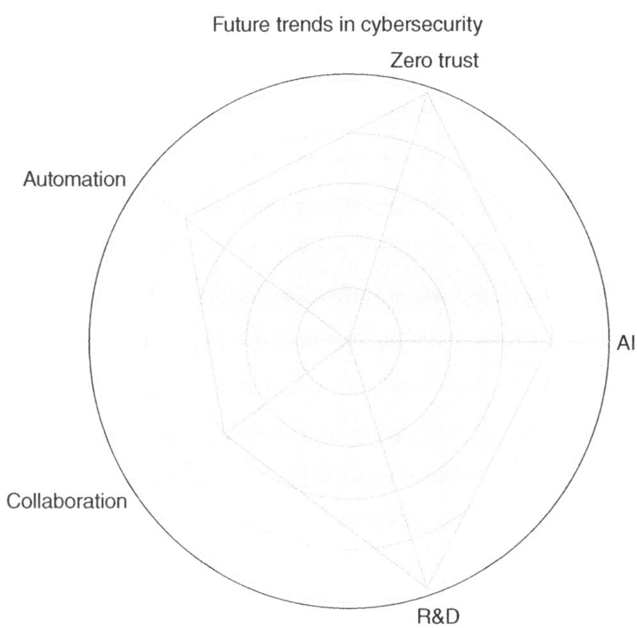

Figure 1.10 Future trends in cybersecurity. Source: Hewa Majeed Zangana.

1.8.3 Final Thoughts

Thus, it is possible to synthesize that modern cybersecurity theoretical and practical application is conditioned by its constant evolution and threats. The attacks continue, and organizations have to keep watchful for putting preventive measures that include technology, skilled workforce, sound policies, and interlinkages. Continuing on this path, the maturing of the learning culture, innovation, and collaboration approach will be critical to achieving the future-proof cybersecurity-oriented environment. Cybersecurity is a work in progress, and this paper aims to contribute to the recommended course that will shape the course of the future in enhancing cybersecurity.

References

1. Gohel, H.A. (2015). *Introduction to Network & Cybersecurity*. Hardik Gohel.
2. Dutta, N., Jadav, N., Tanwar, S. et al. (2022). *Cyber security: Issues and Current Trends*. Springer.
3. Gupta, C.P. and Goyal, K.K. (2020). *Cybersecurity: a self-teaching introduction*. Mercury Learning and Information.
4. Diogenes, Y. and Ozkaya, E. (2019). *Cybersecurity–Attack and Defense Strategies: Counter Modern Threats and Employ State-of-the-Art Tools and Techniques to Protect Your Organization Against Cybercriminals*. Packt Publishing Ltd.
5. Aboelfotoh, S.F. and Hikal, N.A. (2019). A review of cyber-security measuring and assessment methods for modern enterprises. *JOIV: International Journal on Informatics Visualization* 3 (2): 157–176.
6. Angyalos, Z., Botos, S., and Szilágyi, R. (2021). The importance of cybersecurity in modern agriculture. *Agrárinformatika/Journal of Agricultural Informatics* 12 (2): 1–8.
7. Manjikian, M. (2017). *Cybersecurity Ethics: An Introduction*. Routledge.
8. Bock, L. (2021). *Modern cryptography for cybersecurity professionals: learn how you can leverage encryption to better secure your organization's data*. Packt Publishing Ltd.
9. Rohatgi, S., Abinash, B., Joshi, S. et al. (2023). Introduction to artificial intelligence and cybersecurity for industry. In: *Artificial Intelligence and Cyber Security in Industry 40*, 1–22. Springer.
10. Mashima, D., Chen, Y., Roomi, M.M., et al. (2024). Cybersecurity for modern smart grid against emerging threats. arXiv preprint arXiv:240404466.
11. Lapshina, I.V. and Kravets, A.V. (2023). Modern cybersecurity from the perspective of cognitive modeling. *Engineering Bulletin of the Don* 1 (97): 80–95.
12. Varbanov, P. (2022). Perspectives in the design of a modern cybersecurity training programme: the ECHO approach. *Information & Security* 53 (2): 177–190.
13. Omar, M. and Zangana, H.M. (2024). *Redefining Security with Cyber AI*. IGI Global.
14. Thakur, K. and Pathan, A.S.K. (2020). *Cybersecurity Fundamentals: A Real-world Perspective*. CRC Press.
15. Alvarez-Teleña, S. and Díez-Fernández, M. (2024). Modern cybersecurity: new era, new strategies. *New Strategies* (September 16, 2024) http://dx.doi.org/10.2139/ssrn.4957894.
16. França, R.P., Monteiro, A.C.B., Arthur, R., and Iano, Y. (2021). The fundamentals and potential for cybersecurity of big data in the modern world. In: *Machine Intelligence and Big Data Analytics for Cybersecurity Applications* (ed. Y. Maleh, M. Shojafar, M. Alazab, and Y. Baddi), 51–73. Springer.

17 Ajayi, W., Ibeto, O., Olomola, T., and Madewa, M. (2022). Analysis of modern cybersecurity threat techniques and available mitigating methods. *International Journal of Advanced Research in Computer Science* 13 (2).

18 Hasib, M. (2022). *Cybersecurity Leadership: Powering the Modern Organization*, vol. 1. Tomorrow's Strategy Today.

19 Ozkaya, E. (2022). *Cybersecurity Leadership Demystified: a comprehensive guide to becoming a world-class modern cybersecurity leader and global CISO*. Packt Publishing Ltd.

20 Kaur, G., Habibi Lashkari, Z., Habibi Lashkari, A. et al. (2021). Introduction to cybersecurity. *Understanding Cybersecurity Management in FinTech: Challenges, Strategies, and Trends* 17–34.

21 Sharp, R. (2023). *Introduction to Cybersecurity: A Multidisciplinary Challenge*. Springer Nature.

22 Kumar, M., Darshan, S.L.S., and Yarlagadda, V. (2023). Introduction to the cyber-security landscape. In: *Malware Analysis and Intrusion Detection in Cyber-Physical Systems*, 1–21. IGI Global.

23 Salem, I.E., Mijwil, M.M., Abdulqader, A.W. et al. (2022). Introduction to the data mining techniques in cybersecurity. *Mesopotamian Journal of Cybersecurity* 2022: 28–37.

24 Hatzivasilis, G., Ioannidis, S., Smyrlis, M. et al. (2020). Modern aspects of cyber-security training and continuous adaptation of programmes to trainees. *Applied Sciences* 10 (16): 5702.

25 Holovkin, B.M., Tavolzhanskyi, O.V., and Lysodyed, O.V. (2021). Corruption as a cybersecurity threat in conditions of the new world's order. *Linguistics and Culture Review* 5 (S3): 499–512.

26 Ekanayake, N., Karunarathna, H., and Miyuranga, R. (2020). *What is cybersecurity: the reality of modern threats*.

27 Kim, S. and Shrestha, R. (2020). Introduction to automotive cybersecurity. In: *Automotive Cyber Security: Introduction, Challenges, and Standardization*, 1–13. Springer Nature.

28 Jadey, S., Girish, S.C., Raghavendra, K. et al. (2022). Introduction to cyber security. In: *Methods, Implementation, and Application of Cyber Security Intelligence and Analytics*, 1–24. IGI Global.

29 Goutam, R.K. (2021). *Cybersecurity Fundamentals: Understand the Role of Cybersecurity, Its Importance and Modern Techniques Used by Cybersecurity Professionals* (English Edition). BPB Publications.

2

Evolving Cyber Threats: Understanding the New Battlefield

Marwan Omar

Information Technology and Management, Illinois Institute of Technology, Chicago, USA

2.1 Introduction

The recent years have dramatically changed the nature of war, making cyberspace as the fifth domain of warfare. Conventional warfare, for the most part, is fought over geographical territories, that is, land, air, and water, while cyber warfare is fought over cyberspace, and the targets here are core structures, data, and society's essentials. This shift has created a completely different officers' field that requires new tactics and protection systems [1]. As a response, governments, military factions, and businesses at the global level are trying to comprehend, trace, and prevent these new forms of cyber threats since the consequences for national security and the overall welfare of societies would be dreadful if such threats were left uncontrolled [2].

2.1.1 Evolution of Cyber Threats and the New Battlefield

The new generation of cyber threats emerges due to the development of new technologies, increased use of Internet of Things, and more motivated cyberattackers. In the current digital world, newer cyber threats have emerged such as ransomware, Advanced Persistent Threats (APTs), artificial intelligence (AI)-based threats, and attacks. For instance, state actors have fashion cyber warfare capacities used for the purpose of rendering critical assets of adversaries unusable, interrupting them, or controlling them with no demand for direct interference [3]. This change is consistent with the change in the goals of the wars, where the targets are not only a physical regime change but also an information and psychological victory [4]. From a strategic point of view, the dynamics and the fact that cyber warfare is becoming constantly more complex and global make the global legal and policy framework for its regulation rather challenging [5]. As much as violations in physical conflict can be seen and touched, cyber warfare is covert most of the time, hence making it very hard to assign the attacks the right source and at the right time. Critics state that these "hidden digital battle interfaces" determine specific outcomes on a fighting field, that is, they form an unconventional but compelling force in modern wars [6]. The evolution of cyber threats is presented in the following timeline, dating back decades. Beginning from simple incidents of computer viruses to technically complex state-led cyber warfare, this graphic illustrates the shifts that define the cyber threat domain (Figure 2.1).

Defense in Depth: Modern Cybersecurity Strategies and Evolving Threats, First Edition. Edited by Hewa Majeed Zangana.

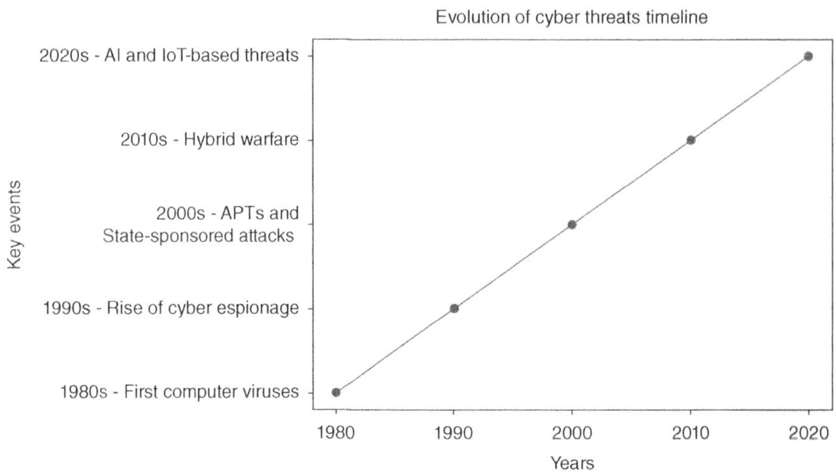

Figure 2.1 Evolution of cyber threats timeline. Source: Hewa Majeed Zangana.

2.1.2 Nontraditional Actors and the New Threat Landscape

Cyber warfare thus brings into the traditional theater of operation such elements not traditionally expected to engage in acts of aggression against an opponent's military might. More and more, it is the non-state actors—including the hacktivists—as well as the organizations from the private sector that run significant risks or, on the contrary, act as key actors engaging in digital conflicts [7]. That said, democratization of cyber capabilities not only enables a broad range of actors to initiate impactful cyber campaign but also brings about upsetting of political and economic balance of the nations [8]. For example, global enterprises have become vulnerable to cyber espionage where acts by state actors try to gain access to the corporations' data, primarily accruing their national interest at the expense of the global business organizations' security [9]. The following diagram represents the nontraditional actors in cyberspace along with their activity and goals in the contemporary threat environment (Figure 2.2).

Figure 2.2 Nontraditional cyber threat actors. Source: Hewa Majeed Zangana.

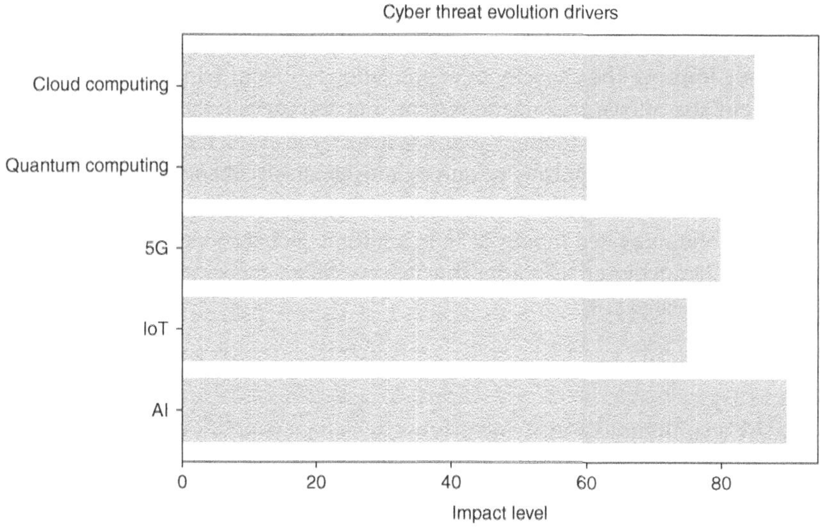

Figure 2.3 Cyber threat evolution drivers. Source: Hewa Majeed Zangana.

Because of such dynamics, the traditional military and defense models of warfare prove somewhat inadequate in capturing the actual cyber warfare. In the globalized warfare space, especially in the digital domain, one cannot point a gun at the other and conduct the operations within the local space. Therefore, the nations must apply a multidomain concept to protect threats that could impact civil infrastructures, the financial system, and other vital assets necessary for protecting state prosperity and security [10]. The following chart points to significant advances in technology that define modern cyber threats and how each of them contributes to the current nature of threats (Figure 2.3).

2.1.3 Technological Drivers of Cyber Threats

The dynamic advancement in technology has changed the possibility, size, and sophistication of threats in cyberspace area. The use of AI, machine learning (ML), and Internet of Things (IoT) components has presented new risks to civilians as well as military organizations since it opened new threats that the adversaries can target [11]. These have gone alongside developing more complex cyberattacks and also means to automate threat management where systems can identify, learn, and counter threats within a given span of time [12]. Specifically, more of the threats predicted to be part of the future threat environment are envisaged to have an AI angle to them. With the advancement of technology, it could become possible for attackers to launch attacks with depth and context awareness of their environment and adapt to the security measures they encounter [13]. For example, AI could enhance sophisticated social engineering schemes since it would be able to identify a user's activities and tendencies rapidly, and this information would be difficult for most security systems to capture [14]. Therefore, there has been an increasing need for defense strategies to embrace advanced technology to offset the realized enhanced capabilities.

2.1.4 The Need for Adaptive Cyber Defense

Due to the nature of cyber threats, static and rigid strategies of cyber defense are not effective enough. As opposed to "traditional" security solutions, where the main approach is based on stopping threats, adaptive cyber defense is designed for defense and recovery, allowing systems to cope, respond, and recover from an extensive spectrum of attacking cyber schemes [15]. This approach does not only improve the capacity of organizations in identifying and preparing responses to cyber threats but also allows organizations to predict and prevent the threats [16].

Adaptive defense is gaining more understanding as an idealistic type of the national systems of protection against cyber threats. States are putting resources into advanced cybersecurity measures that watch for new threats in real time, share information across physical and virtual domains so that threats can be addressed and mitigated rapidly [17]. In addition, global cooperation is a novel paradigm in cybersecurity as distinctive cross-border threats necessitate cooperation and collaboration schemes in order to be defeated [18].

2.1.5 Summary

Therefore, cyber threats are a continuously evolving process, which jeopardizes national security and international peace. If this is the case, then Cyber Incident Detection Systems (CIDS) need to develop ways of handling this rapidly changing and highly complex environment to effectively address the issue at hand. Analyzing motives, techniques, and tools of new generation cyber warfare, stakeholders get an understanding of how the strategies work and can influence the further development of countermeasures against threats. The remaining part of this chapter will therefore explore these dynamics, noting the strategic, technological, and operational features of this tactical cyberspace, as well as how defensive architecture needs to adapt to the reality of the new conflict space [19].

2.2 Historical Context of Cyber Threats

Cyber threats are evolving just as information technology is evolving and proactively changing its form and characteristics. From simple computer-based crimes in the late '90s, various forms of cybercrimes have developed into a complex level where certain states can paralyze entire nations. The following section traces the preparedness timeline of cyber threats, beginning from rudimentary cyber penetrations to advanced, long-term coordinated, and state-sponsored cyber terrorism. Awareness of this progression is key to mastering the nature of their evolution, thus understanding how cyber threats are today's tool active in conflict and geopolitics [14, 20].

2.2.1 The Beginnings: Early Cyber Intrusions and the Growth of Cyber Espionage

Initially, cyber threats appeared sporadic, the acts committed by one or several people with unsophisticated methods. In the early decades of cyber intrusions, the criminals limited themselves to relatively simple attacks on isolated computing platforms. But as technology advanced, the course the aim of the attacks also increased in terms of their scope and design. At the beginning of the 1990s, hackers and cybercriminals began using cyber espionage tactics to steal data from both the public sector and private companies [21]. Some important events of cyber espionage signposted the current grand cyber operations and the growing imperative of comprehensive cybersecurity measures. Cyber spying became a problem for earlier methods of security, which were aimed at the physical security of property in the economy. The change of aims to attack things that are intangible—data and other intellectual property—is the major change in the strategies of the cyber adversaries and the loudest signal that security solutions have to be changed to meet the needs of the digital environment [9].

2.2.2 The Twenty-First Century: Rise of Advanced Persistent Threats (APTs) and State-Sponsored Cyber Operations

The new millennium saw the emergence of APTs and state-backed cyber operations in the early two thousand. Unlike other cyber intrusions, APTs are complex, persistent operations usually set in motion by nation-states for tactical objectives. Such activities may involve espionage on strategic assets, endorsing cyber espionage on government systems, and establishing chronic access to classified information [22, 23]. APATs are described as fundamentally more advanced in their technical complexity and are considered more dangerous than previous forms of cyberattack as they generally require more resources and specialized support teams and are often backed by some sort of state actor.

For example, Stuxnet, seen in 2010, made an example of what could be done in cyber operations by shutting down several physical systems in Iran's nuclear enrichment centers. It also showed how cyber warfare elevated as a method for geopolitical pressure, so other countries stepped up their investment in cyber resources [13]. Therefore, cyber warfare moved from a theoretical idea to a real factor in world politics and became the starting point for an arms race in cyberspace.

2.2.3 The Modern Era: Multi-Domain Conflicts and Hybrid Warfare

With cyber operations being more and more utilized as tactics in larger military strategy plans, a new type of warfare has been created, hybrid warfare, in which rather than solely using military force to defeat an enemy, different strategies are employed, often in conjunction with the use of cyber weapons. This approach allows those subscribed to this modus operandi the ability to sow chaos, mislead, and create divisions in their targets without necessarily having to use military assets and forces, should plausible denial ability be an objective, as well as complicating any further diplomatic actions by the target state [24]. Researchers highlight that these multi-domain conflicts make it hard to distinguish between peacetime and actions of war, and, therefore, provoke ambiguity regarding the justice and suitability of cyber responses in international law [5]. Empirical studies have shown that countries, including Russia, have applied a hybrid warfare system in wars that they employ cyber power together with traditional military forces to accomplish strategic and tactical objectives. These contests suggest that cyber operations are not additive but essential and can, in some circumstances, be the dominant way of accomplishing strategic goals. According to Ref. [18], hybrid warfare entails cyber warfare techniques to destabilize an enemy's infrastructure, communications, and financial systems so as to transform the battleground into a space that lies between cyberspace and the physical world.

2.2.4 Impact of Technological Advancements: Artificial Intelligence and the Internet of Things

Sophistication, meaning the advanced use of technology, especially AI and IoT has brought a new dimension to the aspect of cyber threat. About AI, the attackers get to work with systems and structures that facilitate automation, making it easy for them to increase the complexity of attacks they carry out while also making them highly selective [11]. For instance, AI algorithms can include vulnerability real-time scanning, allowing attackers to have a better shot at contiguous system penetration and reducing the efficacy of the generally practiced generic security tactics and methods, such as Ref. [7]. At the same time, the growth of IoT devices has enlarged the threat exposure due to the fact that any device connected to the internet is another weakness for the enemy [15]. Such developments have led to changes in the technology landscape for cybersecurity since traditional defense measures are generally inadequate in addressing the abilities provided by AI and IoT. This challenge thus calls for the utilization of advanced technologies in cyber defense that accept the emerging threats [17].

2.2.5 The Shift Toward Cyber Deterrence

Due to the increased frequency and complexity of threats, there is a tendency among certain countries to build cyber deterrence policies aimed at preventing the enemy from attacking. Nevertheless, cyber deterrence is different from the concept of traditional deterrence, especially that of nuclear or military based. Due to the virtual and liquid nature of cyberspace, and due to the reasons of assigning the attacks to concrete actors which often remains unclear, it is rather problematic to build credible deterrent threats. In addition, cyber deterrence can be achieved only with a proper understanding of the adversary's purpose for attack, his or her capacities, and the likelihood to react on counteractions. Ahmad and Jahangir [19] have pointed out that its continued dynamism calls for creating a form of cyber deterrence strategy. Yet, given the sometimes confusion and debate around the concept of cyber deterrence, its evolution suggests increasing societal attention and governmental commitment to cybersecurity as an aspect of national security.

2.2.6 Summary

The historical development of cyber threats highlights a consistent trend: over time, the technology used in carrying out the attacks also becomes sophisticated and therefore the effects observed as well. From the first computer viruses or hacks to APTs, hybrid warfare, or AI, threats in cyber warfare have come as a crucial element in both state and non-state actors' operational weapon formations. Proliferation and further development of cyber threats and the development of technologies that are too inconsistent with the existing environment also call for new and layered approaches in order to counter this ever-shifting threat. While the conceptualization of contemporary cyber threats, which violates the basic paradigms providing strategic defense, understanding the historical perspective can offer a better idea about the nature and warfare of cyber threats and the constant endeavors needed to protect state and international security measures [2, 25, 26].

2.3 Types of Modern Cyber Threats

Twenty-first century threats are multifaceted, intricate, and multifarious, depending on technological, geophysical, and tactical circumstances. In the modern world, threats continue to evolve and become more refined; they target various weak spots in cyberspace. This section contains a specific analysis of the most significant types of modern cyber threats that exist in the modern world, as well as those currently threatening organizations and states, such as APTs, ransomware, DDOS attacks, IoT threats, and threats based on AI. Such threats are important to know in order to be able to build up defenses and countermeasures against them. The following diagram presents the main cyber threats grouped by the attack vectors most often used in cyberspace. This gives a broad view of how such threats attack these vulnerabilities (Figure 2.4).

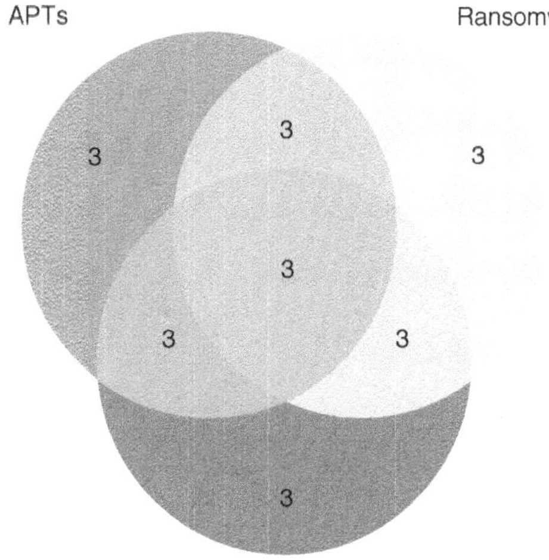

Figure 2.4 Common cyber threat types and attack vectors. Source: Hewa Majeed Zangana.

2.3.1 Advanced Persistent Threats

Thus, APT stands for advanced persistent threats—it defines a class of threats characterized by sustained long attacks made by prosperous state actors or distinct, concerted groups. APTs operate stealthily, covertly entering key infrastructure points such as government organizations, defense industries, and other essential sectors; attackers are long lived at the target site, collecting information. While other cyberattacks focus on the direct damage or rapid downloading of data from a network, APTs focus on stealth, stamina, and manipulation of affected networks. Using APTs, nation-states often leverage them as tools and components in a more massive cyber warfare campaign to destabilize foes and gain leverage. These threats are usually quite hard to deal with because of the great techniques that may include the zero-day exploits, social engineering, and/or the use of custom-built malware [3]. One of the most recent and famous instances of an APT is the Stuxnet worm utilized to sabotage Iran's nuclear plants, showing the capability of APTs to engage physical damage through cyber avenues [13].

2.3.2 Ransomware and Cyber Extortion

Ransomware is the most rapidly developing direction of cyberspace threats and has become one of the favorites of the financially motivated attackers. In a ransomware attack, an unauthorized user installs a program that produces a lock to a victim's files which can only be opened when the attacker is paid for the code, hence the name. Another common propagation strategy is the so-called extortion, which means that the ransomware authors warn the victim to release the stolen data online if they do not receive the demanded amount. This threat has transformed from several loosely associative crimes to well-developed global business, wherein attackers now offer Ransomware as a Service (RaaS) wherein other miscreants can carry out attacks using professionally made ransomware packages [19, 25].

High-profile ransomware attacks that have targeted the healthcare sector and other organizations that provide services which are deemed vital or central to public safety mean that ransomware has the potential to not only bring operations to a standstill but also pose a threat to the safety of the populace. The continuing emergence of ransomware has forced organizations and governments to

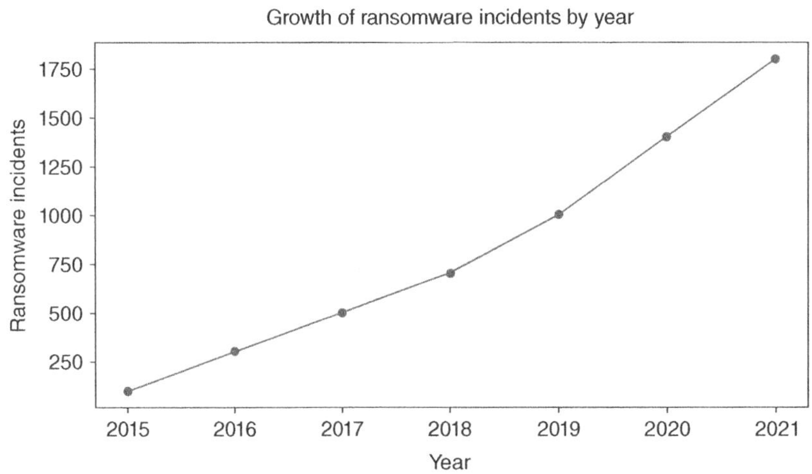

Figure 2.5 Growth of ransomware incidents by year. Source: Hewa Majeed Zangana.

improve their protections and increase their strategies to stop the assaults. Furthermore, advances in the use of cryptocurrency have allowed anonymous transactions such as ransoming data, which places more challenges to the police to apprehend the criminals [1]. Here, the following graph shows the spread of ransomware incidents in the period of several years, which indicates the expansion of growth and escalation of this kind of cyber threat (Figure 2.5).

2.3.3 Distributed Denial of Service Attacks

Denial of service (DoS) and Distributed Denial of Service (DDoS) are cybercrimes where the culprit tries to overwhelm a target's network or servers by sending fill requests which makes the service unavailable for legitimate consumers. DDoS attacks can be devastating, thus often employed to lure the victim or as tactics to instigate disruption of operations during other cyber incidents. Because of the power of botnets, large numbers of compromised client systems are utilized to generate additional attack traffic in the form of DDoS attacks [9]. Presently, DDoS attacks are much more complex, using IoT devices to create large huge botnets with high traffic capabilities. For instance, the Mirai botnet brought one of the largest regular DDoS attacks to light and pilfered the vulnerability of IoT devices and the possibility of flooding these assaults toward an extensive range of organizations [21]. Both governments and companies have recently been using DDoS and interconnecting their systems to enhance protection against this constant and difficult cyber problem.

2.3.4 Internet of Things Vulnerabilities

The growing popularity of IoT technology has led to an increased possibility of new, interconnected devices, thus an increase in access points for malicious attackers. As simple appliances, control boxes, and other smart devices are integrated into our daily life, most of them have been installed with weak or no security measures that attract attackers [11, 15]. Malware infections in IoT devices are beneficial to an attacker as a foothold or can be used directly as part of a DDoS botnet. Issues of IoT security are especially dire in the context of such industries, as attempts to breach systems inherent in critical infrastructures may jeopardize public supply services as well as individual lives. For instance, malicious players may take advantage of the security weaknesses of the insecure industrial IoT devices to cause destruction on water treatment plants, energy providers, or transport systems [24]. It therefore becomes apparent that IoT devices and networks' protection will require a layered security solution of more robust authentication, updated software, and AI-based anomaly recognition systems.

2.3.5 Artificial Intelligence-Driven Threats

The inclusion of AI in cyberspace has presented new and effective classes of cyber threats. AI can boost the impact of cyberattacks by means of automatized reconnaissance, scanning for vulnerabilities, and learning attack patterns that can be changed on the fly. AI attack types are as follows: AI malware, which is able to avoid conventional cybersecurity measures; AI-Phishing, which utilizes ML algorithms to generate ruthlessly personalized phishing emails, texts, and other messages [27].

On the other hand, AI is extensively utilized for cybersecurity, which is the protection against cyber threats, of which AI is employed in the identification of potential threats based on specific patterns, determination of possible breach points, and incorporation of AI into systems for handling the threats [7]. Nevertheless, in its dual applicability as both a tool of the offense and the defense, there stands an emergent set of ethical and strategic concerns with reference to the weaponization of AI in cyber warfare. As derived from this study, it could be deduced that threat actors would leverage the extent of AI and, thereby, making the use of AI in cyberspace engages more heightened attention from cybersecurity professionals as well as policymakers [28].

2.3.6 Social Engineering and Insider Threats

As is well known, social engineering is still the most effective method used in cyberattacks, as it is based on a psychological plan, which encourages a person to provide a critical piece of information or permit an unauthorized individual access. The most common form of social engineering is "phishing", and this is usually used to provide an initial entry point to other forms of cyberattacks including APTs and ransomware. A subtype, spear phishing, is more developed now, with the attackers using specific information about targets to enhance the chances of success [4, 20]. Insider threats also pose a big threat since individuals who have been hired or contracted owe allegiance to the companies they work with, hence becoming a threat to the organizations. In particular, insider threats are often difficult to identify and address for the simple reason that they possess authorized access to the organizational networks and may possess knowledge about their functioning. Businesses are now starting to conduct security awareness training and utilizing behavior analytic programs in an effort to minimize visits from social engineers and threats from insiders [2, 10].

2.3.7 Supply Chain Attacks

Supply chain attacks are focused on exploiting gaps within a target's supply chain; the hackers infiltrate the primary through a third-party vendor, contractor, or service provider. One of the many dangers is that utilizing close connections between digital supply chains, a malicious party can get to what has otherwise been a secure area. Third-party supply chain risks have become more common in the last few years due to breaches like the SolarWinds incident, which emphasizes the looming threats of third-party access and coupling [17]. These attacks are hard to counter because they target actual business partners within the supply chain; hence, it is always hard to diagnose and counter any potential compromises. Measures employed to reduce supply chain

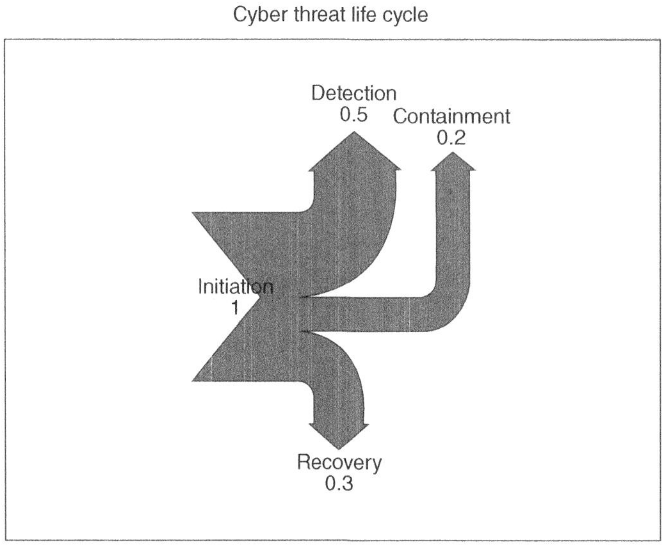

Figure 2.6 Cyber threat life cycle. Source: Hewa Majeed Zangana.

risks include screening third-party suppliers and providing them with access controls as well as installing surveillance systems to continuously monitor for signs of irregularities [18]. It is crucial to know more about the threat cycle so as to protect an organization against those threats. The subsequent flow chart indicates the usual phases of a cyber threat from conception to its control (Figure 2.6).

2.3.8 Summary

The contemporary threat landscape consists of a complex and diverse set of sophisticated threats, each of which brings new challenges for the defender. From the endless stalking of APTs to the devastating impact of ransomware and the ubiquitous DDoS attacks, organizations can only protect themselves if they are willing to develop multi-layered cybersecurity approaches that will fit every form of cyber threat. Furthermore, the incorporation of new technologies like IoT and AI has increased the threat landscape, meaning that there are new angles of attack to consider. It is crucial to know the prevailing forms of the twenty-first-century threats for an organization to formulate protective mechanisms and various countermeasures against emerging cyber risks [8, 12, 26].

2.4 Motivations Behind Modern Cyber Threats

The goals set by the contemporary cyberspace threats are differentiated and correspond to their nature: the desire for money, power, military intent, and ideas [45]. Cyberattackers are either state-sponsored groups, cybercriminal groups, hacktivists, or insider attackers, and all of them have different motives influenced by their background and ends. It is these motivations that need to be fully understood in order to determine the strategies for "countering" the Cyber threats as it is apparent that for many, the 'tools of the trade' and targets share a lot in common with the attackers' goals and desires. As this part of the work has shown, there are the main concerns of the postmodern epoch, cyber threats based on the literature review.

2.4.1 Financial Gain

This is specifically because fifty percent of the cyber threats happen in order to facilitate financial gains. Hackers break into these systems in order to grab information like credit card numbers, personal identification data, or a company's secrets and then sell it to others on the Internet black market. Among those, ransomware attacks in which the attackers encrypt the organization's data and demand a ransom for the release of these data are especially profitable, especially if the organization belongs to a critical industry, such as healthcare or finance [15, 25]. Other cybercrimes that have a financial motivation are also evident since cryptocurrency gives the attacker anonymity and simplicity of the transactions, irrespective of the geography. Cryptocurrencies have become popular and more here to means that cybercriminals have been receiving their ransoms and other payments in a way that cannot be easily tracked by the authorities [18]. Such attacks also contribute to a global underground economy in which the attackers sell data and malware resources [19].

2.4.2 Political Influence and Espionage

Cyberwar is often used in an attempt to gain political or some other kind of advantage over another nation-state. Such operations can relieve intelligence, theft of information, or disruptive actions against foreign governments, usually focusing on state infrastructure or politically intrusion facilities. Cyber espionage practices enable states to gather intelligence with minimal direct political consequences having to do with conventional spying [2, 16]. APTs tend to be conspiratorial in nature and linked to political end than criminal domains since these are typically sponsored by states. For instance, it can be used by state-sponsored actors to interfere with election systems or government databases in order to monitor or manipulate election results and processes [1, 3]. Such campaigns can define the functioning of diplomatic relations and are becoming more and more considered as tools of new generations' war, because they force the states to impose pressure without overt hostility [9].

2.4.3 Military and Strategic Objectives

Hacktivism is now an essential part of any military tactical approach since it enables the breakdown of an opponent via soft-power mechanisms, excluding the use of force. Cyberattacks may be employed by state actors as a way of diminishing an opponent's force coefficients or destroying such elements as supplies, and attacking command and control systems, which can provide the actor with battlefield advantage [13, 14]. For example, disruption of an adversary's communication nets, or satellite control assets, can severely degrade its ability to conduct operations, hence lowering its efficiency. The attack on the Iranian nuclear centrifuges known as Stuxnet is another classical example of state-led cyber operation targeting military goals. Such operations fit well into the large discourse on digital conflict as a replacement or an addition to conventional warfare, with current conflicts characterized by cyberattacks on military and civil infrastructures [17, 29].

2.4.4 Ideological and Social Motivation (Hacktivism)

Hacktivism is any hacking performed by individuals whose primary goal is the advancement of a cause than primarily monetary or strategic. Cybercriminals use cyber terrorism as a form of civil disobedience or as a tactic in support of a civil campaign, fight against organizations, governments, or companies the hackers regard as unfair. They more common attack techniques include website defacement, data disclosure, or DDoS that causes service interruption [5, 10]. Some of the well publicly known hacktivist groups include the Anonymous, who normally attack bodies they feel perpetrate human injustices, spy on the people by authorities, or pull off scams and unlawful acts by companies. These actors therefore use cyberattack tools to bring about a change of attitude or a change of policy within society or organizations. Almost all hacktivists' attacks are not as sophisticated as state-backed ones, yet they are capable of inflicting serious reputational losses and operational disruptions on the target organizations [8].

2.4.5 Technological Superiority and Cyber Deterrence

Some nation-states operate cyber electronically to both superintend and assert technological dominance or set cues of cyber deterrence notice as an authority. These states use perfected cyber skills as a tool to warn off attackers from targeting their structures or interests for fear of being dealt an equivalent blow [7, 11]. Cyber deterrence is the use of threats for a counteraction in the form of proportional or asymmetric cyber operations so as to deter the potential attacker. For example, such states as the United States and Russia spend a lot of money on offense weapons, as well as defense against any actions by an adversary against critical infrastructure. Similarly, capability exhibits in the cyber domain can also bolster a state's geopolitical position and shape norms of cyberspace operations [23, 28].

2.4.6 Disruption and Destabilization

Some cyber actors seek to overthrow unstable governments and economic systems of targeted states for the purpose of the achievement of geopolitical goals. These actors want to disrupt societies, undermine governments, and negate the population's confidence in institutions by using fake news, cyber terrorism, and economic sabotage. It may be in the interest of state actors to use such strategies in order to subvert the competitors without the use of conflict which is in fact latent [6, 12]. Thus, the use of social media and other platforms for the purpose of creating disinformation campaigns is a particularly effective method for accomplishing depriving the targeted population of stability. Such campaigns may include the dissemination of wrong information, fueling social enmity, or even promoting dissenting questions and concerns within a populace. This strategy has been used in different elections and political campaigns all over the world, where opponents use the adversary's weaknesses to cause disorder within their society [20, 26].

2.4.7 Economic Competition

Cyber threats are also motivated by economic competition as the main one among the main categories of threats. Economic spying, in the information age, transpires through cyberspace and allows companies or states to gather data that accord their organizations a competitive advantage. Governments may promote such endeavors to develop their sectors, secure national economic interests, or attain superior technologies to those possessed by other nations [4, 22]. For instance, the piracy of ideas in computer firms may lead to rival firms mimicking products or developing techniques, which took the innovating firms years to develop. This kind of economic espionage could affect a nation's market edge in key markets, most especially in telecommunication, aerospace, and in the manufacture of drugs [15]. As seen in economics competition through cyber espionage, it is thus fitting that international relations and cyber operations in the global economy cannot be understood without considering the respective national interests in [27].

2.4.8 Summary

Modern cyber threats' incentives are also diverse, financial, political, strategic, social, and even economical. As such motivations persist, one anticipates even more growth, creativity, and general compliance that cyber threats will reflect the goals of state and non-state actors. The identification of these motivations is useful in developing counteraction strategies that would help to counter threats from different entities with the right predictions of goals and objectives. As a result of the primary factors of cyber threats, society and government institutions can proactively approach cyber risks in a changing and developmental cyberspace [1, 18, 24].

2.5 Case Studies of Recent High-Impact Attacks

Studying case scenarios provides fundamental understanding about the approach of cyber incidents, their consequences, and the overall implications related to the threat of cybercrime in the modern globalized society. These case scenarios offer a comprehensive and detailed examination of major cyber events that demonstrate threat actor's capacity and intent, in addition to the used techniques and attacked domains. In these cases, generalizing from the current tactics and defenses required to prevent future attacks is made possible by analyzing these case studies.

2.5.1 SolarWinds Supply Chain Attack

The SolarWinds cyber espionage attack was a recently identified attack that targeted several departments of the U.S. government and some companies in 2020. This cyberattack is thought to have been perpetrated by a nation-state actor which sought to infiltrate SolarWinds, an IT management company, by infiltrating its software supply chain. The hackers inserted a backdoor in SolarWinds' Orion update that was sent out to thousands of clients as part of typical updates [13, 28].

This attack shows risks related to supply chain security, in which threats to one trusted party can affect numerous others. The case of SolarWinds shows how nation-state-level attacker operationally uses APTs to conduct espionage without causing immediate alarms [22, 25]. Its size and anonymity demonstrate why supply chain security has become a critical factor in contemporary cybersecurity models.

2.5.2 Colonial Pipeline Ransomware Attack

An example of this is the hacking of the Colonial Pipeline in May of 2021 by the Darkside ransomware group—this knocked out fuel supplies across the eastern United States and caused panic as well as economic consequences. The attackers launched ransomware to lock the company's information and later demanded a ransom to unlock it. In the same regard, Colonial Pipeline made the decision of paying the ransom, thereby revealing one of the difficult choices organizations are put in under cyberattacks [4, 15]. This attack was able to show how leaving critical infrastructure open to attack can lead to problems with ransomware, thus leaving services open to potential threats. The Colonial Pipeline episode demonstrates the physical consequences of a cyberattack and its implications for sociotechnical cybersecurity regulatory norms in critical infrastructure protection [3, 27]. It further focused on the key strategies of cyber deterrence and supply chain risk management in order to reduce the potential effects of ransomware for the country [16].

2.5.3 WannaCry and NotPetya Malware Campaigns

The two main cyberattacks that used malware for dissemination and wreaked havoc are WannaCry and NotPetya of the calendar year 2017. WannaCry is another ransomware that affected hundreds of thousands of computers in the whole world and attacked systems which used a vulnerability in the Microsoft operating system. While blamed on North Korean state actors, WannaCry impacted different sectors, for e.g., health via the United Kingdom's National Health Service [18, 26].

While NotPetya focused on Ukrainian corporations, the attack rapidly extended to worldwide business entities and was extremely costly in terms of trade impact. Compared with typical ransomware, NotPetya aimed more at disruption than at financial extraction: it seemed politically motivated—in its intent [12, 19]. Many cyberattacks starting with limited goals, show how malware, intended for specific purposes, can turn into global campaigns; it clearly underlines the danger of cyberattacks and their potential for reaching across all industries.

2.5.4 Russian Election Interference and Disinformation Campaigns

In recent years, cyber-enabled false information attacks have become a standard tool of state actors seeking to influence political processes. Russian interference in the 2016 US presidential election comprised cyberattacks on political organizations and the leakage of intel on these organizations and the spread of fake news through social media accounts. This kind of influence operation is an excellent example of a synergy between cyber and psychological operations to use technology as a tool to amplify influence on narratives [9, 20]. Another element of such campaigns shows that cyber warfare can go beyond attacking the critical infrastructure and focus on getting around democratic processes. By leveraging social and other platforms, nation states are willing to manipulate politics of the target nation in particular and the world at large in general, hence confirming the role of digital information warfare in the age of cyberspace [26].

2.5.5 Stuxnet and the Weaponization of Malware

The first real-world noteworthy virus that actually produced tangible physical effects in 2010 was the Stuxnet worm. Reported to have been launched to sabotage the nuclear centrifuges in Iranian nuclear power plants, Stux is a known state-sponsored cyberspace operation which introduced software that made the centrifuges malfunction, hence causing a delay in Iran's nuclear program. This cyber-physical attack showed how cyber tools can act as weapons or influence tools as understood by Refs. [5, 14].

Chinese scholars also say that Stuxnet has implications that are not limited to a more effective attack on Iran's infrastructure. It provided ways on how to use cyber power in military and geopolitics, hence highlighting the value of securely protecting critical infrastructures [15, 23]. Further, Stuxnet introduced questions of ethical and legal standards concerning the operation of cyber weapons and motives and restrictions of cyber warfare.

2.5.6 Attack on Saudi Aramco: Shamoon Malware

The Shamoon malware attack in 2012 aimed at the Saudi Aramco company, one of the largest companies in the oil sector, and deleted data from more than 30 thousand computers and stopped work. This attack has been estimated to be politically instigated probably because it occurred at the time of a time of tension in the Middle East. The Shamoon malware erased important business information and left Saudi Aramco offline, and thus, it demonstrated a degree of the cyber risk for any companies, even those possessing ample resources and capital [7, 10]. In essence, the Shamoon attack revealed threats to the psyche of energy sector structures, especially in politically volatile areas. The assault on Saudi Aramco showed how cyber capabilities could be applied as a type of economic warfare that occasioned a big monetary loss on the involved organization [1, 29]. It also points to the possibility of a cyber-domain Network Operations Warfare (NOW) as the region's actors try to harness technology to disrupt rivals and engage in virtual coordinated combat.

2.5.7 Healthcare Sector Attacks During the COVID-19 Pandemic

Throughout the stay-at-home orders of the COVID-19 crisis, healthcare was named one of the most attractive attack vectors for cyber actors and their ransomware phishing campaigns. The Associated Press (AP) revealed that cybercriminals attempted to take advantage of weaknesses in healthcare organizations, with overloaded systems contaminating patient data and abusing the institutions' hospitals and research facilities. These attacks created dire consequences for patients and stalled the fight against this disease [11, 25].

They highlighted real ethics issues of attacking services in the course of a pandemic. The COVID-19 pandemic and the subsequent targeted attacks against healthcare also highlighted the importance of the government and organizations to acknowledge and consider cybersecurity as a critical factor, having regard for necessary fields, one of the disastrous results of cyber threats can entail to public health and safety [17, 19].

2.5.8 Targeted Attack on NATO's Digital Infrastructure

As a result of the changing global political environment, North Atlantic Treaty Organization (NATO)-related digital networks have become more frequently under cyber threats from hostile actors. This particular type of cyberattacks most frequently targets signal control, reconnaissance, and command facilities of NATO, thus eradicating much of its operational capacity and public trust in its protective capacity. An example is the sequence of cyberattacks on NATO member countries and their key infrastructure traced to Russian contractors [2, 24]. Of such attacks, cyber capabilities in hybrid warfare and the role of cybersecurity in military relationships are highlighted. These events are useful for NATO as it progresses in building an effective cybersecurity framework to learn about the necessary perseverance and flexibility needed to protect important defense resources in the twenty-first century [6, 18].

2.5.9 Summary

The case studies presented in this chapter reveal the various goals and numerous implications of more salient cyber operations, from espionage and deception to direct destruction and economic contest. All the examples reveal how significant cybersecurity is for governments, industries, and international associations, all aiming at the idea that the cyber domain represents a strategic battleground between competing powers. By gauging the tactics and consequences of these high-impact events, we are ready for the new threats and are part of designing new, more efficient defense mechanisms as the environment in the cyberspace becomes hostile [8, 22].

2.6 Emerging Technologies and their Role in Cyber Threat Evolution

The growth of emergent technologies has accelerated and brought significant changes to the cybersecurity domain, improving the use of cyber tools both on the offence and defense side. These technologies have raised the level and scale of cyber threats, as well as their potential range, turning into new problems for security experts and states. The most important technological trends, namely AI, quantum computing, the IoT, and 5G networks, are becoming more and more intricately linked with cyber threats.

2.6.1 AI and ML

Automations have formed a promising front in modern cybersecurity, bolstered by AI and ML. On the other hand, AI is also a useful technology for these cyber adversaries since the utilization of AI enables attack and exploitation actions to be integrated and escalated. According to Ref. [19], today's opponents are using AI to develop better and highly developed malware, perform phishing attacks, and even escape detection due to the incorporation of intelligential algorithms. To prevent the prevention of traditional cybersecurity tools from coping up with this correctly, AI tools enable attackers to browse through large datasets to find shortcomings faster [27]. Moreover, the AI in the context of threat hunting and incident response (IR) helps make decisions at the speed of response, while the data-driven nature of such AI also reveals how AI systems remain prone to adversarial attacks, in which the attackers tamper with input data to deceive AI [13].

2.6.2 Quantum Computing and Cryptographic Threats

Quantum computing can be seen as an upcoming revolution in cybersecurity because with the concentration of computational power, the current encryption standards can be easily compromised. Rivest–Shamir–Adleman (RSA) and ECC can be solved by quantum computers, which also means that the current means of data protection are no longer effective [15]. As mentioned by Ref. [18], with the advent of quantum computing can spur a new age of quantum immune encryption. In preparation for this emerging change, cybersecurity researchers are turning their attention to post-quantum cryptography in order to preserve data's invulnerability to quantum-equipped opponents. While quantum computing may not yet be widely available, the race toward its development poses an existential threat to the security of digital information worldwide [12].

2.6.3 The Internet of Things and Network Vulnerabilities

The increasing number of IoT devices raises the attack surface significantly because many of these devices have weak security at best. IoT brings challenging new risks, including to healthcare, energy, and transport systems [28]. Internet of Things Communications (IoT COM) makes management and control possible through a network connection, thereby making physical systems susceptible to cyber means typically referred to as cyber-physical attacks [6]. More recently, Faizan [25] has pointed out that IoT attacks could endanger both personal privacy and national security; therefore, IoT security should have highly strict guidelines for deployment. IoT devices can also be dangerous in military and intelligence settings, with potential uses for spying for reconnaissance or destruction changing the balance of forces in cyber war [11].

2.6.4 5G Networks and the Increased Risk of Cyber Espionage

The deployment of 5G communication technology across the world has improved the way devices connect and the rate at which data is shared, especially in smart cities, self-driving car technology, and tele-surgery, among others. However, bandwidth and low latency resulting from 5G networks have other risks presented next [7]. Other risks arising from the integration of 5G networks include [23]: pointing out that since 5G would create massive interception capability, the cyber espionage could go to another level. Furthermore, the use of decentralized software-defined infrastructure creates an added layer of difficulty for the network's security team to combat and for attackers to gain control of network components [26]. As argued by Ref. [1], 5G may indeed revolutionize military communication tactics and the reliability of defense systems for which a new security paradigm must be adopted.

2.6.5 Blockchain and Distributed Ledger Technology (DLT) in Cybersecurity

Blockchain and also DLT are promoted as tools capable of protecting the data exchange and providing transparency across industries. Some of the main features that give blockchain a secure status are these: unlike other traditional techniques, the attacker cannot post false data onto the system since this requires compromising the majority of nodes in the network [4]. Currently, this technology has significant applications in protecting financial operations, ensuring data integrity, and increasing the use of supply chain solutions' accountability [14]. However, concrete application of technology leads to new problems, among which are cryptocurrencies that focus on anonymity for their users, which makes it difficult to track them for cybercriminal activity. Blockchain being both loved and feared for its security aspect and the fact that it can be used by bad actors to advance their nefarious activities shows that while regulation and governing are important, development of proper, versatile technology should also be encouraged [20].

2.6.6 Autonomous Systems and Cyber-Physical Risks

The possibility of the use of drones or self-driving vehicles means the possibility of cyber-physical risk in the field of cybersecurity. Of all those systems that are of low interaction with the human operators, the most probable are to be manipulated through an AI attack that leads to physical consequences. Pruteanu et al. [24] note that autonomy is a crucial factor in military and strategic procedures, and if these systems get mishandled, their result is devastating. The threat actors are capable of taking advantage of vulnerabilities in the control systems of drones or vehicles to cause disruption in such infrastructure and logistic or defense platforms. These cyber and physical domains are interlinked and represent the complex threat consequences of technological innovations in warfare [2].

2.6.7 Cloud Computing and Data Security Challenges

Cloud computing has emerged as a critical component of enterprise solutions and has defined the management and storage of data assets. However, data migration to the cloud also presents new security risks as cloud services are multitenant by nature and share resources, making cross-tenant attacks possible, according to Ref. [3]. Other risks found in cloud computing are testing or getting unauthorized access to providers where unscrupulous individuals get access to important data through poor or manipulated configurations and phishing, among others [10]. Cloud computing infrastructure also offers adaptable amenities to the attackers in order to conduct DDoS attack and also stressed the importance of an effective cloud security framework [5].

2.6.8 Implications for Defense and Security

The intense adoption of these novel information and communication technologies (ICTs) has reshaped the traditional concepts of implementing and waging cybersecurity and cyber warfare in strategic information technology security. AI, quantum computing, IoT, 5G, and many other technologies are making the new face of cyber threats where adversaries are using new technologies to advance their cyber operations. This shift raises questions about defense approaches and orientations: proactive security, horizontal cooperation, and institutional frameworks at the national and global levels [16]. This is through the lens of Ref. [8], who asserts that the future of cybersecurity lies squarely in deciding the probability and effects of the rising technologies in determining the future of cyber warfare. Such developments do not end with national security impacts, but shape the geopolitics of power and force countries to take measures of defense vis à vis a technologically superior foe. As pointed out by [5], there is a need to adjust laws and policies in 2024 to tackle the ethical and strategic issues presented by sophisticated cyberspace. These data show that there is a constant change in the nature of threats to networks and computer systems and that the process will continue, which means that there is a need to create secure structures and strong protection systems against new technologies' threats.

2.7 Defensive Strategies Against Evolving Cyber Threats

The changes in the type of threats affecting cyberspace have forced governments, organizations, and people to embrace integrated approaches to protect against threats. Cybersecurity is no longer a matter of safeguarding arbitrary networks; it has turned into complex methods of deterrence, intelligence, as well as resilience because cyber threats have evolved and expanded greatly [19]. This section delves into understanding the major defensive measures being taken to combat the advanced trend of cyber threats by analyzing the current existing technical and policy measures. Cybersecurity employs various layers of protection as explained herein next by way of a diagram indicating the layers of protection ranging from perimeter protection to endpoint protection (Figure 2.7).

2.7.1 Cyber Deterrence and Active Defense

Perhaps one of the most significant emerging trends in the cybersecurity environment is the persistence in the pursuit of cyber deterrence, which is the prevention of cyberattacks through deterrence of actual retaliation. Unlike conventional warfare, where the principles of deterrence have been in practice since the past century, this approach has little to do with real world warfare but adapted from old warfare strategies for it to suit the new technological environment of cyber warfare. Digmelashvili and Lagvilava [16] observed that cyber deterrence strategies are coupled with the "use of an actual, ready response to strikes in cyberspace which makes this kind of response uninviting to foes". Cyber deterrence also depends on assigning responsibility for attacks, which is normally difficult due to the nature of cyberspace. As pointed out by Black and Lynch [9], attribution issues require higher intelligence and forensic measures to enhance the threat of retaliation and hence deterrence. Active defense is not limited to the mere higher degrees of deterrence with

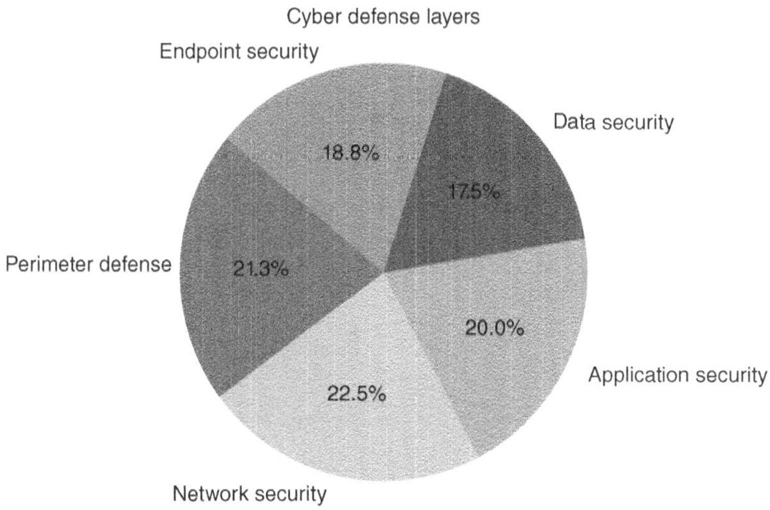

Figure 2.7 Cyber defense layers. Source: Hewa Majeed Zangana.

the use of counter and defense measures to counter threats before they emerge. This includes the use of "honeypots" and "honeynets" that will help organizations capture the method used by attackers as the first alert and independent analysis of new threats [18]. Open-active-type defense tactics, however, are not wholly distinct from offense tactics because they can be questionable under legal and ethical perspectives when performed across different countries [13].

2.7.2 Zero Trust Architecture (ZTA) and Network Segmentation

Zero Trust is a security concept that is different from the principles of perimeter-based security. ZTA works on the foundation that there is no inherently trustworthy device or individual whether or not they are within the context of an organizational network or outside of it. Every request to access is constantly checked, and this means that if any point in the network is penetrated, an attempt to access data is constantly denied [23]. ZTA concerns a constant and user-winning check for enhanced security rather than a single standalone approach against astute threats. Another strong feature is a network segmentation that splits networks into separate areas to stop actors from moving from one segment to another if they have already penetrated the company's perimeter [3]. Subdividing an organization's internal network into segments can help reduce the extent of threats that can be unleashed if a system becomes compromised. According to Ziauddin [29], segmentation is particularly important in high-risk industries, especially where the operational network is separated from the administrative network as a means of avoiding near-disaster experiences.

2.7.3 Threat Intelligence and Information Sharing

Threat intelligence is the concerned flow of timely information which can warn an organization about threats and the methodologies it is utilizing to counter those threats. Threat intelligence, therefore, refers to information about attack tactics, actors, and threats in the global environment that security teams proactively protect against before an incident occurs [12]. Thus, Sharma and Gupta [27] are correct in stating that threat intelligence's value is in the adversary's incapacity to deduce from new knowledge proactive shifts that threat intelligence must make in its opponents.

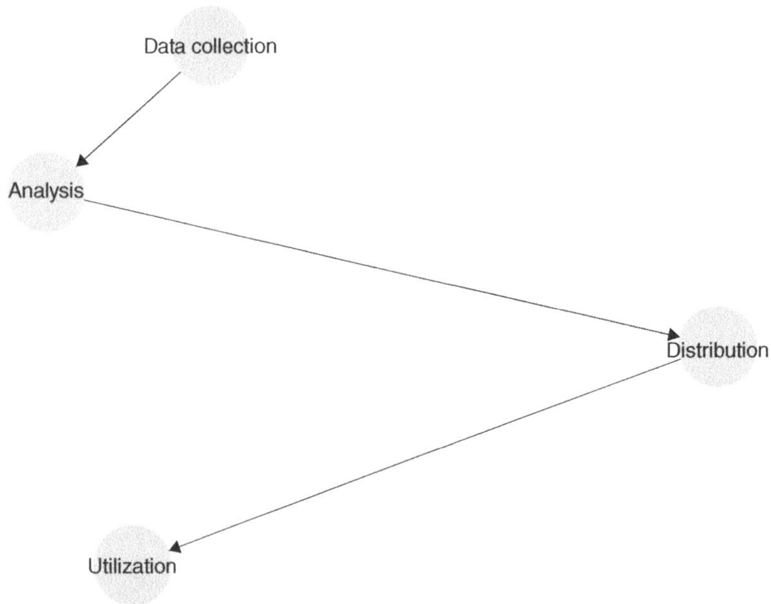

Figure 2.8 Cyber threat intelligence information flow. Source: Hewa Majeed Zangana.

Second, they also developed an idea of the cybersecurity partnership between the government and private companies because information will improve the defense line for all the members. Inter-organization camaraderie is also important, especially because of the cross-boundary issues with cyber interventions. For example, the cybersecurity policy of NATO calls for a sharing of intelligence in cyberspace with member-nations for the protection of mutually understood critical information infrastructure. It makes it easier to share new threat intelligence that can help nations collectively respond to state actor's cyberspace attacks. This flowchart illustrates how the normal flow of cyber threat intelligence works and how data is collected and processed for a better security (Figure 2.8).

2.7.4 Advanced Cyber Hygiene and Security Awareness Training

This makes human error still as one of the biggest threats in cybersecurity, and with tactics like phishing, which [25] noted will still be effective by the year 2024. These are some of the weaknesses in which developments in advanced cyber hygiene practices will seek to reduce these through comprehensive training and security measures. End-user security awareness training informs employees on generic attack schemes thus increasing the ability to ward off potential security threats. Further, a few are also using phishing and feedback for enhancing the employees' behavior toward security [15].

Security hygiene goes further than simply raising the consciousness of the worker; it entails properly managing access throughout a program or fixing and strengthening known software weaknesses and applying updates and patches on the systems [14]. "Updating on demand and using MFA are the ways to avoid breaches due to old systems or poor credentials, thus meeting the goal of strengthen." To quote [29], a good cyber hygiene regime acts as the first line of defense to contemporary cyber threats.

2.7.5 Artificial Intelligence and Machine Learning in Defensive Operations

Advanced technologies like AI with ML have become fully integrated into today's cybersecurity because of their capacity to scour large amounts of data for signs of irregularities. Using big data and other forms of AI, security can be fully automated to detect threats more promptly and with higher precision than analysts who have to do this manually, identify threats, and respond instantly [11]. These systems are most useful in the context of APTs, which otherwise take a long time and are otherwise hard to identify and counter [22]. It is also used in ML algorithms to enhance the predictiveness, which the ML algorithm has used past data to determine attack patterns and possible threats in the future [28]. However, AI-driven defense requires careful management since AI's adversaries can influence it through adversarial attacks. Furthermore, Cunningham [2] said that the application of AI depends on the extension of models to counter the ongoing procedural techniques in defending.

2.7.6 Cyber Resilience and Incident Response Planning

When breaches are inevitable, the next logical thing is for organizations to embrace cyber resilience. Resilience tactics are framed as maintaining operations during and after an assault and establishing as quickly as possible while preventing disruptions [8]. An organization's incident response plan (IRP) is the core of cyber resilience and outlines what needs to be done in case of a breach, from detection, through containment and eradication, to recovery.

IR essentials involve several branches such as IT, legal, and public relations since the fast actions and reporting will help to contain reputational harms. Now as stated by Efe [7], what is important for policy planning is periodic revisits and updating of IRPs in response to new threats and creating awareness of the staff in the implementation of the response protocol under imitation attack. This proactive approach to incident management ensures that organizations are able to return to their optimal state rapidly and minimize the duration a breach will have on an organization [17]. The following diagram presents the normal IR life cycle which highlights the necessary measures needed to address cyber threats (Figure 2.9).

2.7.7 Quantum-Resistant Encryption

More so, with the rise of quantum computing, current modes of encryption can be rendered useless in the future. To this end, all organizations are already trying to search for new ways of preparing themselves and are already considering quantum-resistant encryption algorithms that would be capable of overcoming the possibilities offered by quantum computing. Quantum-safe cryptography is a way forward to prevent the vulnerability of data by quantum computers from quantum computing since quantum computers are expected to break complexity like RSA and elliptic curve cryptography (ECC) in a much shorter time than what is expected from them [4]. As Bardin [18] wrote, such a shift is seen as an imperative need and a priority of information-processing industries that rely on the security of their information, for example, financial or healthcare industries. Because implementing these algorithms is not easy, shifting to quantum-safe cryptography may need the cooperation of the nations of the world and research and development investment [21].

2.7.8 Policy-Based Approaches and Cybersecurity Frameworks

Baldwin and Egelhoff, 2005:147 posit that in an attempt to have standard measures by which to practice as well as enforce cybersecurity, there has been a surge in the use of regulations.

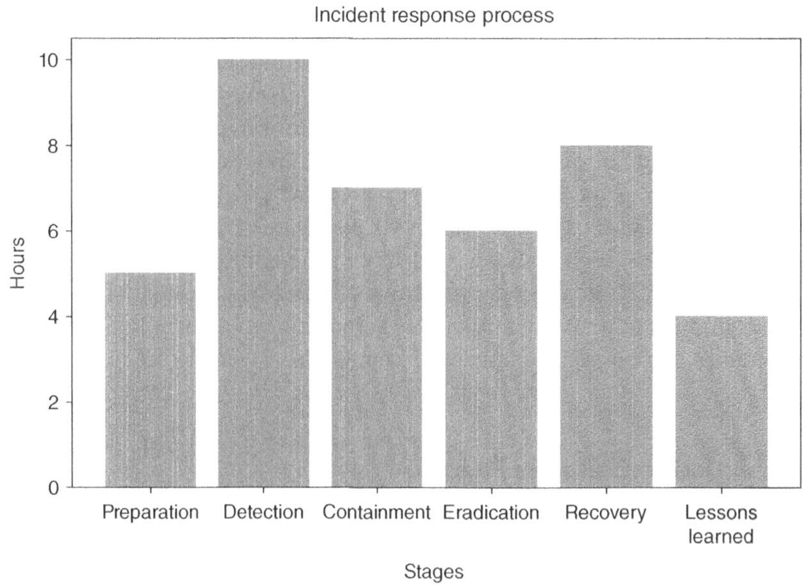

Figure 2.9 Incident response process. Source: Hewa Majeed Zangana.

Currently, global models like the National Institute of Standards and Technology (NIST) Cyber Security Framework and ISO/IEC 27001 offer broad best practice strategies to enforce increased cybersecurity [20]. They give an organization a structured approach for evaluating dangers, applying protection controls, and enhancing security positions consistently.

Global legislation, examples of which include General Data Protection Regulation (GDPR) and the Cybersecurity Act of the European Union is considered under this category owing to its focus on aspects of regulating cyberspace and ensuring the protection of citizens' data [10]. Moreover, international actions such as the Paris Call for Trust and Security in Cyberspace prove that there should be a common understanding of regulating threats in cyberspace among countries [5].

2.7.9 Summary

The measures described above are set and follow an aggressive and informed approach to addressing emerging cyber risks. Thus, because cyber adversaries are constantly developing new and improved methods of attack, civilian governments, organizations, and persons must become correspondingly proficient in their countermeasures. For better understanding, let me define it more clearly: it's a dynamic field not only that yes, there is a cybersecurity procedure but it needs to be updated from time to time. These are among the modern strategies in cybersecurity; technology in computer science including use of AI, quantum-resistant encryption, and others; policy in phrases of collective security and others. With such threats in the cyberspace domain persistently developing, so is the need for strategies to secure cyberspace engaged incessantly.

2.8 Role of Government and International Collaboration

Given the emerging trends where the entire world is embracing digital solutions, government and international organizations have specific responsibilities in addressing cyber risk. Due to the nature and kind of threats posed by cyber espionage, cybercriminals, and cyber war, a concerted effort has become inevitable in order to ensure national security and orderliness in the cyber frontier [4, 14]. Tackling the problem of cyber defense calls for national policies along with international cooperation achieved through collaborative conventional methods in the form of international treaties, conventions, and recommendations.

2.8.1 National Governments: Leading Cyber Defense Efforts

Bureaus are on the frontline in the formation of cybersecurity policies, regulations, and frameworks to safeguard structures important to a nation's security. As several governments have set up centralized security agencies and provided for defense as well as for responders, the respective governments are now capable to handle advanced attacks. In the USA, for example, the Department of Homeland Security and the Cybersecurity and Infrastructure Security Agency (CISA) are the major stakeholders in setting up and applying cybersecurity measures. In the same way, other countries are building capabilities of their own agencies, as well as further improving the private and public interface to enhance the robustness of consequential sectors [7]. It is important to understand that the government's role does not only comprise defense in the field of cybersecurity. Most countries have assimilated offense capabilities with this making it possible for an aggressor to be retaliated in the same manner that he or she attacked [26]. This fits in an emerging paradigm that conceptualizes cyberspace as the fifth operational domain below air, land, and sea domains where a nation's power lies in defense [2, 13].

2.8.2 International Collaboration: Establishing Norms and Cooperative Frameworks

Cybersecurity is inherently an international issue since the origination of the attacks is also across international borders, and the impacts are also borne by more than one country. Consequently, only the unification of the efforts of different countries for countering these threats is possible. Some organizations, such as NATO, have adopted the incorporation of cybersecurity in their strategic plans owing to increased cases of cyber war as a real fight in the current conflict [9]. NATO's strategy for the year 2030 demonstrates a more assertive posture to CYBER defense by focusing on intelligence sharing; joint training exercises; and research on fresh CYBER defense measures [1].

Another essential element is also focused on the United Nations that contributes to sustaining dialogues and recognition of cyber norms. Due to efforts like the UN Group of Governmental Experts (GGE) and the Open-ended Working group (OEWG), member states have deliberated on the theme of responsible behavior in cyberspace. Such has prepared the grounds for setting several norms that frown on any attempt to target critical infrastructure as well as general 2191-word openness and collaboration in managing cybersecurity incidents [15].

2.8.3 Challenges and Future Directions for Government and International Cooperation

However, there are still problems in international cooperation in cyberspace. There is a lot of inconsistency in the approach between the relative national policies and frameworks of the countries and the average general development of the cyberspace authorities. Moreover, ideological and geographical differences contribute to the creation of standard rules regarding cyberspace, more so, given that major cyber actors, including the United States, China, and Russia, have different visions of the internet's governance and users' data protection [5, 19]. The political dimension of cyber incidents, allowing states to blame each other for tampering even when there is no solid evidence also poses a challenge for collaboration [3]. In order to solve these problems, it is recommended to develop a number of approaches to international cooperation, which are nested. A cyber event, which is the development of a multinational standardized information gathering (SIG), to provide a real-time continuous integration (CI) for sharing cyber threat data could also improve global response [17]. In addition, there is another way that governments can promote more formation of regional fellowships like NATO concerning cybersecurity within certain geopolitical domains, which, in turn, can build trust and provide contextual understandings between neighboring countries [16].

2.8.4 The Role of Private Sector and Civil Society in Cybersecurity Collaboration

Hence, governments and international organizations remain valuable but so is the private sector and civil society. A significant number of critical infrastructures are provided and managed by private companies, especially in the areas of telecommunication, banking, and energy, and as such cooperation with these organizations is crucial in any multisectoral security approach [12]. There is a potential to enhance the overall readiness and perform the expressed functions faster in case of a cyberattack since, on average, private organizations own more sophisticated tools and technologies compared to governmental agencies [25]. Last but not least, civil society organizations play a role in promoting affirmative action, accountability, and corporate social responsibilities along with human rights and identity theft within cyberspace. It is those organizations that challenge authorities to be answerable and explain the impact of cybersecurity policies on the freedom of people, especially with regards to surveillance and privacy of data [22]. Cybersecurity strategy as is, therefore, holistic, enlisting research and participation from all cross-sections of society to combat the diverse nature of cyber threats. National governments, global-acting organizations, and the business world can collectively build a safer cyberspace as a result of implemented national policies that support international collaboration. Trends show that as threats become more complex, the role played by collaborative frameworks can only assume even greater importance for global peace and security in the period ahead.

2.9 Future Trends and Threat Landscape

To move on, the advanced current novel threat is traceable to significant improvements in technology and shifts in global politics. While societies develop their infrastructures mainly based on computers, the consequences of cyber war and cybercriminality become even more multifaceted. This section focuses on future trends in the threat environment, new technologies, new tactics, and changes in national and international security measures.

2.9.1 Technological Advancements and Their Implications

The ever-evolving world of Rosetta Stone for technologies, including AI, ML, and the IoT, is changing the character of cyber threats. While these technologies improve defensive outcomes, they also enable malicious actors to efficiently perform more complex attack outcomes. For instance, AI in an attack setting can essentially orchestrate forms of cyberattacks to enable the adversary to exploit effectiveness and efficiency at enormous proportions and tremendously high velocities [21]. Additionally, they argue that, as organizations connect new IoT devices to their networks, the size of potential attack vectors increases as there are more opportunities for the attackers [23]. Cloud computing is gradually becoming the standard mode of computing and has major security implications. When data is moved to the cloud, organizations must deal with challenges like ownership, privacy, and legal requirements of data. Due to this migration, cloud service providers have become the most attractive targets for cyberattackers since a breakthrough in them results in massive data breach [25]. The future cybersecurity business models should aim to safeguard cloud deployments alongside addressing access controls and other encryption techniques that provide defense mechanisms against threats to sensitive data, according to Ref. [19].

2.9.2 Evolving Cyber Warfare Tactics

The strategic behaviors in cyber warfare are dynamic and are influenced by factors of improvement in technology and international relations. Cyber warfare is now frequently carried out by non-state actors, where hackers and cybercriminals act for political purposes, or to gain finances [6]. Subscribing to a modus operandi of versatility, these groups perform actions from utilizing ransomware to strike electricity plants to information warfare to sway people's opinion and overthrow governments [14]. In conventional politics and military, nation-states are utilizing hybrid warfare where they use conventional cyberspace and other forces. This approach enables state actors to accomplish intents during statecraft while not being traced back to them. For instance, based on recent hot international conflicts, states may engage in cyber operations to target an adversary's military command and control networks, thus achieving a superiority on the battlefield [26]. As this trend continues, countries will need to develop more integrated defense strategies that encompass both cyber and conventional military capabilities [8].

2.9.3 The Role of Cyber Deterrence and Defense Strategies

With the accelerating changes in threat actors and their attacks, concepts of cyber deterrence emerge. Nations are gradually seeking to develop effective signals that will in a way prevent the enemy from performing a cyberattack. This means going beyond enhancing security measures while building capabilities of a proactive nature that can be used if faced with major cyber threats [16]. The problem is to determine the correct approach and seek to deter but avoid escalating incidents to the point that they respond with further aggression. It also means that some strategies of cyber defense have to be updated also because of appearing new threats. The use of technological features like AI as well as ML in security strategies has been seen to improve threat recognition and counteraction. Such technologies are capable of detecting faults and threats and predicting them before they actually occur [18, 28]. Furthermore, it is also necessary that organizations implement policies meant for ongoing supervision and planning for incidents to ensure that these organizations could efficiently contain and counter the effects of cyber incidents, as stated by [15].

2.9.4 Implications for Policy and Governance

The future developments in cybersecurity require strong policy frameworks that would address characteristics of a constantly evolving threat space. There is much that governments can do to obtain the best advice and involve stakeholders effectively, including entering into a discussion with the other groups to ensure the formulation of multisectoral strategies designed to foster collaboration and the exchange of information [12]. In addition, there are risks for civil liberties, in the case

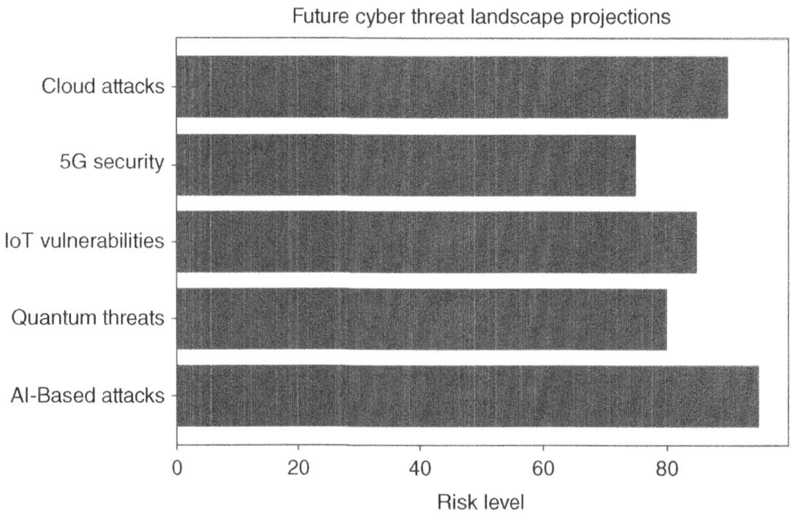

Figure 2.10 Future cyber threat landscape projections. Source: Hewa Majeed Zangana.

of intrusive high-tech surveillance with the increased use of emerging technologies and the impacts on privacy, where cybersecurity solutions should not and cannot violate peoples' rights [22]. On the international level, setting rules and regulations concerning the operations of states in cyberspace is equally important. With increasing frequency, cyber warfare emerges as the new technique of international conflict. Therefore, it requires international cooperation to come up with structures that delineate behavior standards and sanctions in cyberspace in the event of cyber worm attacks [5]. Such cooperation will be critical in fostering order in the global world as it progresses ahead with this integration [17].

With reference to the current dynamic nature of threats in cyberspace, this chart provides a forecast of areas that are most critical for future cybersecurity measures depending on technologies and threat actors (Figure 2.10).

2.9.5 Summary

Today and tomorrow's threat landscape is characterized by the fast growth of technologies, changes in tactics, and constantly shifting geopolitical processes. This is to further stress the significance of pursuing prevention measures on the international level, effective cooperation among countries in terms of cybersecurity, as well as the further strengthening of the policy frameworks. To ensure an effective response to the threats currently facing governments, organizations, and individuals, they should shift and constantly adapt, especially to the fast-growing technologies.

2.10 Conclusion

Therefore, it is accurate to state that the seas and space as the new domains of modern cyber warfare are very dynamic and constantly changing, which is why the traditional perception of security and defense is no longer sufficient. Since digital technologies are evolving with incredible velocity, the techniques and approaches of cyber war are changing at the same pace, too for the state and non-state performers. These risks and consequences increase due to the interactions of the modern world since every country is interconnected with others in some way; therefore, cybersecurity should not only comprise technological solutions, enhanced and effective policies, as well as international cooperation. AI and more broadly, ML and the IoT interconnect, and thus, it will be seen that these emerging technologies have introduced new threats and risks, yet at the same time, they are ones which may be used to better address these. In order to address these complexities, organizations' security implementations must focus on the following aspects: adaptive security and permanent reconnaissance in order not to become a victim of a threat. In this regard, improved hybrid warfare tactics that have become quite common require that state actors set up fused approaches that entail the use of cyberspace capabilities as part of an all-arms conflict since the former prepares for multisector conflict.

As well, the importance of foreign collaboration cannot be overemphasized. Since cyberspace knows no borders, cooperation and integration of states together with the private sector and non-governmental bodies must be achieved in the fight against cyber warfare. The important notion of creating appropriate standards and reference points to regulate the behavioral processes in the context of cyberspace will be critical for creating stability and achieving accountability. There is a need for policymakers to hold productive discussions in order to determine what is ethical in cyberspace security measures while protecting the public's rights, concurrently protecting the security of the state. Contrary to this, the future of cybersecurity is going to be defined more and more by new threats that have yet to emerge. Thus, the strategies, technologies, and governance structure of the digital domain should evolve alongside the ever-expanding digital landscape. Introducing the cultures of resilience and engagement shows the best practices to address the issues arising from cyber warfare to improve the societal standings of our societies.

References

1 Bellasio, J. and Silfversten, E. (2020). The impact of new and emerging technologies on the cyber threat landscape and their implications for NATO. Cyber Threats and NATO 2030: Horizon Scanning and Analysis. p. 88.

2 Cunningham, C. (2020). *Cyber Warfare–Truth, Tactics, and Strategies: Strategic Concepts and Truths to Help You and Your Organization Survive on the Battleground of Cyber Warfare*. Packt Publishing Ltd.

3 Smith, R. (2023). The evolution of cyber warfare strategies: a comparative analysis. *International Journal of Defence and Strategic Studies*, ISSN: 3078-4689 1 (1): 1–11.

4 Kim, S.K., Cheon, S.P., and Eom, J.H. (2019). A leading cyber warfare strategy according to the evolution of cyber technology after the fourth industrial revolution. *International Journal of Advanced Computer Research* 9 (40): 72–80.

5 Zakir, M.H., Allaudin, H., Khan, S.H., and Sultan, M. (2024). Adapting international humanitarian law for the digital battlefield: navigating cyber warfare and technological advancements. *Pakistan Journal of Law, Analysis and Wisdom* 3 (3): 54–66.

6 Kostyuk, N. and Zhukov, Y.M. (2019). Invisible digital front: can cyber attacks shape battlefield events? *Journal of Conflict Resolution* 63 (2): 317–347.

7 Efe, M.N. (2023). The effect of technological transformation on the management of security strategies. *İstanbul Kent Üniversitesi İnsan ve Toplum Bilimleri Dergisi* 4 (2): 65–82.

8 Shahzad, A. (2024). Metamorphosis of warfare: war without warriors or battlefields. *Policy Perspectives* 21 (1): 1–21.

9 Black, J. and Lynch, A. (2020). Cyber threats to NATO from a multi-domain perspective. Cyber Threats and NATO 2030: Horizon Scanning and Analysis. pp. 126–150.

10 O'Hanlon, M. E. (2022). Military innovation and technological change: preparing for the next generation of cyber threats.

11 Song, U., Hur, G., Lee, S., and Park, J. (2024). Unraveling the dynamics of the cyber threat landscape: major shifts examined through the recent societal events. *Sustainable Cities and Society* 103: 105265.

12 Gioe, D.V., Goodman, M.S., and Stevens, T. (2020). Intelligence in the cyber era: evolution or revolution? *Political Science Quarterly* 135 (2): 191–224.

13 Whyte, C. and Mazanec, B. (2023). *Understanding cyber-warfare: politics, policy and strategy*. Routledge.

14 Lehto, M. (2018). *The modern strategies in the cyber warfare*, 3–20. Cyber Security: Power and Technology.

15 Nguyen, M. (2024). Cyber warfare and international security: analyzing threats and defense strategies. *International Journal of Research and Review Techniques* 3 (2): 10–18.

16 Digmelashvili, T. and Lagvilava, L. (2023). Cyber deterrence strategies in the 21st century. *Future Human Image* 20.

17 Goldman, E.O. (2024). Postscript: reflections and future directions for research and practice on cyber in competition, crisis and armed conflict. In: *Research Handbook on Cyberwarfare*, 390–400. Edward Elgar Publishing.

18 Bardin, J.S. (2025). Cyber warfare. In: *Computer and Information Security Handbook*, 1345–1380. Elsevier.

19 Ahmad, S. and Jahangir, J. (2023). Cyber warfare: emerging non-traditional threat to Pakistan's security. *Pakistan Horizon* 76 (2): 39–58.

20 Noel, G.E. and Reith, M.G. (2021). Cyber warfare evolution and role in modern conflict. *Journal of Information Warfare* 20 (4): 30–44.

21 Zhu, L., Majumdar, S., and Ekenna, C. (2021). An invisible warfare with the internet of battlefield things: a literature review. *Human Behavior and Emerging Technologies* 3 (2): 255–260.

22 Sfetcu, N. (2024). Advanced Persistent Threats in Cybersecurity–Cyber Warfare. MultiMedia Publishing.

23 Ciepiela, P. and Venkateshwaran, B. V. (2017). Evolution of cyber threats and the development of new security architecture. World Petroleum Congress. WPC. p. D023S017R003.

24 Pruteanu, I.M., Fechete, L.A., and Gheţău, V.A. (2023). Navigating the complexities of air domain operations: adapting to evolving environments. In: *International Scientific Conference "Strategies XXI"*, 479–492. 'Carol I' National Defence University.

25 Faizan, A. (2024). Guardians of the digital realm: navigating the frontiers of cybersecurity. *Integrated Journal of Science and Technology* 1 (2).

26 Sanders, C.M. (2018). The battlefield of tomorrow, today: can a cyberattack ever rise to an act of war. *Utah Law Review* 503.

27 Sharma, P. and Gupta, H. (2024). Emerging cyber security threats and security applications in digital era. In: *2024 11th International Conference on Reliability, Infocom Technologies and Optimization (Trends and Future Directions)(ICRITO)*, 1–6. IEEE.

28 Lewis, J.A., Lonergan, E.D., Voo, J. et al. (2023). *Evolving Cyber Operations and Capabilities*. Center for Strategic and International Studies.

29 Ziauddin, F. (2024). Network security in modern warfare: the strategic advantage of the US in the digital battlefield. *Law, Policy and Society* 1 (7): 69–92.

3

Defense in Depth: A Multilayered Approach

Jamal N. Al-Karaki

College of Interdisciplinary Studies (CIS), Zayed University Abu Dhabi, UAE

3.1 Introduction

Defense in Depth (DiD) is a strategy of defense in cybersecurity that defines several layers of defense in multiple security domains and layers of protection. Translating from military strategies, which involved the use of multiple barriers in order to slow down and exhaust the enemy, the approach is now applied to computer security as a reliable means to guard against various types of threats. In an environment where cyber threats are emerging and expanding in various contours, DiD offers broad protection comprising various layers of protection, where if one fails, the others still hold for the defense of the organization [1, 2].

The concept behind DiD is the fact that there isn't one solution that can cover all possible threats. This plan weakens the likelihood of adding a passcode to the whole system by incorporating a number of levels that counterbalance the risks involved in the execution of each level independently. For example, network firewalls provide a different layer of security control than intrusion detection systems, access controls, and encryption, each wall that could be structured to cover one weak point in the network security system [3, 4]. Every layer is purposely architected to either stop or at least identify potentially hostile action; that way there is enough time to counteract before assets of value are at risk. The DiD concept is in the implementation of layers of controls where element risks are threatened at every layer. The following graphic displayed presents the hierarchy and shows how each stage of the security concept is an extra layer of security (Figure 3.1).

3.1.1 Core Principles and Benefits of Defense in Depth

The principles of DiD include protection through layers, multiple protection systems, variety, and multiple layers of protection. They all support the others; thus, when implemented, they enhance the security of the whole system. The multitier concept of security adds layers in decision path so that threats that may reach an information target have to go through several hoops. Spare control is efficient since it prevents a single control measure from failing while others fail to offer protection. Diversity in defense mechanisms enables the attackers to be limited in exploiting similar vulnerabilities at various layers [5]. Proactivity can be subdivided into depth of protection; it involves different kinds of dangers/risks and possible ways of an attack which establishes several levels of security from insiders to professional attackers [6].

Several advantages therefore accrue from the implementation of a DiD strategy including freedom from multiple attack vectors, additional time for detection and containment, adaptations to

Defense in Depth: Modern Cybersecurity Strategies and Evolving Threats, First Edition. Edited by Hewa Majeed Zangana.

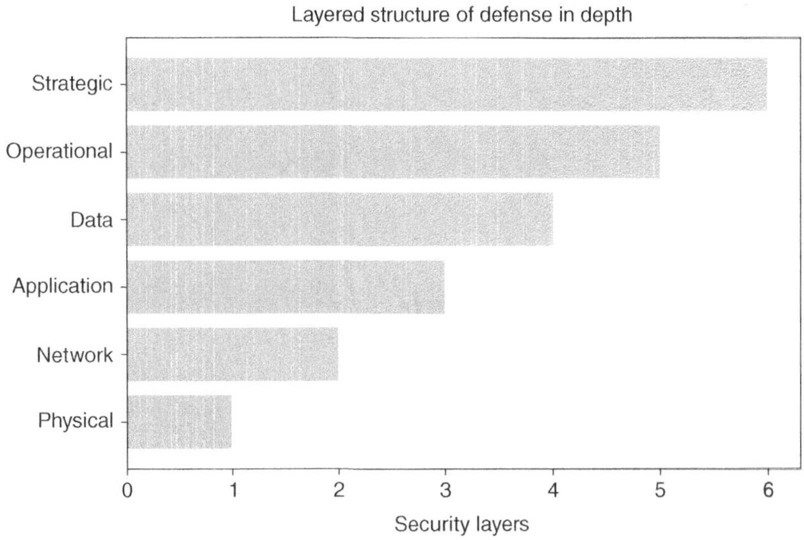

Figure 3.1 Layered structure of defense in depth. Source: Hewa Majeed Zangana.

the emerging threats. For such system environments in an organization especially those within the field of finance or healthcare, this approach shields off the data and other intellectual properties against cyberattacks because the attacker encounters major barriers [7, 8]. In supervisory control and data acquisition (SCADA) systems particularly and the Internet of Things (IoT) at large, where availability trumps everything, DiD takes the hit and shields the operational integrity from disruption by malicious activity [9].

3.1.2 Challenges in Implementing Defense in Depth

As much as the implementation of DiD has numerous benefits, its implementation has a number of drawbacks. First, the use of multiple security layers may present control challenges, where the system implementations, at times, may lead to issues of misconfiguration or inefficient operations. Similarly, organizations have resource limitations as each layer entails expenditure in technology, training, and administrative support [10]. Coordinating such a diverse approach requires striking a fine line between financial constraints and the requirement of offering substantial security. Moreover, stealthy attackers may use one or several high-level techniques to overcome multiple layers of the security mechanism and remain undetected even with the implementation of well-organized DiD systems. For instance, in a setting where the SCADA systems are interconnected, the attackers might use techniques like network hopping and bypassing one protection measure [11, 12]. Hence, each of the mentioned layers requires constant checkups, timely updates, as well as updates regarding newly identified threats.

3.1.3 Evolving Threats and the Need for a Dynamic Defense Strategy

Due to the dynamism of the threats in cyberspace environment, simply applying DiD strategies as a solution doesn't fit current security challenges adequately. Despite the fact that traditional approaches to cybersecurity are considered inefficient as a standalone measure today, firefighters, antivirus software, network segmentation, behavioral analysis, and the Zero Trust model are necessary to protect against Advanced Persistent Threats (APT) and ransomware attacks [13, 14]. Hereby, increasing roles of AI, blockchain, machine learning (ML) bring new innovations in improving DiD as these technologies, along with providing prognostic and real-time threat identification to augment previously existing security perimeter [15]. They also have to analyze the new challenges of the modern DiD implementations such as cloud migration and digital transformation since many organizations use cloud solutions now. Because cloud environments are constantly being changed, it is essential to achieve a change in which security is sent into an adaptive form of authentication, encryption, and identity management in a manner that is both on premises and cloud based [16]. This way, organizations are able to become stable and adapt well to the ever-changing security structure when embracing technologies. Therefore, DiD is an approach that is based on various overlapping layers of protection that are aimed at counteracting complex and frequently changing cyber threats. Studying DiD as a methodology is the way to strengthen the anti-cybersecurity resilience of the organization and protect its valuable assets and ensure organizational continuity in the face of growing cybersecurity challenges.

3.2 The Layers of Defense in Depth

DiD refers to the utilization of multiple security controls uniformly to create a protective shield that makes a hostile penetration difficult or limits the harm it can do. Each of the components constitutes a level of protection, and since all must be breached by an attacker, their implementation enhances the general security. The subsequent part will focus on describing the physical, network, application, and data plane layers of DiD.

3.2.1 Physical Security Layer

The physical layer is the first layer of protection whose aim is to control physical access to IT assets. Physical security controls remain essential in protecting against attackers accessing systems since even the best implemented controls are useless if a bad actor can get direct access to the hardware. Specific physical security means include access control, surveillance, biometric identification, and, where necessary, environmental security to safeguard structures [4, 7]. Appropriate physical security structures are often mandatory because nuclear plants are special facilities and security often requires "defense in depth" principles in order to minimize the potential for attackers to gain unauthorized physical access into the facility [6]. Physical security is the first level in DiD model that involves the protection of physically accessibility of the important components. The following chart identifies the various types of physical security mechanisms to express the relative frequency features of access control, surveillance, and environmental protection (Figure 3.2).

3.2.2 Network Security Layer

There are steps that protect data as it passes through computer networks as made available by network security. This layer is made out of firewalls and intrusion detection and prevention system (IDPS) that can spot the intrusion and prevent it from getting any further into the organization's networks and systems and network segmentation to prevent lateral movement. Furthermore, other sophisticated detection approaches, for example, the use of Bayesian networks to prioritize what needs to be protected on the layer of network, can improve the situation by allocating efforts to the threats most likely to emerge [3]. In the merged modern-world use, DiD for networks also includes

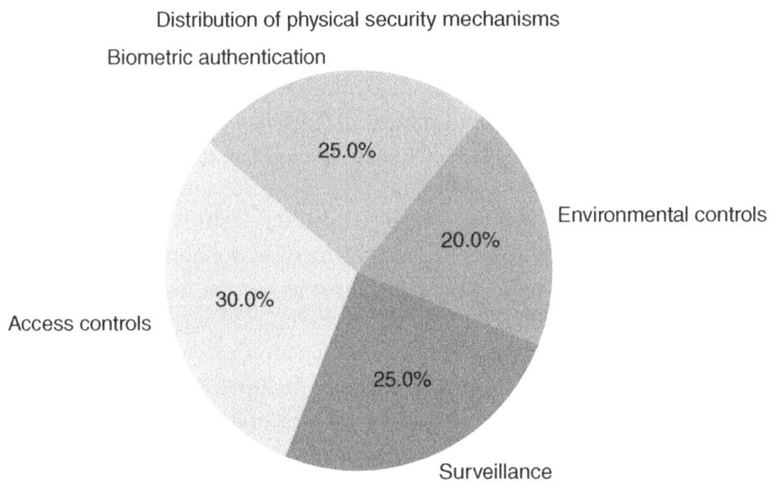

Figure 3.2 Physical security mechanisms. Source: Hewa Majeed Zangana.

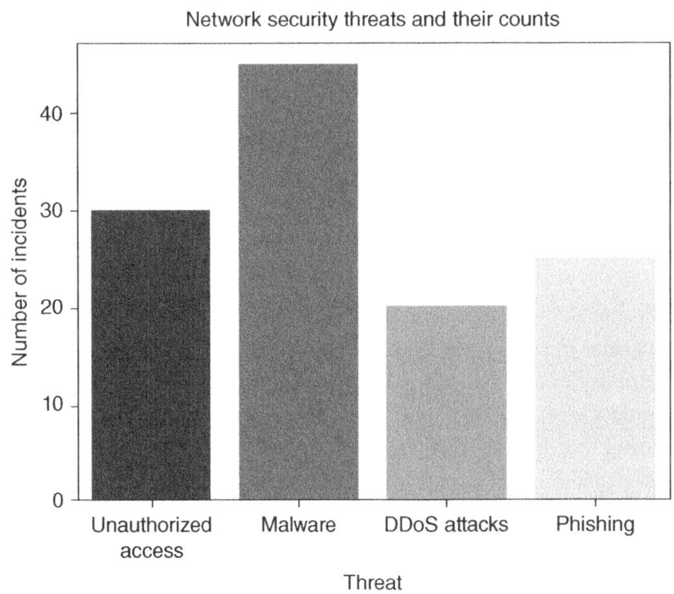

Figure 3.3 Network security threats and countermeasures. Source: Hewa Majeed Zangana.

the Zero Trust architecture (ZTA) so that each request is verified regardless of its source within or external to the network [14]. Network security offers very important layers of security to protect data that is being transmitted. The following chart shows common threats in network security and the defense that goes with them, with much attention given to each security measure (Figure 3.3).

3.2.3 Application Security Layer

Application security is important in ensuring that software is not prone to attacks from the various hackers. Best practices like the use of secure coding standards, routine patching/updates, and use of

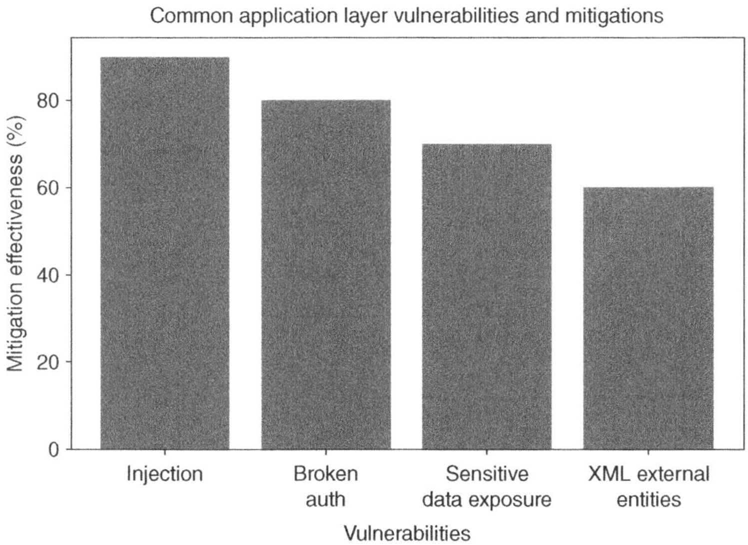

Figure 3.4 Application layer vulnerabilities and mitigations. Source: Hewa Majeed Zangana.

second-factor authentication helps protect the application layer. Data-oriented DiD methodology has been demonstrated to be useful in containing risks in the software-defined systems to mitigate attack presence in applications [2, 17]. Combined with DiD strategies for applications, logic locking can thus be used to prevent unauthorized code execution, thus strengthening the protections against code-based attacks [13]. Application security deals with threats lurking in software applications, which are mostly a favorite for hackers. Shown next is a graph depicting typical weaknesses together with ways in which these threats can be prevented in the application layer (Figure 3.4).

3.2.4 Endpoint Security Layer

Individual nodes that people utilize often are computers, mobile devices, and IoT devices, all of which remain constantly vulnerable to attack. A free global virtual private network (VPN), along with anti-malware software, endpoint detection and response (EDR), and stringent device control, is part of endpoint security, creating this crucial layer [8]. Within IoT solutions, it is crucial to integrate the layered threat-modeling diagrams into DiD models to enhance the endpoint security by predicting the threat in real time [8, 12]. Endpoints, especially those that are the IoT, are vulnerable to such security threats. This flowchart shows how various levels of security may be applied for endpoint protection, starting with the detection process (Figure 3.5).

3.2.5 Data Security Layer

The security of data compromises the protection of information that is in storage, as well as information that is in transit. There is always a need to protect data from unauthorized access as well as any modifications to data since data encryption, access controls, and data masking are some of the ways of protecting the data more effectively. For example, two or more security measures such as encryption and tokenization are useful in protecting personal and financial information especially in a fintech firm whereby the information is usually targeted [15, 16]. In the healthcare

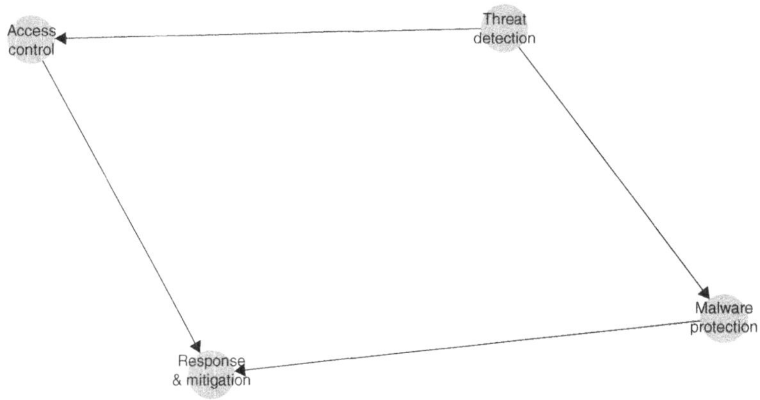

Figure 3.5 Endpoint security solutions in IoT environments. Source: Hewa Majeed Zangana.

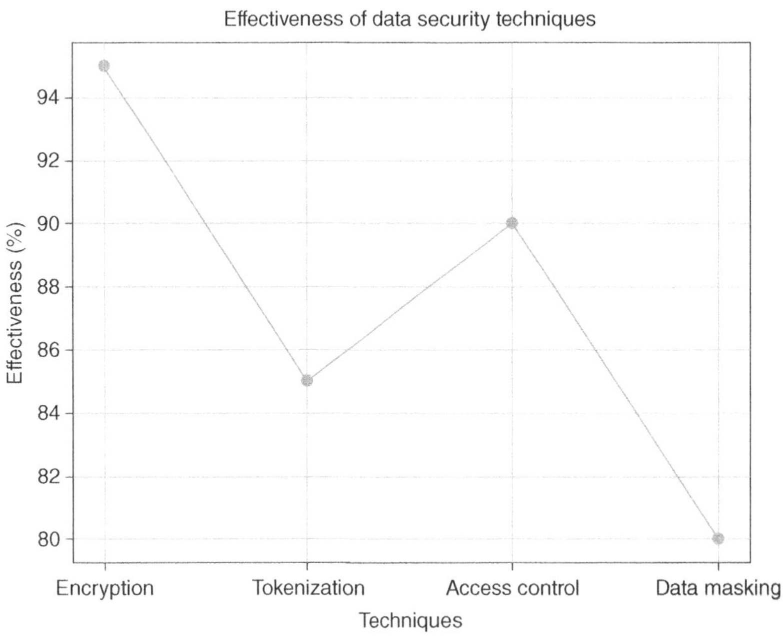

Figure 3.6 Data security techniques. Source: Hewa Majeed Zangana.

and finance industry, the traditional approaches to cybersecurity are not sufficient to protect against ransomware attacks and reduce data loss [18]. Information protection is concerned with conversion of information to a format not easily understandable by unauthorized persons. The following chart provides an organization of different methods of data security with regard to the type and degree of security (Figure 3.6).

3.2.6 Operational Security Layer

Operational security involves controls that deny access to information by only those persons who are authorized to access the information. This layer includes raising employees' awareness of security issues, security incident handling procedures, and disenabling more privileges than

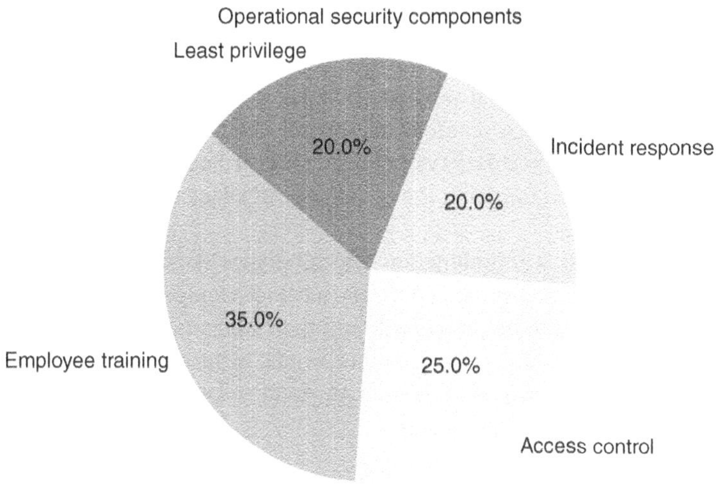

Figure 3.7 Operational security components. Source: Hewa Majeed Zangana.

needed for organizational employees [10, 19]. In sectors such as healthcare, data confidentiality and availability are critical, with a DiD model and training sessions for employees vital to lowering the number of phishing attacks and other human-related perils [7]. Restriction of employee access is part of operational security, consisting of practices in an organization. The following pie chart attempts to exemplify the chosen components and their functions within an effective security model (Figure 3.7).

3.2.7 Strategic Security Layer

Strategically, DiD applies governance and policy-enforced security controls throughout the business organization. This layer incorporates threat identification, risk evaluation, and adherence to best practices from international security standards that promote uniformity and increase security resilience [20]. Furthermore, it elaborates on threat-modeling methodologies adapted for industries with heightened security requirements, including IoT-based structures, involving the DiD framework for identifying security vulnerabilities [21, 22]. By the creation of multiple layers of protection, the DiD concept is flexible to a range of assaults due to the fact that each part is balanced out by other components' inefficiencies. That is why a clearly organized and hierarchical approach to security structures includes the key solutions that improve the effectiveness of protecting information systems and increasing the level of resistance to advanced cyber threats [23].

3.3 Implementing Defense in Depth Across Different Environments

The proper DiD approach results from the proper adjustment of concrete defensive layers and tactics successfully meeting diverse threats and challenges of converging networks, corporate systems, critical infrastructure, cloud systems, and IoT devices. This approach, which is based upon multiple layers of defense mechanisms, is crucial in the contemporary system environment characterized by a high degree of interconnectedness, as it gives a systemic reaction to new threats and reduces the extent of threat coming from a single point of a system.

3.3.1 Corporate and IT Network Environments

Strategically, for corporate networks, the most important security model is a multilayered approach that becomes important for protecting the intellectual and operational secrets, vital information of the company, and its sustainability. As Ajayi [4] has pointed out, precisely a multilayered approach can help to minimize the threats of Internet Protocol (IP) violation and loss of data to a large extent. This is also affirmed by Crossler et al. [10], arguing that the complexity of attacks lowers the risk of a number of attacks on cyberspace.

In practice, DiD in corporate environments is a combination of technologies like firewalls, intrusion detection system (IDS)/intrusion prevention system (IPS), and advanced endpoint protection. According to Alexander [3], DiD measures can be prioritized, and their utilization can be combined with the help of Bayesian networks to reduce risks; in other words, better decisions will be made faster and resources focused more efficiently. This helps organizations to deal with the most probable threats at the expense of overwhelming their assets.

3.3.2 Critical Infrastructure and SCADA Systems

As for mission critical systems and assets like power stations and distribution networks, water treatment plants, and SCADA systems, DiD is usually the only viable strategy to ensure operational continuity. Malware intrusions on such systems pose enormous risk with potential for calamitous cross-sector impacts. In his paper, Holmberg [1] defines DiD as a critical safety approach, which has been widely used for protection against accidents or acts of sabotage in nuclear power plants. For example, Khanna and Ravikumar [20] give a perspective on the DiD framework to safeguard power transmission systems mainly from cyber interference resulting in substation outages. Their research focuses on multilayer protection, aiming to minimize holes or gaps through layers of physical security, networking, and operations. Ghidu et al. [6] also support the notion that the DiD principles apply to facilities such as nuclear power, which require a multilayer protection system to enhance overall system reliability.

3.3.3 Cloud Environments

Some of the new challenges that arise with cloud computing concern data security and data privacy as well as the multiple tenancy and the division of responsibilities. To overcome these, according to the study of Saranya et al. [16], the best practice that should always be enforced to incorporate a data protection strategy includes encryption, access control, and multi-factor authentication (MFA). These measures are some of the many incorporated in a DiD approach targeted for cloud infrastructure where sources of threat may be both external and internal, having the form of a misconfigured asset.

In an attempt to enhance cloud security, Singh et al. [14] encourage adopting Zero Trust security model, combined with DiD security in 5G networks. This approach controls the use of the connected resource in a way that only specific IDs with the correct rights can gain connection. Furthermore, in connection with the discussed issue of protection against phishing and other cyber threats directed at cloud-based services operating in healthcare and other sectors with Health Insurance Portability and Accountability Act (HIPAA) requirements, Cherenko and Williams [7] emphasize the necessity of protecting multiple layers. Hybrid structures must be protected against risks arising from the shared use of the infrastructure of cloud environments. This layered diagram shows preventions and controls within the cloud-computing environments, asserting how each layer prevents risks (Figure 3.8).

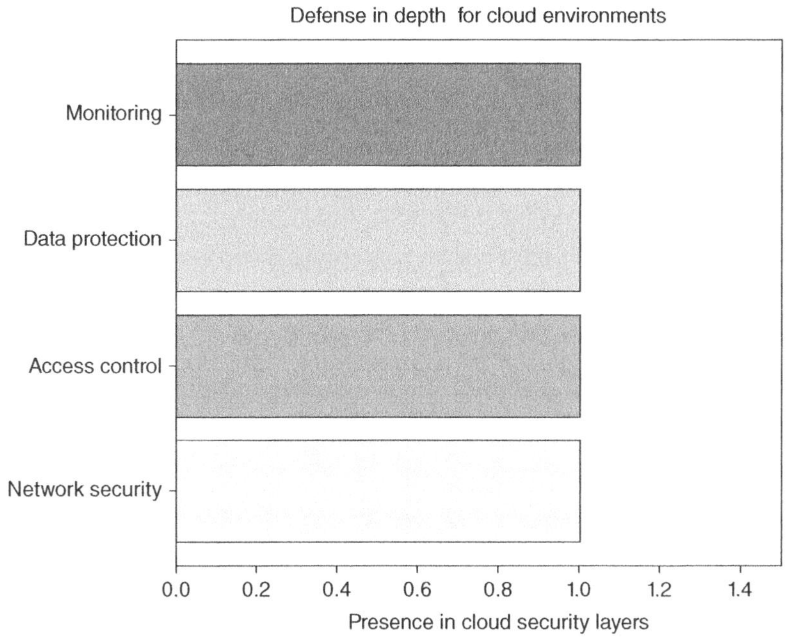

Figure 3.8 Defense in depth for cloud environments. Source: Hewa Majeed Zangana.

3.3.4 Internet of Things and Smart Systems

Primarily, creating a DiD strategy in IoT environments must necessarily consider both the challenges at the network level and at the device level due to the common vulnerabilities of IoT devices. Godakanda [8] uses a threat-modeling scenario to introduce DiD into IoT and note the applicability of DiD for the latter as an attack vector also requires different threat modeling. DiD modules, like those incorporated in pervasive systems as Das [11] for SCADA controllers, enable interdependent IoT detection and reaction to cyberattacks. Likewise, Mofidi et al. [18] point to a layered intrusion detection system (L-IDS) for ransomware detection in IoT networks; this system involves the use of ML algorithms to analyze the behavior of the connected gadgets and respond abnormally.

3.3.5 Autonomous and Industrial Control Systems

Approved scanning vendor (ASV) or automotive, aviation, marine, industrial control or industrial control systems (ICS), railway, drilling utilities, etc., need more than one layer of protection because they are sophisticated, connected systems threatened by an enormous number of cyber threats. In the recent article by Kurkute et al. [24], where the authors describe the security approaches for fully autonomous cars, the authors highlight the necessity to implement DiD mechanisms like layered encryption and secure boot. In the same way, Wai and Lee [9] also offer a DiD approach to SCADA systems in an Industry 4.0 environment, which incorporates the layered protection to combat the Industry 4.0 SCADA cyber risk profile.

Strategies at varying tiers of defense in the different settings underscore that addressing the issue requires scenario-specific, proactive as well as responsive solutions. Every link from the outer circle to the hub increases the systemic security level, so threats cannot go through several barriers [22, 25]. This layered approach makes sure that organizations can be able to prevent risks in the appropriate methods as per the demand within the environments.

3.4 Integrating Cyber Threat Intelligence

Cyber threat intelligence (CTI) has grown to become one of the most diverse and important parts in modern-day security because it makes users to adapt and even identify the threats that are likely to occur in any organization. The usefulness of CTI campaigners can be underlined based on their possibilities to deliver the main kinds of useful information to improve defensive postures based on analyzed present threats and extrapolated futures [15]. This section examines the application of CTI within a complex layered security model, most notably concerning DiD strategies.

3.4.1 Role of Cyber Threat Intelligence in Enhancing Defense-in-Depth

The use of CTI in DiD enhances the capacity of an organization to define, identify, and mitigate threats at all levels of security. It is time-consuming because the DiD concept implies a series of protective barriers, each of which is intended to prevent the occurrence of various kinds of threat and reduce the harm resultant from potential exposure. For examples, in IoT, including CTI can help organizations learn the threats and their trends and prevent or mitigate threats by identifying patterns or signs or compromise [18]. Similarly, CTI also increases the reliability of such interconnected networks including power distribution networks, where by providing accurate prediction of impacts of cyber threats to the substations, necessary actionable defense measures can be deployed in advance [20].

It also has a great responsibility of rationing security controls in line with new type of threat landscapes. For instance, high-impact threats can be taken care of basically by making proper use of Bayesian networks, whereby CTI assists in resource allocation appropriately for security [3]. This prioritization is critical in an environment that can be largely challenging, including the healthcare systems where the CTI can protect the patient information through early threat detection that is likely to degrade the system's confidentiality and availability [7].

3.4.2 CTI and the Layers of Security Defense

When implemented in multiple-tiered security strategies, CTI works at multiple levels and feeds each layer the information it needs to enhance its defensive measures against threats. Layered perimeter intrusion analysis (LPIA), overall outer barrier, beneficiary of CTI in the form of characteristic threat intelligence feeds to identify and lock known risk IP addresses/domains. Lower levels, including internal network segmentation and application-level security, can make use of CTI in order to detect unusual activity indicative of a breach or compromise [9]. Additionally, CTI in SCADA systems which are crucial to Industry 4.0 can be adjusted to look for specific threats such as ransomware or a phishing attack. The integration of CTI enables an organization to adapt security policies and measures on the fly which, in turn, enhances the security of the SCADA systems against disruptions [11]. This proves guarantees that the CTI feeds each layer to ensure that it provides a means for organizations to update as threats evolve.

3.4.3 Predictive Capabilities and Automated Responses with CTI

CTI is not limited to residential use; it also assists in detection and prevention, while additionally enabling predictive and automated responses to threats. CTI systems using threat intelligence as input can learn from the data, find deviation from normal in sophisticated ways, and thus prevent breaches even where it is trying to occur next, [12] say. It is even more helpful for quick reactions to phishing attacks; as such, incidents threaten to leak personal data as soon as possible [25].

CTI-driven automated responses are also useful for protecting financial technologies including Neobank structures, with fine algorithms that constantly watch and respond to threats [15]. They further complement DiD frameworks with the ability to predict threats and prove that the defenses are equally dynamic and preventive.

3.4.4 Challenges and Considerations in CTI Integration

All the same, it is evident that CTI integration has some issues or challenges as highlighted next. Challenges include the need to ensure accuracy of data, timely distribution of intelligence, and compatibility of different systems with those already in place in the organization [22]. Also, CTI gets increasingly developed; organizational privacy-related issues arise, especially when working with or on an individual's sensitive personal data [16]. However, the CTI mechanism, when applied within the DiD strategy, requires considerable proportionality to avoid full automation of communication processes. Some cases may actually be false positives, which means a human must be present to look over the tools and daily check to ensure that what is being presented corresponds with the security goals of the organization [10]. As the abovementioned challenges imply, the best solution is to use automatic systems of CTI integrated with human interaction.

3.4.5 Summary

Cyber threat intelligence is advantageous when implemented with multilayered protection because it increases the speed and effectiveness of the layered system, as well as improves the layer's ability to predict and respond to threats. As cyber threats change, the use of CTI will only expand because organizations can rely on it for the understanding of their security posture and potential threats.

3.5 Adapting to Emerging Threats with Defense in Depth

DiD is one of the axiomatic doctrines that plan the administration of information security and aims at developing multilayered protection from numerous types of threats. This broad approach not only increases reliability since all possible threats are eliminated at these various levels but also carries with it an added layer to protect when one level is compromised. The emerging risk of ransomware, APTs and highly targeted and coordinated phishing attacks means that complex approaches to DiD are required to safeguard numerous structures, including IoT, driverless cars, financial, and SCADA contexts.

3.5.1 The Rationale Behind Defense in Depth

DiD derives from redundancy, which has the basis in the application of barriers that enemy actors need to overcome one by one. Every layer has a role of defense that would delay the would-be attacks, hence increasing the cost and work for the attacker [2]. Due to the constantly evolving threat landscape, incorporating DiD into security models can help avert large data losses, protect ideas and information, and minimize harm to important infrastructure [4]. For instance, a current study shows how DiD in financial systems, when together with emerging technologies that include AI and blockchain, meet the emerging cyber threats [15].

3.5.2 Defense in Depth in Industrial and Critical Infrastructure

The use of DiD is widely adopted across industries that heavily depend on operational technology; energy and manufacturing are among such industries. For example, in nuclear power plants, DiD principle enhancements enhance security because they focus on the weaknesses in access at both digital and physical levels, which increases the protection level of critical infrastructure [6]. With regard to power transmission, a DiD system can help manage risks associated with cyber-stimulated substation blackouts, hence enhancing the stability of power grids [20].

Also, in digital technological processes such as Industry 4.0's SCADA system and IoT interconnectivity, the risk of cyber threats rises. Hence, it is critical that DiD strategies that can be employed to counter these issues be developed for SCADA systems. Various layers of security for SCADA are found to provide a sufficient solution for the protection against intrusions and thus contribute the Industrial Internet of Things (IIoT) ecosystem [9].

3.5.3 Addressing Threats in IoT and Cloud Environments

Alternatively, new opportunities of IoT and cloud technology create new threats and risks that need to be addressed by effective DiD measures that are strong and responsive to change. Earlier, security models did not closely address tightly interwoven interconnected IoT devices, which are not inheritably secure. Some DiD strategies applicable for IoT can seal the above gap through multilayered threat detection. For instance, the integration of DiD modules into IoT devices has been beneficial in the identification and counteracting of ransomware attacks [18]. It should also be noted that protection is essentially multilayered in cloud environments, since cloud solutions are used by cybercriminals to violate protocols for storing and transferring data. DiD applied in cloud environments guarantees that data integrity and confidentiality are preserved at all times and levels, including all breaches. A number of contributions have shared lessons learnt on DiD for cloud security, encompassing key considerations of encryption, network segmentation, and access controls to improve data security and privacy [16].

3.5.4 Advanced Technologies and Defense in Depth

New modus operandi such as ML and blockchain and others like Bayesian networks are now found to be incorporated in DiD strategies to allow for flexibility and the ability to counter new forms of attack. For example, Bayesian networks described have potential in adjustment of DiD measures by organizing security controls in terms of threat landscapes and therefore facilitating sensible distribution of resources [3]. Furthermore, the current AI-based DiD solutions can forecast and respond to new threats with the aid of historical data that makes the proactive defense positions more robust [15].

Advanced cyber threats also require the use of ML applications for early detection and prevention. Local structures in defense frameworks to have multilayered architectures can use ML algorithms for the detection and reporting of suspicious activity that may portray phishing and malware among others. Furthermore, the utilization of blockchain in DiD models gives another secure layer that protects the data from being modified or even forged, which is decisive in more and more sectors as, for instance, finance and autonomous industries as Gubbi et al. [12].

3.5.5 Adapting Defense in Depth to Combat Emerging Threats

Because these threats are evolving in their complexity, it is necessary to enhance DiD strategies and to develop them permanently. When used together with DiD, Zero Trust principles establish a complete security model that assumes none of the users or devices is trustworthy, which improves on the security posture by a notch [14]. Likewise, a method including logic locking improves DiD defense mechanisms by guaranteeing systems are secure from hardware-type attacks in facilities [13]. Therefore, it can be concluded that DiD is not only a defensive concept, but a diverse process which adapts to new threats. It has always been said that layered security does not only strengthen security as a whole, but also minimizes risks from threats in the cyber world. Such flexibility means that should the threat change over time or new ones develop, they, in turn, will be matched by methods of protection for systems, data, and, in essence, organizational credibility.

3.6 Monitoring and Incident Response in a Multilayered Architecture

The incident monitoring and response can only take place within the Layers of Protection Approach when a business has a strong surveillance system that can swiftly address incidents. This system comprises of multiple interrelated subsystems that are created with a purpose of protecting various layers in an organization's architecture, be it the network layer, application layer, the end points, and even data. A system that is protected by multiple layers or barriers is also called DiD due to its all-embracing protection and lack of critical weakness that can be taken advantage of by a would-be attacker.

The best practice of having an initially outlined flow of work regarding security incidents guarantees fast and orderly reactions. The following flowchart captures the main steps in multiple layers of incident response (IR) management process from detection to mitigation (Figure 3.9).

3.6.1 Multilayered Monitoring

In a layered security architecture, continuous monitoring is used at all the layers to try and identify what is abnormal or could pose a threat. A type of continuous detection devices is the Intrusion Detection Systems (IDS) and Intrusion Prevention Systems (IPS); these are appliances that monitor traffic, seeking signs of potential attacker activity. For instance, Mofidi et al. [18] proposed L-IDS which is a multiple-layered technique aimed at detecting ransomware in IoT networks. The extant models require substantial threat intelligence and anomaly detection routines to provide adequate

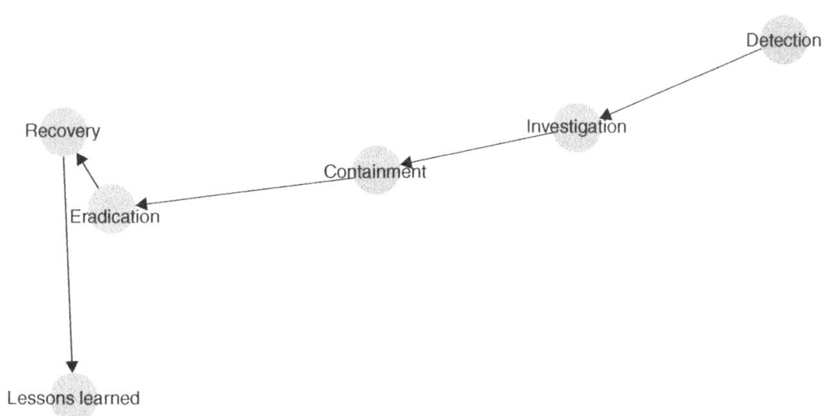

Figure 3.9 Incident response workflow in multilayered systems. Source: Hewa Majeed Zangana.

reactions to new dangers. The layered approach makes it easier to monitor events by layer and identify the presence of malicious activities at the early stage. Further, DiD can be prolonged to detect threats with the help of Bayesian networks as it is suggested by Alexander [3], which can rank and integrate multiple protective measures depending on risks. In addition to enhancing the capabilities of the threat detection component, the method also enables the determination of the allocation of resources for managing incidents to enhance the efficiency and effectiveness of the IR teams.

3.6.2 Incident Response Strategy

An IR plan states possible courses of action that must be taken in case of security incidents so as to prevent the losses that would otherwise be incurred. In a multilayered architecture, often the IR teams struggle to align their responses with the longitudinal platforms and successive levels of security complexities. Cherenko and Williams [7] explained that cyberspace is crucial for defense and safeguarding healthcare data, and system availability requires a multilayered approach. They said that organizations should have response protocols for each layer of security from the perimeter up to the end systems to prevent the spreading of threats throughout the network.

3.6.3 Integration of Threat Intelligence and Automated Responses

Another important development in the expanded concept of response to incidents in multitiered systems is the introduction of threat intelligence and automation. As threat feeds offer the most current risks and attack vectors, the IR team is able to modify its defenses in real time. Security orchestration, automation, and response (SOAR) is a particularly valuable tool for the DiD security model because these technologies are very efficient. While SOAR platforms allow for IR to be more efficient since they reduce repetitive tasks, sorting through notifications, and being able to deal with the threats more quickly. In a DiD environment, the incorporation of automation prescribes to considerable decrease in the time necessary to identify and mitigate threats, adding strength to the relevant critical infrastructures, as written by Holmberg [1].

3.6.4 Cross-Layer Incident Detection and Analysis

A solid-state drive (SSD) also requires elevated levels of incident analysis, utilizing high sophistication to relate occurrences at one layer to events at another layer. This approach focuses on dissecting events happening at each layer of the technology divide including the networks, applications, and endpoint security, before relating them to establish the magnitude of the incident. To enhance the response accuracy and reduce response time, Rendall et al. [25] suggested cross-layer detection mechanism, especially for phishing attacks. The cross-layer incident analysis helps to involve IR teams find out the real cause of the incident, which is critical to design effective remedial strategies. For example, in SCADA systems, the DiD and cross-layer analysis are useful as shown by Wai and Lee [9] in defending possible critical infrastructure components by pointing out possible failure points around the systems' interfaces.

3.6.5 Case Study: Defense in Depth for Financial Services

Hence, the financial services' sector has a strong need for layered security strategies to implement both constant monitoring and quick response. George [15] highlighted how more advanced technologies like AI and blockchain boost the processes of monitoring and managing incidents, especially for digital banking services. With the help of complex figures analyzing user activity and transactions that occur within the process, financial institutions can identify unsafe activities and reduce threats.

Also, to maintain compliance with standards and regulate customers' data, firms in the financial sector have several tiers of incident response. This example reveals a principle of the so-called DiD or multiple barrier security approach as a practical method to build a robust and versatile protective environment against advanced cyber threats.

3.6.6 Defense-in-Depth Strategy and Future Challenges

With the growth in the complexity of cyber threats, the DiD security model will be dynamic and will require new techniques for monitoring and successful handling of events. A primary issue that remains is the level and real-time orchestration of the layers of security. As Ajayi [4] pointed out, this calls for more than just effective security tools; it requires constant adaptation to threats and the integration of layers. Through layering, effective monitoring, and incident response, organizations can increase their level of protection, reduce the extent of possible risks, and make their security even more robust. The threat of inadequate mitigation strategies is particularly significant in critical industries such as nuclear power and defense. In these sectors, a DiD procedure that incorporates robust control mechanisms, along with a IR protocol, is considered essential for maintaining long-term resilience [6, 26].

3.7 Evaluating the Effectiveness of Defense in Depth

Substantial layers of defense that are placed on an asset in a way that, even if one layer is breached, the layers below it will still help protect the asset from being threatened. DiD can be best assessed in terms of response capacities for multiform assaults as well as malleability for emergent threats and scenarios pertinent to an environment as security sensitive as nuclear power plants, financial services, and related critical infrastructures. It is important to assess each layer of the security defense to describe the efficiency of the layers. The following bar chart evaluates the level of strength offered by each layer in DiD model across environments (Figure 3.10).

3.7.1 Layered Security and Threat Mitigation

The fundamental idea of DiD is to have multiple layers of security that are each individual security barriers, ultimately making it hard for attackers to penetrate into the whole system [4]. This approach has been effective especially in organizations with confidential and integrity demands including the financial the healthcare industry, where leakages can cause severe loss in intellectual property and patients' data, respectively [7]. DiD architecture has preventive, detective, and corrective controls at each layer, and they minimize the chances of having ones that is the only option.

3.7.2 Evaluating DiD in Cyber-Physical and Critical Infrastructure Systems

DiD is especially useful in areas where failure is life threatening, such as nuclear power stations, transport, and energy industries. In nuclear establishments, DiD principles safeguard safety through a multilayered approach, whereby several barriers eliminate or reduce the impact of

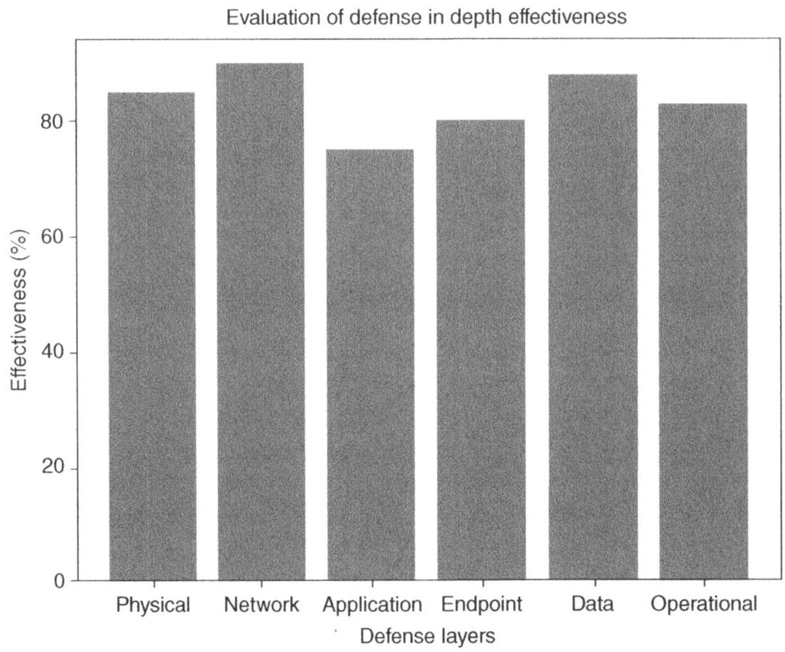

Figure 3.10 Evaluation of defense in depth effectiveness. Source: Hewa Majeed Zangana.

possible risks [5, 6]. It has also been successful in the safeguarding industrial control systems and SCADA systems from cyber threats since the role of each layer is conspicuously distinct in the handling of risks [9]. In the sphere of energy, DiD principles have developed a threat-modeling system and real attack detection mechanisms. For example, Khanna et al. [20] have proffered a DiD framework that is able to check cyber-induced outages of power transmission systems. This framework employs an approach of multiple layers of defense that may be able to adapt to the likely threat in the network space and hence effectively prevent system failure in the face of integrated systems.

3.7.3 Layered Defense in Emerging Technologies

Given the advancement in the emergence of technologies such as AI, blockchain, and 5G among others, a new type of DiD has been developed to combat a new type of risk. In the context of applying AI and blockchain for financial services, George [15] has pointed that only DiD is a key feature to protect the significant and valuable financial operations from fraud and malicious activities. In like manner, Singh et al. [14] propose a layered security approach alongside the ZTA which has emerged as a key approach toward protecting 5G networks against advanced multi-vector threats focused on the layers of the network.

3.7.4 Quantitative Assessment of Defense Layers

Evaluating the quantitative performance of the layers provides better knowledge of DiD to quantify the effectiveness of various layers of defense and measure how well they perform in their individual layers. In general, the authors [21] reveal that mathematical modeling as well as risk analysis tools can quantify the probability of a system getting compromised despite those multiple layers of protection. This way, probabilistic values of each layer can be assigned so that the organizations can analyze the areas of inefficiency and work on improvements. For instance, in critical infrastructure protection, risks of both physical and cyber threats are mitigated through analyses of vulnerabilities, and their compensating controls, armor, are ranked and improved based on the Bayesian networks [3].

3.7.5 Challenges in Implementing DiD in IoT and Cloud Environments

Nevertheless, the outlined specifications of DiD show some challenges that the method faces when adopted to emerging environments such as IoT and cloud computing. Given that IoT consists of interconnected systems of systems, the successful execution of DiD requires security on both the network and the device level. In Godakanda [8], the author advanced a threat-modeling approach based on DiD, specifically for IoT whose multiple layers of security guards against threats that can target the devices' weaknesses. In cloud environments, the implementation of the multilayer security model specifically for data protection is described by Saranya et al. [16] in their work of 2023.

3.7.6 Empirical Studies and User Behavior Analysis

As with every mechanism that is employed to enhance the performance of a system, usability of the instrument involved determines the result of the DiD method, more specifically, how the users engage with the various security layers available. Research shows that as the number of layered defenses increases in a system, users tend to regard these defenses as complicated, leading them to forget to practice safe security measures [10]. This raises the importance of clean interfaces to avoid buttons that complicate use and the need for security awareness programs to also improve DiD by improving the behavior of users.

3.7.7 Adaptations for Defense Against Advanced Threats

They have given DiD a new dimension of threat intelligence and deception techniques necessary when it comes to APTs, among other complex attacks. John [27] said DiD was applied in a faking environment to help in discovering APTs before getting to the critical systems. Likewise, they are the defense mechanisms, such as the one proposed by Das [11] for the SCADA systems, that help in detecting the anomalies in real time. Correspondingly, the incorporation of DiD boosts the latter's protective effectiveness against the targeted attacks.

3.7.8 Summary

As highlighted before, DiD continues to be one of the best security approaches that can still be relied upon in today's world across various domains of operations including critical infrastructures, cloud, and IoT. The flexibility of the strategy comes under its applicability across different industries, and developments of new technology makes it strong approach toward emerging threats in cybersecurity. Nonetheless, it needs to be updated periodically to serve its purpose of protecting against continuously changing and improving threats in cyberspace.

3.8 Challenges and Future Directions

3.8.1 Challenges in Defense-in-Depth Approaches

The DiD model, which is applicable in all the domains of the enterprise, has a number of limitations, which, however, may impede its successful implementation in environments characterized by high levels of competition and dynamic technological change. The first concern that is unique to this area of study is achieving the appropriate security level without sacrificing system speed and ease of use. For instance, DiD may require the use of several layers of security controls that augment latency and use of resources, hence impacting on the efficiency of the system [24]. This can be quite demanding, especially in industries such as self-driving cars' industry where response time is scarce.

The other concern is the ways in which new DiD mechanisms will interact with more recent technologies such as, AI, blockchain, and IoT. All of these technologies create new security challenges that are difficult to address within the framework of a multitiered defense system [8, 15]. For instance, IoT has systems where devices are connected in a large network; this makes the processing of security across all the layers challenging. Furthermore, the heterogenous IoT devices and their sophisticated security measures in each country and region make it difficult for a uniform DiD strategy [9]. Adding to the problem, modern threats are actively changing, especially with increasing the level of endangerment by APT and zero-day threats. The more complex threats are often difficult to counter with traditional DiD metrics, especially in some sectors such as nuclear energy or crucial infrastructure as breaches of such type may be critical [5, 20]. Besides, the issue of dealing with defensive layers may result in such weaknesses or inconsistencies when attackers get the chance to identify them [4, 10].

3.8.2 Future Directions in Defense-in-Depth

In regard to these challenges, the following directions for future development of the DiD framework can be outlined. First, applications of AI and ML (ML) in enhancing defense mechanisms can be regarded as one of the directions for development. DiD owes its flexibility as an AI-based solution that can be easily recalibrated for growing threats, and its applications include smart grids and financial systems [15, 20].

Another important development is that DiD has been integrated with ZTA. Additionally, using some "trust no one, verify everything" policies similar to the protection of diamond deposits, ZTA can strengthen DiD by adding the steps of continuous verification in conditions of high likelihood of insider attacks and unauthorized access. It has the potential to protect today's 5G networks that are very different from traditional wired networks, which based on the perimeter and is no longer reliable [14]. Blockchain technology is also considered to be used for the increased level of interaction integrity for DiD-defined interactions, especially for infrastructure and financial industries. Blockchain's integrated unchangeableness can produce a sealed review, which will assist companies in upholding integrity and responsibility [15]. Further, when it comes to the spheres that demand high reliability, the application of blockchain will allow securely storing the history of access and changes to records [7]. Yet another key research domain is the elaboration of stronger connections between different layers of DiD within different industries. This understanding means that by using norms and recommended measures, more organizations will be able to achieve more interoperability and better defend against a wider array of cyber threats. The effective solutions, like the public-private ones, could help elaborate the requirements of critical sectors like energy, transportation, and finance based on the industry's needs on that specific area [6]. Finally, one needs resilience frameworks geared toward speedy restoration and continuity, especially given the abstract complexities of cyber threats that many organizations face today. When resilience is integrated into the DiD strategy, company's key controls remain operational despite blows at some of the layers [1, 22]. This approach suits DiD aim to keep defense amid the adversities and is especially applicable to fields like power and telecommunications, whose effects are spread [17].

Overall, it may be stated that DiD still remains one of the foundational principles of cybersecurity; however, it still has to be developed and modified further to address the current challenges. AI, Zero Trust, and blockchain, when combined with the DiD model, along with the creation of more concise and robust media, intelligent zero-trust environments and designs (IZED) will be essential steps for tackling the challenges of the contemporary cybersecurity environment and preserving the future of digital infrastructures.

3.8.3 Future Directions in Software Security

As it was described above, the software of security paces dynamic because of progressive developments in technologies and emerging new and sophisticated threats from the hackers. When organizations seek to ensure their assets are safeguarded, there are a number of trends and innovations set to define the future in software security. Among these, there is one potentially highly effective approach, which is the application of large language models (LLMs) in the sphere of software vulnerability detection and addressing. The state-of-the-art LLMs are able to perform splendid natural language processing and therefore can be applied to improve the recognition of security flaws in code repositories. Thus, using LLMs originating from vast data samples, organizations can increase the efficiency of the vulnerability search by automating the code review process. In addition, these models can propose ways and actual code sequences for producing more protective code and instant feedback and coding examples of compliance with security standards. Also, the growth of the market is foreseen in the increased popularity of abstract syntax tree (AST), the application of which is predicted to grow fast. These tools take advantage of ML models to analyze advanced code and identify weaknesses through the software development process (systems analysis and design [SAD], software development life cycle [SDLC]). Such automation does not only consider the efficiency in performing security testing but also gives the developers the chance to center on the main features with no-or-little security negligence.

Two other essential aspects of future software security include compliance requirements as well as adaptability. This is because as governments and regulatory bodies provide the guidelines for the organization, data protection and cybersecurity become stringent. A stronger emphasis will be placed on checking compliance as an integrated part of development, as well as on the compliance of software products with legislative requirements at the time of their creation. However, cloud computing as well as the IoT has their own peculiarities in relation to software security. With the rise of interconnected devices, preservation of the communication lines, as well as stored data, will be an essential issue. Key administration will be crucial to avoid blistering and unauthorized admittance to data secure in these areas, and effective cryptographic schemes and protocols shall have to be extended for secure system communication. Finally, how to address the ethical and privacy questions arising from AI and ML for security applications will also be compulsory. As organizations use LLMs and these automation tools, the question of how to implement these tools in a way that they do not incorporate the wrong bias or intrude personal rights arises. As we have seen, setting of code of ethic and recommendations for the application of AI in security applications will enhance confidence and responsible use of software solutions in security considerations. In conclusion, the future of software security will embrace new technologies and will be regulatory compliant and ethical. Thus, these advancements, when adopted by the organizations, could improve security and help organizations fight off increasingly diverse threats.

3.9 Conclusion

At the end of this chapter, it is therefore inevitable to stress the need to employ DiD strategy, especially given the current and emerging nature of cyber threats. Standardization, physical security, and logical security controls layered together are essential to augment the overall protective capability against variegated cyber threats in organizations. Not only is it critical to safeguard against threats from outside attackers, but it also provides strong protection against attackers inside a computer network, guaranteeing security of all the connection points and all computer and software systems. The ultimate advantage of DiD entails that different cybersecurity challenges can be dealt with comprehensively within an organization, thus minimizing of the incidences of break-ins. One of the main conclusions to be drawn is the ability of DiD to be adaptive and flexible. Unlike the traditional security approach where there is normally a single solution or security mechanism, this approach incorporates several approaches and technologies, and this makes it flexible enough to suit any organization as well as counter changing security threats. This kind of versatility is especially useful in environments that are characterized by continuous technological growth as well as by growing wisdom of unauthorized users. Besides, a multilayered model allows the integration of different types and levels of protection, ranging from IDS's to authentication, so that the overall concept of preventive, detective, and corrective measures is smooth and efficient. In addition, DiD also recognizes the need for constant monitoring and also an assessment schedule. Cybersecurity cannot be considered as an installation process that is done once and for all. The periodic re-assessment of each layer and any subsequent corrected ensures that organizations are at the forefront of threat risks and can easily respond to new exposures. This refine-test cycle lies in the core of the security practice, as the main goal is to ensure confidentiality, integrity, and availability of the necessary data and applications.

Other approaches may give way to it when it comes to the implementation of cybersecurity a DiD that is a strong and well-rounded approach to confronting enhanced cyber threats. Through the use of multiple layers of security that subsume each other, not only does the safeguarding of an organization's assets occur, but also the enhancement of security awareness across organizational members is a distinct possibility. As the complexity of these ecosystems grows, the strategy of DiD guarantees that organizations are ready for further challenges, address security at all levels, and protect their systems from known and unknown threats. Therefore, this layered approach creates the right foundation for a safe future so that safe and sustainable progress can be made.

References

1 Holmberg, J. (2017). Defense-in-Depth. In: *Handbook of Safety Principles* (ed. N. Moller, S.O. Hansson, J.-E. Holmberg, and C. Rollenhagen), 42–62. Wiley.
2 Mughal, A.A. (2018). The art of cybersecurity: defense in depth strategy for robust protection. *International Journal of Intelligent Automation and Computing* 1 (1): 1–20.
3 Alexander, R. (2020). Reducing threats by using Bayesian networks to prioritize and combine defense in depth security measures. *Journal of Information Security* 11 (3): 121–137.

4 Ajayi, O.O. (2023). Layered security defense, a panacea to loss of intellectual properties and damages to information system.
5 Chengcheng, W. (2020). New requirements of defence in depth and extension of its application. *International Conference on Nuclear Engineering*. American Society of Mechanical Engineers. p. V001T02A001.
6 Ghidu, M.A., Ilisescu, I., and Nemes, C. (2023). Improving security in the operation of nuclear power plants using defence in depth principle. *2023 10th International Conference on Modern Power Systems (MPS)*. IEEE. 1–6.
7 Cherenko, I. and Williams, G. (2021). *Reducing the Incidents of Phishing, Protecting the Confidentiality of HIPAA Data and, Ensuring the Availability of Critical Systems Vital to the Success of the Healthcare System Using a Layered-Defense Approach*. Denver: Metropolitan State University of Denver-Department of Computer Sciences.
8 Godakanda, M. L. (2023). Optimising a defence-aware threat modelling diagram incorporating a defence-in-depth approach for the internet-of-things.
9 Wai, E. and Lee, C.K.M. (2024). Depth in defense: a multi-layered approach to cybersecurity for SCADA systems in industry 4.0. In: *Science and Technology: Recent Updates and Future Prospects*, vol. 2, 124–144. SCADA.
10 Crossler, R.E., Bélanger, F., and Ormond, D. (2019). The quest for complete security: an empirical analysis of users' multi-layered protection from security threats. *Information Systems Frontiers* 21: 343–357.
11 Das, R. (2020). An embedded defense-in-depth module for detecting cyberattacks on interdependent SCADA controllers. The University of Alabama in Huntsville.
12 Gubbi, K.I., Latibari, B.S., Chowdhury, M.A. et al. (2024). Optimized and automated secure IC design flow: a defense-in-depth approach. In: *IEEE Transactions on Circuits and Systems I: Regular Papers*, 2031–2044. IEEE.
13 Rahman, M.T., Rahman, M.S., Wang, H. et al. (2020). Defense-in-depth: a recipe for logic locking to prevail. *Integration* 72: 39–57.
14 Singh, K., Kumar, B., Saxena, R., and Lohani, V. A defense in depth with zero trust architecture for securing 5G networks. In: *2023 31st Telecommunications Forum (TELFOR)*, vol. 2023, 1–4. IEEE.
15 George, A.S. (2023). Securing the future of finance: how AI, Blockchain, and machine learning safeguard emerging Neobank technology against evolving cyber threats. *Partners Universal Innovative Research Publication* 1 (1): 54–66.
16 Saranya, N., Sakthivadivel, M., Karthikeyan, G., and Rajkumar, R. (2023). Securing the cloud: an empirical study on best practices for ensuring data privacy and protection. *International Journal of Engineering and Management Research*. 13 (2): 46–49.
17 Matsuoka, H. (2019). The data-centric defense-in-depth approach in the cyberspace operations. In: *Cyber Defense–Policies, Operations and Capacity Building*, 39–45. IOS Press.
18 Mofidi, F., Hounsinou, S.G., and Bloom, G. (2024). L-IDS: a multi-layered approach to ransomware detection in IoT. *2024 IEEE 14th Annual Computing and Communication Workshop and Conference (CCWC)*. IEEE. 387–396.
19 Mui, S., Askin, A., and Banal, R. (2018). *Detection by Defense in Depth*. Livermore, CA (United States): Lawrence Livermore National Lab (LLNL).
20 Khanna, K., Ravikumar, G., and Govindarasu, M. (2023). Defense-in-depth framework for power transmission system against cyber-induced substation outages. *2023 IEEE Texas Power and Energy Conference (TPEC)*. IEEE. 1–6.

21 Netkachov, O., Popov, P., and Salako, K. (2019). Quantitative evaluation of the efficacy of defence-in-depth in critical infrastructures. In: *Resilience of Cyber-Physical Systems: From Risk Modelling to Threat Counteraction*, 89–121. Springer.

22 Patyal, M., Sampalli, S., Ye, Q., and Rahman, M. (2017). Multi-layered defense architecture against ransomware. *International Journal of Business and Cyber Security* 1 (2).

23 Thawani, B., Lim, S.K., Brown, L. et al. (2023). Design of multi-layered protection against guided mortar threats yhrough numerical modeling. *Defence Technology* 29: 55–65.

24 Kurkute, M.V., Selvaraj, A., and Selvaraj, A. (2023). End-to-end cybersecurity strategies for autonomous vehicles: leveraging multi-layered defence mechanisms to safeguard automotive ecosystems. *Cybersecurity and Network Defense Research.* 3 (2): 134–177.

25 Rendall, K., Nisioti, A., and Mylonas, A. (2020). Towards a multi-layered phishing detection. *Sensors* 20 (16): 4540.

26 Iman, K.F., Triharjanto, R.H., Wibowo, H.B., and Ruyat, Y. (2023). Comparative analysis of a multi-layered weapon system for city air defense in the modern warfare. *International Journal of Humanities Education and Social Sciences.* 3 (3).

27 John, J.T. (2017). State of the art analysis of defense techniques against advanced persistent threats. *Future Internet (FI) and Innovative Internet Technologies and Mobile Communication (IITM) Focal Topic: Advanced Persistent Threats.* 63.

4

The Role of Artificial Intelligence in Cybersecurity

Derek Mohammed

College of CARDS, Saint Leo University, FL, USA

4.1 Introduction

Many use it, and what has been witnessed is that with the continuous advancement in digital technology, the connectivity and exchange of data have been highly enhanced. But this has been accompanied by heightened risk and more complex and diverse threats in the cyber world. This results in new types of threats that existing traditional security models cannot handle, hence, such a high demand for better protection. Artificial intelligence (AI) has risen to become the key enabler for cybersecurity as it boosts capabilities for identification, protection, and reaction to systemic threats [1, 2]. AI makes it possible for cybersecurity systems to work better, with faster threat detection, automatic response, and adjustment to evolving threat scenarios.

Applications of AI in cybersecurity are as follows: categories of use include anomaly detection, malware analysis, and threat intelligence. These models of AI like machine learning (ML) and deep learning will allow data mining and be able to detect specific patterns that may signal security risks and breaches. This capability helps in tracing cybertargets six times faster compared to the rule-based methods [3, 4]. Advancements mean that AI supports the ability to forecast or predict future attacks based on past data and trends, making for better proactive defense for organizations. When it comes to the specificity, AI's most successful application is anomaly detection, where the system has to seek out the behaviors that deviate from the norms set for the networks, users, or operating systems. In this process, ML algorithms perform a crucial function because, through big data, they are able to identify normal and anomalous activities [5, 6]. This is especially important for discovering zero days or previously undiscovered security threats attackers can use to exploit before users get updates to fix these threats. AI's capacity to discern these anomalies within real time minimizes the risk exposure time for the attackers, raising the efficiency of the cybersecurity frameworks. Furthermore, by integrating threat data from network logs, social media platforms, forums in the deep web, and others, AI plays a role in threat intelligence. This intelligence helps the security professional to get an understanding of new threats and threat vectors. In other words, by using natural language processing (NLP) and ML, AI systems can analyze a lot of the unstructured data for novel types of attack and improve the situation awareness [7, 8]. Threat intelligence derived from AI assists in identifying trends of an attack and the likely future cyber threats, thus enabling organizations to have adequate information to enable them to make the necessary preparations to counter any threats.

Defense in Depth: Modern Cybersecurity Strategies and Evolving Threats, First Edition. Edited by Hewa Majeed Zangana.

But it also has its challenges that come with adopting AI in cybersecurity. For instance, however, the use of techniques like AI adoption calls for massive computational resources and can be expensive. Moreover, AI algorithmic negligibility and interpretability became a hot topic due to the fact that standard AI approaches may overweight some types of data, potentially leading to bias and misleading threat identification [9, 10]. As a remedy for lack of interpretability of the AI-derived outcomes, a concept known as explainable AI (XAI) has been introduced in security analysis contexts as a way of enhancing the capabilities of AI-based communication [11, 12]. The applicability of AI for cybersecurity for reliability and fairness is an area of discussion. Moreover, as in many other fields, in cyberspace, enemies are also applying AI that makes new and more sophisticated threats of adversarial AI. Cybercriminals use ML in creating advanced phishing scams, malware, and other forms of attacks that can penetrate existing security measures. This has led to up arms race between attackers and defenders, underlining the need for AI to progress continually to match or outdo the perpetrating party [13, 14]. Thus, new and changing with the era of AI, cybersecurity specialists shall stay effective and introduce measures for restoring the two-sided nature of AI as beneficial and powerful in the context of cybersecurity and at the same time malicious and menacing for the cybersecurity specialists and cybersecurity in general. The following figure gives an initial glimpse into the broad domains of cybersecurity that AI has most effects. Some of the more specific categories of use include anomaly detection, threat intelligence capabilities, automated response, as well as vulnerability management (Figure 4.1).

In conclusion, the role of AI is vast for reshaping cybersecurity as a powerful tool for automaticity in threat detection, prevention, and response. Basic cybersecurity tasks such as anomaly detection and threat intelligence as well as more advanced capabilities, including prediction, have become critically reliant on AI. However, the difficulties connected with its implementation, for example, the problems of bias, transparency, and adversarial AI must be solved further more. This chapter focuses on these aspects and considers the ways in which new forms of AI can be included in cybersecurity models to enhance protection against the escalating threat landscape in cyberspace [15, 16].

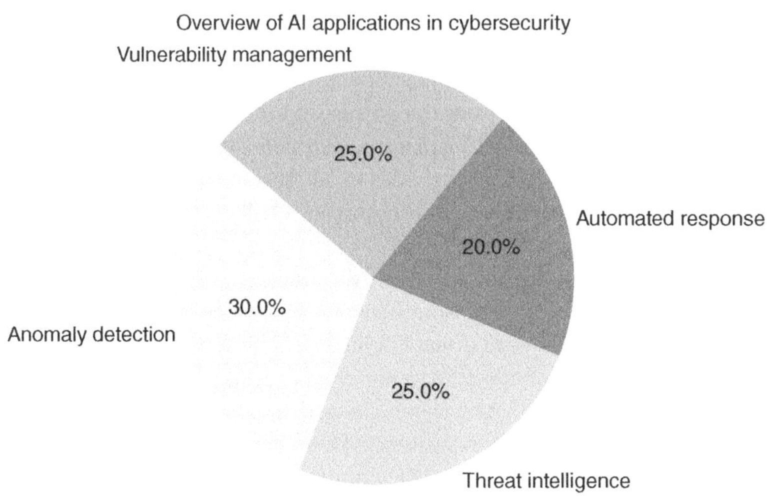

Figure 4.1 Overview of AI applications in cybersecurity. Source: Hewa Majeed Zangana.

4.2 Key Applications of AI in Cyber Defense

It is impossible to discuss modern cybersecurity without mentioning AI since it has improved not only threat identification but also the response to threats and the ability to predict those threats. This section looks at the various AI technologies that are currently espoused in cyberspace defense and security, with major emphasis on threat detection and analysis, response automation, management of vulnerabilities, and behavioral analysis.

4.2.1 Threat Detection and Anomaly Identification

ML is applied here to detect unsafe activity in networks and users' actions due to the recognition of abnormal patterns in the traffic. Combined with deep learning, these algorithms are trained on large datasets of past cyber threats, giving them the ability to identify strange patterns that are indicative of an attack. This predictive capability, often with the help of supervised learning models, includes the capability for real-time detection of malware, phishing, and other cyber threats [1, 3, 5]. Additionally, there are prospect XAI tools that offer interpretability in threat identification so that cybersecurity specialists can comprehend how such models make their choices [7, 11].

For example, applications of neural networks, as well as support vector machines, can assist identifying zero-day attacks since they show anomalous traffic flow as well as the users' behavior [17]. Threats can shift over time, and these algorithms learn and improve the reliability of cybersecurity measures [2, 18]. The following flowchart explains how the elements of AI can be applied for threat detection, starting from the data gathering process to anomaly detection and response (Figure 4.2).

4.2.2 Automated Incident Response

AI can significantly reduce response time as well as reduce possible damages by automating responses to cyber events. Such activities as isolation of affected devices, deletion of malicious files, blocking of unauthorized access can be fully handled by the automated response systems without involving a human being. These capabilities are important in functions like responding to the ransomware attack, where speed to contain the effect or probably reduce the leak of data

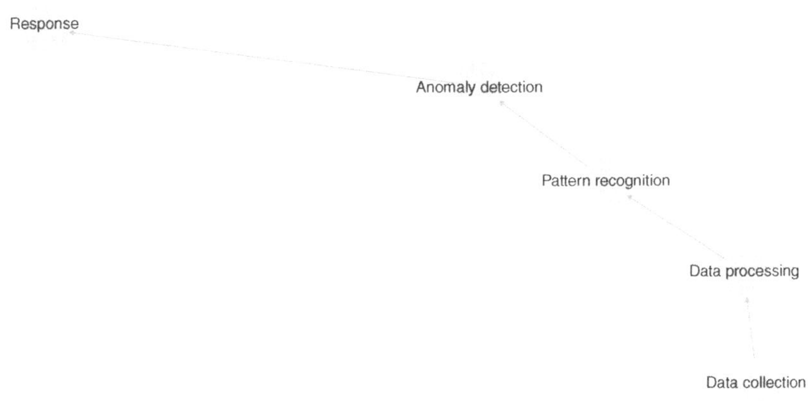

Figure 4.2 AI-driven threat detection process. Source: Hewa Majeed Zangana.

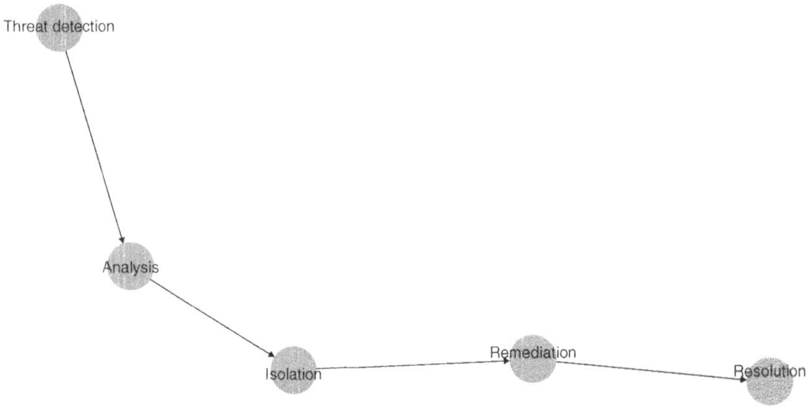

Figure 4.3 Automated incident response workflow. Source: Hewa Majeed Zangana.

is essential [9, 13]. AI used in conjunction with Robotic Process Automation (RPA) can write simple tickets, such as reporting a security incident or making changes to a threat database, so that analysts devote their time to more sophisticated problems. In the same way, ML-based security orchestration, automation, and response (SOAR) work on automating the process of collecting incident information from different sources to improve the speed of detection and response [10]. The organization's system flowchart for the automated response to an incident is detailed in the following flowchart (Figure 4.3).

4.2.3 Vulnerability Management and Patch Prioritization

AI helps in the determination of risks which is involved with software and the selection of appropriate software patches. AI understands the code repositories, identifies security concerns, and estimates the possibility of their exploitation. This application helps organizations effectively manage risks and, more importantly, vulnerabilities that often persist longer in large systems. This is in contrast to what one might expect when using traditional vulnerability management tools and methods [19, 20]. AI-based vulnerability management tools prioritize the vulnerabilities based on the risk factor associated with them, so that these can be solved as per the priority [14]. Such a prioritization is particularly beneficial in such fields as healthcare and finance because frequent updates are necessary to safeguard the information [21]. This chart shows how AI tools sort out risks in vulnerability management and how cybersecurity teams are able to fix the highest severity problems at the first place (Figure 4.4).

4.2.4 Behavioral Analysis and User Authentication

AI improves cyber guardians by monitoring and analyzing user activity to identify compromise and unauthorized inside access. AI-embedded behavioral analytics can track typing patterns, mouse movements, login spots and detect behaviors representing credential harvesting or insider threats [4, 6]. Another facet of security in an AI-based system is the use of biometric scans to act as confirmation of the user by means of some type of biological measurement or pattern such as retina scans, fingerprints, and voice scans. The following systems minimize the possibility of other individuals accessing the system, especially in regions where they have no right to access, by incorporating both the physical characteristics and behaviors of users [15, 22]. Here is the radar chart of the indexes used in AI-driven behavioral analysis to identify users by typing patterns and login location, and so on (Figure 4.5).

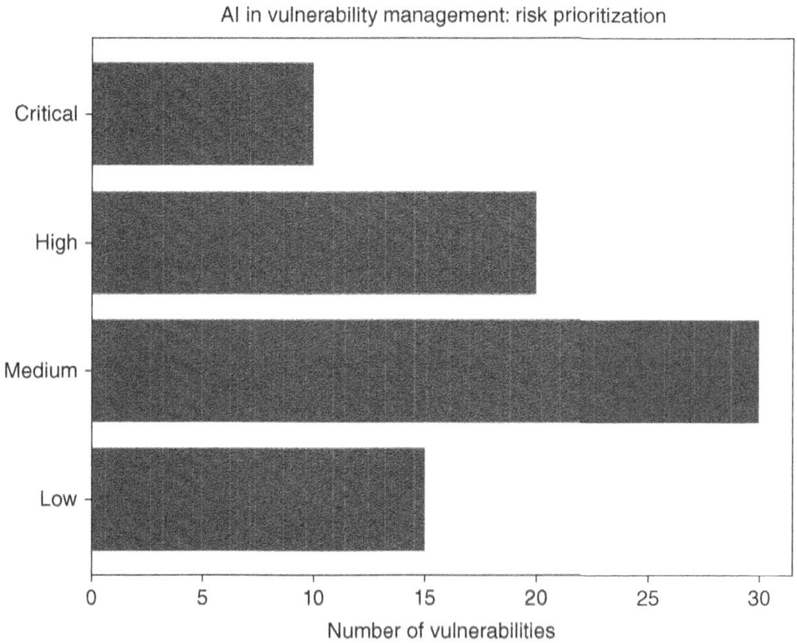

Figure 4.4 AI in vulnerability management: risk prioritization. Source: Hewa Majeed Zangana.

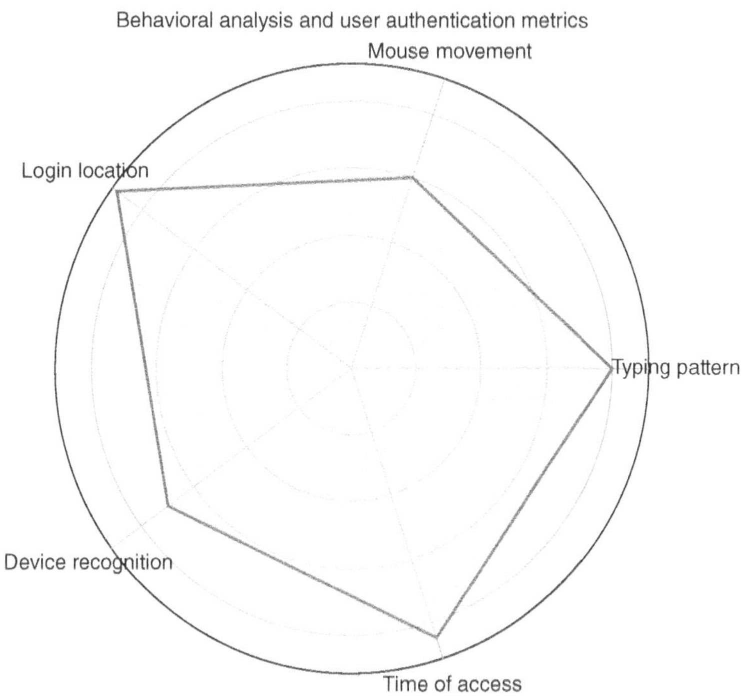

Figure 4.5 Behavioral analysis and user authentication metrics. Source: Hewa Majeed Zangana.

4.2.5 Threat Intelligence and Predictive Analysis

Threat intelligence is a crucial task of many AI systems; these systems gather threat information from all over the world and make recommendations. These systems collect threat data from various sources and analyze them in order to forecast additional threats in the near future. The AI tools can locate threats and vulnerable areas by using the NLP algorithm to read through the news, forums, or social media content without any prior structure [23, 24]. Predictive analysis means that, by creating profiles that outline how a specific organization would be breached traditionally, organizations can plan a defense before an attack. For instance, anomaly detection methods can identify undesirable patterns that analysts formally define as "abnormal" by comparing them with past patterns, thereby enabling security analysts to prevent threats from escalating [25, 26]. The following Figure 4.6 illustrates the relevant data sources for AI-based threat intelligence and indicates where to collect each type of data.

4.2.6 Artificial Intelligence in Internet of Things Cybersecurity

AI has found its application in the cybersecurity aspects of the Internet of Things (IoT) because of the immense connections between several devices. Many IoT systems remain open to threats such as distributed denial of service (DDoS) attacks and data theft owing to weak security measures in most IoT devices. The use of AI algorithms can also be applied in identifying the traffic patterns with specific attacks targeting the IoT systems for improved security measures in smart homes, industrial systems, and healthcare devices [16, 27]. AI-assisted cybersecurity in IoT can assign devices into categories, track for suspicious behavior, and quarantine compromised devices to stop the malware's proliferation. Looking at the layered defense approach is crucial in this context but mostly in sectors like critical infrastructure, where IoT devices control critical processes [28].

4.2.7 Summary

AI has revolutionized the act of cyber defense through early and accurate threat identification and quick response as well as generally improving the field. However, like all features that AI brings,

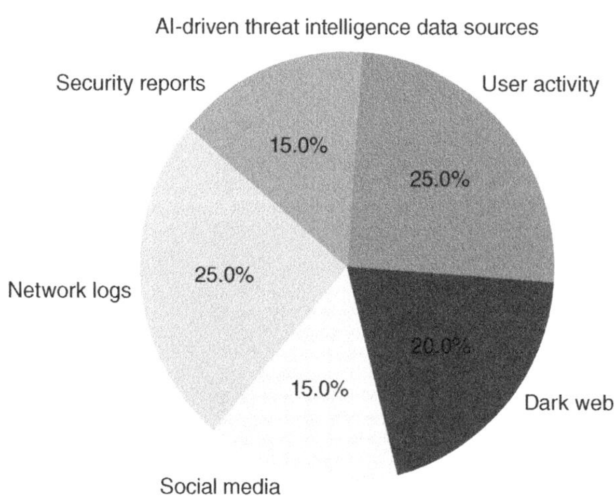

Figure 4.6 AI-driven threat intelligence data sources. Source: Hewa Majeed Zangana.

there are also deficits at the same time, such as bias in AI algorithms, the dependence on data quality, and the need for constant updates and control. Continued advances in cyber threats mean that AI is gradually set to become an even more critical component of defending digital assets across industries, though its adoption needs to be done in a way that deals with the challenges that come along with it [29, 30]. As a result of their predictive, detection, and response features, AI-based cybersecurity systems represent a significant innovation in protecting not only against conventional, but also against advanced forms of cyber threats.

4.3 Artificial-Intelligence-Powered Tools and Technologies in Cybersecurity

AI is widely integrated into cybersecurity systems as fresh approaches to threat identification, counteraction, and prevention. AI, in its basic form of big data analytics and finding patterns, as well as making predictions, has brought into the set of available instruments and methods that enhance the efficiency of cybersecurity operations. In this section, we will present some of the most widely presented examples of AI-based tools and technologies and their use in cybersecurity; we will highlight the new achievements in the application of AI and cognitive computing, including ML with NLP, as well as XAI and reinforcement learning (RL).

4.3.1 Machine Learning for Threat Detection and Prevention

A branch of AI known as ML finds broad application in identifying cyber threats and combating cybersecurity incidents. By pattern matching, which is characteristic of the ML algorithms, one may have data on past events, which may be used to determine security threats. For example, supervised learning is a form of learning that is used to classify between credible and invalid activities aimed at improving intrusion detection systems (IDS) [1, 17]. While unsupervised learning methods provide real-time detection of outliers, making them ideal for identifying zero-day attacks—attacks that target vulnerabilities unknown to the public—they operate without labeled data and can uncover previously unseen threats [9]. Besides, the ML-driven systems can learn new data and updated models by themselves which is a good strategy to face the new threats while lending themselves to the constantly evolving world of cybersecurity [5].

4.3.2 Natural Language Processing for Cyber Threat Intelligence

NLP is quite relevant for extracting knowledge from text, which includes social networks, forums, and other Open Source Intelligence (OSINT) resources in which information about cyber threats is published. Applying NLP means that large volumes of unstructured data can be analyzed, and the necessary trends and specific threats may go unnoticed [22]. However, through the sentiment analysis, these NLP tools can analyze the proactive intent of some of the communication that is very vital in the prediction of the behavioral profile of the cybercriminals and responding to their psychological tendencies and motives [26, 28]. Further, threat intelligence through NLP assists in the development of automated chatbots and virtual assistants for handling threats where the system would always be active to observe the threats in real time and provide the report whenever any threat is identified [15].

4.3.3 Explainable AI in Cybersecurity

XAI intends to enhance AI interpretability, summarizing the "black box" problem that has limited the usage of AI in domains such as cybersecurity [7, 11]. XAI is important to cybersecurity professionals who should explain the rationale of AI-driven decisions in situations including threat detection and prevention of user access, among others. However, XAI not only brings trust from the cybersecurity point of view but also helps validate an AI model and troubleshoot the system and its models easily [6]. XAI also improves the aspect of compliance with the legal and ethical results of AI decisions [3]. The following flowchart provides insight onf how XAI enhances the transparency and analysis of cybersecurity through AI decision interpretability for the analyst (Figure 4.7).

4.3.4 Reinforcement Learning for Adaptive Security Measures

In this context, RL can be deemed a dynamic model of cybersecurity by allowing AI agents to update their decisions with regard to the environment in which they exist based on the feedback that is received [31]. In contrast to normal rule-based systems, which depend on prescribed procedures, RL-based systems can learn how to create procedures that will help address cyber threats as they emerge. RL has been effective in the area of autonomous network defense to identify and curb complex attacks, thereby minimizing reliance on human inputs and providing quicker solutions [18, 32].

4.3.5 Artificial Intelligence in Automated Incident Response and Mitigation

AI helps those tools to automate the process of handling adverse incidents and containing or reducing their effects on an organization as quickly as possible, thus containing and preventing the spread of cyber threats, fixing the leaked data, and other types of incidents [20]. With automated incident response, automated decision-making occurs by using ML algorithms to learn from past incidents to minimize the time taken so that the damage does not aggravate [13]. In addition, by analysis of the potential threats or risks, which is a function of AI, the most probable points of attack can be determined and preventive measures put in place before an attack happens [27, 33].

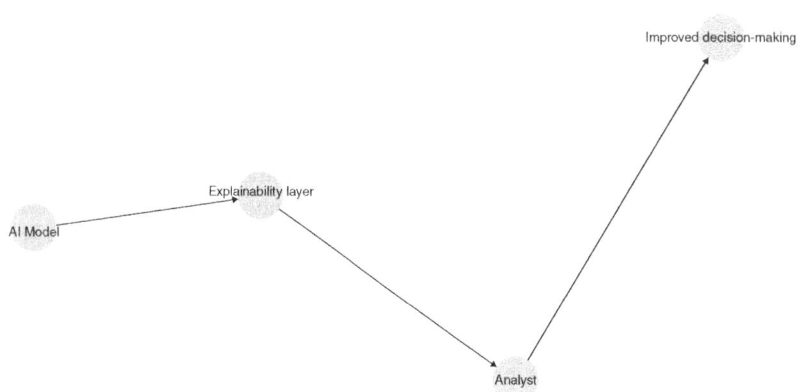

Figure 4.7 Explainable AI (XAI) in cybersecurity: trust and transparency. Source: Hewa Majeed Zangana.

4.3.6 Artificial-Intelligence-Powered Security in the Internet of Things

The emergence of more and more IoT devices imposes new risks both for insiders and strangers as every device acts as a weak link in a system. Today, IoT networks utilize AI-based tools for monitoring, threat identification, and prevention. Anomaly detection and behavior-based threat modeling are employed to identify alarming signs within IoT ecosystems [16]. Second, AI helps with the handling of large amounts of data produced by IoT devices to identify threats as they occur across multiple devices [21]. AI also improves the security of IoT networks by automating security monitoring, giving those systems a level of security against coordinated assaults and shortening the amount of time required to address breaches.

4.3.7 Cybersecurity in the Metaverse: Artificial-Intelligence-Driven Safeguards

With the growth of the metaverse, AI is used in cybersecurity to guard against numerous threats in virtual space. The constant interaction with the digital world, increasing with the inclusion of the metaverse, means that cybersecurity needs to address several problems such as identity theft, data leakage, and hacking. AI approaches are constantly able to observe and safeguard virtual environments using NLP to analyze attitude, identify exceptional cases, and promptly moderate interactions [3]. They enable safe navigation and interaction in metaverse platforms, thus adding critical protection layers for this constantly expanding component of human lives.

4.3.8 Future Directions for Artificial Intelligence in Cybersecurity

Further, the future of AI in cybersecurity is positive, with new developments targeting more advanced threat modeling, better incorporation of AI and blockchain for secure solutions, and better coordination between AI-guided systems and analysts [2, 6]. High ethical and regulatory concerns will remain the primary drivers of AI in cybersecurity, thus increasing pressure on the use of explainable and legal AI. In addition, the interdisciplinary synergy between AI and cybersecurity will create a venture to address new threats and contribute to a safer sociotechnical environment for citizens and businesses [25, 34]. In conclusion, the use of AI tools and technologies helps in improving the cybersecurity capabilities in the detection, prevention, and response mechanisms. However, the effective implementation of AI in this field depends on some factors where technology, innovation, and ethics of AI are far benefits, significant to establish genuine and reliable cybersecurity solutions for the population.

4.4 Enhancing Defense in Depth with Artificial Intelligence

In the context of defense in depth in cybersecurity, which refers to the concept of implementing multiple layers of protection to against possible weaknesses, the addition of AI to these layers enhances the organizational defense strategy. Traditional security measures can be supported by AI; threat identification and response may occur faster, while response actions may be automated, all of which helps save time and resources to counteract threats [9, 14].

4.4.1 Artificial Intelligence-Driven Threat Detection and Prevention

In the threat detection context, the AI techniques are ML, deep learning, and NLP, which have enabled the detection of threats, especially because of handling a huge volume of data and state detection of threats that may be a sign of security threats. Complex computations can analyze the traffic and activity on the network as well as the users to notice any anomalies for cyber threats like phishing or ransomware, as noted by Refs. [3, 4]. This proactive identification of threats enhances the defense-in-depth model by bringing in an intelligent, real-time monitoring layer that notices threats as they develop and not in isolation from the development.

4.4.2 Artificial-Intelligence-Enhanced Intrusion Detection Systems

Conventional IDS technologies are capable of producing a very high number of alerts, which can cause alert fatigue to cybersecurity personnel. AI improves IDS in that it filters out false alerts, and it has the ability to analyze the patterns of attack that may not be well understood by conventional methods [29]. Owing to this characteristic of learning, the AI-based IDS are able to respond to novel threats as they are better suited to new threats than currently active threats [2, 31]. For instance, anomaly detection algorithms are able to highlight scripts that go against the typical patterns in network traffic, which might point toward insiders or compromised devices [13, 16].

4.4.3 Automated Threat Response

Incorporation of AI in the defense in depth means that the response to the incident can be easier. Sophisticated threat response allows for quarantine devices, block Internet Protocols (IPs), and trigger recovery processes with no human input being necessary in such a situation. This is especially essential in preventing the impacts from emerging fast attack types such as the DDoS attacks that call for a fast responding system [17, 33]; as De Azambuja et al. [10] discuss, this integration of automation ensures that threat actors cannot take advantage of poor response time from human beings.

4.4.4 Explainable AI for Enhanced Cybersecurity

XAI is particularly important in the cybersecurity domain as it offers both interpretability and models for which cybersecurity personnel are able to comprehend and have faith. XAI increases an expert's awareness of the reasons behind threat notifications, thus enabling faster and precise decision-making [5, 11]. It is especially valuable in industries with legal constraints as well as auditability, as it provides the ability to track threat identification steps in a transparent manner [12, 32].

4.4.5 Artificial-Intelligence-Driven Security for the Internet of Things

In general, the IoT environment requires stepping up the defense in depth using AI means. Because IoT devices have open connections to the internet and can have low levels of protection, IoT devices are prone to cyber threats. AI serves as one of the ways through which IoT security can be strengthened as it becomes easy to notice when a device deviates from normal behavior and fix any security vulnerabilities lying in its path. For instance, ML models can never overlook traffic from IoT devices and can alert the system on intrusions or access attempts, which complements perimeter security of IoT environments [16, 26]. In the context of the present chapter, this diagram illustrates the main aspects regarding the impact AI makes on IoT device security at the stages of monitoring, identification of anomalies, and response to these threats (Figure 4.8).

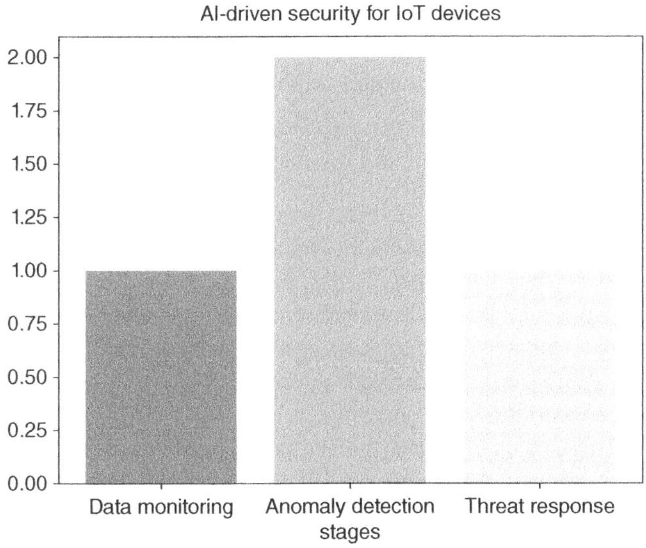

Figure 4.8 AI-driven security for IoT devices. Source: Hewa Majeed Zangana.

4.4.6 Enhancing Endpoint Security with Artificial Intelligence

That's why endpoints are often under cyber threat as they remain the weakest links in a network. AI solutions enhance endpoint protection through the ability to identify malware, ransomware, and other viable activities at the endpoints. It is possible to detect emerging threats, not requiring a signature database. The advanced algorithms are capable of detecting malware based on a behavioral rule [1, 6]. EDR coupled with AI helps one determine where endpoint compromises are influential and act promptly, making defense in depth have another essential facet [28, 35].

4.4.7 Ethical Considerations and Challenges of Artificial Intelligence in Defense in Depth

As much as AI has proven beneficial in improving security, there are ethical issues and downsides to think about. The main disadvantages of the AI models as potential obstacles to privacy are the need for vast datasets for training AI and the fact that biased data produce unfair or inaccurate threats detection. In addition, business dependence on AI systems also invites threat actors to engage in adversarial techniques to compromise AI models; this suggests that there is an urgent need for model validation [22, 25]. In order to overcome these challenges, the researchers are designing frameworks for making the AI applications for cybersecurity not only ethical but also less susceptible to adversarial attacks [7, 24]. When workers integrate AI utilities in various defense levels and layers, organizations are likely to develop sophisticated and elastic security measures. AI's incorporation into defense in depth greatly enhances the status of cybersecurity from a method that reacts to harm to one that prevents the harm from occurring in the first place.

4.5 Integrating Artificial Intelligence with Cyber Threat Intelligence

There is no doubt that the adoption of AI with cyber threat intelligence (CTI) can be considered as the new way of improving cybersecurity. CTI pertains to the collection and analysis of information on threats, risks, and adversaries to enable organizations to prevent real cyber threats. CTI incorporated with AI such as ML and deep learning will help to improve the processing of threats as well as the effectiveness and capability of processing large amounts of threat-related data.

4.5.1 Role of Artificial Intelligence in Threat Detection and Analysis

AI algorithms in CTI work can also analyze huge quantities of threat data in real time to notice patterns that suggest forces, which often present considerable difficulty for analysts to detect on their own. For example, ML models can cross-correlate many threat feeds, utilizing data from various sources to detect threat anomalies and suspicious activities in clusters which are not achievable by conventional means [1, 5]. This capability is valuable in the complex space where nontrivial attack forms like Advanced Persistent Threats (APT) cannot be detected by conventional means. ML is the flavor of the decade coupled with deep learning being employed as a strategic tool to identify complex relationships in huge datasets. These models improve threat detection systems to uncover other forms of threats that conventional systems cannot trace out [2]. They can find new attack patterns using large historical datasets, and they can certainly provide a good understanding of the tactics, techniques, and procedures (TTPs) that adversaries are likely to use.

4.5.2 Predictive Intelligence Through Artificial Intelligence

Predictive intelligence is one of the main areas in which CTI has benefited from the application of AI. AI models can derive this information from the historical data available in the system and identify fresh trends in attack patterns and provide preventive measures. For instance, risk assessments can predict possible threats from actions performed by threat agents, so that organizations can strengthen their protection before an attack [3, 6]. This is quite different from other approaches to cybersecurity, where interventions are only made after the threats have compromised security. In addition, predictive intelligence using AI technology contributes to decreasing the mean time to detect (MTTD) and the mean time to response (MTTR) in cybersecurity operations. Through the use of technology, organizations can respond to these cyber threats and perhaps avoid turning them into big embarrassments [4].

4.5.3 Real-Time Threat Intelligence Automation

The following are some of the ways that AI in CTI yields great benefits; one of the benefits is the automation of threat intelligence processes. AI models can also periodically or in real time analyze the data stream from the network traffic and respond to these threats autonomously without the need to involve a human being [9]. Automated threat response systems may perform auto-executable activities, including preventing specific suspicious IPs or isolating compromised systems, containing the range of the threat [11]. Also, such automation frees up the time of cybersecurity teams, as, for instance, categorizing threat alerts is a rather monotonous task.

4.5.4 Enhancing Decision-Making with Explainable Artificial Intelligence

XAI in cybersecurity entails providing the security analysts with ways in which to follow, interpret as well as understand the AI insights in order to enhance trust as well as accountability in the AI threat intelligence systems. With the growing reliance on AI in threat intelligence solutions, the identification of decision-making mechanisms is essential for decision outcome verification when countermeasures to threats are applied [7]. For example, XAI models can explain why specific alerts have been triggered, allowing analysts to make better decisions and explain their actions to the stakeholders [14]. XAI integration in CTI provides for the rationale since where decisions are to be auditable particularly in highly regulated fields. Compliance and organizational accountability require detailed rationales for threat detection and response decisions that it can offer [13].

4.5.5 Case Studies and Applications

Alleviated by CTI automation and security engineering (SE) + AI integration, CTI has been reported to yield considerable results in many scenarios. For instance, ML in IDS has enhanced the capacity for detecting malware and phishing attacks [16]. Also, through the use of AI in threat intelligence systems, it has been possible to identify threats early in the financial industry which the adversary focuses on since data is highly sensitive there [15].

4.5.6 Challenges and Ethical Considerations

When implemented, therefore, integrating AI with CTI also has its drawbacks. These are the demand for large and clean training data and the uncertainty of adversarial manipulation or deceit of AI systems [22]. Moreover, the marginalization risks including the privacy aspect and the probability of using AI in the sphere of cybersecurity abuse also have to be solved for the proper AI application [25, 34]. AI-driven CTI also has high computing power and sophistication, and it has high costs and may be difficult to deploy. While it is clear that more and more organizations are turning to AI to provide their cybersecurity, they must be aware of these constraints and begin to work on formulating strategies to combat them.

4.5.7 Future Directions

Further studies can be directed toward the increase of the further utilization and application of XAI in the CTI to make the explanation's function even better. Continued research can also be devoted to the application of AI-based threat intelligence in new challenging areas, for example, IoT and cloud as traditional CTI methods may not work as efficiently in these environments [27, 32]. Furthermore, bearing in mind that threats in the cyberspace are constantly advancing, there will be a need to come up with artificial intelligence models that adapt to the environment and self-develop. In sum, CTI augmented with an AI approach offers important potential for boosting cybersecurity defense. Due to its capability of detecting threats quickly, predicting, or making informed decisions, and responding automatically, AI-based CTI offers a solid protection solution to the increasingly complex threat environment. However, organizations need to solve the related ethical, technical, and operational issues to make full use of AI in cybersecurity in the future [26].

4.6 Artificial-Intelligence-Driven Security Operations Center (SOC)

The new generation of AI-based SOC will significantly revolutionize the world of cybersecurity—switching focus to speed, efficiency, and accuracy of threat actions. When integrated into an organization's SOC, AI and ML can help organizations sort through large volumes of data coming in from various sources, identify advanced threats in real time, and forward the information to the cybersecurity personnel for appropriate actions. In this section, we discuss the current state of AI implementation in SOCs, the opportunities and risks associated with this approach, as well as how AI-driven SOCs can positively impact cybersecurity in responding to the constantly growing number of threats.

4.6.1 Enhancements Brought by Artificial Intelligence in Security Operations Centers

AI as a concept in an SOC changes the perception of performing cybersecurity operations by providing a more efficient response to threats compared to manual methods. Conventional SOCs embrace fragmented hardware (HW) processes and rule-oriented tools, which fall short of dealing with the increasing and diverse threat levels. AI-based SOCs, on the other hand, employ improved formulas to analyze and correlate the data contents of the network activities and endpoints and other interaction points to improve threat visibility and perspectives [9, 17]. For instance, ML models can identify and detect any new patterns such as zero-day attacks, with fresh behavioral baseline data collected from the real-time streams [5, 15]. A valuable attribute of AI in SOCs is its application to predictions. AI can also analyze historical attack patterns, and thereby, SOC can be ready for future attacks in advance since the AI is self-learning. Predictive analytics will make a distinction between serious threats that must be addressed and low-priority incidents that need not be acted on Refs. [3, 7]. Moreover, AI also assists in the lower-level duties, including log analysis and anomalous activity identification, thereby sparing the analysts for significant threats [2, 29].

4.6.2 Role of Explainable Artificial Intelligence in Security Operation Centers

XAI is becoming a crucial factor for enhancing AI-based SOCs since it aims at demystifying the actions of AI. Unlike conventional approaches of AI that may be obscure, XAI ensures the decisions made by AI applications are comprehensible to the SOC analysts and other stakeholders. Such transparency is critically important in complex scenarios, such as cybersecurity, as the background for the alert can affect the strategies for further actions [7, 11]. XAI also supports compliance as it gives an understanding of how an AI system arrived at some conclusions; this is very important in meeting data protection and cybersecurity standards [5, 13]. Nevertheless, certain factors make the integration of XAI within SOCs possible. It would take time to provide many details and elaborations, large and small, so quickly responding is the main challenge. This might cost organizations too much transparency and an information overload that defeats the very purpose of decision-making processes that are supposed to be made easy [12, 26]. Nevertheless, XAI is a critical component of the trust-building process that can directly target cybersecurity specialists already concerned about the AI decision-making process in SOCs.

4.6.3 Automation and Response

With automation, AI SOCs are also following this evolution while delivering incident response. The consequence is an opportunity to liberate SOC analysts from low-severity threats, which still occur frequently. For example, it can also independently quarantine infected endpoints, prevent hackers from moving laterally through the network, and launch preliminary mitigation actions [22, 32]. Such high levels of automation will help avert the delay of time between detection and confirmation of such attacks, thus minimizing the impacts.

Systems that use AI for advanced response also utilize it to assess the importance of incidents much more effectively, giving way to a more accurate incident management approach [27, 28]. With machine help, SOC teams can better understand which assets are most valuable and which instances are most dangerous, thus making the most of available resources. The automation of threat response corresponds to the need for a highly coordinated response to huge volumetric attacks targeting infrastructures [1, 10].

4.6.4 Limitations and Challenges

Nonetheless, the integration of AI in SOCs has its share of challenges as highlighted below. There is one big barrier, namely the unreliability of data. It is one of the most significant barriers to successful knowledge management implementation. AI models need loads of labelled data, and obtaining such data is cumbersome because of issues of privacy and sensitivity of the data [31, 36]. In addition, adversarial manipulations in engineered AI models are also under threat; the adversarial inputs are designed to smuggle in threats into the system or trigger unnecessary alarms [25]. Another problem deals with the lack of experienced specialists who could oversee and analyze the activity of AI-based systems. Analysts who are conversant with cybersecurity and at the same time have data science and ML skills are still scarce in the market when operating AI-based SOCs [13, 26]. It is also important to note that the use of AI in SOCs also brings out ethical and privacy issues, especially when handling data of individuals or organizations [6, 34].

4.6.5 Future Prospects of Artificial-Intelligence-Driven SOCs

The future is even brighter for AI-enhanced SOCs as improvements are most likely to be made in many areas such as: first, self-learning threat identification system; second, predictive risk management system; third, the integration of new trending technologies such as IoT and edge computing [16, 33]. Moreover, advancements in quantum computing could soon facilitate improvements in the processing rates and the functionality of the elements of SOC operations that apply more sophisticated algorithms and return even more precise threat prediction and response measures [18, 24]. In addition, emerging forms of federated learning approaches might let SOCs to train the AI models across organizations while keeping most of the raw data private, which will ensure an adequate level of privacy protection but still provide sufficient learning information for AI algorithms [37, 38]. Explaining and federated AI-based SOCs could usher in a new era of collaboration and mark the next frontier for AI cybersecurity, increasing trust and cooperation across organizations. In conclusion, the AI-based SOCs are on the way toward integration into a modern security system as tools that have capacities exceeding the traditional SOCs based on speed, accuracy, and flexibility. But with those opportunities, there are corresponding issues that need to be solved in order to maximize the benefit such as data quality issues, ethical issues, and workforce skill issues. The use of advanced AI and thinking on how to overcome these hurdles will likely place the next generation of AI-centered SOCs at the cutting edge of cyber protection solutions and tactics.

4.7 Challenges in Implementing Artificial Intelligence in Cybersecurity

AI in cybersecurity is simply employing automation of threat intelligence and improved response time to risks. Nevertheless, there are major barriers to the integration of AI in cybersecurity. This section examines the AI/automation journey, potential issues to consider, and barriers such as technical issues, ethics, data reliance, and explainability.

4.7.1 Data Quality and Dependency

AI systems involve huge datasets, and good quality data is very important in cybersecurity. Nevertheless, it is sometimes difficult to gather the necessary, clean data as they are sparse, and their uptake varies in the cybersecurity domain [1]. The data quality affects the performance of the ML methods that were mentioned herein, rendering some of the results inaccurate or even biased if the dataset used was of poor quality [2, 4]. In addition, privacy restrictions like General Data Protection Regulation (GDPR) also hinder data access and reduce the potential for perfect model training and thereby AI applications within real-time threat detection [22].

4.7.2 Adaptability to Evolving Threats

Thus, cyber threats are actively developing, and new types can appear more often than experts can train AI models against them. Some examples of the limitations of models based on the historical approach include models trained on limited data that may lack the ability to perform well with new and unique attacks that are yet to be captured in the dataset, or when they are frequently employed that often, they may need to be retrained to prevent overfitting [27]. AI-based systems face the dynamic nature of cyber threats where new types of threats appear and existing ones improve; in response, AI systems update continuously with new versions, which requires time and skills [6, 9].

4.7.3 Explainability and Transparency

The concept of AI is particularly crucial in cybersecurity as the outputs of AI have to be trusted by cybersecurity analysts who use them; understanding the patterns behind decisions will assist in such a process. However, many AI models, especially those of the deep learning group, remain opaque or "black boxes," that is, they are difficult to understand how the decision the models reach their conclusions [5, 7]. The problem arising from explainability is that it is still challenging for cybersecurity personnel to comprehend or defend the AI system's choices; this gradually raises concerns about AI-based system implementation [6].

4.7.4 High False Positive Rates

AI applications within cybersecurity are also vulnerable to false positives, typical of cases when benign activities are marked as suspicious. High false positive numbers make it difficult for cybersecurity personnel on the watch to be as sensitive and attentive to real infections or attacks because their alarms have increasingly turned into noise or false alarms [8, 17]. This problem becomes worse in environments that are susceptible to changes from time to time such as the IoT where data incessantly flow in and different network activities go on, thus complicating the aspects in the AI systems [16].

4.7.5 Ethical and Privacy Concerns

The use of AI technologies in cybersecurity also comes with some moral dilemmas when it comes to user privacy and how personal user information is processed. For example, surveillance systems to identify unusual patterns in the network traffic could well collect personal details, thus contravening privacy standards [25, 34]. Moreover, utilizing AI in the processes of controlling and supervising the activity of employees and using their personal gadgets also has ethical issues related to privacy and informed consent; therefore, it is critical to establish a strong policy and act transparent [3, 13].

4.7.6 Vulnerability to Adversarial Attacks

AI models themselves are susceptible to adversarial which are instances that involve actors trying to feed the model with wrong data. Adversarial ML involves making small modifications to the inputs given to a ML model such that the model produces a wrong output regarding threats or entirely misses an attack [29, 32]. These attacks target the process through which the model was trained, making AI the very threat it was designed to combat—as development researchers call the "AI security paradox."

4.7.7 Cost and Resource Requirements

Introducing AI in cybersecurity solutions involves significant computational processing, human expertise, and continuously recurring expenses that can prove very expensive to most organizations [5, 19]. Other problems include higher dependence on high-performance hardware and cloud-based solutions for handling huge datasets in real time, which adds more pressure on organizational cost, particularly on organizations with limited budgets with their implementation, perhaps smaller firms [33]. Further, talent acquisition and talent retention are problem because there is tough competition for the best AI specialists in the market [28].

4.7.8 Regulatory Compliance and Legal Risks

AI deployment in cybersecurity must meet regulatory requirements that are sometimes standard across regions or industry specific. For instance, applying AI for surveillance or monitoring has to look at legal requirements for user consent and processing of data [37]. Legal consequences make the fourth challenge in the implementation of AI; failure to adhere to these laws results in sanctions. This aspect also affects the process of data collection as regulatory measures are inconvenient for AI in some cybersecurity applications [21].

Consequently, there are lots of barriers to AI implementation in cybersecurity: technical, ethical, and regulatory. These issues must be addressed for organizations to deploy and realize AI benefits while protecting the cybersecurity steps ventured, ethical, and transparent with corresponding adaptability to the continuously emerging threats.

4.8 Case Studies: Real-World Applications of Artificial Intelligence in Cyber Defense

Use of AI in cyberspace is a recent development which has transformed cybersecurity from simply reacting to threats to featuring proactive measures that are intelligent. This section covers various scenarios and best practices illustrating the adoption of AI technologies for various industries, explained through different success stories of AI-driven cybersecurity, threat detection, and response possibilities. These case studies highlight the positive uses of AI and emphasize that the main focus should be on how AI can and should be harnessed for cybersecurity. However, it is also important to consider the role that AI plays and the challenges that must be addressed.

4.8.1 Artificial Intelligence in Threat Detection and Anomaly Detection

AI has thus been proven to augment the threat detection systems by detecting anomalous patterns of behavior indicative of security threats, for instance, the banking sector since it is the recent target

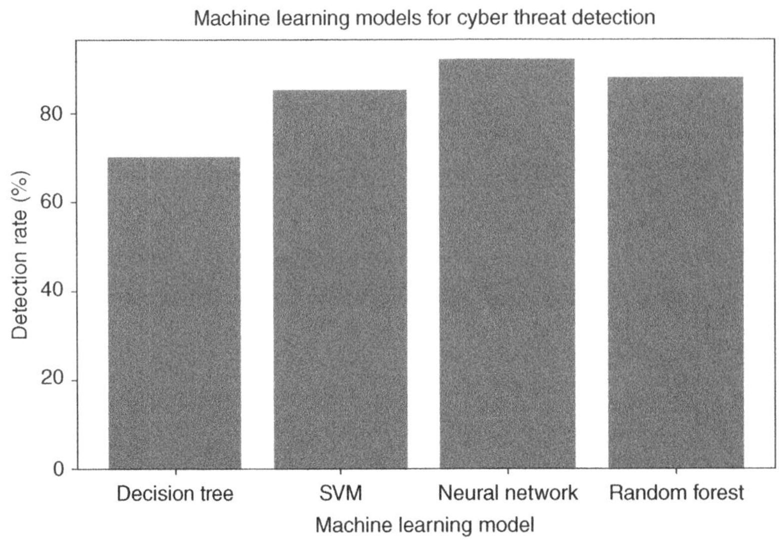

Figure 4.9 Machine learning models for cyber threat detection. Source: Hewa Majeed Zangana.

for phishing and malware and it uses ML for anomaly detection. AI models, which work with historical data, see small changes in users' behavior and identify those that may point to fraud. Ali et al. [1] note that such systems minimize false positives and are great for operations because analysts can then center their efforts on legitimate threats. Another example is telecom networks that use anomaly detection for real-time detection of DDoS attacks [3]. Such systems that largely depend on AI models are capable of fast detection and response since they mimic the historical trends of network traffic, hence minimizing service interruption. The following bar chart contrasts the performance of several ML models in identifying cyber threats and demonstrates the detection level of each model (Figure 4.9).

4.8.2 Autonomous Response Systems

Again, along with the exceptional identification, AI has allowed for the deployment of automatic reaction systems which respond as soon as a security threat is identified. For instance, some AI-based security applications are able to contain affected systems from the network on their own to curb the spread of any malware. An example can be found within the healthcare industry and looks into how AI applications can protect patient data through detecting unauthorized access, processing the necessary actions to cancel such access in the process [15]. This automation helps in minimizing the amount of time it takes to handle possible data breaches common in areas where data is often compromised. As pointed out by Chakraborty et al. [6], self-sufficient response systems increase organizational readiness and also take part in the initial identification of threats to offer support to overwhelmed security personnel.

4.8.3 Artificial-Intelligence-Enhanced Endpoint Security

On the contrary, securing endpoints like the computers, the servers, and the many mobile devices that connect to a network has been boosted by AI. Smart endpoint security solutions always perform constant surveillance over the device, identify suspicious activities, and sometimes—potential risks in terms of the observed usage patterns. For instance, in the financial sector, the endpoint security solutions employ ML to check fraudulent financial transactions [2]. Through analyzing the transactional data as well as user activities, ML algorithms can identify inconsistencies and prevent fraudulent activity. AI policies in Industrial Internet of Things (IIoT) devices enable end-point protection in these environments where devices are self-installed, a situation seen in case studies pointed out by Belani [4].

4.8.4 Explainable Artificial Intelligence in Cybersecurity for Compliance and Trust

XAI has therefore emerged as an important element in cybersecurity, especially for industries that require explainability such as finance and healthcare industries. By using XAI, human analysts can better understand how and why threats have been detected and the actions taken by an AI-enabled system. In finance, XAI models help institutions meet regulatory compliance by explaining the processes that identify specific transactions as suspicious; thus, institutions develop trust in such automatic approaches [5]. Similarly, in the field of healthcare, XAI-based systems for cybersecurity prevent data breaches in downstream systems as regulations demand clear justification of any intervention that modifies the permissions of the data pertaining to patients [11]. According to Charmet et al. [7], there is growing enthusiasm for reinforcement from regulators to resolve problems caused by AI, with interpretability and traceability provided by XAI.

4.8.5 Artificial Intelligence for Threat Intelligence and Predictive Analysis

AI is capable of processing large data, hence enhancing rich threat intelligence that will help organizations to detect and counter new threats. Big businesses utilize threat intelligence systems driven by AI to collect info from several sources and determine probable kinds of attacks. For example, the energy sector, which has become increasingly targeted by ransomware attackers, is using AI to integrate patterns depending on past attacks' data to protect critical assets from cyber-attacks [8]. These predictive analytics platforms involve the use of AI algorithms combined with past data to indicate the dangerous periods when organizations need to know preemptive measures to take [24]. According to Das and Sandhane [9], these systems minimize dependency on manual analysis, allowing organizations to shift from simple threat detection to prevention.

4.8.6 Artificial Intelligence in Securing the Internet of Things

This situation raises many cybersecurity issues because IoT devices are increasingly being used throughout the world and frequently have weak security protections. Expert systems, specifically in IoT cybersecurity, were developed with the primary purpose of boosting IoT protection and deterring intrusions. For example, Kuzlu et al. [16] describe how AI algorithms for smart-city IoT structures observe device traffic and detect signs of attacks. These algorithms are especially beneficial to smart grid systems where AI comes in enhancing the security of the data, thereby protecting important services. In another case, AI-based security systems in smart homes watch device behaviors, which will alert threats and safeguard users' data privacy independently [26]. AI also plays an important role in increasing protection for IoT devices that function mostly on autopilot since data is reviewed frequently.

4.8.7 Challenges and Considerations

AI undoubtedly improves cybersecurity, but, like with any tool, it offers its share of difficulties that need to be resolved. Ethical issues as well as challenges such as state bias and adversarial attacks that exploit the weaknesses in the system are concerns among cybersecurity experts [25]. Its integration for cyber defense is, however challenged by some limitations that, according to Wiafe et al. [33] must be understood to ensure system integrity. Furthermore, large resource requirements for AI training can be expensive, especially for organizations of small capacity [19]. In addition, there is a requirement for professional people to monitor and analyze the information and insights created with the use of AI, as noted by Truong et al. [32].

4.8.8 Summary

The purpose of these case studies is to show that AI advances cybersecurity across industries. Whether humans like it or not, threat detection and even immediate responses in some cases, and managing IoT devices, or improving the endpoint, AI offers strong tools with the right functionality to mitigate the increasing challenge of cyber threats. But it is not that easy to implement AI in the present structure of cybersecurity; still, organizations have a lot of barriers in terms of technologies, ethical concerns, and resources to efficiently apply AI. Overtime, AI applied to cybersecurity has been enhanced and refined; it is therefore expected to play even more crucial roles within cybersecurity and data protection pervasively across essential domains.

4.9 Future of Artificial Intelligence in Cybersecurity

It means that the use of AI is relevant for the consideration of further development of cybersecurity measures due to the intensification of threats in the context of the modern IT landscape. AI has been expected to bring not only better ways of identifying the threats as well as preventing them but also enhance the systems' protection. The literature review highlights several trends, challenges, and potential developments in this area of practice.

4.9.1 Enhanced Threat Detection and Response

AI has been used in proactive cybersecurity for the simple reason that it is capable of identifying cyclic patterns which may precipitate a cyberattack. For instance, ML models can go through loads of data in order to identify that there is something wrong, and thus, threat detection comes earlier. New developments in deep learning ways, especially the neural networks, improve the detection rates for complex threats which include APTs, zero-day exploits, and ransomware [1, 26]. Moreover, threat intelligence systems based on AI use data from various sources to give complete information instantly and reduce potential losses [27].

4.9.2 Explainable AI for Greater Transparency

One research theme at the intersection of AI and cybersecurity is explainable AI or XAI for short. Deep learning models, in particular, do not provide clear understandability, although their configurations are complicated; this is an issue for human operators in need of clearer instructions from the AI systems. AI for cybersecurity is one of the applications of the XAI approach, which explains to these professionals how an AI model comes to a decision [5, 7]. In the future, as the demand for model explainability rises, XAI might become integrated into future systems to enhance both trust and interpretability to help analysts rediscover why some alerts or recommendations were flagged in the first place [11].

4.9.3 Autonomous Security Operations

This means that future development of cybersecurity is predicated on instituting autonomous systems that are AI controlled and require little human oversight. Improving isolated cybersecurity operations yields a strong view into specific threats and timely incident response using AI entities. Such systems might use RL, a type of ML approach, for constantly learning and enhancing the kind of protection strategies implemented against changing threats [13, 24]. Autonomous security systems decrease dependency on human operators, so they can enhance organizations' ability to respond to attacks in high volume.

4.9.4 Integration of Artificial Intelligence in Internet of Things and Cloud Environments

The new risks emanating from IoT and cloud systems are rendering traditional approaches to cybersecurity ineffective. AI can effectively contribute to securing these environments through an analysis of device behavior, access controls, and performance of security checks to define abnormality. Research data suggest that the use of AI algorithms in regard to IoT security can assist in managing the threats raised by the growing number of connected devices in the future [16, 19]. For cloud computing, issues with threats can be addressed intelligently by adopting AI-based solutions because of their ability to adjust to changes in the structure of cloud computing as well as the behaviors of the users in near real time [10].

4.9.5 Ethical and Regulatory Considerations

As AI gradually gets integrated into cybersecurity more and more, ethical and regulatory issues will arise. The integration of data in AI models to work out complex issues forces a breakdown of data ownership and security, surveillance, and malicious use of AI power. Other ethical issues include issues to do with bias within the chosen AI models which are more likely to affect some groups or regions negatively [25]. In response, future frameworks are expected to focus more on the aspects of regulation and compliance and ethical use of AI, thereby promoting transparency in order to ensure that AI technologies are not misused by organizations [6, 25].

4.9.6 Artificial Intelligence for Predictive Cybersecurity

Another effective use includes preventive cybersecurity where AI is employed to envision possibilities of risk within a system before being exploited. ML gathers crime stats and threat information to give regions a score and advice on possible countermeasures. They were also expected to improve organizations' concepts of how the threat actors are likely to attack and how vulnerabilities could be handled a priori, which would, in turn, reduce the risk of exploitation [14, 18].

4.9.7 Human–Artificial Intelligence Collaboration

The idea of displacing all human analysts in cybersecurity is dismissed by experts who opine that it will evolve toward a more combined automation and analyst hybrid workforce system. AI is capable of processing data and performing routine analysis and scanning through large volumes of data that, in contrast, human analysts can work with complex problem-solving and decision-making [28, 37]. Integrating human skills and AI can lead to the formation of a strong cybersecurity system that can empower both qualitative and quantitative results of the cybersecurity system [33].

4.9.8 Challenges and Future Research Directions

However, AI in cybersecurity still has numerous problems: adversarial AI, for example, and AI where attackers try to feed models inputs that will mislead them, and the costs related to the complexity of complex model training. The future work will have to solve these issues by designing better algorithms that would be more immune to adversarial attacks and by losing unnecessary computational redundancies without losing efficacy [2, 8]. Also, AI-driven cybersecurity will advance in future by improved data and model quality, more efficient models, and ethical AI applications [22]. This graph represents potential futuristic research domains of AI for cybersecurity such as adversarial defense and ethical AI (Figure 4.10).

Last, AI's function in cybersecurity is set to increase because it provides sophisticated means to combat new cyber threats. Through tapping into AI, the cybersecurity discipline has been expanding toward a more preventive, self-evolving, and self-healing field. Nevertheless, to achieve greater AI agility, it shall be noted that there are still hurdles in terms of ethical, technical, and regulatory issues that need to be overcome before AI not only enhances cybersecurity but also reflects societal and ethical imperatives.

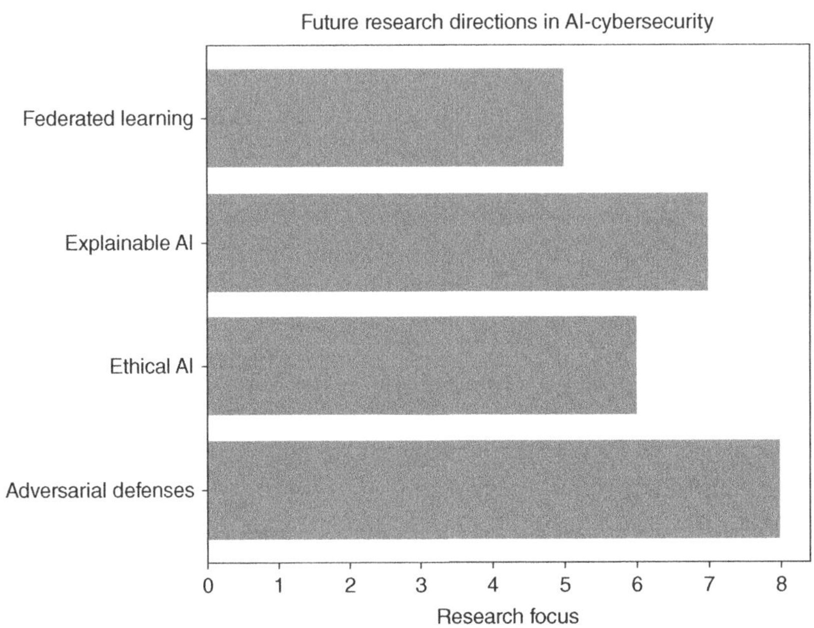

Figure 4.10 Future research directions in AI-cybersecurity. Source: Hewa Majeed Zangana.

4.10 Conclusion

Cybercrime, as one of the primary issues of modern society, is navigated by AI and cybersecurity as an innovative breakthrough in countering threats. Since the attackers have become more famous and aggressive and since they use better technologies to perform their activities, there is a need to develop intelligent and effective methods that counter the cyberattackers. With threat identification, response automation, and analysis, AI presents organizations with new and powerful methods for improving organizational security strength and addressing consequences related to cyber threats. But, unlike various AI benefits, there are emerging additional concerns as well as ethical issues to consider. It is also risky if not well controlled since it can create new forms of vulnerability; the use of algorithmic methods can also be unfair and perhaps nontransparent. Also, with AI system assets having become targets for adversaries, the security of such technologies cannot be overlooked in a bid to make them secure lest they become the uncontrolled catalysts undoing the systems they have been designed to protect. The prospects of AI applications in cybersecurity are quite promising but with a strong focus on equilibrium. Businesses need to place effort into adopting and implementing XAI to improve the level of transparency and trust among the user base. Frequent research and involvement from all stakeholders including technologists, policymakers, and ethicists will be immensely valuable as the reality of this setting unfolds. It is crucial to emphasize the security importance of the AI subject and take into account its innovative and ethical capacity to make a better selection of the digital environment. Therefore, the application of AI into cybersecurity is not just an addition but rather a vital component to cybersecurity at present. As we look ahead, the goal must be to build upon these technologies in a wise and constructive manner to help underpin a strong and sustainable approach to cybersecurity that will stand up to present and future threats. AI and cybersecurity are therefore expected to revolutionize the style of protection against cybercriminals to help establish a more secure and credible internet space for every user.

References

1 Ali A, Khan MA, Farid K, et al. (2023). The effect of artificial intelligence on cybersecurity. *2023 International Conference on Business Analytics for Technology and Security (ICBATS)*. IEEE. 1–7.

2 Ansari, M.F., Dash, B., Sharma, P., and Yathiraju, N. (2022). The impact and limitations of artificial intelligence in cybersecurity: a literature review. *International Journal of Advanced Research in Computer and Communication Engineering* https://ssrn.com/abstract=4323317.

3 Awadallah, A., Eledlebi, K., Zemerly, J. et al. (2024). Artificial intelligence-based cybersecurity for the metaverse: research challenges and opportunities. *IEEE Communications Surveys & Tutorials* 27: 1008–1052.

4 Belani, G. (2021). *The Use of Artificial Intelligence in Cybersecurity: A Review*. IEEE Computer Society.

5 Capuano, N., Fenza, G., Loia, V., and Stanzione, C. (2022). Explainable artificial intelligence in cybersecurity: a survey. *IEEE Access* 10: 93575–93600.

6 Chakraborty, A., Biswas, A., and Khan, A.K. (2023). Artificial intelligence for cybersecurity: threats, attacks and mitigation. In: *Artificial Intelligence for Societal Issues*, 3–25. Springer.

7 Charmet, F., Tanuwidjaja, H.C., Ayoubi, S. et al. (2022). Explainable artificial intelligence for cybersecurity: a literature survey. *Annals of Telecommunications* 77 (11): 789–812.

8 Chaudhary, H., Detroja, A., Prajapati, P., and Shah, P. (2020). A review of various challenges in cybersecurity using artificial intelligence. *2020 3rd International Conference on Intelligent Sustainable Systems (ICISS)*. IEEE. 829–36.

9 Das, R. and Sandhane, R. (2021). Artificial intelligence in cyber security. *Journal of Physics: Conference Series*. IOP Publishing 042072.

10 De Azambuja, A.J.G., Plesker, C., Schützer, K. et al. (2023). Artificial intelligence-based cyber security in the context of industry 4.0—a survey. *Electronics (Basel)* 12 (8): 1920.

11 Hariharan, S., Velicheti, A., Anagha, A.S., Thomas, C., Balakrishnan, N. (2021). Explainable artificial intelligence in cybersecurity: a brief review. *2021 4th International Conference on Security and Privacy (ISEA-ISAP)*. IEEE. 1–12.

12 Sharma, D.K., Mishra, J., Singh, A. et al. (2022). Explainable artificial intelligence for cybersecurity. *Computers and Electrical Engineering* 103: 108356.

13 Jonas, D., Yusuf, N.A., and Zahra, A.R.A. (2023). Enhancing security frameworks with artificial intelligence in cybersecurity. *International Transactions on Education Technology* 2 (1): 83–91.

14 Kaur, R., Gabrijelčič, D., and Klobučar, T. (2023). Artificial intelligence for cybersecurity: literature review and future research directions. *Information Fusion* 97: 101804.

15 Kumar, S., Gupta, U., Singh, A.K., and Singh, A.K. (2023). Artificial intelligence: revolutionizing cyber security in the digital era. *Journal of Computers, Mechanical and Management* 2 (3): 31–42.

16 Kuzlu, M., Fair, C., and Guler, O. (2021). Role of artificial intelligence in the Internet of Things (IoT) cybersecurity. *Discover Internet of Things* 1 (1): 7.

17 Bhatele, K.R., Shrivastava, H., and Kumari, N. (2019). The role of artificial intelligence in cyber security. In: *Countering Cyber Attacks and Preserving the Integrity and Availability of Critical Systems*, 170–192. IGI Global.

18 Jun, Y., Craig, A., Shafik, W., and Sharif, L. (2021). Artificial intelligence application in cybersecurity and cyberdefense. *Wireless Communications and Mobile Computing* 2021 (1): 3329581.

19 Mijwil, M. and Aljanabi, M. (2023). Towards artificial intelligence-based cybersecurity: the practices and ChatGPT generated ways to combat cybercrime. *Iraqi Journal For Computer Science and Mathematics* 4 (1): 65–70.

20 Namiot, D., Ilyushin, E., and Chizhov, I. (2022). Artificial intelligence and cybersecurity. *International Journal of Open Information Technologies* 10 (9): 135–147.

21 Omar, M. and Zangana, H.M. (2024). *Redefining Security With Cyber AI*. IGI Global.

22 Lysenko, S., Bobro, N., Korsunova, K. et al. (2024). The role of artificial intelligence in cybersecurity: automation of protection and detection of threats. *Economic Affairs* 69: 43–51.

23 Juneja, A., Juneja, S., Bali, V. et al. (2021). Artificial intelligence and cybersecurity: current trends and future prospects. In: *The Smart Cyber Ecosystem for Sustainable Development* (ed. P. Kumar, V. Jain, and V. Ponnusamy), 431–441. Wiley.

24 Tao, F., Akhtar, M.S., and Jiayuan, Z. (2021). The future of artificial intelligence in cybersecurity: a comprehensive survey. *EAI Endorsed Transactions on Creative Technologies* 8 (28): e3–e3.

25 Taddeo, M., McCutcheon, T., and Floridi, L. (2019). Trusting artificial intelligence in cybersecurity is a double-edged sword. *Nature Machine Intelligence* 1 (12): 557–560.

26 Zeadally, S., Adi, E., Baig, Z., and Khan, I.A. (2020). Harnessing artificial intelligence capabilities to improve cybersecurity. *IEEE Access* 8: 23817–23837.

27 Zhang, Z., Ning, H., Shi, F. et al. (2022). Artificial intelligence in cyber security: research advances, challenges, and opportunities. *Artificial Intelligence Review* 1–25.

28 Verma, S. and Gupta, N. (2020). Application of artificial intelligence in cybersecurity. *Innovations in Computer Science and Engineering: Proceedings of 7th ICICSE*. 65–72.

29 Morovat, K. and Panda, B. (2020). A survey of artificial intelligence in cybersecurity. *2020 International Conference on Computational Science and Computational Intelligence (CSCI)*. IEEE. 109–115.

30 Wirkuttis, N. and Klein, H. (2017). Artificial intelligence in cybersecurity. *Cyber, Intelligence, and Security* 1 (1): 103–119.

31 Zarina, I.K., Ildar, R.B., and Elina, L.S. (2019). Artificial intelligence and problems of ensuring cyber security. *International Journal of Cyber Criminology* 13 (2): 564–577.

32 Truong, T.C., Zelinka, I., Plucar, J. et al. (2020). Artificial intelligence and cybersecurity: past, presence, and future. In: *Artificial Intelligence and Evolutionary Computations in Engineering Systems* (ed. S.S. Dash, P.C.B. Naidu, R. Bayindir, and S. Das), 351–363. Springer.

33 Wiafe, I., Koranteng, F.N., Obeng, E.N. et al. (2020). Artificial intelligence for cybersecurity: a systematic mapping of literature. *IEEE Access* 8: 146598–146612.

34 Taddeo, M. (2019). Three ethical challenges of applications of artificial intelligence in cybersecurity. *Minds and Machines* 29: 187–191.

35 Pattyam, S.P. (2021). Artificial intelligence in cybersecurity: advanced methods for threat detection, risk assessment, and incident response. *Journal of AI in Healthcare and Medicine* 1 (2): 83–108.

36 Mohammed, I.A. (2020). Artificial intelligence for cybersecurity: a systematic mapping of literature. *Artificial Intelligence* 7 (9): 1–5.

37 Patil, P. (2016). Artificial intelligence in cybersecurity. *International Journal of Research in Computer Applications and Robotics* 4 (5): 1–5.

38 Soni, V.D. (2020). Challenges and solution for artificial intelligence in cybersecurity of the USA. Available at SSRN 3624487.

5

Blockchain Technology: Enhancing Security in a Decentralized World

Marwan Omar

Information Technology and Management, Illinois Institute of Technology, Chicago, USA

5.1 Introduction

Blockchain is increasingly being recognized as a revolutionary tool in many industries because of the manner in which it addresses issues related to data storage, accessibility, and protection. Starting as the foundational approach to cryptocurrencies, blockchain has evolved and expanded its performance reach to cover a vast array of industries that may include finance, healthcare, IoT, and others [1, 2]. Blockchain, emerging as a technical innovation in the domain of cybersecurity, provides new approaches to solving traditional issues and strengthens the system against aggressively evolving threats such as identity theft and cyber fraud. In essence, blockchain is a type of distributed ledger technology (DLT) that is used to ensure the secure decentralization of data records. In contrast to a centralized database where one party owns both the data and its access, blockchain distributes permission management across multiple nodes within the blockchain; every node hosts a complete copy of the ledger. In this way, there is no emphasis on a centralized element, which makes blockchain extremely immune to fraud and cyberattacks [3, 4]. Moreover, the elements of cryptography in the block make data unchangeable since each block is anchored to the previous one through a cryptographic hash [5].

Blockchain is not an innovation confined only to the financial world. The following figure illustrates the current state of industries that use blockchain technology and the extent to which they do so (Figure 5.1).

In detail, since blockchain favors a decentralized structure, it is advantageous when it comes to cybersecurity since risks associated with central points are eliminated. For instance, with reference to an IoT environment where several devices communicate and share information, centralized approaches to security fail to adequately mitigate security threats. Blockchain eliminates these problems due to its multiple layers and decentralized nodes, which help distribute trust through accountability while reiterating data security [6, 7].

5.1.1 Key Features of Blockchain for Cybersecurity

1) **Decentralization**: Blockchain disrupts the manner in which data is stored and shared since the system is decentralized. The various data recipients in a traditional system either have full access to data or are dependent on central servers or authorities that store the data, which gives the attacker a greater opportunity to manipulate the system. On the other hand, blockchain

Defense in Depth: Modern Cybersecurity Strategies and Evolving Threats, First Edition. Edited by Hewa Majeed Zangana.

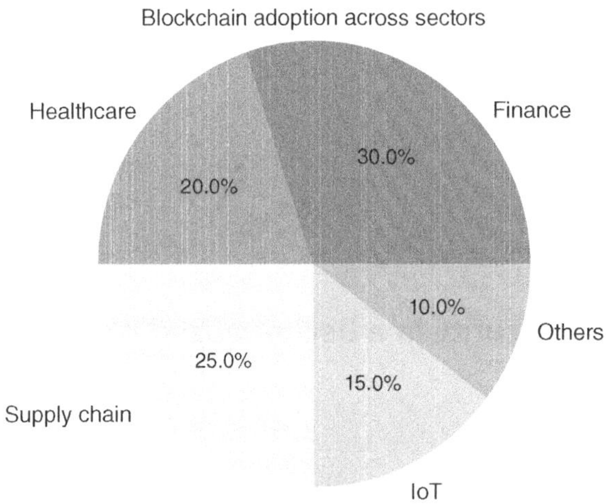

Figure 5.1 Adoption of blockchain across sectors. Source: Hewa Majeed Zangana.

maintains a decentralized architecture for storage of data in which data is spread across the many nodes of the system and which makes it hard for hackers to instigate an attack [8, 9]. Such a structure presents increased reliability and guarantees that the system will persist in its functioning, whether one or several of the nodes are inoperable.

2) **Immutability and Data Integrity**: In connection with cybersecurity, one of the most valuable properties of blockchains is data invariability. Any time data is written to the blockchain, it is permanent, and any alteration will affect every following block in the chain and will require consensus from the network participants. This feature makes blockchain well-suited for use in the protection of sensitive information, guaranteeing data authenticity, especially in fields like health and finance [10, 11]. For example, in decentralized healthcare data systems, blockchain offers the protection of patient records from modifications and fraud.
3) **Transparency and Accountability:** Blockchain is unlike centralized systems in that it is barely possible to cover up inefficiencies, given the checks and balances that enforce transparency of activities in a blockchain. The actions taken on the blockchain are recorded to be transparent, where every participant can conduct reviews on the carried out activities. In cybersecurity, this increases responsibility and frowns upon any form of deception in deeds and actions, as it facilitates an increased ability to fight fraud. One major group for which the technology is important is businesses where traceability and accountability play essential roles, including supply chain management and product IP protection [12, 13].
4) **Enhanced Privacy through Cryptographic Protocols**: Blockchain uses a cryptographic approach to create and maintain the security of data propagated on the platform. In blockchain, cryptography is significant for needed purposes like validating transactions, encrypting data, and authenticating messages so that illegitimate players cannot gain access to the necessary information [14, 15]. Other budding solutions like Zero-Knowledge Proofs (ZKPs) superimpose more privacy by enabling the confirmation of information without presenting the original information.
5) **Trustless Transactions**: Another unique aspect of blockchain is that it can enable, by and large, trustless transactions. Previously, agreements entailed trust between business people or third parties to facilitate compliance with the agreement. Most blockchain applications resolve the need for middlemen with designs like consensus mechanisms, including proof of work (PoW) or proof of stake (PoS), thereby providing transaction authenticity from within the chain.

This view of a direct, "trustless" connection eliminates dependence on third parties and lowers concerns regarding third-party data processing [16, 17].

6) **Scalability and Interoperability**: With the increasing use of blockchain, issues of scalability and interoperability are some of the main areas of focus. In many applications, more so in those that involve high transaction throughput, scalability has been an issue. Nevertheless, improvements in consensus algorithms and the capability of blockchain architecture, such as sharding and multichain framework, address these issues and hence the applicability of blockchain in large-scale cybersecurity solutions.

5.1.2 Challenges and Future Potential of Blockchain in Cybersecurity

Thus, despite numerous benefits implementation of blockchain in supply chain management brings, it comes with some difficulties. These challenges pertain to scalability, energy consumption, and compatibility as problems again for large-scale scenarios [18]. For instance, some consensus protocols, like PoW, cause high energy consumption. Solving these issues opens the need to enhance new algorithms and protocols for more efficient energy consumption. However, much hope still lies in blockchain in terms of revolutionizing cybersecurity practices, especially in next-gen blockchain models that use artificial intelligence (AI), enhanced cryptography, as well as next-gen consensus systems [19, 20]. Remarkably, consensus mechanisms come with different levels of energy consumption. The bar chart shown below presents the energy consumption of different consensus models of the most-used blockchain protocols, whereby PoW is significantly higher than other models (Figure 5.2).

Finally, applying the results of the study, it is possible to note that the technical component of blockchain technology can be considered as a set of tools to improve cybersecurity in a context of strengthening the role of the cyber environment in human life. Because of its distributed, open, and

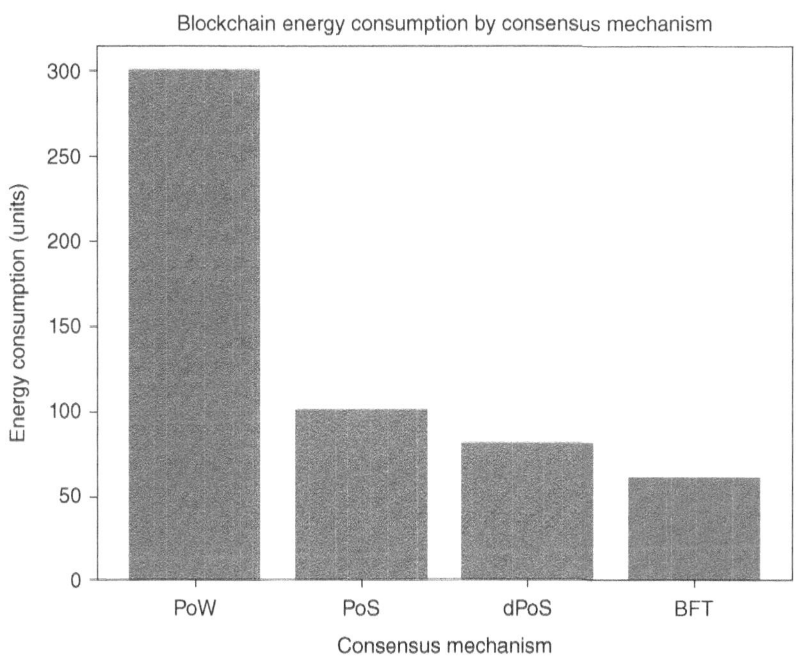

Figure 5.2 Blockchain energy consumption by consensus type. Source: Hewa Majeed Zangana.

unalterable properties, blockchain can be used to protect vital infrastructures and prevent complex cyber threats, according to the study. Blockchain solutions are already being proposed for cybersecurity use, and as the underlying technology develops, the effects of usage are going to change the paradigm of security across industries.

5.2 Blockchain Architecture and Security Fundamentals

Blockchain is an open-sourced distributed ledger platform designed especially for the secure exchange of value across multiple sectors. The structure at its base is based on a line of blocks holding the data, and that makes it reliable and safe. The blocks consist of a cryptographic hash of the previous block, the time of creation for every block, and the transactions done, which make sure that the data has not been altered. Such a structure can do without a strong center and increase the level of openness, which is beneficial in such sectors as financial services [1] or IoT security [6].

In order to provide a clear vision of the architectural strengths of blockchain, the subsequent representations of the basic elements, such as transactions, hash, time, and connections between the different elements of a block, are illustrated in Figure 5.3.

5.2.1 Decentralized Network and Distributed Ledger

The distribution of data is intrinsic to the blockchains since they have several nodes or copies of the data stored in them. Every participant in the network saves a copy of the ledger, and since there is decentralized control, altering a record is almost impossible without the alteration affecting all copies of the ledger in the entire network [5]. This decentralization increases the level of trust and security in the system since there is no one central place that can be so easily hacked [21]. Especially

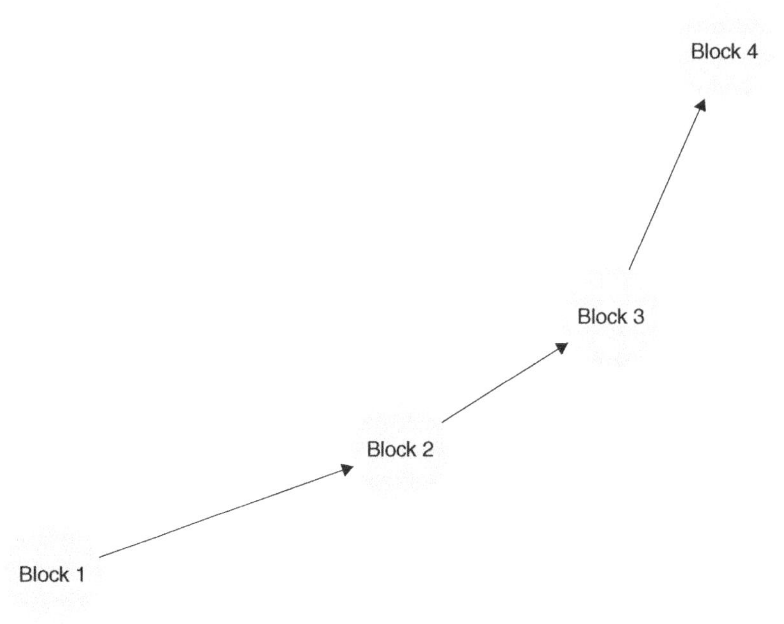

Figure 5.3 Blockchain architecture overview. Source: Hewa Majeed Zangana.

in healthcare, decentralization of data is beneficial because it increases data security and data privacy [2]. The characteristic of the distributed ledger in blockchain also helps build a transparent and indelible framework. This is done by consensus mechanisms that check the authenticity of the transactions in the network to make it applicable in financial and healthcare fields, as pointed out by Refs. [11, 15].

5.2.2 Consensus Mechanisms

An enlightening aspect of consensus mechanisms is that they offer a way through which nodes come to an agreement on the validity of the transactions. A number of these include PoW and PoS. In Bitcoin, PoW requires participants to solve complicated mathematical problems before the validity of a transaction is proven and it is included in the ledger [4]. Being an energy-efficient double of PoS, the validators are allowed to propose blocks according to the number of coins owned. This method is preferred where a lower energy consumption and better scalability are desired when applied in specific applications such as IoT [7].

Furthermore, new consensus methods such as delegated PoS and Byzantine fault tolerance (BFT) are gradually adopted in those systems that value high throughput and scalability [22]. The given mechanisms help in bringing flexibility to blockchain requirements in corresponding fields like industrial applications or digital healthcare, where transaction verification is fast and secure [20]. The key consensus mechanisms vary in their features, benefits, and downfalls. Below, I have provided a bar chart showing several important metrics like energy usage, size, and the security level of selected consensus types (Figure 5.4).

5.2.3 Smart Contracts and Interoperability

Smart contracts are digital contracts where the terms of the contract are written in code to be implemented automatically without the need to involve third parties. They remove the need for

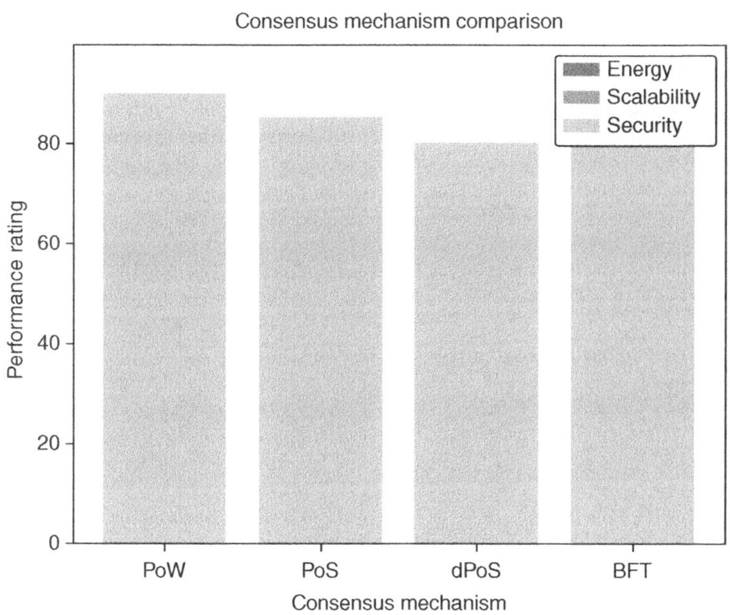

Figure 5.4 Consensus mechanisms comparison. Source: Hewa Majeed Zangana.

middlemen, which makes them cheaper and more secure [17]. In DeFi systems, smart contracts are useful to provide secure financial transactions without much interference [8]. In energy systems, smart contracts can be used to enable decentralized energy trading, thereby increasing efficiency and transparency [22]. Another element of blockchain security architecture is compatibility, which facilitates the ease of data sharing between one blockchain system and another. This is done through concepts such as interoperability solutions—in this case, cross-chain solutions that enable the exchange of information and value within different blockchains [23]. Interoperability becomes more important when dealing with multiple layers of blockchain systems, improving security in decentralized healthcare and other financial applications [24, 25]. Smart contracts have the feature of adapting certain actions as per a particular state or occurrence. This flowchart captures a reduced procedure that is followed when executing a smart contract in a DeFi transaction (Figure 5.5).

5.2.4 Cryptographic Techniques

Blockchains rely heavily on cryptographic algorithms to secure data, using two primary methods: hashing and asymmetric cryptography. Hashing produces a different unique number for every transaction to imply the genuineness of the data. Since the beginning, this hash changes with any small change in the input data, making it easy to tell if the data has been tampered with (Zheng et al.) [18]. The public and private key pairs within the blockchain are the basis of asymmetric cryptography for secure and private exchange of data and identity checks [26]. These cryptographic techniques offer secure security, particularly in areas that deal with important information such as health records and copyrights [12].

5.2.5 Privacy and Security Challenges

Nevertheless, blockchain has some privacy and security issues related to user data protection and platform scalability. For instance, openness in a blockchain can compromise people's identity by revealing transaction information that is undesirable [3]. One solution lies in permissioned blockchains, where access rights are limited; in this way, companies can specify who has the right to join and view the network [27]. But this approach may hinder the decentralization that is attributed to blockchain technology. Despite the numerous benefits of blockchain, scalability fails to realize its true potential due to challenges arising from large traffic. Proposals such

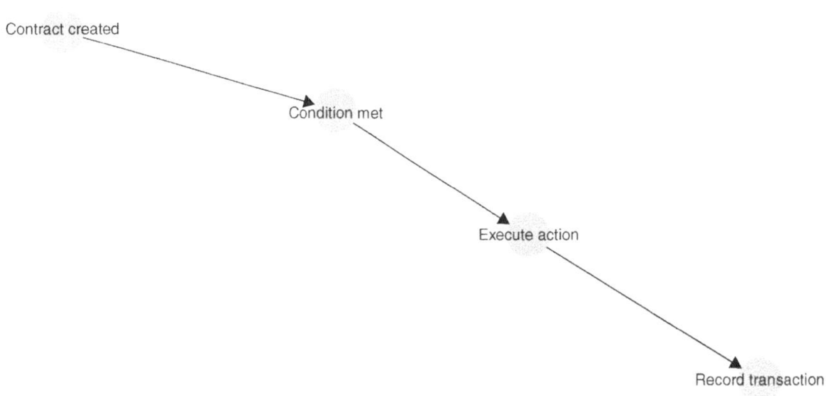

Figure 5.5 Smart contracts workflow. Source: Hewa Majeed Zangana.

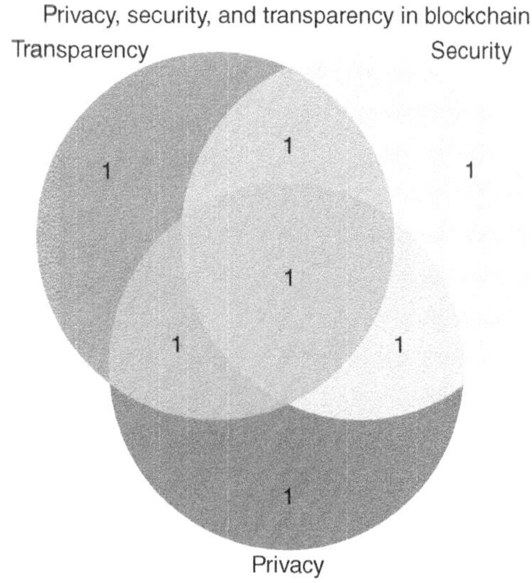

Figure 5.6 Privacy in blockchain transactions. Source: Hewa Majeed Zangana.

as sharding, which is a partial scaling approach, and off-chain transactions, which are easing the expansion of the Layer-2 solutions, have been proposed to overcome these challenges [28]. Secondly, socio-technical security that takes into account human stakeholders can help address security weaknesses of blockchains. Users must embrace updated control measures in combating social-engineering plans, and strategies must be adopted by companies to effectively prevent such attacks [29]. This Venn diagram seeks to show how these three features of blockchain solutions, transparency, security, and privacy, can complement and compete with each other. It shows ideal situations where all three are optimized as well as situations where transparency is optimal but security and privacy are suboptimal, or where security is optimal but transparency and privacy are suboptimal, and so on (Figure 5.6).

As a result, the system of blockchain architecture presupposes the application of several key principles, including decentralized communication and consensus, as well as cryptographic methods that contribute to enhanced levels of security of various transactions across numerous fields. But maintaining the level of openness, growth, and confidentiality is still an essential problem of blockchain to this day. Blockchain is already making waves in areas such as healthcare, finance, and the Internet of Things (IoT), as organizations across different industries consider it a solution to the growing demand for improved data security and decentralization.

5.3 Blockchain in Decentralized Security Models

Blockchain technology has revolutionized decentralized security models, providing technological solutions to secure decentralized systems in places that previously relied on central authority. A decentralized security model decentralizes both authority and responsibility, minimizing control with any one party. Thanks to the distinctive features of smart technologies based on blockchain, including DLT, cryptographic security, and consensus mechanisms, industries including finance, IoT, healthcare, and data management have incorporated efficient decentralized security measures. This is the case since decentralization reduces the risk of a data breach and simplifies control of data, as it is not centralized in one particular location. The next pie chart depicts the ratio of the effects of decentralization on data integration, access authorization, and robustness (Figure 5.7).

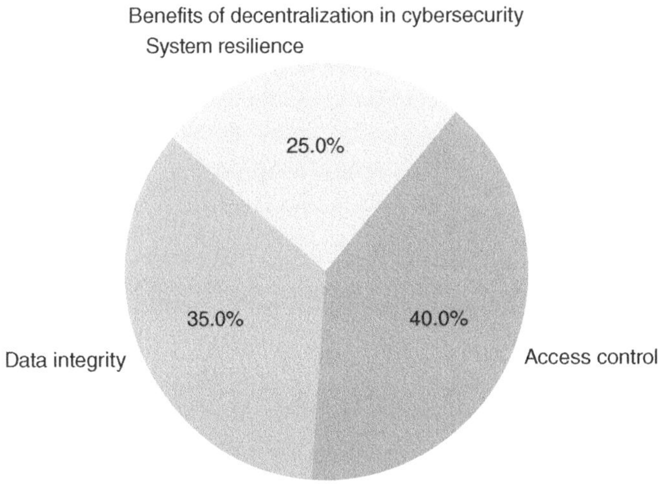

Figure 5.7 Decentralization benefits in cybersecurity. Source: Hewa Majeed Zangana.

5.3.1 Distributed Ledger Technology and Data Security

In decentralized security models, one of the most important features of blockchain is DLT, through which data is replicated in different nodes to boost data security and data consistency. Every transaction in a blockchain is checked and placed in a block that includes a time and a cryptographic hash of the previous block. This chain structure has the advantage of not allowing interference and is fully transparent. Other areas that rely on distributed ledgers include decentralized finance (DeFi), which enhances trust and operational accuracy by sharing information through an unalterable ledger [1, 8].

5.3.2 Cryptographic Security and Data Privacy

In other words, the cryptographic underpinnings of blockchain make it possible to maintain data security in decentralized systems. A blockchain consists of transactions that are encrypted using cryptographic algorithms, thus safeguarding its information. For instance, in IoT networks, blockchain has cryptographic solutions that mitigate cyberattack risks through the decentralization of data, as revealed by multilevel frameworks for safeguarding decentralized IoT systems [6, 30].

5.3.3 Consensus Mechanisms in Decentralized Security

Blockchain integrates concepts of distributed consensus, such as PoW, PoS, and new concepts like the ZeroTrustBlock for unifying consensus on the validity of data and transaction processing. Consensus algorithms are crucial in any distributed system as the system does not require centralized control; instead, the nodes can make decisions altogether [27]. In a decentralized payment system, for instance, consensus mechanisms are applied whereby only transactions that pass specific tests are incorporated into the ledger, making the solution more secure and scalable simultaneously [15].

5.3.4 Decentralized Applications (dApps) and Security

Decentralization is a principle applied using the properties of blockchain, wherein applications that can be created without the command from a single center are termed dApps. dApps are managed by smart contracts, which are capable of executing agreements programmed into code. These contracts also automatically impose laws and decrease the chances of fraudulent acts, making them suitable for industries such as trading. For example, the energy sector employs blockchain smart contracts based on dApps for decentralized power management and service, minimizing reliance on centralized power grids and increasing both organizational and security outcomes [22].

5.3.5 Applications in Health Security

Blockchain has been identified to have significant value when it comes to improving security and data accuracy in healthcare, which embraces decentralized system models to securely exchange large amounts of data for disease tracking. For instance, blockchain can be implemented in the healthcare industry, serve as a secure system to manage patient data, preserve data privacy, and ensure clear and shared records between organizations [2, 24]. These applications maintain the security and integrity of patient data as it is transferred across different entities within the healthcare network.

5.3.6 Decentralized Security in Finance and DeFi

It must be mentioned that the application of blockchain in decentralized security models is one of the most revolutionary implications in DeFi. In this kind of DeFi, parties deal directly without involving third parties such as banks, through a blockchain. Thus, DeFi systems via smart contracts ensure intermediary-free financial processing, including lending, borrowing, and trading, and contribute to a constructively built decentralized financial environment [8]. The elements of transparency supported by blockchain, as well as the immutability of the solution, have raised confidence in the DeFi industry by minimizing fraud potential and maintaining traceability of transactions [31].

5.3.7 Challenges and Future Directions

Despite the prospect of the application of blockchain in decentralized security models, there are challenges involved, which include scalability issues, energy consumption challenges, and even privacy issues. Indeed, as blockchain solutions and ideas become more popular, some problems, in particular those related to consensus algorithms and power demand, especially in PoW networks, need solving. There are new consensus models like PoS and hybrid models to address such issues. For handling privacy and scalable solutions for sensitive data, there are techniques like ZeroTrustBlock [27, 28].

Finally, the combination of blockchain with other innovative technologies like AI and machine learning (ML) can provide scope to improve decentralization security in a more enhanced way. For instance, the concept of blockchain-based AI provides structures with reference by which AI can be decentralized and the possibility of data falsification minimized, while improving the model's purity [19]. All these kinds of developments are expected to increase the use of blockchain technology in a broad range of industries and sectors to enhance decentralized security frameworks [20, 32].

5.4 Applications of Blockchain in Cybersecurity

Blockchain can primarily be described as an innovative technology that was initially used to support cryptocurrency and is now one of the most important assets in cybersecurity that tackles the problems of data alteration, identity, and access to different systems. Blockchain technology, being decentralized, immutable, and transparent, has proved useful in solving many cybersecurity issues, and this practice is changing the approach to the protection of data, privacy, and networks. This section further covers important areas of focus in the blockchain cybersecurity field, together with the strengths and weaknesses of these applications, as well as the future prospects.

5.4.1 Data Integrity and Tamper Prevention

Data control is one of the key concepts in cybersecurity as it keeps data unmodified and accurate. Blockchain's DLT increases the credibility of data through blocks where data is linked through cryptography. Because of the hash linked with previous blocks, any change in a single block is easily recognizable, making it extremely challenging to tamper with records [4]. This capability is mandatory for fields that require data handling and computation, where errors can have serious consequences, including finance and healthcare [2]. For example, in healthcare, blockchain offers the opportunity to guarantee the integrity of patients' records and enhance their trust [11, 24].

5.4.2 Identity and Access Management (IAM)

Security is arguably the greatest utility of blockchain; one of the ways it has been applied within this field is on user identity and network privilege management. Older IAM systems are centralized, and that is the reason why they can easily be compromised. Blockchain provides a mechanism for decentralized identity; hence ,users can create, manage, and own their identities without the intervention of a centralized authority. In combination with decentralized identifiers (DIDs), blockchain provides a better level of privacy and security, minimizing the threat of unauthorized access [12]. Additionally, smart contracts can easily handle authentication in blockchain networks, thereby enhancing security in cases of access control by eliminating human involvement. The comparison between the traditional approach to identity management with the use of blockchain gives blockchain an edge in preserving the privacy of users and controlling user data. Shown following is the flowchart of the identity management process within the blockchain environment (Figure 5.8).

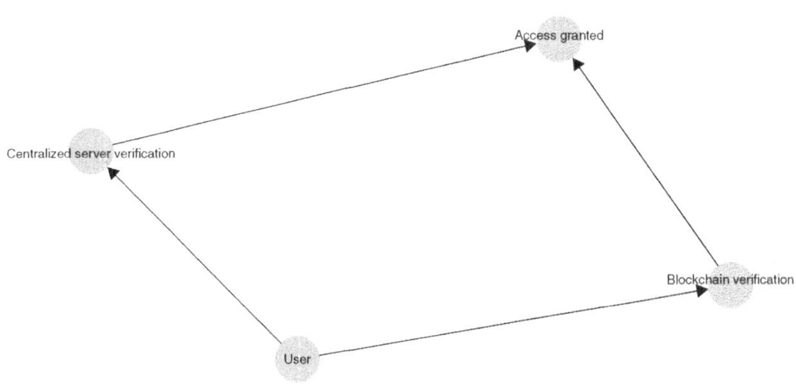

Figure 5.8 Blockchain in identity management. Source: Hewa Majeed Zangana.

5.4.3 Internet of Things (IoT) Security

The increase in the number of IoT devices has increased exposure to cyberattacks, as traditional security continues to grapple with numerous and different adapting devices. Blockchain's structure makes it usable to create reliable P2P networks for IoT devices, negating the requirement to centralize control of the IoT system [14]. Thus, the use of blockchain enables IoT networks to improve privacy, data sharing security, and device identification [33]. The use of multilayered blockchain has implications for handling IoT data, and it provides round-the-clock protection against cyber threats [6].

5.4.4 Supply Chain Security

Supply chain networks are complicated and involve several participants who may be situated in various provinces and states, and are therefore not easily protected against cyber risk. To reduce such risks, blockchain technology creates clear and incorruptible records of every interaction within the chain [20]. Another benefit is that it records all activities, making blockchain ideal for products that require high traceability, such as pharmaceuticals and electronics, which need verification of origin and integrity.

5.4.5 Decentralized Finance (DeFi) Security

In the financial segment, blockchain has led to decentralized finance or DeFi, which aims to do away with middlemen in exchanges of value. Yet, this model is decentralized, which highlights the necessity for a proper security system against threats. The cryptographic method of blockchain makes the process of financial transactions transparent, fixed, and secure, and hence difficult for hackers to compromise, as it uses records of the transactions that have been made [1]. However, as DeFi gains more traction, it undoubtedly encounters security issues, such as compromised smart contracts, thus calling for more advancements in blockchain security solutions [15].

5.4.6 Enhanced Data Privacy through Zero-Trust Models

Blockchain works seamlessly with zero-trust security frameworks in which users, devices, and applications are consistently authenticated before being allowed to connect to any network platform. As for record management, blockchain can securely store cryptographic keys, identity credentials, and authentication records, so that systems can allow access according to a more comprehensive decentralized audit trail established through this model [27]. They noted that industries with numerous compliance burdens should benefit most from this application, especially in the healthcare and finance industries, where the protection of data is sacrosanct [5].

5.4.7 Blockchain in AI Security and Model Verification

ML-based applications call for high data quality, especially in industries such as finance, healthcare, and cybersecurity. Blockchain also provides a decentralized means of confirming the data in AI models, so models can be trained and updated only with the data verified to be accurate and untainted [26]. Second, model training of AI using blockchain in a decentralized manner helps avoid data leaks as only encrypted, authenticated data is shared between models [19].

5.4.8 Future of Blockchain-Based Cybersecurity: Metaverse and Beyond

Blockchain is set to become a major factor in the security of emerging internet realms such as the metaverse. Thus, with an increasing number of organizations operating in virtual environments, threats and risks connected to digital identity, assets, and secure transactions are also increasing. Blockchain can offer a distributed platform, independent of central authority, for asset regulation, identity verification, and real-time money transactions in the developing metaverse, thereby improving its credibility among users and within its ecosystem [16]. Consequently, blockchain's flexibility could become a key factor in protecting future-generation digital environments as the metaverse expands [32].

5.4.9 Summary

Blockchain clears up many of the most pertinent cybersecurity issues in the present era of advancing technology, including IoT, identity, DeFi, etc. Reflected in the growing number of threats, blockchain can serve as a robust antidote to highly centralized cybersecurity risks with its distributed, transparent, and secure paradigm, albeit at the cost of scalability, standardization, and legal compliance issues [8]. Certainly, as both technology evolves and the number of new applications for blockchain grows, it will help build security and resilience into digital systems, in turn helping to create more trust-based systems.

5.5 Blockchain-Based Solutions to Emerging Cyber Threats

Unfortunately, new threats appear constantly and rapidly, so conventional security tools struggle to cope with the task of adapting to the growing cyber threats. Technology, specifically through blockchain, can proffer novel solutions to these new impending challenges by proposing a more decentralized, secure, and clear approach that hinders weaknesses in many interfaces.

5.5.1 Decentralized Identity Management

Among one of the most important and successful areas touched upon, where the potential of blockchain technology is being actively used to improve the cybersecurity situation, is the sphere of identity management. Centralized identity mechanisms are very vulnerable to things such as a single point of failure; therefore, the solution is often targeted. Blockchain decentralized identities are identified by distributed ledgers that ensure the safe management of identities. Due to decentralization in systems, with the users owning their identity data, these systems help minimize data breaches [5]. Due to decentralization in the system, blockchain creates a system-specific, decentralized identity information storage system where the alteration or deletion of data is impossible to perform without authorization and is detected by a network of other nodes [6]. This same concept of decentralized digital identity management also aligns itself with the idea of self-sovereign identity, meaning one owns their data and can control when and how it is used. Such an approach complies with privacy legislation like GDPR and at the same time reduces the use of central server databases, which are easy to hack [29].

5.5.2 Enhancing IoT Security

The IoT is expanding at a high rate, bringing many opportunities, but threats are also enormous. Most IoT devices have poor security solutions and can easily be attacked, for instance, by distributed denial of service (DDoS) attacks. Blockchain provides a secure architecture for controlling IoT device interactions and communication, which improves IoT security and prevents insecure endpoint threats [7]. This is because, through the use of blockchain, IoT network security is established with the ability to support device-to-device relationships rather than going through a central authority. This minimizes large targets and weak points and improves robustness against DDoS and other varieties of attacks [30]. Furthermore, applications that apply blockchain technology enhance data authenticity as device transactions are stored in the blockchain, creating a difficult environment for hackers to corrupt data or disrupt a device's functions [33].

5.5.3 Securing Decentralized Finance (DeFi) Systems

Cryptography as a subcategory is intertwined with DeFi, and as DeFi grows in acceptance and usage, smart contracts used in DeFi have become prone to cybercriminal attacks such as hacks and scams. DeFi platforms are based on blockchain technology that offers more reliability and a chance to turn middlemen into a thing of the past. Yet they are not immune to smart contract hacks. In response, DeFi protocols aim to implement a variety of enhanced blockchain security features, as outlined below: multi-sig wallets, decentralized oracles, and audits on smart contracts. Smart contracts must be audited by DeFi protocols, self-executing contracts, or programmers who are responsive to code. Higher-degree blockchain security measures are needed in DeFi, as noted in "Five protocols" [1].

Blockchain, mostly used in decentralized autonomous organizations, helps DeFi systems through its intrinsic trait of offering transparency to purge fraudulent actions. For example, smart contracts enforce the rules of the contracts and execute the related transactions without human intervention and by avoiding human weakness such as manipulation [8]. In addition, consensus mechanisms make transactions on DeFi applications safe across the nodes to reduce information manipulation by attackers, which makes data immutable and difficult for an attacker to manipulate financial transactions [15].

5.5.4 Protecting Healthcare Data

Due to the high levels of security and the decentralized nature of blockchain technology, the use of the technology in the healthcare industry is continuously being adopted for the secured storage of patient data as a means of enhancing health system security. Protected regions of healthcare organizations, mainly databases, contain the patients' personal and medical information, and are therefore vulnerable to cyber/data breaches. Traditional systems offer some solutions in this regard. Blockchain technology offers a solution in that it allows interoperability of data between the various healthcare providers while at the same time preserving the privacy of the patient [11]. Blockchain should also be used in conjunction with AI because AI can identify risks, such as a potential security threat, and send alerts to help stop such threats [26]. Moreover, self-sufficiency or decentralization of the blockchain protects medical data from being violated or tampered with, since any data recorded and verified on the blockchain cannot be changed again. For instance, health records contain a hash of the patient information and are stored on the blockchain, only accessed by individuals included in the patient's circle, such as doctors [13]. This affords health information the much-deserved legal bounds under regional regulations, including the HIPAA, among others, while at the same time safeguarding patients from any misuse of their information.

5.5.5 Enhancing Data Security in Industrial Applications

Core business systems and industrial applications mean more rigorous security measures are necessary because, in many cases, their disruption leads to catastrophic outcomes. Blockchain attracts attention in industrial applications because it provides decentralized data control and secure multiparty communication. In smart grids, blockchain can be applied for the authenticity of data, for tracking the usage of energy, and for protection of the system against any illegitimate intruders [22].

Blockchain technology cannot be hacked and altered like centralized systems, which renders it ideal for the protection of foundational sectors from cybercriminals [10]. It also has the capability to preserve log data from activities, so the activity to access affairs in Industrial systems could be checked in case, thus increasing accountability in organizations [34].

5.5.6 Addressing Data Privacy in Digital Transformation

As a result of the digital revolution, most cloud services are dependent on centralized servers, which create privacy and security challenges. The current concerns relate to the decentralization of data storage and minimizing the reliance on cloud solutions, which have been solved by introducing blockchain technology. By integrating the use of complex codes, blockchain ensures the proper sharing and control of access to information [12]. Blockchain also offers possible solutions for Zero Trust architectures, as these architectures assume all incoming and outgoing traffic is dangerous and has to be validated at every stage. In cases of using blockchain-based DLT, one can improve different Zero Trust models of cybersecurity risk management by means of real-time check-ins of access attempts and lowering the probability of unauthorized data access [27]. This approach greatly enhances protection of networked applications, particularly for finance and healthcare companies and organizations, as well as other industries [28].

5.5.7 Securing Metaverse and AI-Driven Applications

Combining blockchain with the metaverse and the further use of AI is a trend that is emerging because it considers specific cybersecurity concerns of the virtual world. The decentralized structure of blockchain technology makes it secure and capable of authenticating users who are crucial in the booming metaverse markets. By leveraging blockchain, developers can secure and safeguard virtual goods, avatars, and content in metaverse use cases [16].

In addition, privacy and security can benefit from blockchain in training AI, as blockchain enables users to decentralize datasets and AI algorithms, thereby eliminating biased data and increasing model integrity [19]. This is particularly important in areas that require careful handling of sensitive information and data, such as ride-hailing, self-driving cars, and smart city frameworks [20].

5.5.8 Summary

The blockchain-based solution offers a suitable method to tackle new cyber risk challenges in finance, healthcare, IoT, industrial uses, and virtual worlds. This characteristic makes it suitable for use in modern-style protection as it has a decentralized and largely unalterable structure that diminishes the extent of data vulnerability to a wide array of threatening counteractions. People use blockchain technology in identities, IoT, DeFi, healthcare, industry, and virtual worlds to make digital worlds safer, to match the enhancement of digital environments and connected living.

5.6 Challenges and Limitations of Blockchain in Cybersecurity

Nevertheless, there are still many strengths and shortcomings in the applications of blockchain in increasing cybersecurity, which influence its improvements and implementation in different fields. Such understanding is crucial for forming practical expectations of what can be achieved in cybersecurity using blockchain technology.

5.6.1 Scalability Issues

The primary concern many researchers have with blockchain distributed ledgers is scalability, which creates great difficulties in supporting high-transaction environments. Permissionless blockchain networks generate lower throughput and higher energy utilization as the members in the network increases. This is because each transaction must go through several nodes in the network, leading to traffic jams in networks such as Ethereum and Bitcoin, during busy periods [4]. Thus, the solutions include new generations of blockchains, as well as Layer-2 solutions, like sharding and sidechains. But these approaches are complicated and still under exploration, which is why scalability remains a real problem for them [15].

5.6.2 High Energy Consumption

The second problem is high computational requirements due to the complexity of blockchain systems and PoW consensus algorithms. PoW, which is the basis for many legacy blockchains, requires a lot of energy to maintain, leading to environmental unsustainability in the future [5]. This has led to the search for other consensus algorithms such as PoS and proof of authority (PoA), which, although they have lower scalability and are less secure, also enable less decentralization [22].

5.6.3 Privacy Concerns in Public Blockchains

There are inherent privacy concerns within a public blockchain system because most of the interactions occur in a distributed ledger where everyone can see the record. Thus, public or open blockchains provide transparency that may go against data owners' willingness, while compromising user anonymity and resulting in data leakage threats [3]. Current blockchain applications for privacy include dissident currencies, like Monero or Zcash, which use methods such as ZKPs. However, such solutions remain marginalized and have not seen massive implementation, thus making them less relevant in general use cases [29].

5.6.4 Security Risks and Vulnerabilities

In point form, the following can be stated about blockchain practices as potential targets. In spite of its security features, blockchain is not invulnerable to attacks. Threats like the 51% attack, vulnerabilities in smart contracts, and Sybil attacks are some of the contributing factors. A 51% attack, in which a user takes control of over 50% of the network's processing power, allows a double-spend attack or reverse the transparency of blockchain records, hence negatively affecting data authenticity [33]. Likewise, smart contracts—self-executing agreements—can be riddled with imperfections in coding and programming, leading to loss of funds and security breaches [7].

5.6.5 Regulatory and Compliance Challenges

This is due to the centralization of blockchain operations, where the business may compromise specific legal and compliance structures. As the transactions on a blockchain cannot be altered or deleted, the possibility of reaching data protection regulations, including GDPR and the right to be forgotten, is very limited [11]. Moreover, there are also challenges that regulatory authorities experience when implementing the laws in a decentralize system, a problem that makes blockchain challenging to implement in areas with more regulations. like the financial sector and the health sector [1].

5.6.6 Data Storage Limitations

Writing a large number of blocks in a blockchain presents a couple of challenges; the major downside is that a large volume of data storage is not very efficient because the storage of blocks demands a decentralized nature. Traditional blockchain systems, in general, keep all the data in each of the nodes, meaning that as the data continuously accumulates, storage becomes a major problem. For instance, when integrating blockchain in gross data storage, like medical records, the architecture features mixed solutions whereby blockchain preserves the core test transaction records while relying on off-chain storage to accommodate the remaining data [2]. However, these systems are hybrid and complicate applicability by having off-chain storage with third-party providers, which brings in new vulnerabilities [28].

5.6.7 Limited Interoperability

Tokens today work within an individual ecosystem, and this has developed compatibility problems for different ecosystems. For instance, Bitcoin and Ethereum do not easily interoperate; hence, cross-chain trade or efficient conversion of assets is impaired. Although atomic swaps and cross-chain bridges have been suggested as solutions, they are still at the experimental level and have security issues [14]. The enhancement of compatibility will make blockchain more useful, particularly in such segments that depend on interoperability, including the IoT [6].

5.6.8 Usability and Complexity

Blockchain technology is still technical, in that it requires technical know-how to implement and to maintain. This is a problem because the average user may be unable to comprehend the workings of these blockchain-based systems, thereby limiting their use. Furthermore, it is challenging to manage cryptographic keys that are required to access blockchain accounts for users, which could be potentially dangerous if the keys are lost or hacked [31]. Integrating user interfaces and creating friendly applications will be critically important to expand the usage of blockchain more broadly [9].

5.6.9 Summary

Nonetheless, there are countless impediments, and research and development efforts continue to find solutions to these limitations of blockchain. The actions in existing consensus mechanisms, scaling solutions, and interoperability frameworks are expected to help address many such problems in the long run. However, it is imperative to understand that blockchain cannot offer an end to all cybersecurity issues and should accordingly be understood in terms of its limitations when operating within large systems. With regard to these challenges, stakeholders are in a better position to build on the strengths of blockchain while addressing some of these areas of weakness with the aim of improving the state of cybersecurity.

5.7 Case Studies of Blockchain Implementation in Cybersecurity

The cases of using blockchain in different fields demonstrate the versatility and effectiveness of this approach in increasing cybersecurity. Through this section, which focuses on case studies drawn from sectors like finance, health, IoT, and energy, this publication documents how blockchain has turned challenges traditionally associated with security around and brought a new definition of privacy and data protection to bear on these applications.

5.7.1 Decentralized Finance (DeFi) and Financial Security

Business entities, particularly those in the financial industry, have been adopters of blockchain technology because of its merits, which make it secure, transparent, and tamper-proof. DeFi , which aims at providing an elaborate solution to the current financial system, has leveraged blockchain to enhance security and help the unbanked population gain entry into the financial system [1]. Built on blockchain technology, dApps deploy smart contracts to enable peer-to-consumer transactions, thereby eliminating fraudulent activities besides protecting consumer data from hackers [8]. This has led to increased financial secrecy and personal user data control in the decentralized payment system [15], revealing the capability of blockchain in the successful and secure handling of sensitive transactions.

5.7.2 Healthcare Data Security and Privacy

Healthcare is another important domain where blockchain has been found to play a role in the protection of sensitive information. Combined, these solutions create a suitable system that lets healthcare providers protect records and their data integrity as well as privacy. For example, the application of blockchain disease surveillance has increased global health security, since it permits safe and real-time information exchange between entities in public health [24]. In another case, it has promoted medical data security by preventing access by unauthorized parties while providing data access to only authorized parties [11]. Further, to this, HealthAIChain is a blockchain-based platform that has improved data protection and security in AI healthcare and is an example of how blockchain complements AI to address emerging security needs [26].

5.7.3 Enhancing Security in the Internet of Things (IoT)

IoT networks, as systems designed for the high connectivity of various devices and the unity of an enormous amount of various networks, have issues with security maintenance. Hosting IoT on a blockchain has offered a tiered, distributed structure that increases IoT security [6]. By incorporating blockchain, IoT systems can reduce the risks of data alteration and unauthorized access, as it does not require a centralized controller for data exchange between devices [14]. For instance, blockchain has been used to succeed in protecting 5G IoT networks through smart contracts and cryptographic hash functions, indicating the applicability of blockchain in protecting next-generation networks [7].

5.7.4 Industrial Applications: Smart Grids and Energy Management

The energy sector is one of the areas that has embraced the idea of blockchain for application in managing distributed energy systems. Blockchain has the potential to provide an optimal means of tracking energy transactions, handling distributed resources, and establishing the authenticity of the energy-related data [22]. For instance, blockchain-based decentralized systems can also involve secure peer-to-peer selling and buying of energy, offering transparent and appropriately modified control over energy resources [10]. Moreover, as for the energy systems, a predominant and widely known application of blockchain might be of use in managing the distribution of renewable energies, which may help facilitate the shift toward more sustainable models.

5.7.5 Intellectual Property and Additive Manufacturing

Blockchain has been especially helpful to IP management, especially in areas related to additive manufacturing, as it can deliver a trustworthy system of documenting IP rights. Blockchain provides ownership verification and recording in real-time, thus safeguarding a designer's or manufacturer's creations and products against emulation or copying. By applying a blockchain-based system, the validation of ownership of the IP will be more open, the likelihood of infringement will be lower, and the whole process of manufacturing will be more efficient and reliable.

5.7.6 Blockchain in the Metaverse and Digital Identity Verification

With the development of the metaverse, it is now clear that there is a need for the decentralization of identity systems. Metaverse security structures, which are implemented based on blockchain, are intended to protect objects in the metaverse, enable identification, and further facilitate authorized interactions of the users, as well as secure the transactions [16]. Blockchain can also incorporate Zero-Trust security paradigms, where individual users or devices perform identity checks independently, reducing the related risks of unauthorized access and improving trust in digital contexts [27].

5.7.7 AI-Driven Cybersecurity and Model Training

The combination of AI with blockchain is a perspective in the context of cybersecurity because blockchain's properties can protect AI's training data from changes. For instance, a decentralized model of training AI models, simply by leveraging the principles of blockchain to act as a virtual record of data transactions, improves the reliability of the model development process [19]. To a greater extent, this kind of application may be valuable in fields closely related to data protection, including finance and healthcare, as the data can be securely shared without compromising its trainability.

5.7.8 Government and Public Services

Due to the ability of blockchain to provide government services simply and securely, it is applied in voting, identification, and records. When records are made unalterable through the use of such a distributed ledger, institutions that are implementing the change can earn the trust and participation of the public [3]. For instance, blockchain solutions for digital identity help governments provide citizens with secure digital identities as well as make identity management both secure and more accessible [20]. Such a level of transparency is crucial to minimize fraud and corruption and at the same time protect the citizen data as much as possible.

5.7.9 Cybersecurity in Supply Chain Management

Cyber risks and fraud present themselves in supply chains, as most supply chain operations today are in complex global networks. This digital technology increases supply chain stability through trust since every process involved in the supply cycle of a product is recorded, from its production to the delivery process [9]. The use of an underlying network of blockchain in the supply chain means that every transaction is validated, and the product origins and other aspects are checked to ensure that no incorrect data is entered in the supply chain, hence the difficulty that hackers, fraudsters, etc. encounter in inputting wrong data into the supply chain records. Detailed analysis of these cases clearly demonstrates the many and varied uses for blockchain across industries and their specific security requirements that blockchain is perfectly positioned to solve with its decentralized, secure governance model. From financial systems through the IoT, healthcare and many others, blockchain for cybersecurity is becoming more apparent as it aims to set a standard in data security and privacy in future society.

5.8 Ethical and Privacy Considerations in Blockchain-Based Security

The adoption of blockchain technology in cybersecurity has raised moral and privacy issues since organizations depend on decentralized systems to prevent attacks and ensure safe transactions. Despite its reference to security, blockchain has lots of considerations with reference to data privacy, ethical transparency, and even the future unscrupulous use of dApps. This section will describe the ethical use of blockchain in cybersecurity and privacy concerns it poses for organizations and how they might be managed.

5.8.1 Privacy Challenges in Blockchain

In addressing one of the most crucial issues with blockchains, which is managing privacy in an environment that does not allow for anonymity, blockchain networks and other P2P ledgers are both decentralized and public by default. While individual transactions are not known to the external world, all nodes on the network have visibility into the transactions. This results in vulnerability to data exposure despite the fact that the information might be pseudonymous [3]. Unlike other existing databases where access can be put under certain controls, the incorporation of blockchain makes it hard to delete or change records. This is particularly the case concerning data protection rules, including the European Union's GDPR, which enshrines the right to be forgotten—a principle inapplicable to the basic structure of most blockchain platforms [4].

5.8.2 Ethical Implications of Decentralization

Thus, decentralization has rather prosaic but still good ethical consequences concerning data control, but new problems arise with such decentralization. Cutting off centralized control results in a lack of responsibility, which the central authority used to enforce on intermediaries. Though this might create great value for organizations when implementing blockchain in their organizations, it leads to ethical issues because it makes it possible for certain activities to be conducted without the necessary regulatory oversight [6]. Ethical transparency becomes more significant as the technology is integrated into modern finance through DeFi—which seeks to offer suitable solutions to underserved clients but also has significant risks of exploitation and scams because of its lack of regulation [1].

The ethical aspect seems even more problematic when blockchain technology is used for actions that would be unlawful when performed on traditional platforms, although legal in the distributed digital space, for instance, in dApps, where people can do everything they want without any repercussions [9]. Hence, despite its attribute of decentralization being one of its most-admired features, blockchain raises different but significant ethical dilemmas on how to apply decentralization in making participants accountable and transparent.

5.8.3 Privacy-Preserving Mechanisms in Blockchain

There have been a number of works in literature that are focusing on integrating privacy-preserving techniques like ZKPs, homomorphic encryption, and ring signatures in smart contracts to address privacy issues of blockchain-based security systems. The staking methods are supposed to improve privacy since it is possible to ascertain transactions without compromising on any sensitive data [27]. For instance, ZKPs' applications can include providing capabilities of proving identity without revealing personal details, which privacy protection objectives pertain to. As for homomorphic encryption, the notion allows for computations on encrypted data, while blockchain remains open and tamper-proof as before [2]. Permissioned blockchains also offer another option in cases when higher privacy is needed, as well as when permission is granted only to specific participants. This is quite beneficial in areas like health, because although patient data can be transferred between authorized parties, they are protected from public scrutiny [11].

5.8.4 Balancing Transparency and Privacy in Blockchain Networks

One of the most imperative ethical considerations in the use of blockchain for security is the issue of openness and confidentiality. On the one hand, one of the defining characteristics for which blockchain is famous, namely that it is transparent, can become a violation of people's privacy. Various drawbacks arising from decentralization of data include, as in the case of public blockchains, transparency of all transaction data which, while enhancing accountability, may allow third parties to monitor user activities and possibly associate pseudonymous addresses with actual identities [21]. This leads to a conflict between the principles of blockchain and values of decentralization and privacy preservation among blockchain users.

New architectures such as Zero-Trust permissioned blockchain possess a capacity to solve this problem by applying fastidious identification procedures and permissions controls while maintaining complete openness [27]. Furthermore, there is healthAIChain, which points out how blockchain technologies can enable the secure management of HHC data, including the creation of an anonymity-preserving yet an open ledger for such data [26].

5.8.5 Regulatory and Compliance Challenges

As with other technologies, blockchain also regulates with respect to privacy and data sovereignty. As predictors integrate blockchain technology into their applications, they find it hard to meet international data protection laws such as GDPR because blockchain technology is inherently unpredictable in some ways, such as data deletion [5]. For instance, authorities may find it easy to censor information on blockchains where information is supposed to remain permanent. As solutions based on blockchain technology grow worldwide, understanding regulatory frameworks that contain various levels of data protection becomes crucial [29]. Also, as DeFi emerges, the blockchain structure has to face AML and KYC issues to prevent misuse in financial processes. These regulations are designed to eliminate fraud and ensure accountability for funds; however, implementing them in a decentralized structure considerably increases the risks of compromising blockchain's principles [8].

5.8.6 Ethical Design for Privacy-Respecting Blockchain Solutions

Moreover, privacy must be incorporated into the design of blockchain systems from the beginning, and not be an addition that is considered later on. This can include writing ethical rules directly into the algorithms in question or defining restrictions on data, stating rules for the work of smart contracts with significant information, etc. For instance, the ethical design of blockchain in IoT and healthcare can be trialed from data privacy without minimizing data usefulness [30, 33]. Blockchain developers can follow an ethical approach by conforming system protocols to ethical frameworks to prevent harmful outcomes for users of this technology [34].

5.8.7 Summary

Although blockchain technology offers significant opportunities for improving cybersecurity, its ethical and privacy factors should be defined to unleash its full potential in applications. Privacy-preserving mechanisms, permissioned blockchains, and regulatory compliance frameworks are the first necessary success iterations in building ethical blockchain-based security solutions. Blockchain-based applications should provide transparency while doing so with respect to users' and ethics' importance in applications such as health and finance. With thought, proper regulation, and significant effort put into its workings, blockchain can mature as an incorruptible, moral innovation designed to maintain users' anonymity while enlisting the power of an open and transparent system.

5.9 Future Trends and Innovations in Blockchain for Cybersecurity

With further development of the digital environment, blockchain technology will be able to solve new challenges in the sphere of cybersecurity by virtue of new advancements. The following subtopics outline the future evolution of blockchain with regard to strengthening security architecture, data privacy, and distributed organization in various industries. Blockchain technology, on account of its decentralized and unalterable characteristics, is revolutionizing global sectors like finance, health, and IoT to provide safe settings for data sharing and data storage [1].

5.9.1 Integration with Decentralized Finance (DeFi) and Decentralized Identity Solutions

Blockchain's effect on DeFi systems is massive since it offers a shared financial structure that is difficult to meddle with or hack. Such features include the fact that by the use of smart contracts, DeFi does not involve the use of middlemen, which makes the deal secure and transparent [8]. With the improvement of the blockchain-implemented identity verification platforms, cybersecurity improves through building a secure digital identity environment that cannot be exploited for identity deception and scams [6].

5.9.2 Blockchain and IoT Security

IoT technology has crept into most sectors that are considered sensitive, and therefore, these networks need to be protected. Blockchain appears to be a solution to such issues due to its decentralized architecture that enables IoT devices to authenticate and communicate securely, without having to rely on centralized infrastructures [33]. Future development may concern technologies providing multileveled decentralized IoT, which increases the security of connected environments and addresses inherent flaws in traditional network paradigms [7]. In the same way, the integration of IoT with blockchain will improve IoT security by offering distribution and using hashing to keep a record of interactions. The following diagram illustrates a multiple-layered blockchain model in an IoT network (Figure 5.9).

5.9.3 Blockchain in Healthcare and Data Privacy

It is also notable to note how blockchain technology is finding application in the healthcare sector in areas such as data sharing, data management, and integration. In healthcare, records on the blockchain are relatively more secure and private when it comes to patient data and medical records [2]. Implementations in the healthcare sector of the future may combine AI with blockchain in order to guarantee better security and insights for the interpretation of the data [26]. These technologies have the potential to enhance the practice of managing health data especially in the context of public health surveillance and disease prevention [24].

5.9.4 Enhancing AI Model Training with Blockchain

There is an increasing significance of AI in cybersecurity, but there are also emerging risks that contribute to the range of threats identified, including model manipulation. It means that with blockchain, the training data lineage to AI can be tracked in a secure manner, thus the integrity of the data used is better protected. When using blockchain to train AI models on a decentralized basis, those who apply the results will be able to exclude unauthorized changes to the data, thus ensuring the creation of responsible and, therefore, safe AI applications [19]. It is especially suitable for enhancing the method of developing predictive models in the cybersecurity domain, while ensuring safe and clear cooperation.

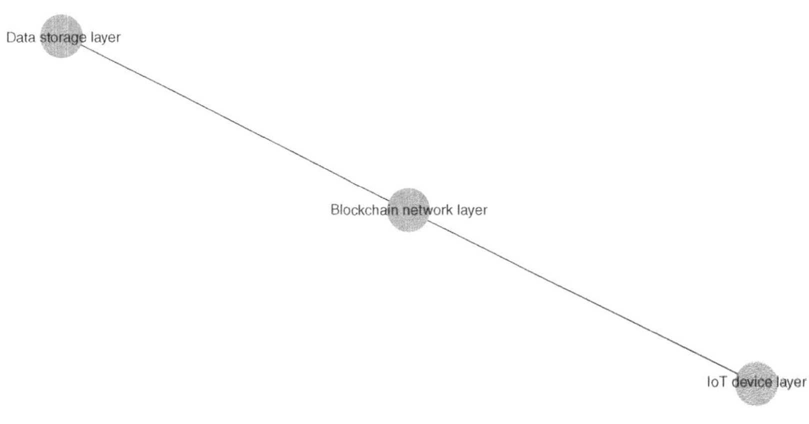

Figure 5.9 IoT security with blockchain. Source: Hewa Majeed Zangana.

5.9.5 Blockchain in Supply Chain and Intellectual Property (IP) Management

They include supply chain security, which is emerging as important for many enterprises as they seek to minimize risks of fraud, counterfeiting, and data leakage. The characteristics of blockchain provide users with clear and open supply chains, making it difficult for fake products to infiltrate markets [12]. In addition to the issues of user-based design (UBD), blockchain offers better protection of intellectual property (IP) rights ownership and secure, verifiable transactional rights in digital products and services [25]. All of these innovations are expected to expand into digital content delivery, offering better IP protection mechanisms in the digital market [31].

5.9.6 Blockchain in the Metaverse and Virtual Environments

Thus, with the launch of the metaverse, blockchain is promoted as one of the main fundamentals of safe decentralized communication. The application of blockchain technology in the metaverse provides people with immediate, transparent, and secure management of virtual assets and control over their transactions. Blockchain-based consensus mechanisms guarantee that metaverse platforms are immune to adversarial attacks, hence providing a safe space for user engagements [32]. With the rise of virtual space, blockchain will have a crucial function in the preservation of user identities and the safety of online transactions [16].

5.9.7 Innovations in Consensus Mechanisms for Scalability and Efficiency

What's next has to do with future improvements in consensus algorithms to further improve the blockchain framework, its performance, and its environmental performance. New consensus mechanisms, including PoS, PoA, and methods of sharding, testify that the necessary computations can be done while preserving security. By solving the issues of scalability, these improvements allow blockchain to manage the growth in transactions while maintaining levels of security and decentralization [4].

5.9.8 Blockchain for Secure Digital Voting Systems

Digital voting is now seen as a good use case for blockchain, as it is an effective approach to openly cast votes and record the same. Blockchain can offer the actualization of complete audit trails, which makes the electoral processes safe from interference [5]. The division of the current voting system into a decentralized blockchain structure could help eliminate the danger of interference, which would make digital voting a realistic option compared to the current systems.

5.9.9 Blockchain as a Foundation for Next-Generation Internet Architectures

Moreover, the architecture of a new generation of the internet is being formed with the help of blockchain. Also known as the decentralized web, this web model foresees users owning data, information, assets, and identities without the need for centralized structures [21]. Safe dApps also provide blockchain as an opportunity to create a protected open net, which enhances cybersecurity in internet business dealings and communications [17, 23]. New advancements with blockchain intend to prototype problems with scalability, energy, and connectivity. A timeline of some expected developments in blockchain technology is shown in Figure 5.10.

In conclusion, it can be said that the further evolution of blockchain in cybersecurity will depend on its capability to distribute important tasks, improve the quality of work with information, and

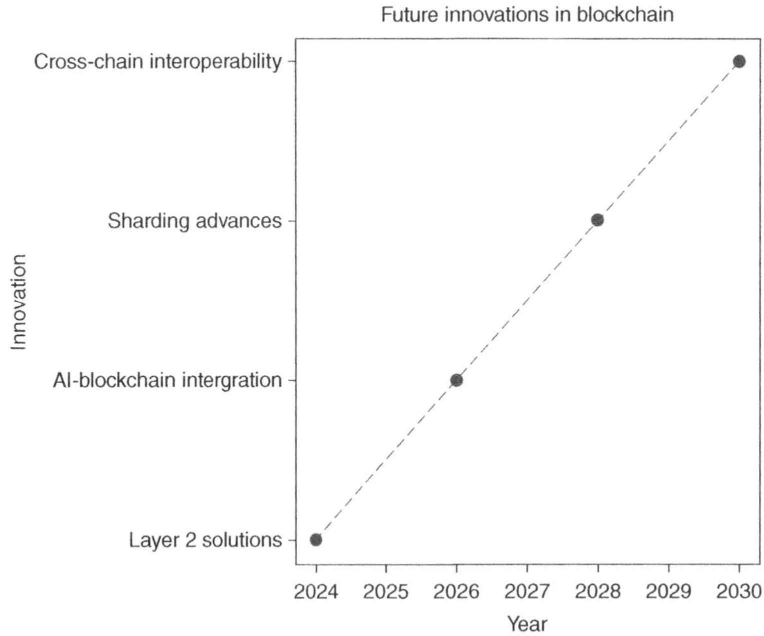

Figure 5.10 Future innovations in blockchain. Source: Hewa Majeed Zangana.

ensure secure exchange of data within various spheres. Blockchain has the potential to revolutionize cybersecurity applications across industries through enhanced consensus mechanisms, AI incorporation, and improvements to address emergent technology considerations [18].

5.10 Conclusion

One of the most important transitions that blockchain technology has brought into the concept of cybersecurity is the ability to protect the data and transactions of an organization. Blockchain also has the potential to improve security, openness, and reliability of business data while at the same time minimizing the vulnerabilities characteristic of centralized database systems. But this promising technology also has its limitations, and the major ones include ethical issues and privacy issues.

While blockchain solutions gradually enter the organizational context, companies have to focus on the questions of user anonymity and data security. This feature presents the problem that the very attributes that make blockchain an attractive technology are also a danger to individual identity. As a result, there is a need to have privacy-preserving solutions and architectures that facilitate secure trading without necessarily revealing personal details. However, questions of ethics related to decentralization have to be met to come up with accountable and responsible blockchain systems. There is no supervisory authority overseeing the usage of the technology, and this could therefore result in abuse, which means that there needs to be stringent policies and measures in place that encourage the right use of the technology and adherence to set legal measures. The fact is, as the blockchain technology is still developing rapidly, all participants should focus on developing systems that ensure the data security, as well as remain ethical. In the end, the use of blockchain in cybersecurity can only be successfully implemented if the benefits blockchain offers are balanced by ethical considerations inherent in its regular use. If organizations embrace transparency and ethical design, they will receive all the benefits blockchain has to offer without compromising user's confidentiality and trust in the emerging digital world. As this field grows, discussion and exchange between technologists, ethicists, and regulators will remain crucial to developing a safe and ethically sound use of blockchain technology.

References

1 Abdulhakeem, S.A. and Hu, Q. (2021). Powered by Blockchain technology, DeFi (Decentralized Finance) strives to increase financial inclusion of the unbanked by reshaping the world financial system. *Modern Economy* 12 (01): 1.

2 Haleem, A., Javaid, M., Singh, R.P. et al. (2021). Blockchain technology applications in healthcare: an overview. *International Journal of Intelligent Networks* 2: 130–139.

3 De Filippi, P. (2016). The interplay between decentralization and privacy: the case of blockchain technologies. *Journal of Peer Production* (7).

4 Guo, H. and Yu, X. (2022). A survey on blockchain technology and its security. *Blockchain: research and applications.* 3 (2): 100067.

5 Islam, S. and Apu, K.U. (2024). Decentralized vs. centralized database solutions in blockchain: advantages, challenges, and use cases. *Global Mainstream Journal of Innovation, Engineering & Emerging Technology* 3 (4): 58–68.

6 Alhusayni, A., Thayananthan, V., Albeshri, A., and Alghamdi, S. (2023). Decentralized multi-layered architecture to strengthen the security in the internet of things environment using blockchain technology. *Electronics (Basel).* 12 (20): 4314.

7 Haris, R.M. and Al-Maadeed, S. (2020). Integrating blockchain technology in 5G enabled IoT: a review. *2020 IEEE International Conference on Informatics, IoT, and Enabling Technologies (ICIoT).* IEEE. 367–371.

8 Chen, Y. and Bellavitis, C. (2019). *Decentralized Finance: Blockchain Technology and the Quest for an Open Financial System.* Stevens Institute of Technology School of Business Research Paper.

9 Lee, J.Y. (2019). A decentralized token economy: how blockchain and cryptocurrency can revolutionize business. *Business Horizon* 62 (6): 773–784.

10 Khan, F.A., Asif, M., Ahmad, A. et al. (2020). Blockchain technology, improvement suggestions, security challenges on smart grid and its application in healthcare for sustainable development. *Sustainable Cities and Society* 55: 102018.

11 Sharma, P., Borah, M.D., and Namasudra, S. (2021). Improving security of medical big data by using Blockchain technology. *Computers & Electrical Engineering* 96: 107529.

12 Sekerin, V.D., Slepov, V.A., Gayduk, V.I. et al. (2021). Blockchain technology development as tool for enhancing security in management and protection of intellectual property rights in additive manufacturing. *Revista Geintec-Gestao Inovacao E Tecnologias* 11 (2): 1184–1200.

13 Tariq, M.U. (2024). Revolutionizing health data management with blockchain technology: enhancing security and efficiency in a digital era. In: *Emerging Technologies for Health Literacy and Medical Practice*, 153–175. IGI Global.

14 Simaiya, S., Lilhore, U.K., Sharma, S.K. et al. (2020). Blockchain: a new technology to enhance data security and privacy in Internet of things. *Journal of Computational and Theoretical Nanoscience* 17 (6): 2552–2556.

15 Bhurgri, S.S., Ali, N.I., Korejo, I.A., and Brohi, I.A. (2024). Enhancing security and confidentiality in decentralized payment system based on blockchain technology. *The Asian Bulletin of Big Data Management* 4 (1): https://doi.org/10.62019/abbdm.v4i1.119.

16 Rajawat, A.S., Goyal, S.B., Goyal, A. et al. (2023). Enhancing security and scalability of metaverse with blockchain-based consensus mechanisms. *2023 15th International Conference on Electronics, Computers and Artificial Intelligence (ECAI)*. IEEE. 1–6.

17 Raval, S. (2016). *Decentralized applications: harnessing Bitcoin's blockchain technology*. O'Reilly Media, Inc.

18 Zheng, X., Zhu, Y., and Si, X. (2019). A survey on challenges and progresses in blockchain technologies: a performance and security perspective. *Applied Sciences* 9 (22): 4731.

19 Satish, S., Meduri, K., Nadella, G.S., and Gonaygunta, H. (2022). Developing a decentralized AI model training framework using blockchain technology. *International Meridian Journal* 4 (4): 1–20.

20 Nimmagadda, V.S.P. (2021). Artificial intelligence and blockchain integration for enhanced security in insurance: techniques, models, and real-world applications. *African Journal of Artificial Intelligence and Sustainable Development* 1 (2): 187–224.

21 Kremenova, I. and Gajdos, M. (2019). Decentralized networks: the future internet. *Mobile Networks and Applications* 24 (6): 2016–2023.

22 Cali, U. and Fifield, A. (2019). Towards the decentralized revolution in energy systems using blockchain technology. *International Journal of Smart Grid and Clean Energy (SGCE)* 8 (3): 245–256.

23 Tyagi, A.K. (2023). Decentralized everything: practical use of blockchain technology in future applications. In: *Distributed Computing to Blockchain*, 19–38. Elsevier.

24 Chattu, V.K., Nanda, A., Chattu, S.K. et al. (2019). The emerging role of blockchain technology applications in routine disease surveillance systems to strengthen global health security. *Big Data and Cognitive Computing* 3 (2): 25.

25 Rajawat, A.S., Goyal, S.B., Solanki, R., et al. (2023). Blockchain-based security framework for metaverse: a decentralized approach. *2023 15th International Conference on Electronics, Computers and Artificial Intelligence (ECAI)*. IEEE. p. 1–6.

26 Kshetri, N., Hutson, J., and Revathy, G. (2023). healthAIChain: Improving security and safety using Blockchain Technology applications in AI-based healthcare systems. *2023 3rd International Conference on Innovative Mechanisms for Industry Applications (ICIMIA)*. IEEE. p. 159–164.

27 Thantharate, P. and Thantharate, A. (2023). ZeroTrustBlock: enhancing security, privacy, and interoperability of sensitive data through ZeroTrust permissioned blockchain. *Big Data and Cognitive Computing* 7 (4): 165.

28 Sharin, F.H., Hernandez, M.S., and Sentosa, I. (2023). Future trends of blockchain technology in the technological fields. *2023 3rd International Conference on Advance Computing and Innovative Technologies in Engineering (ICACITE)*. IEEE. p. 1307–1313.

29 Nabben, K. (2021). Blockchain security as "people security": applying sociotechnical security to blockchain technology. *Frontiers of Computer Science* 2: 599406.

30 Spathoulas, G., Negka, L., Pandey, P., and Katsikas, S. (2021). Can blockchain technology enhance security and privacy in the Internet of Things? *Advances in Core Computer Science-Based Technologies: Papers in Honor of Professor Nikolaos Alexandris* 199–228.

31 Yerram, S.R., Goda, D.R., Mahadasa, R. et al. (2021). The role of blockchain technology in enhancing financial security amidst digital transformation. *Asian Business Review* 11 (3): 125–134.

32 Mourtzis, D., Angelopoulos, J., and Panopoulos, N. (2023). Blockchain integration in the era of industrial metaverse. *Applied Sciences* 13 (3): 1353.

33 Muzammal, S.M. and Murugesan, R.K. (2018). A study on leveraging blockchain technology for IoT security enhancement. *2018 Fourth International Conference on Advances in Computing, Communication & Automation (ICACCA)*. IEEE. p. 1–6.

34 Idrees, S.M., Nowostawski, M., Jameel, R., and Mourya, A.K. (2021). Security aspects of blockchain technology intended for industrial applications. *Electronics (Basel).* 10 (8): 951.

6

Human Factors in Cybersecurity: The Weakest Link

Hewa Majeed Zangana

IT Department, Duhok Technical College, Duhok Polytechnic University, Duhok, Iraq

6.1 Introduction

Cybersecurity is not a stand-alone system that depends solely on technology, but largely depends on its occupants. Human factors are now considered the weakest link in the security chain, affecting general compliance with security, as they encompass the capability to engage in established security practices and the vulnerability to security-related tricks such as social engineering and other related insider threats. That means, as a society becomes more technologically inclined and modern, so do the schemes and tricks that seek to take advantage of individuals. Hence, to build effective protection systems, specialists cannot ignore the human aspect of cybersecurity [1, 2]. Behavioral, psychological, and cultural characteristics are all fundamental components of the human side of cybersecurity. Technical enablers are necessary, but it is the approach the organization adopts in handling the human aspects that defines the success of cybersecurity, according to Aksoy [3]. Mistakes made by end users and system administrators can also result in the worst kinds of breaches, such as phishing scams. Furthermore, human weaknesses can be exploited even in psychological procedures, including social engineering, which cannot be prevented with purely technology-based measures [4].

Research evidence shows that the strength of the workforce plays a key role in enhancing secure practices within the workforce environment to support organizational security [5]. In addition, Hughes-Lartey et al. [6] opine that potential threats to an organization's information technology are most likely to arise when the human element is not well addressed, especially in IoT systems. This goes to prove that human behavior is instrumental in influencing several aspects of cybersecurity and, therefore, not a one-dimensional issue. In the words of Corman [7], the human element can be managed only through a twin-track approach that combines technology and behaviors. With the growing research on the social dynamics of technology use, it becomes easier to design a more holistic approach toward policy implementation. In the same regard, [8, 9] posit that trust frameworks, in conjunction with organizational awareness, must rise to the challenge of this weakest link and turn human factors into a strength within the prevailing cybersecurity systems. Thus, the flow of technologies and human behavior can be connected to enhance the organization's cyber resilience and minimize the chance of being penetrated by insiders with the intent to cause harm.

Defense in Depth: Modern Cybersecurity Strategies and Evolving Threats, First Edition. Edited by Hewa Majeed Zangana.

6.2 Understanding Human Factors in Cybersecurity

Human factors in cybersecurity are thus defined as the roles individuals and people play in either making or breaking the security of organizations and systems. Due to these principles, cybersecurity threats are known to take advantage of human failures such as ignorance, fatigue, and carelessness, making the human the essential weak link in cybersecurity [1]. Technology and risk mitigation involve a complex web of technical and social factors that can only be understood holistically, where human factors are not overshadowed by technology [10].

6.2.1 The Role of Human Factors in Cybersecurity

In its essence, the human factor in cybersecurity refers to people's comprehension, conduct, and activities regarding computers and the internet. Research indicates that human violations contribute to a large percentage of cases where employees contribute to the vulnerability of security systems by being victims of phishing or by performing unauthorized security actions [11, 12]. This has led to the appreciation that while other strategies, such as firewalls and encryption tools, are critical solutions, they can only work with a knowledgeable and aware staff [13]. Some common criticisms of humans as the weakest link include that they are easily compromised through social engineering, they are rarely trained on the best practices to observe, and they often violate laid-down protocols [7]. These risks, therefore, make it necessary for organizations to enhance cybersecurity training and education [14]. Hughes-Lartey et al. [6] opined that the human factor can greatly endanger IoT by either poorly managing the IoT devices or by configuring them wrongly. The knowledge of human factors that result in cybersecurity risks and threats is valuable for filling these gaps. Figure 6.1 outlines the interactions between human factors and awareness, behavioral, and technological aspects within cybersecurity environments.

6.2.2 Human Vulnerabilities and Cybersecurity Threats

Another major threat is the susceptibility of people to acts that cybercriminals take advantage of in social engineering [9]. These attacks involve exploiting the target into revealing information, opening a link, or downloading malware [15]. It becomes quite difficult to differentiate between

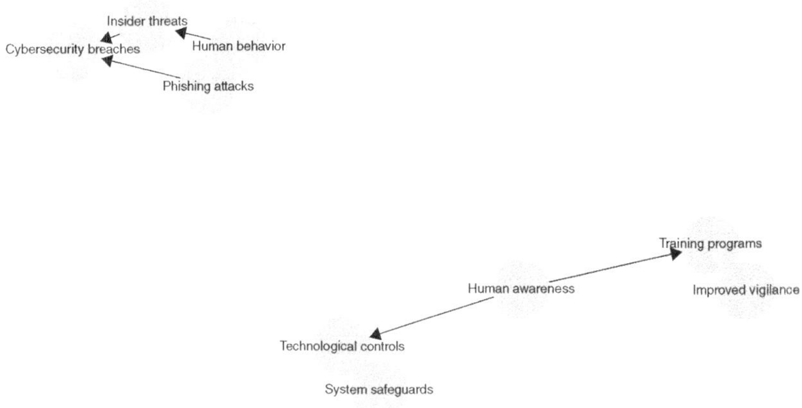

Figure 6.1 The role of human factors in cybersecurity. Source: Hewa Majeed Zangana.

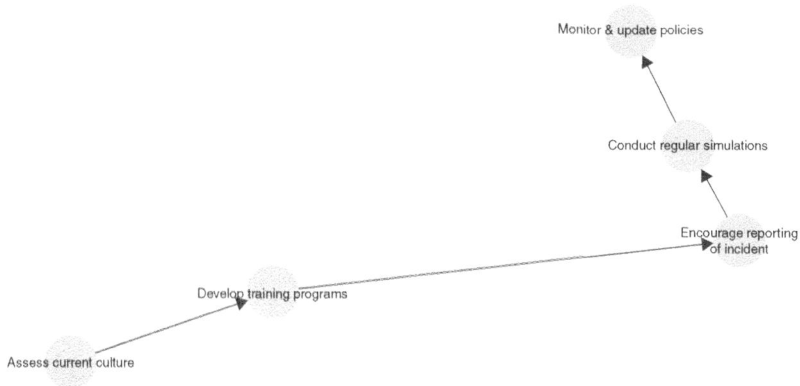

Figure 6.2 Steps to building a cybersecurity culture. Source: Hewa Majeed Zangana.

actual and fake communication due to human cognitive limitations, especially during busy hours when quick decisions have to be made [11].

In Aksoy's [3] work, the protection of cybersecurity is not solely a function of how good the technical solutions and technologies being implemented are, but necessarily involves the human dimension as well. The perception of risks, the understanding of security procedures, and the compliance of employees with safety measures substantially determine the efficacy of cybersecurity measures at the organizational level. For those reasons, the number of attacks involving human factors, such as misconfigurations and failure to patch vulnerabilities, is estimated at sixty percent of all successful attacks [2, 16].

6.2.3 The Importance of Cybersecurity Culture

[2] proposes the development of a strong cybersecurity culture as the framework for addressing human factors. A positive cybersecurity culture fosters helpful security attitudes in employees and encourages them to practice security in their day-to-day business, and becoming stakeholders in the protection measures employed in the organization [17]. In the view of Campean [2], such measures should include cybersecurity awareness programs through which organizations develop the right culture and build the attitude that encourages employees to embrace personal responsibility for protecting the information. Organizations should ensure that they are conducting frequent updated training sessions to ensure that their employees are exposed to the new threats [8]. In turn, it is important to note that these programs should provide both knowledge and understanding of the program and employee decision-making processes related to security incidents, rather than being purely technical. For example, simulated phishing provides an insight into recognizing relevant emails, while practice and exercises enable the employees to determine the correct action to take when faced with a breach [18]. The only way to address human factors in cybersecurity is by constructing a strong cybersecurity culture. A flowchart is presented that may help to identify the major activities that must be performed for creating a cybersecurity-aware workforce within organizations (Figure 6.2).

6.2.4 Stress, Burnout, and Security Fatigue

Another area of significant concern regarding the human element is stress and burnout in employees who are charged with the responsibility of defending an organization against cyber threats.

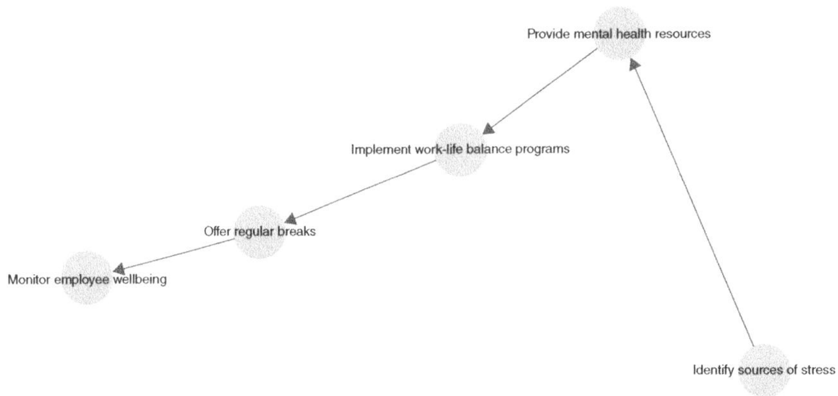

Figure 6.3 Addressing stress and burnout in cybersecurity teams. Source: Hewa Majeed Zangana.

Security practitioners work under such stressful conditions because the risk of cyber threats is continually present, which can lead to security desensitization and carelessness [18]. Indeed, as Sangwan [19] pointed out in his work, stress-related challenges have to be solved to ensure the cybersecurity teams' efficiency. Fatigued and stressed workers can make mistakes, and since system criminals know this, they are likely to attack such workers [7]. It is very important to pay close attention to stress and burnout issues of the teams working in the cybersecurity field. The following flowchart describes a process that will help manage stress and minimize its effect on the performance of cybersecurity teams (Figure 6.3).

6.2.5 Bridging the Gap Between Human Behavior and Technology

Between human behavior and the production of adequate mechanical solutions for cybersecurity, a definite issue persists. According to Corman [7], organizations have to overcome this gap by designing work processes that require minimal input from users, and at the same time, are less likely to involve errors. In this section, [20] rightly points out that technology cannot address cybersecurity problems unless it is supported with people-centered approaches to its use. According to Young et al. [21], cybersecurity has to be seen as a complex system, with humans as important stakeholders and actors whose behaviors should be actively observed and managed in response to new threats. Furthermore, it increases knowledge of the cognitive processes that may underlie human behavior in cyberspace through the application of findings from cyber forensic psychology [4]. Thus, psychological knowledge helps create better policy and training approaches to provide individuals with greater resistance to cyber threats.

In the case of human factors in cybersecurity, there is a need to use both technical and people-focused interventions for an organization to succeed. The key actions and strategies for identifying human vulnerabilities and for developing relevant mitigation measures are shown in the flowchart (Figure 6.4).

6.2.6 Summary

This paper focuses on human factors in cybersecurity to develop better ways of addressing threats in cyberspace. Although technical solutions are vital, it is critical to address the vulnerabilities associated with individual actions. Companies should work on enhancing cybersecurity by constantly

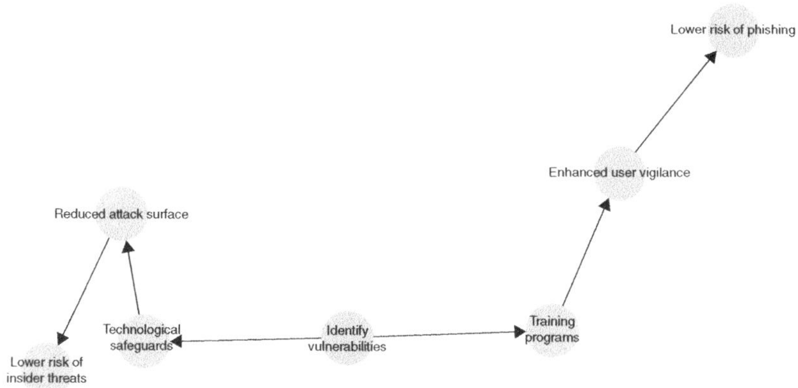

Figure 6.4 Mitigating human vulnerabilities in cybersecurity. Source: Hewa Majeed Zangana.

training personnel and reducing the consequences of stress and fatigue. When human factors are incorporated into cybersecurity plans, organizations' vulnerability to human errors is lowered, and there is enhanced security.

6.3 The Role of Human Error in Cybersecurity Breaches

It is worthwhile to stress that human mistakes continue to be one of the primary causes of cyber threats, often overpowering the technical solutions meant to prevent them. While organizations today have good security tools and standards in place, most cyber-related threats stem from operational or human error at their core. To be able to understand the contribution of people factors, it is important to determine how cognitive biases, stress, ignorance, and social engineering take advantage of the failures and produce opportunities for attackers. The study also reveals that most cybersecurity incidents are directly attributable to human activities. The following graph indicates the percentages of breaches caused by different types of individual mistakes, as per different kinds of research (Figure 6.5).

6.3.1 Cognitive Limitations and Decision-Making Errors

This is due to the fact that, in daily decision-making processes, humans always try to balance between effectiveness and security, which can lead to errors. Under stress, people make wrong decisions, making data security a challenge in high-pressure organizations. Tactical blind spots, such as overestimating one's knowledge of possible phishing scams or underestimating the dangers of relying on automated tools and technology, only amplify these threats. According to Zhang [22], people depend heavily on technology, which results in low oversight and, as a consequence, many faults. In addition, decision fatigue caused by weariness of making decisions drains people of energy, leading them to overlook protocols within the organization and making them prone to security breaches.

6.3.2 Stress, Burnout, and Security Fatigue

Stress and burnout are leading factors in human interference in the case of cybersecurity. Nobles [] points out that individuals' security fatigue becomes noticeable when people start to ignore all

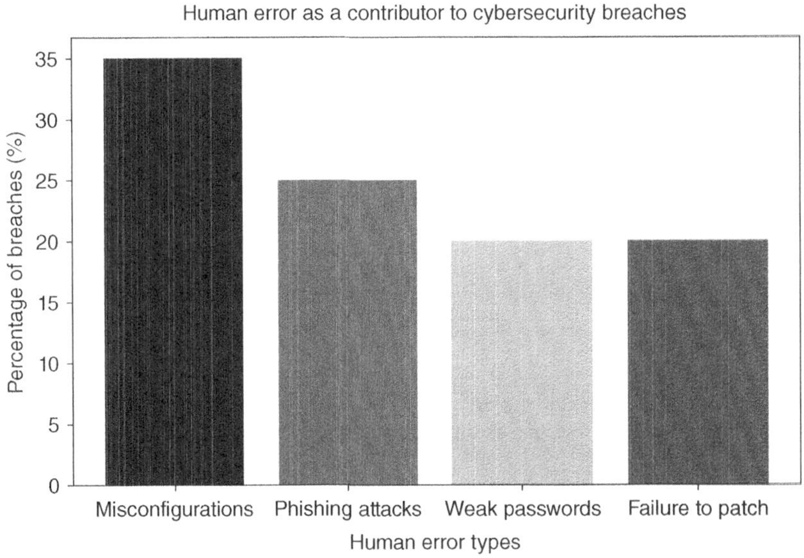

Figure 6.5 Human error as a contributor to cybersecurity breaches. Source: Hewa Majeed Zangana.

security measures due to excessive alerts. This fatigue leads to creating weak passwords, often neglecting security measures, or becoming a victim of a phishing scam. Furthermore, increased pressures from job activity, especially in healthcare or financial organizations, result in hasty approaches to work, where the act of working assumes precedence over the aspect of security sensitivity [20]. Stress and burnout contribute to increased security risks, indicating a direct link between stress and security risks. The following line chart presents experimental results from various findings of subpar performance under tense conditions over time (Figure 6.6).

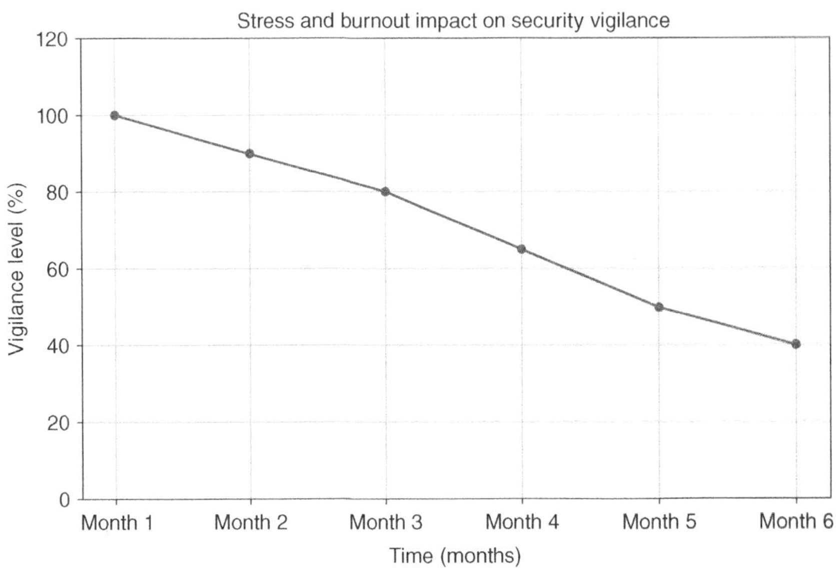

Figure 6.6 Stress and burnout impact on security vigilance. Source: Hewa Majeed Zangana.

6.3.3 Social Engineering and Human Vulnerabilities

Social engineers often try to take advantage of psychological biases such as trust, fear, and time. In their study, Ref. [1] offers a rather clear definition of social engineering attacks, explaining that they are attacks on cognitive security, in which individuals are manipulated and forced to share sensitive information or to bypass the security system. Phishing, pretexting, and baiting are all highly effective even on the most professional employees because people fundamentally trust their technology. Denno [11] notes that social engineering scams tend to bypass technical security measures by focusing on people. This is an innate human weakness in which individuals tend to obey authority or quickly respond to emergency appeals, a trait that attackers exploit. Corman [7] supports this by explaining how cyberattackers combine psychological tactics with technical skills to develop a very effective attack that, rather than depending on the weakness in a system, depends on the foolishness of humanity.

6.3.4 Insufficient Training and Awareness

Insufficient training on implementing protections makes human mistakes accountable for most cyber threats. According to Hughes-Lartey et al. [6], an organization becomes vulnerable and easily penetrated by threats when it lacks the capacity to provide constant and realistic simulations of emerging hazards. An employee who is not well informed about new techniques used by hackers may fall prey to fake emails or even ransomware, thus making mistakes. Similarly, Campean [2] declares that a cybersecurity culture that leaves out human factors is a culture doomed to collapse. Annual training programs that focus on inputs to create better awareness and adoption of better practices are key among strategies for minimizing the effects of human errors in cybersecurity. In the words of Kadena and Gupi [13], adding practical, real-world simulations and practical training aids will assist individuals in identifying cyber threat incidents. Furthermore, strategies for decreasing cognitive load, such as simplifying security processes and creating more comprehensible interfaces, can decrease human mistakes in cybersecurity.

6.3.5 Trust and Misplaced Confidence in Technology

Unfortunately, humans tend to overtrust technology by thinking that the systems in place are enough to provide security. Daudi [9] describes how a false sense of immunity develops, resulting from a reliance on artificial cognitive shields that do not protect people when new attacks or oversights in the systems invalidate these defenses. When applied or understood incorrectly, trust frameworks magnify the chances of human-factor failures because people blindly rely on them, overlooking the risks their actions may cause [5].

6.3.6 Addressing Human Error Through Cybersecurity Leadership

Cybersecurity leaders need to acknowledge the role that humans play in the breaches. According to Triplett [17], it is critical for organizations to move away from a reward/punish mindset—where mistakes are punished. This approach involves the creation of a security culture that acknowledges the limitations of human beings and fosters a positive approach to cybersecurity.

6.3.7 Summary

There can be human errors in data protection measures taken in cybersecurity incidents, but they are preventable. When the social-technical aspects of human behavior are looked at in terms of limitations, stress, and vulnerabilities, organizations have a great chance of minimizing human cyber vulnerabilities. Cognitive biases may be countered by a human-centered approach, which includes both human and technical aspects of cybersecurity complemented by regular training, well-defined procedures, and management oversight.

6.4 Social Engineering and Insider Threats

In the case of cyber threats, social engineering and insider threats are among the greatest threats facing organizations today. Both depend mostly on preying on human vices, hence are very cumbersome to be solved by technical means alone. These threats point to the fact that current and emerging cybersecurity threats cannot be solved by technology alone but also require a human-focused approach to cybersecurity management. The main psychological manipulation techniques are used in social engineering attacks. The birthday cake-looking pie chart (Figure 6.7) categorizes most of the social engineering tactics deployed by hackers to take advantage of human behavior.

6.4.1 Social Engineering: Manipulating Human Behavior

Social engineering attacks rely on psychological tricks to make people reveal some information or perform actions that are unsuitable from a security standpoint. These attacks can be of many kinds, among which are phishing, pretexting, baiting, and the rest. Social engineering, therefore, thrives when the attacker is able to manipulate man's basic emotions like trust, fear, or perceived urgency. According to Corman [7], a chief peculiarity of social engineering is that it is highly likely to get around classical security measures like firewalls and intrusion detection systems (IDSs). Attackers learn to trick the employees into doing something they shouldn't do, like clicking a link or responding to a phone call. Based on Nobles [8], the increase of social engineering proves the fact that the human factor remains paramount in cybersecurity, even with sophisticated systems in place that can be exploited. Also, Hughes-Lartey et al. [6] stress that these cyber threat actors are exploiting the

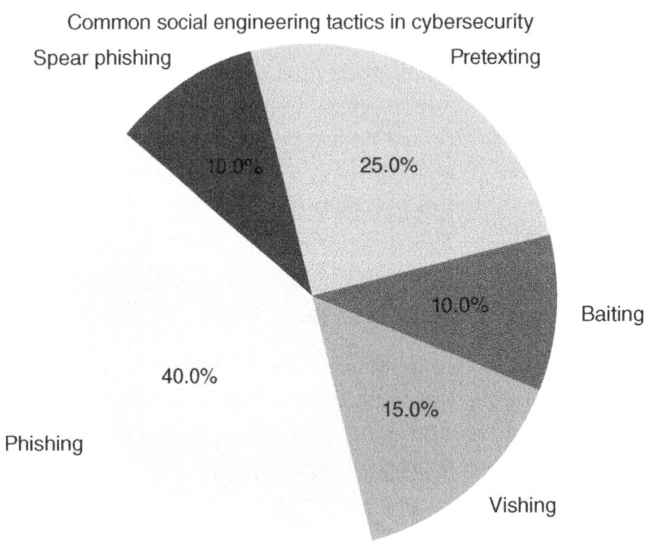

Figure 6.7 Common social engineering tactics in cybersecurity. Source: Hewa Majeed Zangana.

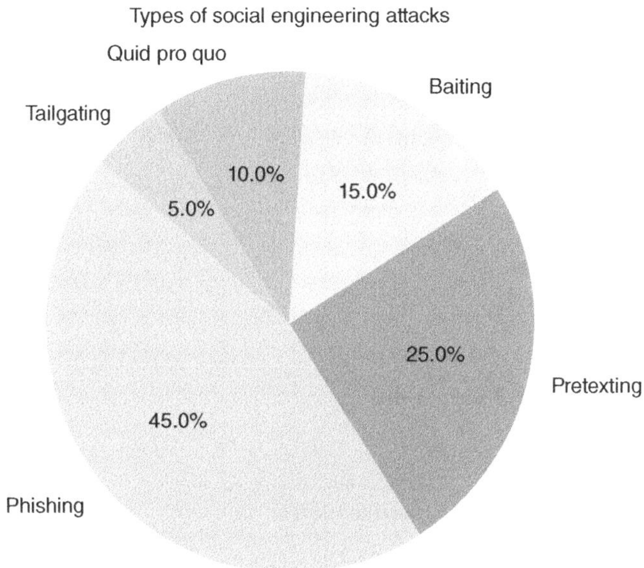

Figure 6.8 Types of social engineering attacks. Source: Hewa Majeed Zangana.

IoT devices leveraged by these organizations since IoT devices often have poor security measures in place to protect them from manipulation. The complication of these attack vectors makes social engineering even more effective as organizations grow interlinked and dependent on technology. Social engineering attacks make use of psychological aspects in their execution. The pie chart illustrates the different types of social engineering attacks with a focus on frequency in current world attacks (Figure 6.8).

6.4.2 Insider Threats: The Human Element Within

All too often, the most formidable source of security threats arises from within an organization due to the acts of a malicious or careless employee or other trusted personnel. Employees of the organization have authorized access to the company's information, making them more difficult to detect. Ani et al. [5] also successfully argued that insider threats are overlooked mainly because organizations pay higher attention to external threats, while internal threats remain rife.

Insider threats can broadly be categorized as malicious insiders, unintentional insiders, and facilitated insiders. Motive: Malicious insiders knowingly and deliberately seek opportunities to inflict harm on their organization and/or individuals and, in the process, benefit either financially or by holding a grudge. Inexperienced workers, in contrast, do not have malicious intent but may cause harm by not adhering to security policies and procedures, for example, leaving important information exposed or becoming victims of phishing scams. According to Nobles [18], burnout and security fatigue are possible aggravators of insider threats because workers under pressure are bound to make more errors that threaten organizational security. Another article [4] describes the process of creating cyber resilience in humans as critical for combating insider risks. This is done through raising staff knowledge concerning the impacts of risks and training them to be part of the protection layer of an organization. As highlighted by Poehlmann et al. [10], overall, enterprises with good cybersecurity awareness programs and a strong security culture within the workplace are prepared to mitigate the threat of insider threats. In these respects, insider threats

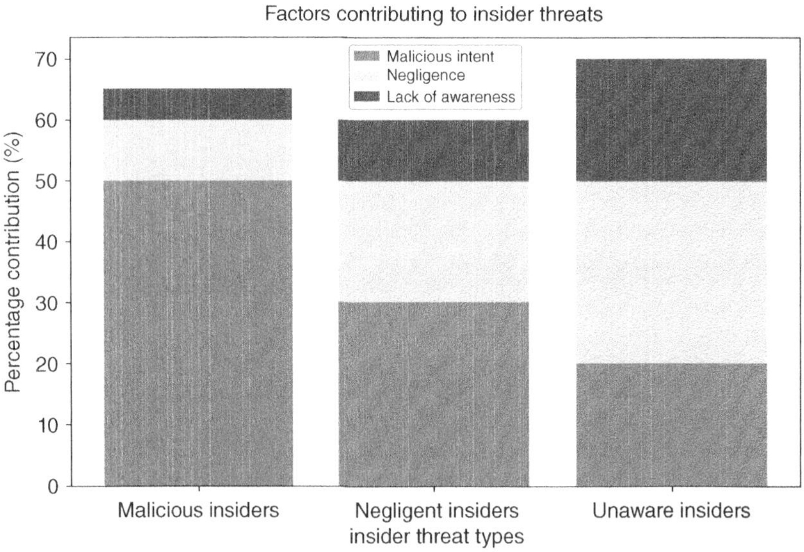

Figure 6.9 Factors contributing to insider threats. Source: Hewa Majeed Zangana.

may be caused by different reasons that include intentional and unintentional insiders. This hidden factor forms the basis of insider threats in cybersecurity as presented in the stacked bar chart (Figure 6.9).

6.4.3 The Intersection of Social Engineering and Insider Threats

These two concepts are always related, with social engineering becoming the tactic used by an insider threat. For instance, a social engineer may, as a result of manipulation, transform the organization's employees into an insider threat by making them reveal passwords or engage in other activities that are unlawful or dangerous to the organization. A similar analysis is provided by Aksoy [3], suggesting that Limerick also states that maintaining human factors in cybersecurity is significant because both social engineering and insider threats stem from the same flaws in human behavior.

In a recent article, Rahman et al. [15] have proposed a complex approach to combine both technological measures to counteract social engineering and insider threats, as well as psychological and behavioral changes. Most social engineering attacks are successful because employees are not trained to identify them, or they do not know how to stop them. In a like manner, controlling access to company resources and paying attention to employee activity can prevent incidents and avoid considerable losses due to such threats.

6.4.4 Summary

Social engineering and insider threats are two of the most complex issues for any contemporary cybersecurity campaign. It is suggested that both take advantage of human factors, making cybersecurity an area where technical, organizational, and human factor aspects need to be addressed. According to Daudi [9], more trust frameworks that are characterized by an inclusion of human behavior models in cybersecurity can curb such risks. As experts in cybersecurity and threat mitigation continue to warn organizations of the dangers of outside manipulation and internal betrayal, creating an organizational culture that takes social engineering and insider threats seriously is critical for strengthening the security posture of an enterprise and promoting the resilience of the company against powerful and malevolent forces.

6.5 User Awareness and Training

In cybersecurity, the category of user awareness and training is the link that connects the technical and social walls of protection, yet remains one of the most understudied and overlooked areas. As evident from Aksoy [3], the effectiveness or otherwise of cybersecurity strategies depends not only on the technologies involved and their implementation but also on people's roles in the management of these systems. With low awareness and training, users are likely to fall victim to a myriad of cyber risks, thus being the weakest point in an organization's cybersecurity architecture.

6.5.1 Importance of Awareness Programs

It is, therefore, unequivocal that cybersecurity awareness programs are of enormous importance. It is important for organizations to embrace constant and inclusive training programs to create awareness among users of dynamic threats. As explained by Poehlmann et al. [10], awareness training enables the user to acquire the best knowledge and essential steps required to avoid phishing attempts, social engineering activities, and other dangerous incidents. This chapter argues that through extending an understanding of security to all members of an organization, organizations can reduce the likelihood of unintentional insider threats occurring. Also, Rahman [15] stresses that training must address the issue of maintaining the user's attention and keeping them updated over time. User awareness is also a factor that greatly helps in building the "immunity" of an organization. Jeong et al. [16] claim that increasing the knowledge of users in areas such as cognitive bias and decision making can improve user behavior during a security event. It is recommended that training should demonstrate real-life examples; for example, the user should consider how they would protect their accounts against threats like suspicious emails or prevent insecure behavior.

6.5.2 Tailored Training for Different User Groups

The strength of IT literacy varies from user to user, and as a result, security awareness training must be designed to cater to all distinct groups of employees in an organization. Alsharif et al. [1] show that errors can not only occur from a lack of knowledge, but employees may also disengage or prefer not to engage by denying themselves participation in security training, ignoring that they do not understand most of the technicalities used therein. The personalization of training information to the user's occupational standing and IT literacy enhances the training's relevance and comprehension.

Moreover, Nobles [8] also emphasized that high-risk user groups, including employees who have access to work-related sensitive information, require special training addressing their risks. These involve providing training and reinforcing aspects of information, security, passwords, and the use of multi-factor authentication, as these are critical elements of the organization's security protocol.

6.5.3 Continuous Training and Testing

Cybersecurity is definitely not stagnant; indeed, it is a field with constantly evolving new threats. In support of this, Hughes-Lartey et al. [6] opine that training programs must therefore be presented as continuous, and not occasional affairs, with periodic updates on the latest trends in cyber threats. Occasional training sessions do not suffice in preparing users for new risks because ad hoc training sessions are inadequate. Instead, organizations should apply a cyclical training process of methods, supported by refresher courses, workshops, and practice scenarios with real attacks. Examples of such phony attacks include simulated phishing attacks that have been found to be rather useful in evaluating the level of user awareness and to define how many of them require training [4]. These simulations enable users to familiarize themselves with threats in a controlled environment and therefore minimize cases of actual phishing attacks. The comments given during such a scenario can be very useful in enhancing the utilization and reaction rates among users. Cybersecurity training also greatly improves awareness among employees of the various activities performed on the corporation's network. This line chart shows the trend of cybersecurity awareness, comparing two groups of employees: those who have been trained on this subject and those who have not (Figure 6.10).

6.5.4 Challenges in Implementing Effective Training

However, there are various issues that limit the success of the above-mentioned efforts aimed at enhancing user awareness and training. Denno [11] explained that one of the key challenges includes user disengagement and the belief that cybersecurity is the sole mandate of the IT department. It takes a paradigm shift for an organization and all its users to embrace security as part of the common responsibility to achieve. Also, lack of visibility into the effectiveness of training programs is explained by Zhang and Ghorbani [22]. Although users can be given quizzes or assignments to check how much they retain of what has been learnt, it is quite impossible to conduct

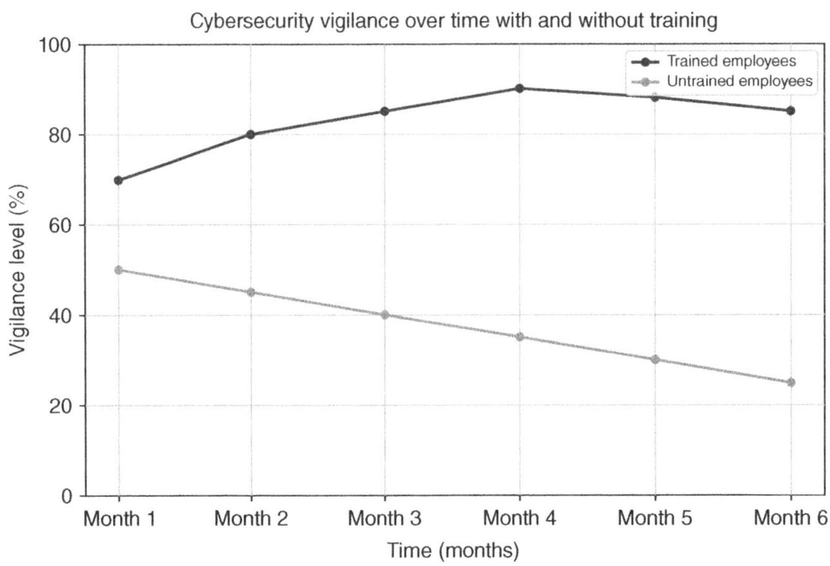

Figure 6.10 Cybersecurity vigilance over time with and without training. Source: Hewa Majeed Zangana.

an assessment as to whether the user will apply the learnt knowledge practically. Hence, there exists a need for undertakings to adopt a variety of techniques to measure the effectiveness of their training processes, such as user satisfaction, behavior change, and behavior during a realistic cyber-attack [23].

6.5.5 Role of Leadership in Promoting Awareness

Management commitment as a global best practice is essential in the promotion of overall cybersecurity. In his study, Triplett [17] finds that leaders should champion and invest in training exercises to ensure they signal their dedication to cybersecurity. This entails defining the necessary resources for training programs and guaranteeing that cybersecurity is a frontline at every level of the business. This way, the leaders make the users understand the seriousness of security training and the need to apply it at work. Daudi's [9] trust framework also points to a significant point of communication from leadership to users concerning the significance of cybersecurity literacy. If users consider themselves part of the organization's security, they will be willing to participate in training activities and adopt security measures.

6.5.6 Summary

Consequently, the cybersecurity plan needs to involve controlling the awareness and training of users. It remains clear that the threats active in the information space are developing, and so too are the training and awareness programs. In this way, the probability of human threats decreases significantly, allowing an organization to adequately protect its assets from loss due to employees' carelessness. This is supported by studies from Refs. [1, 3] and others, which show that active user awareness is key to transforming users from the weakest link into a compelling force against cyber threats.

6.6 Human-Centric Security Design

Human-centered security involves making the human element a part of the security system as a way of dealing with security issues associated with people's actions and contact with technology. Since employee negligence remains one of the most significant factors in cyber incidents, this aspect is crucial for creating reliable, versatile, and efficient security structures.

6.6.1 Understanding Human Vulnerabilities

The level of exposure of human actors within cybersecurity environments is also apparent, with previous studies showing that, more often than not, cybersecurity incidents stem from user-related issues, including wrong decisions, carelessness, or ignorance. Refs. [1, 3] specifically notes that organizational protection from risks cannot be achieved solely with technology; people's weaknesses must also be understood for cybersecurity to be adequately controlled. One is cognitive overload—a condition that arises when users cannot efficiently process and engage with a flood of information with real-time responses. In complex security environments, this can lead to decision fatigue, making users more vulnerable to cyberattacks [16]. This requires security designs that are user-friendly and the type that will help reduce cognitive overload.

6.6.2 Designing for Usability and Security

A good human-oriented design is not only about strengthening technical protection measures, but also about simplicity, because users will follow rules if the interface is comprehensible [10]. Usability and security are two areas that are inextricably interconnected; any OS that is overly complicated can lead to noncompliance, while one that is oversimplified can put in additional vulnerabilities. Giaocomello and Pescaroli [12] say systems must incorporate security practices that are as stringent as they are friendly from the viewpoint of the human element. Supplementing this analysis, Refs. [8, 11] also reveal that human behavioral analysis has to be incorporated into designs for risk mitigation to be effective. For instance, the inclination of users to set up poor password standards or neglect software updates is addressed and countered by a security system design that creates incentives and controls that guide users toward the appropriate security advisories.

6.6.3 Adaptive Systems and Human Error

However, one of the significant problems in the context of cybersecurity design is the presence of the human factor. As Danet [23] noted, cultures that involve trying to apportion blame for an error are likely to lead to defensive actions like not reporting them. A more realistic approach would be to align the system with user behavior rather than to expect the best from people. According to Rebensky et al. [24], stress, fatigue, and even distractions in humans produce far from optimal actions. Based on this assumption, one should design systems capable of responding and adapting to expected human errors. For example, machine learning techniques help forecast and respond to users' behavior, which can be useful in terms of detecting when one deviates from the normative flow and, thus, can be potentially a source of an error or a security violation [19]. It is possible to cultivate the out-of-sight, out-of-mind mentality, trusting the platform to become less hospitable to a hacker's craft, and simultaneously create systems that learn with and from the users in order to lower the possibility of successful attacks and augment the likelihood of a kinder and more cooperative atmosphere in cybersecurity.

6.6.4 Trust and User Empowerment

I have established that trust is an important facet of human-centric security design. Engaging systems that aim for users' trust are apt to be compliant rather than engaging systems that just put across their compliance messages. More to this point, Daudi [9] identified the problem by proposing that there should be a trust framework in which users have the perception that they are acting under the support of the system rather than being policed. This not only enhances the morale of the workers but also decreases stress and security fatigue issues that have raised questions within organizations [18]. Furthermore, Corman [7] rightly postulated that people's behavior and technology need to be brought closer by means of understanding. It increases the level of users' awareness about the system's provided and required capabilities and characteristics, as well as the extent of their personal control over security issues, resulting in a proper decision-making process.

6.6.5 Leveraging Behavioral Insights

Security appliances can be built in a manner that takes into account how people behave when in contact with any device. Pollini et al. [25] proposed the use of models derived from cognitive and psychological theories to describe the likely behavior of users and to design measures that would enhance safe behaviors. This approach echoes with the research proposed by Young et al. [21], where they posit that cybersecurity systems should be active in that they sense the behavior of users and subsequently provide a follow-up to address the problem, such as providing notifications about password changes or reminders about the necessity to install security patches. Similar to the above researchers, Marble et al. [20] suggested an incorporation of strong and wise defense systems, which can detect human errors and prevent a breach before it happens. Such action-oriented development methods, coupled with friendly interfaces, improve both security and ease of use of the system.

6.6.6 Building Resilience through Human-Centric Design

Finally, for cybersecurity, it is crucial to be human-oriented and aimed at improving cyber resilience, that is, the organization's capability to withstand, operate through, and recover from cyber threats [2]. This involves developing enablers that do more than prevent threats but also assist users to identify, counteract, and rebuild from threats. Hughes-Lartey et al. [6] note that resilience is an organizational process and exists at both the technical and human aspects of an organization and involves all the organizational hierarchy levels. The combination of training, usability, and behavioral adaptation within human-oriented designs helps to enhance overall cybersecurity defenses. It is also important to understand that humans are insiders in the security process and to minimize their risks through proper design [5].

6.7 The Role of Leadership and Organizational Culture

Cybersecurity, especially in human factors, requires efficient leadership and a sound organizational culture. It is a known fact that leadership defines the emphasis placed on a particular issue, the organizational tolerance levels, and gives direction for the implementation of necessary measures. Furthermore, the overall organizational culture greatly affects the employees' approach toward cybersecurity; it can either stoke up or put out efforts with the goal of boosting up the organization's security postures.

6.7.1 Leadership's Influence on Cybersecurity

Any strategy regarding cybersecurity necessarily involves leadership because people and organizations respond directly to their superiors. When leaders prioritize cybersecurity, they set the tone that results in the culture of security being a foundational element. Organizational learning, along with understanding and responsiveness of the organization at all levels, is an important part of this approach. Based on Aksoy [3], leaders should know that cybersecurity is not solely a technological problem but rather a human problem. When leadership doesn't support cybersecurity or information security, and there is no proper communication, employees may overlook or put into practice measures that may harm the organization.

It also affects the level of support the company gives in terms of resource commitment to cybersecurity. Triplett [17] notes that cybersecurity leadership focuses on the use of technology that enhances a culture of protection and compliance and the recruitment of human resources. Managers have to properly train staff, make sure they obtain necessary security tools, and let cybersecurity personnel perform their work well.

6.7.2 Organizational Culture and Cybersecurity

This chapter argues that an organization's culture guides the perception and response to cybersecurity among its employees. When the culture supports a lack of security measures, then the employees themselves will be unmotivated to pay much attention to security measures. A sound cybersecurity culture is one where every worker, irrespective of their rank or status as a rookie or a manager, has adequate knowledge of the role they play in warding off cyber threats [11]. Such a culture helps organizations be more secure in the face of attacks or any form of invasion seen within the organization's perimeter. In the opinion of Campean [2], the implementation of cybersecurity as an organization's culture involves the development of a culture of security responsibility among employees. This shared responsibility is important because the human factor is always the greatest vulnerability in cyberspace security. Goh [4] agrees with this, noting that achieving cyber resilience in humans means this has to become a cultural norm and not an add-on to regular protocols of a system.

6.7.3 Building Cyber-Resilient Organizations

For an organization to become cyber resilient, leadership must advocate for a new culture that embraces security. This culture is cultivated through constant training, communication, and constant reminders of the cybersecurity policies in use. Hughes-Lartey et al. [6] pointed out that human factors, such as a lack of awareness and proper training, play a crucial role in raising the security threats and risks where employees are exposed to IoT devices. Hence, organizations must set their levels of cybersecurity education high and ensure that their workforce recognizes threats that may be prevalent in regular operations.

Also, the organizational culture speaks to the level of stress and burnout of cybersecurity professionals, either positively or negatively. Nobles [18] points out that an intolerant culture could inevitably result in security-skepticism, and the workforce becomes dispassionate to the security initiatives due to pressure. Managers need to stay vigilant when it comes to burnout, rotate schedules, create a healthy workplace, and provide help with stress levels.

6.7.4 Integrating Leadership with Security Practices

The application of leadership with cybersecurity polices ensure that the security polices in the organization are not just a checklist to be complied with as a formality but rather as a policy to be implemented and functioning within the organizational structure. According to Poelhmann et al. [10], cybersecurity success at the organizational level depends more on the leadership's effectiveness in getting people on board and imparting the right practices at the workplace, and being keen on security in the organization. This has the effect that leaders need to be aware of new threats and technologies and adjust security measures according to this cyberspace threat landscape. Jeong et al. [16] underscore that the establishment of open communication platforms between technical personnel and leaders is critical in cybersecurity leadership. This way leaders are always informed of these issues while the cybersecurity team receives support in mitigating these issues. Leadership involvement in security decisions likewise ensures a signal to employees that cybersecurity is a concern at the senior staff level and throughout the company.

6.7.5 The Role of Trust in Leadership and Cybersecurity

Leadership must maintain trust with their employees in order to create a strong cybersecurity program. Daudi [9] discussed the role of trust in cybersecurity frameworks, especially in addressing human exploitation. As a result, trusting employees will tend to report suspicious activities and follow security policies. Conversely, when patients do not trust their physicians, they may fail to report any likely security threats, and the threats continue lurking.

The same meaning is also attached to how leaders handle cybersecurity issues. During a breach, leadership should work to reduce panic and enhance coordination. Therefore, leadership should promote cybersecurity by valuing input from employees and appreciating their work on cybersecurity [23].

6.7.6 Summary

Cyber human factors can be managed through leadership and organizational culture. Exploiting human vulnerabilities remains a major threat to organizational cybersecurity, but through the promotion of cybersecurity, but with effective security responsibility, sharing, and trust, leaders can minimize the threats posed by human elements. This paper concludes that, with emerging forms of cyber threats, leadership is set to become a critical factor within organizations in leading on aspects related to IT security implementations as well as moderating human factors.

6.8 The Impact of Organizational Policies on Human Behavior in Cybersecurity

An organization's policy and attitude toward cybersecurity vastly influence the employees, and vice versa. Policies not only state what is expected in regard to security but also outline the working environment for employees. This section aims at explaining the features of a well-developed organizational policy as a safeguard against vulnerabilities, to promote sound practices, and improve security.

6.8.1 The Foundation of Cybersecurity Policies

Adopting cybersecurity policies should be preconditioned by the best understanding of the organization's environment in terms of security risks and legal obligations, as well as valuable assets. A mechanistic or "strong" approach does not work; policies must fit into the organization like pieces of a puzzle [4]. Through qualified measures of risk analysis, important and probably dangerous aspects of human activities can be identified, and corresponding policies that interact with these threats can be created.

Policies should then outline how employees are expected to commit to undertaking their activities with respect to cybersecurity. This includes setting the acceptable use of technology, policies on passwords, and measures on methods of alerting authorities of suspicious activities. It is quite stimulating when employees comprehend their duties and are inclined to adhere to security-oriented behaviors.

6.8.2 Encouraging Compliance Through Clear Communication

Availability is hence crucial when preparing for cybersecurity policies for implementation, so as to enhance communication. It needs to be clear in any organization that all workers are well informed of the given policies and the reasons behind setting those particular policies. It is possible to organize training sessions during which employees will be reminded of the necessity to follow compliance and learn more about the possible consequences of security protocol violations [17]. Furthermore, policies should be clear and understandable to those who intend to implement them. Some authors mentioned that using overly technical language may lead to the disengagement of participants, including employees. Two strategies that could help people learn more can be applied: reducing cognitively complex language and using graphics.

6.8.3 Building a Culture of Accountability

Organizational policies should effectively promote organizational accountability, making employees feel that they are accountable for the results of their actions and decisions, and helping them appreciate the results of their actions on the security of the organization. Accountability culture entails forcing individuals to accept responsibility for their actions as well as stick to certain program norms [6]. Another way to enhance accountability is by establishing the connection between a number of key performance indicators directly linked to cybersecurity compliance. This way, one can both pinpoint specific problems that arise during work and motivate people who demonstrate proper information security measures. Among these, CIP not only encourages the enforcement of policies among employees but also promotes the formation of shared responsibility.

6.8.4 The Role of Incentives and Consequences

This chapter has found that incentives can work as one of the ways of encouraging people to adhere to the configured cybersecurity policies. This includes incorporating measures that can encourage employees who always follow information security regulatory measures or provide their contributions in improving the organization's security status [18]. Employees may be rewarded through verbal appreciation during company meetings or presentations, framed identification, or even by offering some form of monetary incentives.

On the other hand, organizations have to design and implement consequences for noncompliance with the organization's policies. This does not mean that punitive measures should now dominate; consequences should merely be presented as part of the learning experience. For example, if an employee violates a regulation, the organization may offer more lessons rather than reprimanding the employee. This approach encourages improvement and reinforces the notion that cybersecurity is everybody's responsibility.

6.8.5 Continuous Policy Review and Adaptation

There is always something changing in the cybersecurity environment, and policies should also reflect such an environment. The policies should therefore be reviewed at least annually to determine whether they are still up to date. It is crucial that organizations establish a structured approach for assessing and revising security policies in tune with new risks, tools, accessories, and changes in laws [2]. Involving employees in the efforts will also make it easier to know how some of the policies are interpreted and practiced in the working environment. Mechanisms, for example, polls or group discussions, can reveal which areas of the policy are weak and which solutions are not very efficient, so adjustments can be made in time.

6.8.6 The Integration of Technology and Human Factors

Although policies are important in organizations, they should not run independently of technology. It is recommended that organizations aim at achieving a policy/technology/human factors solution. This integration can help develop a stronger stance against cybersecurity threats, as the employees will have what it takes to follow policies strictly [3]. For instance, an organization can integrate automatic compliance checks to systems to ensure security compliance is achieved. Some of these systems are able to warn employees if they go off-color and reorient them, and hold them accountable in the process. Also, technologies such as password managers help to address countervailing psychological pressures and unburden employees to follow policies.

6.8.7 Training as a Policy Enforcement Mechanism

Training is an essential part of how organizations implement cybersecurity policies. If it is necessary to train people frequently, those training sessions should not only involve policy explanations but should also present how those stated policies are going to be implemented in the organization's activities. Another form of training is the live simulation of cyber events by which workers practice compliance at the workplace [11]. In addition, the necessity for education as a continuous process should be stressed by organizations. IT security risks are ever-changing and should be communicated to the employees, highlighting new threats and the practices to be adopted. The heads of an organization can build a culture of L&D by providing constant training, conferences, and knowledge updates on cybersecurity.

6.8.8 Promoting Psychological Safety

In teaching and learning in schools, the foundation of the teaching profession, policies work best when people feel comfortable to report security issues and risks on the company's policy without facing repercussions. Employers should create a culture that would allow the employees to speak out their concerns and report experiences of cyber events [18]. If employees are encouraged to report on missteps, or seek clarification, they are more likely to behave in ways that improve security. The absence of punishment for reporting means that mistakes can be corrected through reviewed and adjusted policies. To help support this, anonymous reporting channels can be utilized to help inspire people to come forward about probable misconduct without the worry of being persecuted.

6.8.9 Summary

To address the second research question regarding organizational policies, it can be stated that these policies are a crucial factor in directing behavior related to cybersecurity [2]. Clear, accessible, and enforceable enforceable policies can help an organization reduce human risks and create an accountable and compliant environment. Additionally, individuals should regularly engage with security, cybersecurity, and IT, integrating these aspects with technology training and open communication. People should be in touch with security, cybersecurity, and IT regularly, which should be integrated with technology training and open communication. Therefore, as the organizational operating environment changes with challenges such as new threats and evolving policy expectations, the readiness of the organization to implement and adapt policy and policy changes will be highly effective.

6.9 Technological Solutions to Mitigate Human Weaknesses

Considering the research on human factors in cybersecurity, humans are considered to be the weakest link in defense [7, 11]. However, training people to become better and enhancing human assets are key areas. Technology can be leveraged to cover up for human shortcomings by providing solutions that reduce the effects of human failings, or in some cases, eliminate them altogether.

6.9.1 Automation and Artificial Intelligence

Both automation and AI have become pivotal assets in fighting against the weaknesses that the human factor has brought to the table in cybersecurity. Such technologies eliminate the occasions that require human interventions, thereby reducing the probability of mistakes due to forgetfulness, tiredness, or misunderstanding [1]. Moreover, certain peculiarities in the process might not be easily noticed by operators if AI is not used. For instance, AI-based systems may classify traffic on the social network in real time, and flag suspicious activities sooner than manned teams (Nobles, 2022). Of all use cases, the intersection of AI in cybersecurity has revealed some success in features such as detecting phishing, especially where AI can analyze and detect malicious links before human interaction [15].

6.9.2 Multi-factor Authentication (MFA)

A proactive measure of how powerful simple technological measures can be when it comes to overcoming human vices is multi-factor authentication (MFA). MFA goes beyond requiring users to input a password before they are granted access to sensitive systems. On the same note, MFA can as well prevent the access by an unauthorized person even if he or she knows the user's password and thus minimizes use of passwords, which are usually weak due to human error [12]. Even though MFA can still fall victim to phishing attacks, it causes more problems for the attackers, who must now gain access to multiple factors rather than just one [26].

6.9.3 Endpoint Detection and Response (EDR)

Endpoint detection and response effectively enhance the protection processes as the EDR system constantly checks endpoint devices for any malicious activities. EDR tools incorporate live tracking along with response mechanisms, thereby closing the loophole that was previously left by human intervention in the detection of cyber threats [10]. These systems run independently to identify specific behaviors likely to be connected with the prohibited actions, including unauthorized access of data or transferring files. This is because through automated responses that are provided by EDR tools, organizations are in a position to contain threats before they advance [5].

6.9.4 User Behavior Analytics (UBA)

User behavior analysis (UBA) uses big data analytics and machine learning methods to analyze user actions that may pose threats for an organization. Since UBA systems establish individual user profiles and compare inputs to them, UBA can identify suspicious actions such as logins a new geographical area or accessing restricted folders after normal working times [25]. These systems are especially good at handling insiders, since standard approaches to perimeter security may not be sufficient [24]. By doing so, UBA enhances security decision-making by recognizing risky behaviors that may be hard for these personnel or other approaches to detect [9].

6.9.5 Secure Access Service Edge (SASE)

The secure access service edge (SASE) framework is a relatively emerging architecture with prospects in the sphere of cybersecurity; it merges network security services, embracing firewalls and secure web gateways, with a WAN service style to account for flexible, efficient access. The essence of integrating all these technologies under SASE is that complexity and human errors that might be caused by human administrators are also eliminated [13]. It also guarantees that security policies are applied across latitude, longitude, application, etc., to reduce risks caused by human elements [21].

6.9.6 Data Loss Prevention (DLP) Tools

DLP stands for data loss prevention and is a set of products that depict the ability to detect or prevent the transmission of confidential information. These tools are more effective in preventing human error mishaps, such as sending the wrong documents to the wrong recipient [16]. DLP technologies, apart from incurring costs, also enforce the compliance of the organization's data-sharing policies [11]. In other words, DLP tools are a second-level control since they complement the efforts of a human being in the process of protecting data.

6.9.7 Continuous Security Training Tools

As training is considered a human solution, we have a technological one in continuous security training platforms. These tools are used to teach current threats to employees in a more efficient manner, using nanodegrees personalized for each employee's performance and behavior. Through setting users to solve quizzes like phishing mimics or other forms of interactive programs, the application ensures that such training is current and dynamic to new threats [3]. Such a constant feedback system can help to greatly decrease the likelihood of human error, as long as cybersecurity remains a matter of focus among users [8].

6.9.8 Threat Intelligence Platforms (TIPs)

A threat intelligence platform (TIP) is the integrated collection of threat feeds from several sources offering timely threat information. These platforms are important in reacting to cybercriminals by pointing out susceptibilities that may be exploited. TIPs help minimize the workload of threat intelligence by allowing human analysts to rely on automated systems to extract intelligence from the internet, leaving them with the work of categorizing and prioritizing intelligence [2, 4]. Moreover, TIPs enable organizational cyber defense by identifying the behavior of cybercriminals, which could be used to help organizations shift from reactive to proactive [20].

6.9.9 Summary

That's why it is important to study technological solutions of the human factor in cybersecurity. These tools prevent the role of human error and increase organizational robustness in terms of process automation, multitier security provisions, real-time monitoring, and response. But even such technologies work best when they are supported by an informed and protective human workforce. Hence, integrating people factors with technology is the core to tackling cybersecurity threats [17, 22].

6.10 Challenges and Future Directions

6.10.1 Evolving Threat Landscape and Increased Complexity

A major problem in practicing defensive cybersecurity measures against human factors is that traditional threats change over time. Attackers use the human aspects of security by using advanced social engineering schemes or advanced persistent threats (APTs). The continually evolving threat environment poses a challenge for security officers, who must prevent and mitigate brand-new types of attacks that leverage personnel [4]. However, the integration of IoT, artificial intelligence, and cloud computing makes these challenges worse, as these new technologies introduce new opportunities for attacks [6]. Whereas in the past, technical countermeasures may have been sufficient throughout the evolution of cyber threats, these are generally insufficient. Corporate culture has a major influence on enhancing or provisioning cover for existing cyber risks from individuals [21]. To overcome them, cybersecurity strategies should change and develop as a set of strategies coordinated by the intersectionality of technology and people.

6.10.2 The "Human Firewall" and Organizational Cybersecurity Culture

While organizations invest significant resources in technical defenses, commonly known as perimeter defenses, recent findings highlight the need to strengthen the human aspect—often referred to as the human firewall—through security awareness and training programs [3]. But there are challenges in the implementation and subsequent functioning of such programs. For example, there are questions of employee concern and motivation, for example, where many employees simply ignore cybersecurity as a mere second job. One of the major challenges that most organizations face today is the inability to develop an organizational culture that involves employees in dealing with cyber risks [2, 8]. To counter these difficulties, management in such organizations must change their approach toward cybersecurity by developing a cybersecurity culture where everyone is aware of their responsibilities. More effective engagement might be achieved by improving the visibility of training opportunities and enforcing learning and simulation activities tied to the specific job responsibilities where engagement is low [16]. According to Pollini et al. [25] psychologically, educationally, and organizationally, incorporating human factors into cybersecurity frameworks improves overall system protection.

6.10.3 Overcoming Security Fatigue and Burnout

Briefly, the three threats to human involvement in cybersecurity are security fatigue, burnout, and desensitization. Studies show that annoying security signals and numerous procedures inhibit crucial employee security control, in particular, cause negligence and various mistakes [18]. This issue is especially concerning where attention to security is inherent in the business; the key sectors affected are finance and healthcare. Future plans should be directed toward easing the security workload on employees by automating processes and enhancing the usability of technology systems of security [27]. For instance, implementing artificial intelligence (AI) solutions that can also help in threat identification and detection of unusual patterns without generating false alerts also relieves the issue of security burnout [10].

6.10.4 Regulatory and Compliance Challenges

Thus, cybersecurity is still an emerging field, adding new complexities regarding regulatory rules and regulations. Organizations must abide by many standards, including GDPR in Europe and other regional cybersecurity regulations [15]. Implementing these compliance norms effectively while simultaneously managing the human factor in cybersecurity presents numerous difficulties because people may never grasp the details of these regulations or may rationalize bypassing security steps for the sake of efficiency [11]. To this end, regulators need to promote awareness of compliance requirements among the employees of organizations. This can be done by including compliance-centered modules as a part of the more extensive cybersecurity and privacy modules [17]. Also, future security frameworks require more sophisticated instruments that regulate processes without involving many people, considering the risks of errors [23].

6.10.5 Future Directions: Leveraging Emerging Technologies

It was found that the key to the future of cybersecurity will be the effective integration of human elements alongside other advances in advanced technologies like artificial intelligence, machine learning, and blockchain. AI solutions can serve as an important means of preventing human failures by detecting threats and risks in the process and minimizing paper-based approaches [21]. Machine learning models can also analyze someone's behavior and provide indications of abnormal behavior to the security teams, making the human factor even more valuable in cybersecurity frameworks [22]. The most significant ideas for the use of blockchain technology in solving human factors are ensuring record retention and providing decentralization due to the system's transparency [13]. In addition, by introducing blockchain as a key component of identity management and authentication, it is possible to avoid a range of dangers related to technical mistakes, for instance, poor password protection or phishing [5].

As cybersecurity trends evolve further, such technologies have to be incorporated into human endeavors in order to minimize as much as possible the possibility of errors and to take advantage of opportunities not exploitable by traditional forms of security. Businesses need to spend more money on the development of AI-based cybersecurity technologies, with the emphasis placed on the analysis of their relationships with some human actions [7].

6.10.6 A Multidisciplinary Approach to Human-Centered Cybersecurity

The nature of cybersecurity risks and threats is now taking on a post-modern nature, so there is a definite need for more integrated action. The knowledge from psychology, sociology, and behavioral sciences, when integrated into the cybersecurity plans, can provide a better view of people's behavior in cyberspace [12]. As Thron et al. [26] pointed out, the major areas of research will include defining human-centered cybersecurity in a social-contextual way, elucidating the potential threat surface of people, and benefiting from multi-sector cybersecurity education programs to aid cybersecurity professionals in understanding socio-technical structures and human behavior. Further, organizations should also go further to develop strategies to enhance cyber resilience that involve employees' flexibility, adaptability, and constant learning [24]. Subsequent cybersecurity frameworks can improve overall security by directly addressing the human element that current frameworks do not treat as solely a technical problem. Thus, the issue of human factors is critical in cybersecurity, but there are significant opportunities for improving the overall security of technology systems through the adoption of technologies, improvements of educational programs, as well as through collaboration between professionals from various fields. In the future, therefore, organizations need to strike a balance between human intervention and the use of technology in order to counter newer forms of threats.

6.11 Conclusion

As the world becomes more dependent on digitization, cybersecurity has become one of the biggest issues that companies and businesses in all industries face. From the current levels of sophistication and diversification of threats within the cyber world, it becomes clear that it is only possible to get a functional handle on the situation by addressing human factors. The concept of humans as the main vulnerability in cybersecurity points to events that should happen in organizations, which are associated with people's activities, perceptions, and organizational practices, besides technological measures. This combined approach acknowledges the fact that technology is indeed important in developing a solution, and at the same time acknowledges the fact that technology alone cannot ensure that protection is accorded to the relevant facets of a business. The study outlined in this chapter demonstrates the critical roles played by human factors in exacerbating the problem of cybersecurity. Cognitive security's main challenge includes security fatigue and burnout, vast challenges posed by compliance work, among other issues that organizations encounter when propounding cybersecurity responsibility among the workforce. Furthermore, when considering how emerging technologies interact with people's behaviors, both threats to cybersecurity and ways to improve its strength may be identified. Vital system solutions, including AI and machine learning, help prevent workers from making mistakes while engaging employees in monitoring and protecting organizational capital. Therefore, for an excellent cybersecurity implementation, an organization needs to undertake continual training education for its employees and motivate them to be responsible for organizational security. When behavioral science concepts are incorporated into cybersecurity plans, an organization will be able to account for its employees' behavior and actions. This human domain enhances a security culture within employees; not only do they know the threats, but also know how to handle them.

Finally, only the symbiosis of technical and nontechnical factors will determine the development of cybersecurity in the future. While organizations seek to grapple with and gain mastery over the multifaceted sphere of cyberspace, it will be critical to engage a systems approach that encompasses not only the technological but also the human dimensions if the goal is to experience enduring security. With that in mind, organizations need to reintegrate the concept of the human factor and by doing so, increase their ability to provide cybersecurity protections to their valuable data, promote overall security awareness of their employees and customers, and engage them in creating a secure zone between the organizations and cyber threats. So, by this combined action, the cybersecurity environment can slowly transform into a more protective and less vulnerable space for organizations and people.

References

1 Alsharif, M., Mishra, S., and AlShehri, M. (2022). Impact of human vulnerabilities on cybersecurity. *Computer Systems Science & Engineering* 40 (3): https://doi.org/10.32604/csse.2022.019938.

2 Campean, S. (2019). The human factor at the center of a cyber security culture. *International Journal of Information Security and Cybercrime (IJISC)* 8 (1): 51–58.

3 Aksoy, C. (2023). Critical success factors for cybersecurity just technical? Exploring the role of human factors in cybersecurity management. *Research Journal of Business and Management.* 10 (2): 51–57.

4 Goh, P. (2021). Humans as the weakest link in maintaining cybersecurity: Building cyber resilience in humans. In: *Introduction to Cyber Forensic Psychology: Understanding the Mind of the Cyber Deviant Perpetrators*, 287–305. World Scientific Connects.

5 Ani, U.D., He, H., and Tiwari, A. (2019). Human factor security: evaluating the cybersecurity capacity of the industrial workforce. *Journal of Systems and Information Technology.* 21 (1): 2–35.

6 Hughes-Lartey, K., Li, M., Botchey, F.E., and Qin, Z. (2021). Human factor, a critical weak point in the information security of an organization's Internet of things. *Heliyon* 7 (3): e06522.

7 Corman, A. (2023). *The Human Element in Cybersecurity-Bridging the Gap Between Technology and Human Behaviour*. AKITRA.

8 Nobles, C. (2018). Botching human factors in cybersecurity in business organizations. *HOLISTICA–Journal of Business and Public Administration* 9 (3): 71–88.

9 Daudi, M. (2023). Trust framework on exploitation of humans as the weakest link in cybersecurity. *Applied Cybersecurity & Internet Governance* 2 (1): 1–26.

10 Poehlmann, N., Caramancion, K. M., Tatar, I. et al. (2021) The organizational cybersecurity success factors: an exhaustive literature review. *Advances in Security, Networks, and Internet of Things: Proceedings from SAM'20, ICWN'20, ICOMP'20, and ESCS'20*. 377–395.

11 Denno, J. (2016). *Attacking the Human-the Weakest Link in Cybersecurity.* Utica College.

12 Giacomello, G. and Pescaroli, G. (2019). Managing human factors. In: *Cyber Resilience of Systems and Networks* (ed. A. Kott and I. Linkov), 247–263. Springer.

13 Kadena, E. and Gupi, M. (2021). Human factors in cybersecurity: risks and impacts. *Security Science Journal* 2 (2): 51–64.

14 Wiechetek, Ł. and Mędrek, M. (2022). Human factors in security–cybersecurity education and awareness of business students. *Annales Universitatis Mariae Curie-Skłodowska, sectio H–Oeconomia* 56 (1): 119–142.

15 Rahman, T., Rohan, R., Pal, D., and Kanthamanon, P. (2021). Human factors in cybersecurity: a scoping review. *Proceedings of the 12th International Conference on Advances in Information Technology*. 1–11.

16 Jeong, J., Mihelcic, J., Oliver, G., and Rudolph, C. (2019). Towards an improved understanding of human factors in cybersecurity. *2019 IEEE 5th International Conference on Collaboration and Internet Computing (CIC)*. IEEE. 338–345.

17 Triplett, W.J. (2022). Addressing human factors in cybersecurity leadership. *Journal of Cybersecurity and Privacy* 2 (3): 573–586.

18 Nobles, C. (2022). Stress, burnout, and security fatigue in cybersecurity: a human factors problem. *HOLISTICA–Journal of Business and Public Administration* 13 (1): 49–72.

19 Sangwan, A. (2024). Human Factors in Cybersecurity Awareness. *2024 International Conference on Intelligent Systems for Cybersecurity (ISCS)*. IEEE. 1–7.

20 Marble, J.L., Lawless, W.F., Mittu, R. et al. (2015). The human factor in cybersecurity: robust & intelligent defense. In: *Cyber Warfare: Building the Scientific Foundation* (ed. S. Jajodia, P. Shakarian, V.S. Subrahmanian, et al.), 173–206. Springer.

21 Young, H., van Vliet, T., van de Ven, J. et al. (2018). Understanding human factors in cyber security as a dynamic system. In: *Advances in Human Factors in Cybersecurity: Proceedings of the AHFE 2017 International Conference on Human Factors in Cybersecurity*, July 17–21, 2017, The Westin Bonaventure Hotel, Los Angeles, California, USA 8. Springer. 244–254.

22 Zhang, X. and Ghorbani, A.A. (2021). Human factors in cybersecurity: issues and challenges in big data. *Research Anthology on Privatizing and Securing Data* 1695–1725.

23 Danet, D. (2021). *Punish and Perish: The Human Factor in Cybersecurity*, 1–8. ITASEC.

24 Rebensky, S., Carroll, M., Nakushian, A. et al. (2021). Understanding the last line of defense: human response to cybersecurity events. *International Conference on Human-Computer Interaction*. Springer. 353–366.

25 Pollini, A., Callari, T.C., Tedeschi, A. et al. (2022). Leveraging human factors in cybersecurity: an integrated methodological approach. *Cognition, Technology & Work* 24 (2): 371–390.

26 Thron, E., Faily, S., Dogan, H., and Freer, M. (2024). Human factors and cyber-security risks on the railway–the critical role played by signalling operations. *Information & Computer Security* 32 (2): 236–263.

27 Rohan, R., Funilkul, S., Pal, D., and Chutimaskul, W. (2021). Understanding of human factors in cybersecurity: a systematic literature review. *2021 International Conference on Computational Performance Evaluation (ComPE)*. IEEE. 133–140.

7

Advanced Defense Techniques: Beyond Traditional Security Measures

Rebet Keith Jones

Cyber and Information Security Department, Capitol Technology University, Laurel, Maryland, USA

7.1 Introduction

As the nature and intensity of threats evolve, basic security solutions like firewalls and antivirus can no longer withstand new-generation threats like Advanced Persistent Threats (APTs), ransomware, and zero-day exploits. Conventional protection strategies are often passive and act as barriers against specific and identifiable forms of attacks but cannot adapt to emerging threats as fast. Such a divergence now calls for higher levels of defense mechanisms that can also prevent threats alongside responding to them [1].

7.1.1 Evolving Cyber Threats and the Need for Advanced Defenses

There are new and complex risks such as APTs, which are long-term and organized cyberattacks that do not follow the traditional models of attack and evade simple security measures. According to Alshamrani et al. [1], these threats are still active and few organizations have worked out measures for early identification and prevention. Sophisticated approaches such as the case of machine learning (ML) for threat detection and artificial intelligence (AI)-based security provide new footholds to identify threats and distinguish between normal and malicious behaviors that were virtually imperceptible previously [2]. However, these threats are fast evolving and hence require organizations to take a number of layered and precautionary measures which transcend a simple defense-in-depth model.

For a better perspective of the advancement of cyber threats, the following timeline outlines major milestones of modern threats that have developed from simple threats to APT and ransomware threats (see Figure 7.1).

7.1.2 Core Elements of Advanced Defense

7.1.2.1 Artificial Intelligence and Machine Learning for Predictive Defense

ML models are extremely useful when it comes to creating threat intelligence models that will predict threats. Using big data, these models are capable of identifying potential signs of an attack, and with them, organizations can prevent the occurrence of a weakness. Government networks

Defense in Depth: Modern Cybersecurity Strategies and Evolving Threats, First Edition. Edited by Hewa Majeed Zangana.

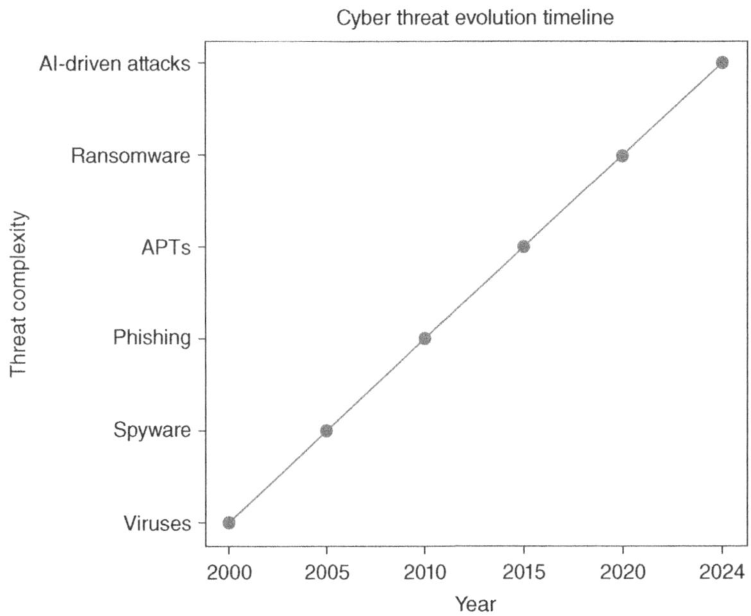

Figure 7.1 Cyber threat evolution timeline. Source: Hewa Majeed Zangana.

mentioned that AI and ML improve the accuracy of threat intelligence to predict threats and minimize the workload of detecting threats [3]. The following chart also shows the improvement in threat detection and in the accuracy of AI and ML models. It also points out early detection as one of the strengths of automated systems because it takes less time than most other techniques (see Figure 7.2).

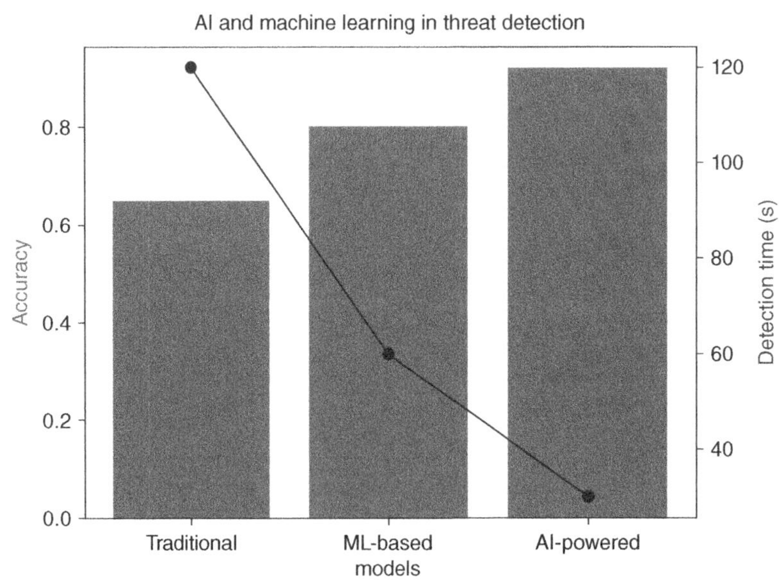

Figure 7.2 AI and machine learning for threat detection. Source: Hewa Majeed Zangana.

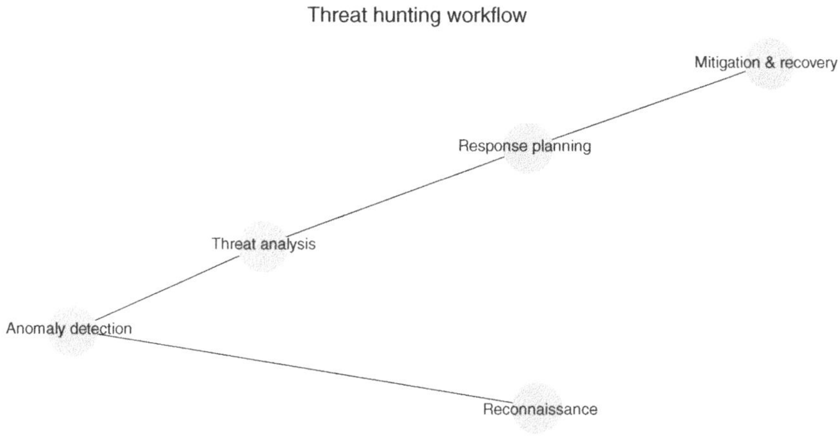

Figure 7.3 Threat hunting workflow. Source: Hewa Majeed Zangana.

7.1.2.2 Threat Hunting and Proactive Monitoring

Threat hunting is the proactive process of searching for threats and indicators of compromise (IOCs) in a system before they are observed in a network. This is different from being reactive in nature which is based on alerts derived from automatic systems. As Badva et al. [4] observed, threat hunting should be seen as a valuable activity aimed at stopping APTs and other covert attacks that may not be detected within a traditional analytical and monitoring system. Based on the analysis of threat-hunting activities and the model shown below, the common phases include sampling, threat analysis, and identifying indicators of compromise. These phases generally fall under reconnaissance, anomaly detection, and response preparation (see Figure 7.3).

7.1.2.3 Zero Trust Architecture

Zero trusts work under the principles of never trust and always validate. This approach means that every user and every device attempting to access resources must be authenticated with confirmation of identity each time, irrespective of whether they are within the network boundary or outside it. In their paper, Patil et al. [5] explain how and why of zero trust architecture (ZTA). It has gained importance especially for securing cloud-based financial services and data that resides in multiple platforms and systems. However, there is still a place for the model called ZTA which is described in detail with the flowchart that shows how strict access to all the devices and users is to be controlled and checked nonstop (see Figure 7.4).

7.1.2.4 Moving Target Defense

This makes a system difficult to attack because with moving target defense (MTD), the targets are shifted often enough. Such methods include internet protocol (IP) formulation, network restructuring, and software heterogeneity. In the paper of Sengupta et al. [6], there is information that exactly MTD makes attacks more complex and dynamic and thus poses significant challenges to attackers. MTD portrayed in the following diagram demonstrates that through dynamic reconfiguration of the target, security increases assailant unpredictability (see Figure 7.5).

7.1.3 Integrating Artificial Intelligence and Automation in Defense

AI and automation are standard parts of cyber defense at the moment; one of the primary areas where they apply is the data processing of data collected from threat intelligence systems.

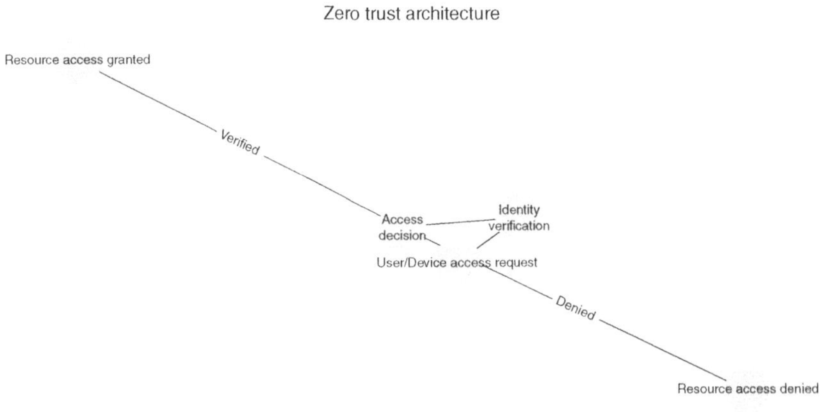

Figure 7.4 Zero trust architecture. Source: Hewa Majeed Zangana.

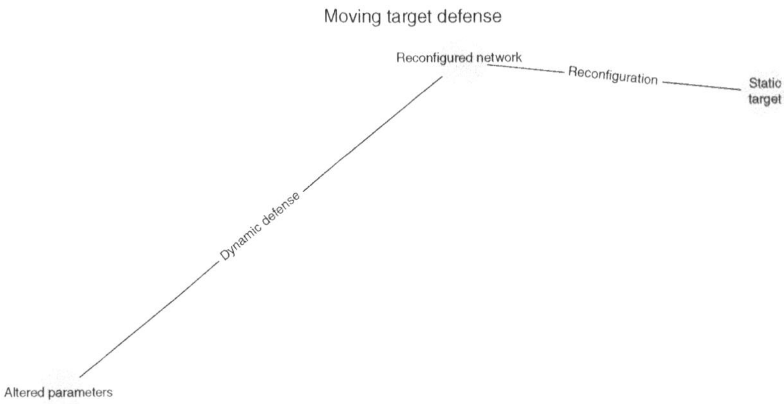

Figure 7.5 Moving target defense conceptual diagram. Source: Hewa Majeed Zangana.

Security may be better accomplished with automation substrates, given that they can perform mundane security tasks faster and more accurately than security operators. AI can also improve these systems by using AI based on prior attacks and using the attack data for next-level defense [7, 8]. Such integration minimizes their detection period and improves the preparedness for organizations to counter them in the shortest time possible, as opposed to having to operate on a reactive basis once an attack has happened. The following pie chart which illustrates the automation ratio in the contemporary cybersecurity processes, highlights the fact that AI has become the cornerstone of efficient security processes (see Figure 7.6).

7.1.4 The Role of Cyber Resilience

Cyber resilience incorporates the aspects of cybersecurity by adding a focus on precise recovery as a way of having minimal operational disruption once breached. In our study, AL-Hawamleh [9] proposed a strong cyber resilience model and stressed the potential threats posed by cyber disruption on business continuity planning. The component called resiliency is characterized by the presence of proactive and reactive layers that can help the organization continue the functioning of the key

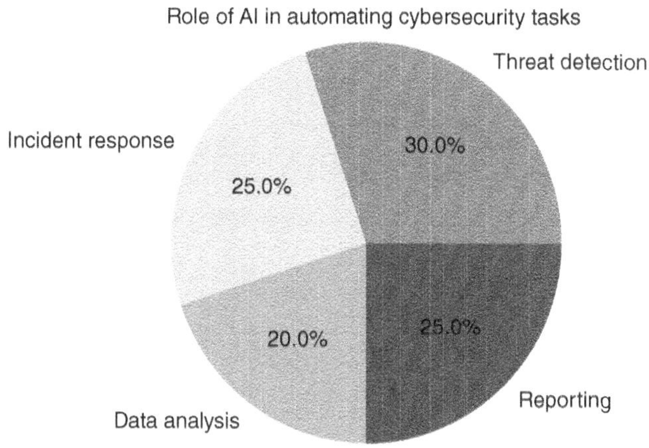

Figure 7.6 Integration of AI and automation in defense. Source: Hewa Majeed Zangana.

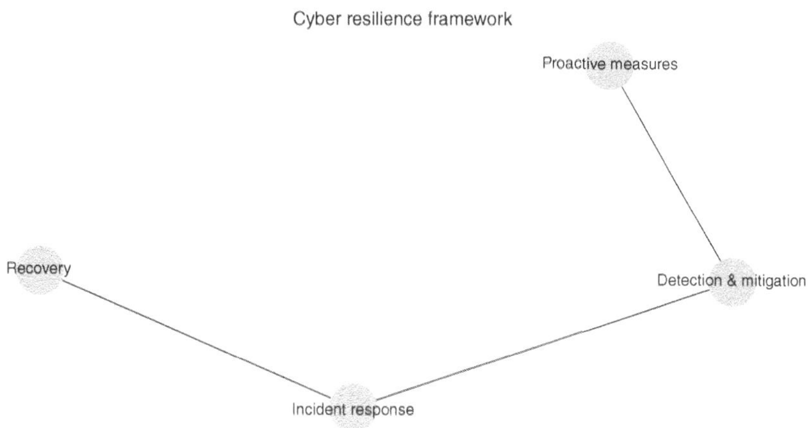

Figure 7.7 Cyber resilience framework overview. Source: Hewa Majeed Zangana.

processes in the context of a breach. This chart shows proactive, reactive, and recovery aspects of the cyber resilience framework that would reduce their impact features as much as possible (see Figure 7.7).

7.1.5 Looking Beyond Perimeter Defense

Using a perimeter approach has proven to be ineffective against the current-day cyber threats. McMahon [10] posited that synchronous measures of securing the IT system should be in multiple layers rather than just around the network perimeter. Today's attackers do not necessarily get past physical security measures such as firewalls and intrusion detection systems because many choose to attack users directly. As a result, high-level methods focus on internal surveillance and control, which can recognize insidious threats that cannot be stopped by outside protection. Besides the implementation of a layered defense-in-depth, the security system employs various layers of security. This layered model shows different security measures at different hierarchy levels of IT structures as a strong defense mechanism (see Figure 7.8).

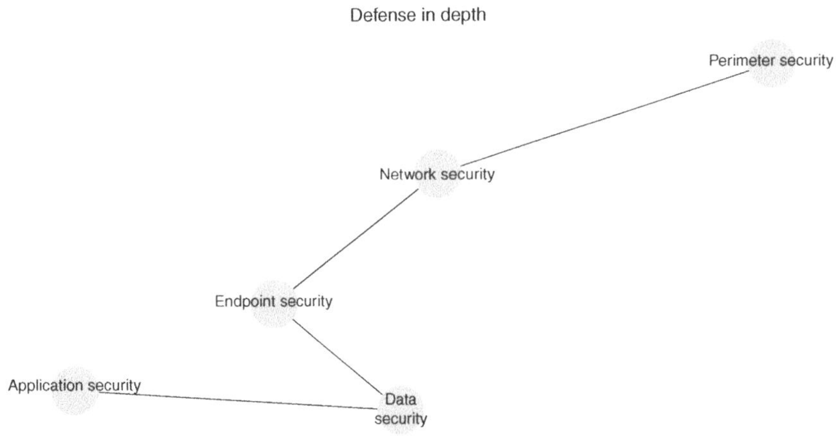

Figure 7.8 Defense-in-depth layered. Source: Hewa Majeed Zangana.

7.1.6 Summary

Sophisticated ways of defending against attacks are emerging from such barriers and rigid security systems. All the strategies outlined here center on flexibility, adaptability, and overcoming challenges because cyber threats are constantly changing. According to Mahboubi et al. [11], the use of such techniques reflects modern, intelligence-initiated, security efforts to prevent threats rather than simply deny them access. This evolution is very significant for organizations that strive to develop an efficient and effective defense strategy that will enable react and be prepared for contemporary complex and constant cyber threats.

7.2 Behavioral Analytics and Anomaly Detection

Behavioral analysis and anomaly detection have become almost indispensable at the present time within the frameworks of contemporary cybersecurity, as these methods allow organizations to act upon anomalies that violate set behavioral patterns. This is because the likelihood of APTs, sophisticated cyberattacks, and the overall shift from known attack behaviors has made it imperative to detect the most subtle behavioral deviations. Behavioral analytics is the process of monitoring and analyzing users' and systems' "behaviors" to set up normal activities and detect further behavior or events that correspond to possible threats. Currently, the use of sub-techniques based on AI and ML opens the ability to learn and classify, subsequently enhancing the view of potentially malicious actions. For example, ML can be programmed to look for different patterns of logins at certain times of the day or week, different patterns of data access, or traffic on a network that would be would be a sign of possible intrusions or security breaches [7, 8]. The last major benefit of behavioral analytics can be found in protecting against insider threats and stolen/misused credentials. These threats were previously addressed by traditional security solutions since these rely heavily on known threat signatures or attack vectors [3]. Nonetheless, behavioral analytics is a more proactive solution incorporating an enhanced method by identifying anomalous activities done within typical user's accounts which makes its detection a lot better, as Chastain and Smith [2] put much stress on behavioral approach, pointing to the fact that application of AI helps increase the system's chances to identify suspicious behavior that signals the intention to conduct a cyberattack.

It must be noted that anomaly detection works alongside behavioral analytics by pointing out that there are deviations from baseline behavioral profiles. This technique has been useful in identifying APTs, always used in long duration, and who uses concealment methods [4, 12]. For example, threat-hunting techniques which are modern involve anomaly detection techniques to highlight activities, which may not be easily noticeable, for instance, the movement from one layer of the network to another or changes in system parameters [11]. Newer developments in the world of AI have brought novel anomaly detection methods, which include features of context awareness, making threat detection even more elaborate. The former can distinguish between normal dynamic in behavior, from one that may arise out of a change of position within an organization and other real outrightly anomalous behaviors, which may point toward potential threats [13]. According to Edwards [14], AI anomaly detection procedures combined with monitored networks enhance real-time analysis and increase block response, enhancing cybersecurity status. In general form, the concepts of behavioral analytics and the identification of anomalies are not only useful for reducing threats to a business but also for increasing the overall organizational robustness. In this case, organizations can detect specific behaviors that indicate a more significant problem that needs to be addressed to counteract the possible breaches earlier in their development [9]. Furthermore, the elements of the presented predictive behavioral models help to improve the threat intelligence that is used in cybersecurity threat assessment in order to strengthen proper security measures and resist new and more complex cyber threats [15]. The bar chart shown next depicts the success rate of behavioral analytics in detecting different categories of cyber threats, including login profile and network traffic (see Figure 7.9).

Further developments in the field will likely to be directed toward improving the algorithms for the detection of anomalies. These improvements will be crucial in organizing huge datasets and in decreasing the incidences of false positives, which are still major limitations evident in behavior-based detection models [16]. Therefore, the use of behavioral analytics and anomaly

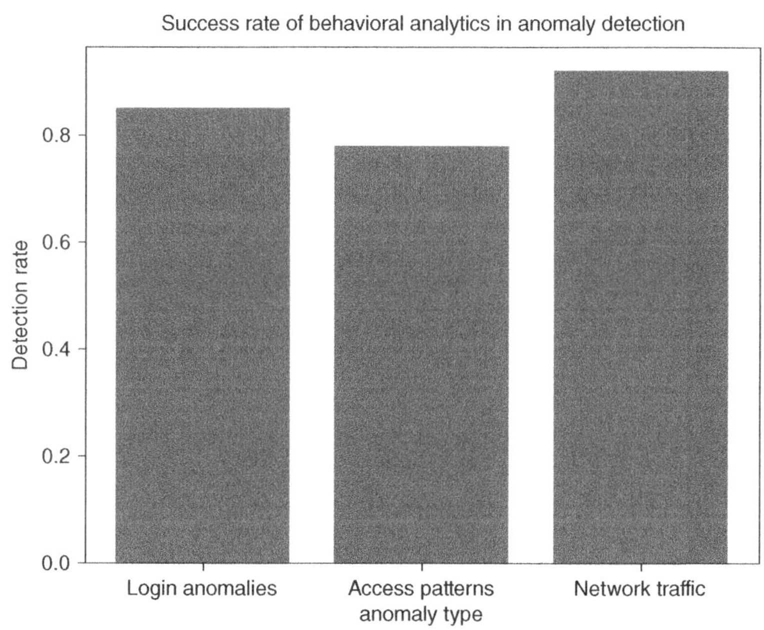

Figure 7.9 Behavioral analytics for anomaly detection. Source: Hewa Majeed Zangana.

detection will also be very integral as threat actors adapt by utilizing new and sophisticated methods of infiltration in line with organizational proactive defense measures and shift toward the resilient security framework enabled by AI [17, 18].

7.3 Zero Trust Architecture

ZTA is a security model that moves the perimeter security focus from being perimeter based where the majority of security can be accomplished at the perimeters of the network to being a requirement that identity and access controls have to be checked regardless of whether an item is inside or outside the network perimeter. As Patil et al. [5] illustrate in their work of 2023, this approach focuses on the issues which cloud services may pose and encourages the utilization of a security model that does not include trust, but rather considers all attempts to gain access a threat. ZTA is gradually becoming relevant as organizations shift toward work from home, shift to the cloud, and grapple with new threats [14, 19].

7.3.1 Core Principles of Zero Trust

Key assumptions for the Zero Trust model are always verify, never trust, and microsegment. In more detail, Nair [12] explains that it is structured by means of continuous authentication mechanisms that occur at regular time intervals and adaptive security policies that function in real time, adjusting to identified threats at the core of ZTA. Moreover, McMahon [10] also revealed that ZTA conveys defense in depth that involves the stacking of security controls to preemptively accredit the identities of an individual without the restriction of network location.

1) **Continuous Authentication and Identity Verification**: Of all the principles the ZTA has instituted, one has to emphasize that the users are always expected to authenticate themselves and their privileges every time they try to gain entry. According to Edwards [14], constant identification reduces lateral movement threats in a network because user credentials are frequently checked for authorization for the requested service.
2) **Least Privilege and Access Controls**: The least privilege principle is one of the main principles of ZTA, through which users are granted access only if it is necessary for their position. This principle reduces the impact of an infringed account in the system [13]. Pham and Xiong further note that when privileged access is being granted only based on dynamic factors such as time of access or device used, it makes ZTA even more exceptional by making it almost impossible for a privilege to be gained by a wrong doer.
3) **Network Segmentation and Micro-Segmentation**: In ZTA, segmentation limits exposure of particular sections of a network to threats, hence curtailing their flow. The technique explained by Alshamrani et al. [1] helps to reduce the possibility of an attack gaining access to an organization. Micro-segmentation improves ZTA through a highly granular and software-based approach to access control, meaning that even within micro-segments of the infrastructures described by El-Amir [20], network interactions remain heavily constrained.

7.3.2 Implementing Zero Trust in Modern Infrastructure

In practice, identity and access management (IAM) processes, endpoint protection, network monitoring, along with encryption, become effective methods that need to be incorporated as part of ZTA. These include, for instance, the technologies like multifactor authentication (MFA), role-based access control (RBAC), and continuous endpoint monitoring are useful in the attainment of ZTA goals. In their work, Gudumetla [21] has mentioned that ZTA, if combined with advanced firewall strategies, strengthens the network security and also pulls the trigger with the help of proactive threat intelligence as suggested by Rodriguez and Costa [3].

7.3.3 Advantages and Challenges of Zero Trust Architecture

ZTA provides various advantages, for instance, improved defense against breaches and increased visibility of security points in the network. However, one notes that there are problems in terms of implementation. One challenge they face is the integration of ZTA in legacy systems, where massive infrastructure changes are usually required to meet the ZTA security posture [11]. Also, the constant checking and identity authentication can lead to the formation of performance hitches and, worst, in observational robust environments of immediate access request [19].

Uchiyama and Oroy [17] opine that the advent of AI can help reduce some of these problems by automating normal monitoring activities as well as adapting security policies depending on users' behaviors. Likewise, advanced threat detection mechanisms, as seen from Tan [15] can support a ZTA model by responding to emerging threats in real time.

7.3.4 Zero Trust Architecture's Role in Future Cyber Defense

ZTA is a relatively novel solution compared to classic approaches to information technology (IT) security, where the focus is on boundary security. Given the burgeoning threats from APTs and ransomware, among other contemporary threats, ZTA is further driving robust and persistent access control, constant monitoring, and micro-segmentation, making it a suitable model for modern organization security [4, 22].

7.4 Deception Technology and Honeypots

Deception technology is becoming more and more crucial for contemporary cyberspace protection and defines the use of decoy systems, files, and environments aimed at engaging malicious users and tracking their activity without using real assets. The core of this approach is honeypots, which are the dispersed, specially designed systems representing the valuable network assets. A honeypot is designed to lure the unauthorized user into spending his or her time with irrelevant information, while at the same time, data on the activity is being recorded. This not only assists in preservation of the real resources, but also contributes to the improvement of the increase in situational awareness through the analysis of the methodologies of attack as well as potential weaknesses. Honeypots can be developed with different levels of interaction, with a basic type which can imitate a single service or a complex one which imitates a full system. Since the targeted individuals have no actual reason to engage with the defenses set up by the traps, it becomes easier for defenders to detect malevolent actions [23]. The intelligence collected through these engagements gives defenders actual data about the attackers' TTPs, enabling the defensive side to counter these threats.

This makes honeypots, in their conception as a foundational element of deception technology, also be easily adopted and employed in conjunction with other security measures such as firewalls and intrusion detection systems [24]. For instance, new generations of honeypots are normally combined with AI for analyzing patterns which may presage imminent breach [15, 25]. Together, this enhances threat detection capability and enables defenders to engage in what is known as predictive threat intelligence, an element of threat prevention that can, in turn, shorten incident response time and aid in defense preparations [3]. A specific application of deception technology is to run actual honeypots using cloud simulation inside virtual frameworks. This approach enables organizations to develop believable though manufactured contexts within the social structures, or networks, which form their organizations, often relying on AI and ML for surveillance and control. As such, the creators can modulate their answers depending on the threat level and even alter structural makeup, creating the honeypot even more effective [17, 18]. These MTD strategies make predictive movements and actions very difficult for the attackers, thus enhancing difficult operations which may discourage attackers from achieving their intended goal. Another attribution of the use of deception technology with the broader cybersecurity paradigm is the mitigation of APTs constitute long-term and complex attacks, honeypots present themselves as useful instruments to interfere and analyze such threats while keeping intrusions from actual systems [1]. This approach can enhance current resilience models by highlighting attack paths during the early phase of penetration [9].

The applicability of honeypots does not end with the areas of interest highlighted above but further goes to areas like healthcare that have to deal with data breaches but at the same time have to adhere to certain set regulations. By deception technology, organizations in specific and attacked industries can build better protection walls and apply superior threat characterization, increasing the security of data within structures of vital importance [13]. Concisely, deception technology and honeypots are the development of cyber defense in evolving and moving ahead by harvesting intelligence from the actions of the attacker. As the threats evolve over the course of the years, incorporating deception technology with AI solutions will become ever essential for protecting an organization's digital resources across industries [2, 4].

7.5 Threat Intelligence and Proactive Security Measures

Threat intelligence as well as successful prevention measures are among the significant components of modern security strategies. Threat intelligence is the process of researching, processing, and analyzing data on prospective threats to help prevent a cyberattack. Tactical security activities are closely related to threat intelligence, referring to the security activities that seek to prevent events from occurring, instead of merely reacting to them. Both models support the development of a sustained position that prepares organizations to counter new threats. The following line chart helps to stress increased periods of threats' mitigation as a result of threat intelligence and other proactive security measures (see Figure 7.10).

7.5.1 Importance of Threat Intelligence

Therefore, threat intelligence forms the foundation of proactive cybersecurity because the involvement helps organizations to gain insight about potential security threats. Through the availability of new and increased threat exposure data, threat intelligence teams are capable of offering information that assists in decision-making and improves threat identification. For instance, Mahboudi et al. [11] point out that there are changing approaches in threat hunting which, in essence, focus on new strategies of threat intelligence in hunting threats and eliminating them before they affect systems. Preventative cybersecurity is called threat hunting, and, when done well, can find threats that standard protection might overlook due to adversary tactics, techniques, and procedures (TTPs) [4].

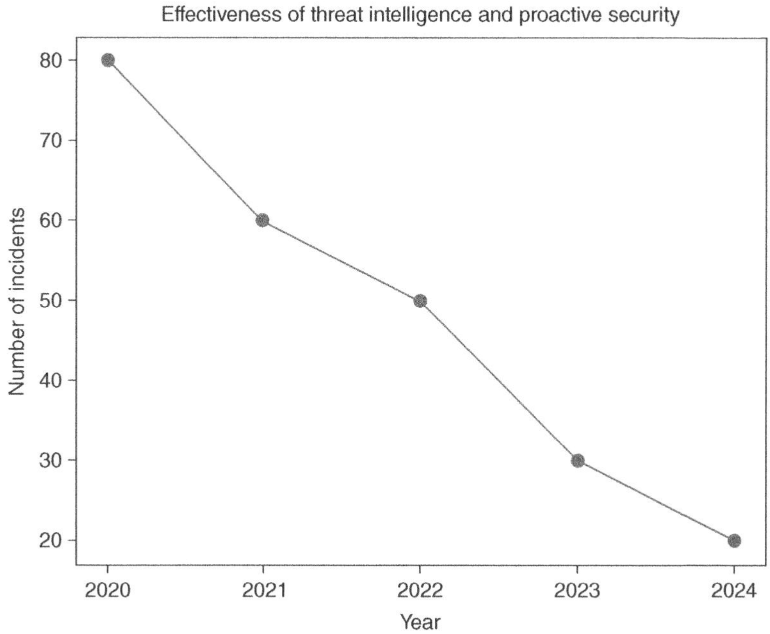

Figure 7.10 Threat intelligence and proactive security measures. Source: Hewa Majeed Zangana.

In the contemporary world of digital processes, organizations are confronted with such threats as, for instance, APTs. Alshamrani et al. [1] explain how APTs use advanced strategies for utilizing systems, and this may need a preemptive defensive approach. These threats point to the need for a constant procurement of threat intelligence in order to provide IOCs to enhance existing detection.

7.5.2 Integrating Artificial Intelligence and Machine Learning in Threat Intelligence

AI and ML are now crucial in upgrading threat intelligence because they gather data and render data prognosis on probable threats from previous data instances. Chastain and Smith [2] as well indicate how the use of AI offers mechanism supports, real-time identification of threats, and response to threats which is very vital in cases of cyber defense. Through AI, organizations are able to decode massive threat information and report deviations much faster than analysts could accomplish alone [15]. Moreover, Rodriguez and Costa [3] give an insight into applying the predictive threat intelligence in government networks that use ML to analyze data and anticipate threats.

The application of AI in cybersecurity creates improvement in several defense mechanisms such as network monitoring and intrusion detection. According to Edwards [14], dynamic network analysis is a powerful tool in which AI-based monitoring and identification of suspicious patterns can be employed and followed by more efficient and quicker action from the organization. In addition, AI and ML in threat intelligence enforce a zero-trust model, assuming every network request is malicious until proven otherwise, which improves protection from unauthorized access [5].

7.5.3 Proactive Security Measures for Enhanced Defense

Innovative paradigms of security management are shifting to actions that address threats before they actually occur and include MTD and deception technologies. MTD is more effective in network security, which involves constant changes of settings to make it hard for the attacker to penetrate the system. It also limits the reconnoiter capability of the potential attackers as well as adds confusion for any potential attacker as their defense model is constantly in a state of evolution [18]. Another proactive measure in cybersecurity is cyber deception, where an organization develops fake environments or decoys in order to ensure attackers do not harm real assets. This technique, as proposed by Steingartner et al. [23], is particularly helpful in industrial control systems with the primary goal of protecting the vital assets. Misleading situations consume the attacker's resources and can otherwise expose the ways as well as the goals he or she has.

7.5.4 Threat Hunting and Advanced Monitoring Techniques

Threat hunting is a complex, proactive security activity that assumes the existence of threat intelligence within an organization. It entails constantly hunting for risks that cannot be dealt with by normal security measures. According to Tahmasebi [16], the threat intelligence data improves threat hunting by giving information on present threats, making it easier for hunters to uncover latent or inactive threats. This approach enhances network monitoring since it attempts to identify possible security flaws by conducting an extensive study [20].

Portal monitoring, also blended with proactive defense mechanisms, including firewalls and IDS, is important approach to combating cybersecurity threats. Firewalls commonly functioning as the first layer of defense are enhancing with promising performances in responding to advanced threats [21, 24]. Contemporary IDS tools integrate AI and ML to continuously analyze traffic data to identify malicious actions, thus helping organizations respond to threats as soon as possible [8].

7.5.5 Cyber Resilience and Business Continuity

Cyber resilience has become an important objective for today's organizations as it focuses on the availability of adequate preventive and responsive mechanisms to support organizational functions in the context of cyber threats. AL-Hawamleh [9] has also described cyber resilience that looks at enhancing the relevant defense with the continuation of business operations. Different from previous ones, this framework not only focuses on the issues of security controls but the factors of detecting and responding mechanisms to security incidents so as for organizations to continue their operations after incidents with the least impact. Thus, threat intelligence and the activities that are pursued in its framework are of great importance if one wants to maintain a sufficient level of cybersecurity. Therefore, the use of AI, ML, and other techniques, such as MTD and deception, assists organizations in containing emerging cyber threats. The implementation of the presented strategies contributes to the development of a strong and flexible defense that is capable to overcome and overcome critical actions.

7.6 Endpoint Detection and Response and Extended Detection and Response

The basic programs of the present protection systems, endpoint detection and response (EDR) and extended detection and response (XDR) are used to detect and investigate sophisticated cyber threats. As threats in cyberspace change, EDR is seen to offer increased insight and innovation with an entirely new XDR offering, even greater control over network protection, which allows organizations to be proactive against complex attacks.

7.6.1 Endpoint Detection and Response: Capabilities and Limitations

EDR deals mainly with identifying and mitigating risks at endpoints that include but are not limited to computers, servers, and mobile devices. EDR works in real time for data collection and follows the behavioral analysis and other automated features to detect any threats. Nair [12] highlighted that some EDR solutions include capabilities such as behavioral monitoring, malware analysis, and incident response workflows. These features help mitigate threats arising from the rapid expansion of network environments. In fact, the strength of EDR is the identification of behaviors associated with attacks unique to endpoints, which is effective for dealing with zero-day vulnerabilities and other endpoint-related threats [20]. But the use of EDR solutions also has its drawbacks. For example, they may not have the comprehensive picture across various layers of the organization's environment to identify polymorphic attacks, including those that target both endpoints and the cloud concurrently. As Alshamrani et al. [1] note, EDR is rather good in endpoint threats, but it often fails to detect threats which move through layers of the network outside the endpoint, such as APTs that target complex interconnected systems.

7.6.2 Extended Detection and Response: Expanding Beyond the Endpoint

XDR was introduced and designed to advance from EDR and improve the capabilities of detecting threats throughout the layers of IT infrastructure. The approach of XDR is to collect data from different layers of security such as network traffic, cloud services, mail services, among others, in order to provide a consolidated threat detection and response solution. This holistic view enhances threat detection and response in various contexts, since data from different sources is correlated and analyzed collectively, as discussed by Chastain and Smith [2].

XDR offers centralized access possible because that personal visibility is crucial in its capacity to identify innovative approaches to circumventing current endpoint security measures. For example, Edwards [14] explains that XDR covers threats by applying deep analytics and ML for identifying threat patterns in various domains and offers better chances of discovering lateral motion and synchronized attacks across an organization's whole digital environment. This ability to correlate data sources also makes XDR give context-aware alerts that will help reduce the time and effort needed for investigation.

7.6.3 Endpoint Detection and Response vs. Extended Detection and Response in Threat Detection and Response

EDR and XDR are both designed for improving threat detection capabilities in organizations; however, the efficacy depends on the type of threats that exist or the organization's infrastructure. EDR is better at endpoint protection and dealing with endpoint threats, so it is loved for the spaces where most threats originate from endpoints. On the other hand, cross-layer adaptability of XDR as a tool enforces it as a solution for organizations that have intricate, fractured network that requires a comprehensive security solution [13]. As for the APT incidents, XDR has an effective approach. Alshamrani et al. [1] provide an illustration of how APTs shift from one domain to another as a technique of avoiding detection and hence the need to have a solution such as XDR. The above benefits of XDR are, however, countered by a higher complexity that renders integration difficult and attracts higher levels of expertise for implementation [3].

7.6.4 Advances in Endpoint Detection and Response and Extended Detection and Response Technologies

EDR has now evolved to XDR and AI and ML are being added to both to increase the efficacy of threat detection and minimize false alarms. Therefore, Oroy and Anderson [7] have identified that integration of AI allows these systems to learn progressively new forms of attack on their own, the more complex threat forms, since such forms change frequently. Since the attackers themselves are prone to following certain patterns, ML-based EDR/XDR provides more effective means for proactive defense due to the historical data analysis.

Additionally, the use of threat intelligence feeds and predictive analytics in EDR and XDR solutions further strengthens their defense mechanisms by providing timely information on emerging threats and known indicators of compromise [26]. These capabilities are essential for addressing increasingly complex attack vectors that leverage AI to evade detection.

7.6.5 Summary

EDR and XDR are such significant innovations in the domain of cybersecurity, which provide value for cybersecurity solutions in today's digital world. Though EDR is still a fundamental component of endpoint security, XDR offers the level of visibility required for fighting more complex threats. This study demonstrates the importance of AI and ML to organizations as they act to develop sophisticated cybersecurity solutions to counter complex cyber threats [8]. Implementing both solutions as part of a total cybersecurity plan means that the organization will hedge its bets against deeper attacks by cyber hackers.

7.7 Cloud Security Posture Management and Cloud Workload Protection

Consequently, Cloud Security Posture Management (CSPM) and cloud workload protection (CWP) are the two new models that should be implemented in cloud settings. These are management frameworks used to assess cloud security risks and the level of compliance with security standard practices through visibility and conformance features and the capability of identifying emerging security threats in real time.

7.7.1 Cloud Security Posture Management

CSPM is a method and tool that addresses cloud security management by highlighting misconfiguration, policy breaches, and security issues in cloud infrastructure. CSPM tools scan cloud infrastructures against compliance and security policies, performing a continuous configuration check against benchmarks and policies to decrease the potential of vulnerabilities impacting cloud settings [14, 20]. It is noteworthy that proper CSPM is very important for decreasing the probability of APTs, since the misconfigurations in the cloud environment are popular among them [1].

They are most useful where the organization uses multiple clouds or a mix of private and public clouds, since a large-scale setup has more inherent risks of misconfiguration. CSPM can create the handling of security assessments, which may, in turn, reduce the general workload on security professionals since policy infringements can be perpetrated in real time without being detected. This continuous assessment approach fits well with the current threat-hunting model that is proactive and fully automated to detect possible breaches within cloud structures [4, 11].

7.7.2 Cloud Workload Protection

Compared with CWP, cyber workforce development (CWD) is intended specifically for workloads and applications that operate within cloud environments on virtual machines, containers, or in serverless environments. CWP tools enable runtime protection, malware, and vulnerability control with CWP for modern distributed cloud workloads. When deployed with sophisticated defense mechanisms, Cloud Workload Protection (CWP) solutions safeguard applications against both known and emerging attacks, thereby strengthening cyber-resilience in cloud computing environments [3, 9]. Implementations of CWP solutions bring in elements of zero trust and network segmentation to promote adherence of the workloads only to trusted networks. This approach improves defense by compartmentalizing the workloads to reduce the blast radius in the unfortunate scenario of a breach. Furthermore, today's CWP applications may use ML algorithms to detect suspicious activity in cloud workloads, known for their high effectiveness in early threat identification [2, 15].

7.7.3 Integrating Cloud Security Posture Management and Cloud Workload Protection

Integration of CSPM and CWP ensures the cloud infrastructures and workloads are secure at the same time. CSPM and CWP together can act as the multilayer protective shield by the external cloud scheme and the internal protection aspect in the working of clouds [26]. This can be classified as the defense-in-depth principle, a concept that mainly involves creating multiple layers of defense to combat distinct threats [10, 12].

For organizations, CSPM and CWP have a synergy since they provide improved visibility into the current state and activity of cloud resources. With the visibility and threat intelligence available in real time, organizations are well placed to prevent threats before they act, something critical when operating in cloud environments where threats are constantly emerging or changing [17, 27].

7.7.4 Challenges and Future Directions

However, there are various issues that are still unaddressed in ensuring complete cloud environment security, even with the strengths of CSPM and CWP. While cloud architectures grow more extensive, so does the challenge of managing security at different layers and services, and this results in challenges in achieving congruency of security stances [19]. Additionally, the risk of embedded vulnerabilities in automation within CSPM and CWP tools is also changing as are current and future threat environments [13]. The future trends for CSPM and CWP would be to integrate it with "Artificial Intelligence—AI" and "Machine learning" in order to forecast the threats and plan to control and manage the security more efficiently to analyze the further depth of the threats that forms part of cloud security management [5, 28]. Also, the research with regards to MTD solutions for cloud infrastructures has been continuously emerging and could enhance cloud security by gradually hardening environments against new forms of threats [6, 18]. Faced with further increase in the complexity of cloud environments, the role of CSPM and CWP will only increase in the future. The incorporation of the above solutions enables to realization of strong cloud security frameworks and the flexibility required to counter growing cloud threats [24, 29].

7.8 Artificial Intelligence and Machine Learning in Cyber Defense

The use of AI and ML in cybersecurity has made advances for threat identification, reaction, and instantaneous adaptation to new threats. These technologies combine to allow cyber defense systems to be predictive in nature, not only in their ability to detect threats, but in being able to prevent possible attacks from occurring.

7.8.1 Predictive Threat Intelligence

Some of the most commonly used AI and ML methods for discovering cyber threats are focused on using predictive analytics. They include methods of looking at large volumes of data in order to identify exceptions that may represent a threat. For example, Rodriguez and Costa [3] explain that AI predictive threat intelligence is more common in government networks to prevent cyber terrorism act by predicting threats before they happen. This predictive capability then not only further expands the defensive veil but can also predict threats well before compromising assets of critical systems.

7.8.2 Advanced Threat Detection

The use cases of AI in cybersecurity include superior threat detection, which reinforces the process of differentiating between complex activities, including various scams like phishing and ransomware. As Nair [12] has noted, the characteristics of these threats can be analyzed through ML models, specifically to help an organization notice and counter an attack. This capability is especially useful in identifying more subtle and less “loud” threats that typical architectures may well miss, including APTs [1]. The employment of AI in threat hunting has been described in several reports. To illustrate, Badva et al. [4] reflect upon how AI is utilized in present-day threat hunting, which is a proactive endeavor of searching for threats intranet. It advances these practices by boosting the detection of sophisticated patterns of attack, allowing cybersecurity teams to act more effectively.

7.8.3 Real-Time Network Monitoring and Adaptive Defense

AI and ML also play their part in credible network monitoring on a real-time basis that would allow organizations to take action against credible cyber threats in real time. Edwards [14] also mentions that AI helps in having constant vigilance on networks and whence it prevents threats as they take their course by having defenses that counter them. Utilization of smart defense measures that can change the course of the preferred safety methods depending on the assessed level of danger makes organizations stronger against attacks. On this premise, Chastain and Smith [2] provide a view on how AI is used in cyber defense changes and grows to deal with emerging threats. This flexibility is important in order to counter cyber threats which may pose a new threat that needs to be anticipated and countered.

7.8.4 Automating Incident Response

Another essential change that the AI brings to cybersecurity is the automation of reactions to security incidents. AI systems can themselves assess the extent of an attack, determine the areas under threat, and set the response mechanisms in motion, all of which can be done in considerably less time than is conceivable in human effort, thus keeping the losses in check. For instance, Oroy and Anderson [7] describe the implications of AI-enabled technologies, in incident response systems in particular, that deal with incidents on which significant manual interaction is needed. This automation is necessary to address huge cyber calamities while maintaining business continuity.

7.8.5 Enhancing Defense-in-Depth Strategies

AI also brings about defense in depth techniques by acting as an extra layer to improve the defense of a particular system. As McMahon [10] explains that defense-in-depth is an approach to security that puts in place a number of protective barriers and layers that interconnect, and AI adds the value of providing more information that might go unnoticed when using other forms of defense. For instance, it can recognize the flow from one part of a network to another, which is typical of APTs, and initiate a corresponding response [6]. AI, when used as a part of a multilayered security strategy, can enhance the effectiveness of organization's security measures.

7.8.6 Artificial-Intelligence-Driven Cyber Deception Techniques

Another area, where AI is proving to be very useful is cyber deception. Thus, the AI-based deception techniques encompass chimerical systems or networks that resemble valuable targets, thereby giving data regarding attackers' methods [23]. This approach not only protects real assets but also provides valuable insights into the methods attackers may use in the future.

7.8.7 Moving Target Defense

The idea known as MTD makes systems more dynamic and makes them harder for attackers to penetrate. MTD strategies are constantly changing the settings of systems and networks so as not to allow the attacker to take root [18]. When implementing AI into MTD, attackers are likely to find it challenging to breach due to these changes being made dynamically in real time.

7.8.8 Implications for Future Cyber Defense

AI use in cybersecurity is making advancements in defense systems and structures more effective. AI technology is gradually developing, and the application of this technology in an organization's cybersecurity is poised to move up a higher level, incorporating more protective measures. As observed by Mahboudi et al. [11], future studies may investigate applying the general performance enhancement principle through improvements that could enhance the AI-based techniques deployed on cyber defense so that it is more adaptive, secure, and resistant to threats that it has yet to encounter. In conclusion, both AI and ML bring a new approach to the world of cybersecurity and cyber defense. These technologies have become effective means of threat identification, response, and adaptation, allowing organizations to address the current and future threats more effectively. Hence, using advanced concepts such as predictive intelligence, automated incident response, and real-time monitoring, AI has brought a strong and concrete framework for better cybersecurity protection and a defense system.

7.9 Secure Access Service Edge and Network Security Innovations

Thus, there is a progressive development of fresh concepts in cybersecurity as a result of higher levels of threat complexity. This has seen the emergence of what has been described as the secure access service edge (SASE) model. SASE is a solution that combines elements of networking and security to give organizations a single solution for end-to-end protection, with no regard for the user's location or the device they are using. In this part, let us examine what has been described as SASE's essential fundamentals and how the concept offers improvements to the security of networks, as well as newer innovations that can contribute to this model.

7.9.1 The Fundamentals of Secure Access Service Edge

SASE consolidates what has become several essential capabilities into a cloud-delivered architecture, such as software-defined wide area network (SD-WAN), secure web gateway (SWG), Cloud Access Security Broker (CASB), and zero trust network access (ZTNA). When integrated, these technologies are delivered through SASE to give organizations an integrated solution that maintains high levels of security, and at the same time offers better performance and the ability to scale.

1) **Cloud-Native Architecture**: Due to SASE's cloud approach, security and networking can be delivered to users and devices at the edge, reducing latency and increasing access time [1]. This architecture allows for real-time change in security policies and access controls necessary to counter new cutting-edge threats [19].
2) **Zero Trust Security Model**: Zero-trust security model is one of the fundamental concepts of SASE that aims to authenticate every person and device, which seeks to gain access to any resource regardless of the location of the person or the device behind the access request. This approach reduces possible harm from insider threats and stolen credentials [5].
3) **Unified Security Policies**: SASE enables one policy to be administered to all the users and devices and is the right approach because otherwise, mistakes can be made in the configuration of the security policy. This is necessary to ensure compliance and interoperability as well as offer high level and homogenous security across disparate networking settings [14].

7.9.2 Enhancing Network Security Through Secure Access Service Edge

SASE brings dramatic changes in the network security paradigm, taking into account the deficiencies of perimeter security models. The following are key innovations that enhance network security within the SASE framework:

1) **Advanced Threat Detection**: Most SASE solutions will include AI and ML as elements to help improve threat detection. These technologies scan through large traffics in real time to find out peculiarities that may be overlooked by usual protection systems [8, 25].
2) **Integrated Threat Intelligence**: Integrated threat intelligence feeds help SASE solutions offer active protection from APTs and other intelligent cyber threats. This intelligence assists companies to estimate the breaches and modify their security policy in advance [2, 11].
3) **Enhanced Visibility and Monitoring**: As SASE solutions are built to support networking, they come with extensive visibility and monitoring features with which security professionals are able to monitor user actions or potential threats and respond to them in real time. Visibility is critical in the recognition of risks and compliance with the principles set legislation [12, 13].

7.9.3 Innovations in Cybersecurity Complementing Secure Access Service Edge

SASE is not only remodeling how networks are safeguarded but also creating solutions that support a better security environment for every brand. Some noteworthy advancements include:

1) **Threat-Hunting Practices**: Cyber defense strategies in today's world are heavily subjugate to threat hunting, which is the process of actively seeking signs of compromise or IOCs. This proactive approach enables organizations to be in a position to discover threats before they grow out of proportion and cause much havoc [4, 20].
2) **Moving Target Defense**: Other protective measures that supplement the mentioned methods are MTDs, where the attack surface is constantly in a state of change. This approach makes the task of cyber adversaries difficult and is thus effective in preventing attacks [6, 18].

3) **Comprehensive Cyber Resilience**: Companies are switching to frameworks concerned with cyber resilience which is the ability to carry on operations in the face of a cyberattack. This involves the alignment of security measures to business continuity planning and disaster recovery plans [9, 16].
4) **Integration of Quantum Cryptography**: Kinds of risks change over time and so do the practices of handling and addressing them. The integration of quantum cryptography gives potential for enhancement in securing communication and data for the future [30].

7.9.4 Summary

SASE is among the most recent innovations in the cybersecurity world that puts a framework at the center of securing an organization's networks and improving the flexibility and performance of networks. In addition to the present problems, SASE is a new architecture that incorporates ML, threat intelligence, and zero-trust principles to protect against presently existing as well as future threats. Hence, while organizations remain committed to establishing processes suited to the contemporary world, the adoption of SASE and related solutions will be crucial to protecting processes from new threats and being on the same level as cyberattackers.

7.10 Security Orchestration, Automation, and Response

A security operation center (SOC) and security operations are ways of describing procedures for incorporating technology to analyze security threats and risks in organizations. The key objective of Security Orchestration, Automation, and Response (SOAR) is to help reinstate control and automate processes involved in incident response and expedite the overall security response for any threat that may occur in an organization. Integrated security operations and risk solutions enable the consolidation of processes, giving the security group rich automation capabilities, seamless integration of work, and a means of improving organizational alignment and security cooperation.

7.10.1 The Need for SOAR in Modern Cybersecurity

With intensification of the cyber threats, the management and response to such incidents are a challenge to organizations. The number of alarms provided by numerous security technologies can be staggering, along with filter fatigue and the time taken to recognize and respond to each attack [31]. SOAR solves these challenges in the following way since it automates the process of filtering, prioritization, and response to threats. This is not only helpful to the security analysts since they're relieved of the burden of having to sort through numerous threats but also convenient since important threats are easily dealt with. Further, Alshamrani et al. [1] pointed out that APTs has changed a lot, and much more powerful means need to be deployed to protect from the threats. Originally, SOAR was designed to offer organizations the ability to incorporate threat intelligence, respond to threats automatically, prepare and execute incident response plans, which could help employees deal with more challenging security issues.

7.10.2 Components of SOAR

SOAR solutions typically consist of three key components:

1) **Security Automation**: This is the process of pre-scripting or preplanning how the security team will respond to a security event. For example, if phishing is identified, then SOAR can

immediately block the account which was compromised, notify the actual user and the security team, and minimize response time [2].

2) **Orchestration**: This component also provides the possibility of nesting the existing security tools and platforms into a single system. With the integration of various systems, SOAR makes it easy to pass data and information from one tool and transfer to another such as the security information and event management (SIEM) systems, threat intelligence platform (TIP), and Endpoint Protection (EP) solutions [10].
3) **Incident Response**: SOAR solutions help within the general approach to security incident management. The guidelines of the sample plan also involve different incident severity levels, a communication plan, and post-incident analysis to improve successive reaction [19].

7.10.3 Benefits of SOAR

The implementation of SOAR solutions offers several advantages to organizations, including:

- **Improved Efficiency**: Another advantage of using SOAR for security operations is in displacing most conventional repetitive tasks and leaving the analysts with more fulfilling roles. This results in enhanced timeframe and swifter resolution of security events [12].
- **Enhanced Threat Detection**: Using ML and AI, SOAR solutions can analyze security data and look for patterns or any anomalies which ultimately helps them to quickly determine the potential threats [8].
- **Consistent Responses**: Automated responses put into action ensure the management of every incident is guided by common procedures without the probability of inconsistency resulting from human mistakes [26].
- **Collaboration Across Teams**: SOAR improves the overall communication between the security, IT, and business aspects, thus evolving a collaborative approach to cybersecurity [2].

7.10.4 Challenges in Implementing SOAR

As we shall learn, there are a number of challenges that organizations face in the implementation of SOAR. Sharing of data and information across security tools may be cumbersome, and organizations may experience interconnectivity problems between the existing security tools and new SOAR platforms [11]. Furthermore, there are always one or two challenges every time SOAR solutions are being deployed; sufficient training and change management plans are needed for the successful implementation [13]. In addition, when organizations pursue optimal performance and dynamics continue to unfold, there is always a requirement to review and update the playbooks for automation and the response strategies to address the growing threats at regular intervals [16]. Thus, it is worthwhile to assume that the efficiency of the solutions provided by the SOAR approach may decrease over time if updates are not made regularly.

7.10.5 Summary

Security orchestration, automation, and response or SOAR is an evolutionary leap in this sphere that gives organizations tools that can help them improve their security posture with a constantly evolving threat environment. SOAR helps in creating features that extend, automate, orchestrate, enhance, plus triage across security operation centers and rallying abilities for representing and mitigating cyber threats. Thus, the necessity of utilizing the SOAR approach in order to create adequately protective cybersecurity strategies increases with threats' further development.

7.11 Post-breach Detection and Response Techniques

In the fast-changing security environment where a breach is inevitable, the implications insist on strong detection and response capabilities. The problem also reveals that organizations can not only manage the direct consequences of a cyberattack but also build their capacity to address future threats. The following section discusses further post-breach detection and response methods related to the topic of the chapter while taking into account the findings of the recent literature and real-world experiences.

7.11.1 Importance of Timely Detection

Cyber breaches should therefore be detected as early as possible in order to reduce the impact and come up with a solution early enough. Modern organizations apply technologies of automated monitoring in order to stably react to anomalies and possible threats. Edwards [14] says that monitoring of the network is essential in early detection of a breach since traffic is continuously analyzed to identify a security breach. In the same way, Alshamrani et al. [1] also talk about APTs and the problem of their concealment, saying that more complex detection methods have to be employed in order to notice such threats.

7.11.2 Threat Hunting Practices

Threat hunting is an important activity during the post-breach phase; one of the engineering functions that has been identified is proactive threat hunting. This practice is focused on the search for threats which have somehow escaped the efforts of an organization's security systems. In the following paragraphs of this writing, Badva et al. [4] provide a comprehensive analysis of threat hunting and different approaches that organizations may adopt as well as some of the difficulties organizations are likely to encounter when executing the methodologies. Through threat intelligence and context data, one can even track and dismantle threats as they occur, instead of waiting for them to grow into a full-blown cyberattack.

7.11.3 Incident Response Frameworks

Hence, it is critical for organizations to have a well-coordinated plan for managing the breaches commonly referred to as an incident response framework. Thus, regular protection measures need to be developed for the detection, containment, elimination of viral outbreaks, as well as the subsequent recovery. AL-Hawamleh et al. [9] offered a cyber resilience framework that not only builds up a business's protection but also optimizes its functioning during a cyberattack. This framework focuses on the management of various approaches toward the response, such as automatic and manual response mechanisms, which together ensure incidents are addressed through both preprogrammed systems and human-led interventions.

7.11.4 Leveraging Artificial Intelligence

AI is already reshaping the post-breach response in the cybersecurity industry through its integration. Since the use of AI entails massive capabilities of analyzing data, it is possible to detect incidents within a short span that show some system compromise. According to Oroy and Anderson [7], AI plays a key part in the contemporary cybersecurity environment as it optimizes the capabilities of threat detection. Moreover, Tan [15] explained AI and ML solutions and approaches in addressing danger since they are dynamic and can change in response to new threats to help improve security status.

7.11.5 Continuous Improvement through Analysis

An examination of the incident aftermath usually helps in knowing the reasons behind the incidents in order to avoid a repeat in the future. The vulnerability must be examined in order for organizations to perform forensic investigations to make the necessary alterations. Blogger McMahon [10] is in favor of defense-in-depth model that uses multiple layers of security controls to establish a reliable network system. It also assists in identifying breaches and improving security policies and procedures learned from previous security breaches.

7.11.6 Risk Modeling and Contingency Planning

The greater the amount of data and the more centralized its storage, the more complex the risk modeling and contingency planning for post-breach recovery. In order to address the above threat factors, according to Salami et al. [13], new sophisticated threat-modeling frameworks can also be employed for identifying the risks and developing the relevant risk management plans. It is strategic in the sense that threats are identified ahead of time, and strategies for dealing with them are readied in advance so that they can be unleashed the instant the breach take place.

7.11.7 Utilizing Cyber Deception Techniques

Cyber deception is a relatively new concept in developing better methods for detection and response processes. According to Steingartner et al. [23], it is suggested to trick the attackers through deception so that one can learn from them. Emphasizing this particular approach can greatly improve an organization's capacity for insight into threat planes and management of breaches.

7.11.8 Summary

Those methods that are used in the process of post-breach detection and response are valuable to improve the cybersecurity of an organization. In this way, with the help of new technologies, fast and effective reaction, such as the structural implementation of the incident response patterns, constant update of the organizational practices based on best practices and lessons learned, one is confident about the ability to prevent future threats. Given the rapidly changing character of cyberspace, the incorporation of cutting-edge approaches to protection will remain a critical need to sustain security and business operations.

7.12 Emerging Defense Techniques and Future Directions

More and more complex and frequent are the cyber threats to an organization, more important it becomes to constantly adjust the strategies used for protection. This section discusses new trends of defense mechanisms and possible proliferation of anti-APT and other malicious penetrations to increase organizational cybersecurity readiness.

7.12.1 Advanced Threat Hunting Practices

The process of threat hunting is gaining popularity as an early predictive action to take against threats before they compromise an organization's assets or functions. In the chapter, Badva et al. [4] explore the practices of threat hunting and difficulties that arise with the requirements of hiring specialized personnel and implementing modern instruments. The IOCs that are received from threat intelligence feeds help organizations prevent advanced threats [11].

7.12.2 Integration of Artificial Intelligence in Defense Mechanisms

The application of AI and ML in cybersecurity defense is a notable development. These technologies allow for real-time threat detection and proactive handling of incidents [2]. What makes AI useful is the capability of scanning through large quantities of information to search for some patterns that could suggest the possibility of a cyber threat, and the defense measures are enhanced. For instance, Rodriguez and Costa [3] highlight how, through the use of AI, predictive threat intelligence can be improved to strengthen the protective measures in government networks.

7.12.3 Zero Trust Architecture

That is why such a security model as ZTA is rapidly developing, which is based on the denial of trust of any user and device, including those located behind the network perimeter [5]. This does mean that the user identities and device health need to be verified on a constant basis, which offers a strong anti-insider threat and account compromise. ZTA can be achieved in organizations to minimize the attack surface to promote the organization's cybersecurity.

7.12.4 Dynamic Defense Strategies

The ongoing sophisticated threats require dynamic defense mechanisms that are adaptable, and their ground may shift depending on threat intelligence gathered in the field [31]. Strategies like MTD hide the system components, which can by complicated for the attackers to infiltrate the system weaknesses [18]. They must be able to devote time and resources in order to adapt the organizations' defense mechanisms to counter the new threats that are arising.

7.12.5 Cyber Deception Techniques

Cyber deception is a modern approach to anticipating and synthetically leading attackers into decoys and traps. Therefore, through baiting these attackers into interacting with the fake components, organizations are in a position to gather significant information on the mode and purpose of attack [23]. It is also a form of active defense measure that not only redirects threats but also increases visibility and revenue-containing information.

7.12.6 Enhancing Cybersecurity in Emerging Technologies

As cyber-physical systems emerge with devices including the Internet of Things (IoT) and connected vehicles, enhancing security for these systems draws high priority as there are no common approaches adapted for them [28]. As Patel et al. [30] have already stated, there is a need to incorporate higher layers of defense mechanisms into those technologies, taking into consideration the confrontation of possible threats. The use of these technologies is steadily on the rise, and countering cyber threats that target these technologies is a requirement.

7.12.7 Future Directions

Looking forward, the following directions should be prioritized to enhance cybersecurity resilience:

1) **Investment in Cybersecurity Workforce Development**: The development of a force of human capital in cybersecurity is essential for the deployment and governance of sophisticated security solutions [20]. The educational programs should therefore concentrate on threat hunting, AI, and deceptive strategies that are likely to be encountered in the near future.
2) **Collaborative Defense Strategies**: There is a concern with organizations and the need to coordinate with each other, as not all threats and the defenses against them are isolated to one business. It can increase joint safety and develop better protection against cyber threats [26].
3) **Continuous Research and Development**: New ideas and approaches need to be developed all the time, and the research in this regard is vitally important in order to outcompete the enemies in cyberspace. Just like threats change over time, it is important that dealing with threats also changes over time [1, 8].
4) **Focus on Regulatory Compliance**: Formerly, the particular regulation and compliance issues in cybersecurity have been sensitive for organizations to always be alert to changes in the laws or rules within the business. The knowledge of these regulations is crucial for the purpose of creating successful security strategies for organizations in the future [12].
5) **Resilience Planning**: It is imperative to stress the disaster recovery and resilience planning because it will prepare organizations for effectuating the best response strategy. Presumably, the use of information concerning previous mishaps will improve future responses [16].

7.12.8 Summary

Current and emerging cyber threats are highly diverse, which means that traditional and conventional defense methods alone are no longer sufficient to address them effectively. However, organizational involvement of higher technologies, having trained human capital, and cooperation between entities are helpful in improving the organization's position toward growing threats. Also known as adaptive cybersecurity, the three aspects of AI, ZTA, and dynamic defense strategies will be key to developing the future of cybersecurity.

7.13 Conclusion

In the context of globalization, the general importance of strong information security systems cannot be overemphasized. Indeed, as cyber threats change in terms of sophistication and scale, the urgent requirement for new approaches to protection surfaces. Identifying innovative approaches, including AI, ML, and advanced threat hunting, shows how these novelties can bolster the credibility of cybersecurity frameworks. This way organizations are not only better equipped to mitigate threats and respond to risks, but they are better placed to identify future trends of threats and risks in the changing dynamics of the cyberspace. Implementing modern approaches to protection, including zero-trust security and MTD mechanisms, is utterly new to the security paradigm. These strategies state that ongoing monitoring and the adaptation to emerging threats are key to keeping organizations ahead of the curve with the enemy. Furthermore, the emergence of the human factor into complex cybersecurity discussion means that the training and education of stakeholders need proper attention for satisfactory cybersecurity assurance. As we look to the future, a multisectoral approach, ideas from technology, policy, and end-user behavior will be crucial for constructing the resilient cybersecurity environment. When organizations pursue the creation of elaborate defenses, one must remember to strive for a flexible security environment. In recognizing innovation and collaboration, the cybersecurity community will be able to move in a direction that will make the digital platform secure, not only for important data, but also for users and stakeholders. All in all, the threats rooted in cyberspace are very significant even if they are sophisticated; the shift in defense mechanisms and active participation of organizations altogether ensure a secure future. Focused efforts to embed new and advanced technologies in the line of duty, together with a clear perception of the threat environment, will, in the long run, improve the strength as well as the impact of cybersecurity approaches in the global markets.

References

1 Alshamrani, A., Myneni, S., Chowdhary, A., and Huang, D. (2019). A survey on advanced persistent threats: techniques, solutions, challenges, and research opportunities. *IEEE Communications Surveys & Tutorials* 21 (2): 1851–1877.

2 Chastain, K. and Smith, J. (2024). Cybersecurity reinvented: the integration of AI defense mechanisms. *EasyChair*.

3 Rodriguez, P. and Costa, I. (2024). Artificial intelligence and machine learning for predictive threat intelligence in government networks. *Advances in Computer Sciences.* 7 (1): 1–10.

4 Badva, P., Ramokapane, K.M., Pantano, E., and Rashid, A. (2024). Unveiling the {Hunter-Gatherers}: Exploring Threat Hunting Practices and Challenges in Cyber Defense. *33rd USENIX Security Symposium (USENIX Security 24).* 3313–3330.

5 Patil, K., Desai, B., Mehta, I., and Patil, A. (2023). A contemporary approach: zero trust architecture for cloud-based fintech services. *Innovative Computer Sciences Journal* 9 (1).

6 Sengupta, S., Chowdhary, A., Sabur, A. et al. (2020). A survey of moving target defenses for network security. *IEEE Communications Surveys & Tutorials.* 22 (3): 1909–1941.

7 Oroy, B. and Anderson, J. (2024). Cyber Sentry: How AI Shapes Modern Cyber Defense Strategies. EasyChair.

8 Iqbal, S., Rizvi, S.W.A., Haider, M.H., and Raza, S. (2023). Artificial intelligence in security and defense: explore the integration of AI in military strategies, security policies, and its implications for global power dynamics. *International Journal of Human and Society.* 3 (4): 341–353.

9 AL-Hawamleh, A. (2024). Cyber resilience framework: strengthening defenses and enhancing continuity in business security. *International Journal of Computing and Digital Systems* 15 (1): 1315–1331.

10 McMahon, D. (2014). Beyond perimeter defense: defense-in-depth leveraging upstream security. In: *Best Practices in Computer Network Defense: Incident Detection and Response*, 43–53. IOS Press.

11 Mahboubi, A., Luong, K., Aboutorab, H. et al. (2024). Evolving techniques in cyber threat hunting: a systematic review. *Journal of Network and Computer Applications* 104004.

12 Nair, S.S. (2024). Securing against advanced cyber threats: a comprehensive guide to phishing, XSS, and SQL injection defense. *Journal of Computer Science and Technology Studies* 6 (1): 76–93.

13 Salami, A.A., Igwenagu, U.T.I., Mesode, C.E. et al. (2024). Beyond conventional threat defense: Implementing advanced threat modeling techniques, risk modeling frameworks and contingency planning in the healthcare sector for enhanced data security. *Journal of Engineering Research and Reports* 26 (5): 304–323.

14 Edwards, D.J. (2024). Network monitoring and defense. In: *Critical security controls for effective cyber defense: a comprehensive guide to CIS 18 controls*, 371–404. Springer.

15 Tan, A. (2024). Enhancing cyber defense mechanisms: AI and machine learning-based threat mitigation strategies. *Journal of Quantum Science and Technology* 1 (3): 90–93.

16 Tahmasebi, M. (2024). Beyond defense: proactive approaches to disaster recovery and threat intelligence in modern enterprises. *Journal of Information Security.* 15 (2): 106–133.

17 Uchiyama, N. and Oroy, K. (2024). Sentinels in the digital realm: AI's influence on cyber defense strategies. EasyChair.

18 Soussi, W., Christopoulou, M., Xilouris, G., and Gür, G. (2021). Moving target defense as a proactive defense element for beyond 5G. *IEEE Communications Standards Magazine* 5 (3): 72–79.

19 Ogungbemi, O.S., Ezeugwa, F.A., Olaniyi, O.O., et al. (2024). Overcoming remote workforce cyber threats: a comprehensive ransomware and bot net defense strategy utilizing VPN networks. Available at SSRN 4911878.

20 El-Amir, S. (2023). Comprehensive cybersecurity review: modern threats and innovative defense approaches. *International Journal of Computers and Informatics* 1: 30–37.

21 Gudimetla, S.R. (2015). Beyond the barrier: advanced strategies for firewall implementation and management. *NeuroQuantology* 13 (4): 558–565.

22 Rubio, J.E., Alcaraz, C., and Lopez, J. (2020). Game theory-based approach for defense against apts. Applied Cryptography and Network Security: 18th International Conference, ACNS 2020, Rome, Italy, October 19–22, 2020, Proceedings, Part II 18. Springer. 297–320.

23 Steingartner, W., Galinec, D., and Kozina, A. (2021). Threat defense: cyber deception approach and education for resilience in hybrid threats model. *Symmetry (Basel).* 13 (4): 597.

24 Sipho, N. and Thandeka, M. (2020). Firewall Mastery: Advanced Strategies for Implementation and Digital Defense. *International Journal of Trend in Scientific Research and Development.* 4 (3): 1243–1249.

25 Smith, J. and Anderson, J. (2024). AI's Watchful Eye: Strengthening Cyber Defense as Guardians of the Virtual Gate. EasyChair.

26 Obi, O.C., Akagha, O.V., Dawodu, S.O. et al. (2024). Comprehensive review on cybersecurity: modern threats and advanced defense strategies. *Computer Science & IT Research Journal* 5 (2): 293–310.

27 Foti, E., Musumeci, R.E., and Stagnitti, M. (2020). Coastal defence techniques and climate change: a review. *Rendiconti Lincei. Scienze Fisiche e Naturali* 31 (1): 123–138.

28 Pham, M. and Xiong, K. (2021). A survey on security attacks and defense techniques for connected and autonomous vehicles. *Computers and Security* 109: 102269.

29 Wu, J. and Wu, J. (2020). New approaches to cyber defense. In: *Cyberspace Mimic Defense: Generalized Robust Control and Endogenous Security* (ed. J. Wu), 113–157. Springer Nature.

30 Patel, C.D., Aggarwal, M., and Chaubey, N.K. (2025). Enhancing cyber-physical systems security through advanced defense mechanisms. In: *Advancing Cyber Security Through Quantum Cryptography* (ed. N.K. Chaubey and N. Chaubey), 307–342. IGI Global.

31 Saffar, M. and Naji, H.R. (2022). Increasing the security of advanced metering infrastructure using dynamic defense methods. *2022 12th Smart Grid Conference (SGC).* IEEE. 1–5.

8

Practical Applications and Case Studies

Marwan Omar

Information Technology and Management, Illinois Institute of Technology, Chicago, USA

8.1 Introduction

Security of information is now a fundamental necessity in virtually all fields of endeavor given the interconnectivity of modern society. Cybersecurity strategies make it possible to appreciate how to approach, evaluate, and address actual, real-life security risks. This part explores cybersecurity solutions and products; it overviews consequential defense-in-depth measures; it displays and discusses current and future technologies as well as multiple layers protecting various Internet threats, compromising the Internet of Things (IoT), critical infrastructure (CI), financial information, and more. First of all, it is worth mentioning that the threats in the field of cybersecurity have changed throughout the years. The following is a timeline graph that highlights the main types of cyber threats that have emerged in the years as shown in the following (Figure 8.1).

8.1.1 The Importance of Practical Application in Cybersecurity

As it was mentioned, cybersecurity is facing much more intricate issues and, therefore, requires much more than pure knowledge obtained at university. In this way, it can be seen that organizations allow for various practical implementations, whereas the defense-in-depth approach, which means the use of a series of security techniques, can be evaluated for its efficiency. This approach is supported by real-world examples and highlights the effectiveness and potential weaknesses of cybersecurity measures depending on environment heterogeneity [1, 2]. All these studies demonstrate how threats are managed in real organizations and, hence, provide rich resources for both theorists and practitioners.

8.1.2 Evolution of Cybersecurity Threats and Applications

In the type C world, the threat vectors range from malware, ransomware, and other brand new complex adversarial threats with artificial intelligence (AI) backing up the attacks on key infrastructures [3, 4]. The measures to counter each type of cyber threat depend on each of them individually. Machine learning (ML) and AI have emerged as critical to creating the applications that can effectively and, more importantly, adaptively identify and address these threats [5, 6]. For instance, predicting analytics has become possible to identify deviations that may indicate an attack and allow for a timely response [7]. AI and ML have brought significant improvement to methods

Defense in Depth: Modern Cybersecurity Strategies and Evolving Threats, First Edition. Edited by Hewa Majeed Zangana.

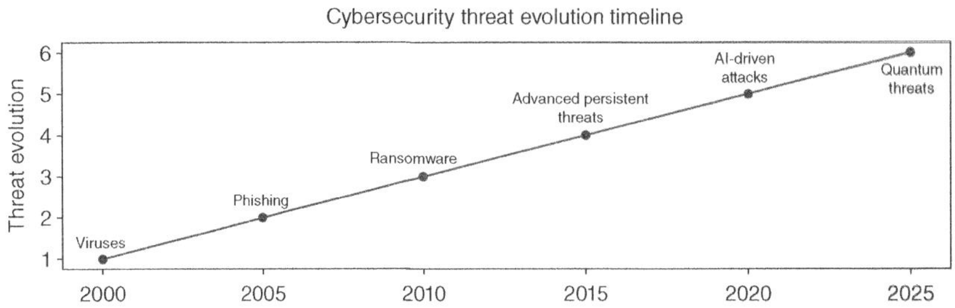

Figure 8.1 Evolution of cybersecurity threats. Source: Hewa Majeed Zangana.

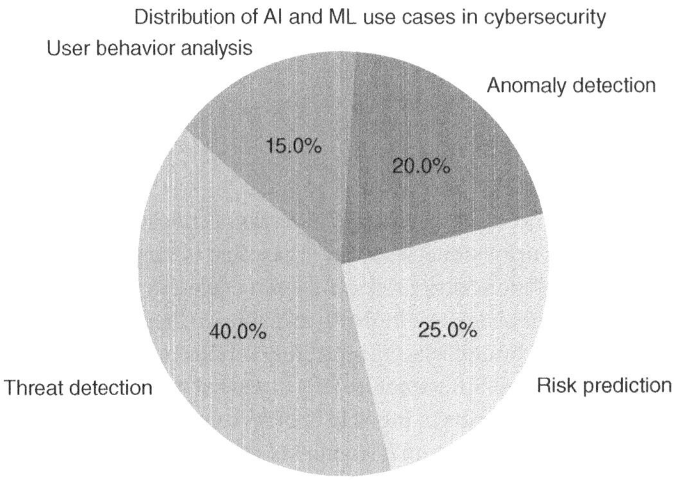

Figure 8.2 Impact of AI and ML in cybersecurity. Source: Hewa Majeed Zangana.

involving the identification of risks and ways of handling them. The following pie chart presents the distribution of AI and ML in organizations' cybersecurity uses (Figure 8.2).

8.1.3 Case Studies as Learning Models in Cybersecurity

The use of case-based method to investigate cybersecurity measures helps close the theory–application divide, whereas an example is shown, providing specific recommendations and proved applications in practice [8, 9]. For example, examples of uses of ML in threat detection importance of AI in quickly identifying threats and addressing cybersecurity threats is discussed [10]. In the same way, realistic case scenarios give an example of how others have implemented and adapted successful security models to fit an organization, depending on the need and threat levels.

8.1.4 Key Areas of Application

Cybersecurity applications span various domains, each with unique requirements:

- **IoT Security**: IoT devices are increasingly being used in homes, businesses, and industries, denoting the weaknesses that they bring in as they require specialized security solutions. For instance, the current research focuses on the need to adopt countermeasures unique to IoT networks in order to enhance security against unauthorized access and data compromise [11, 12].

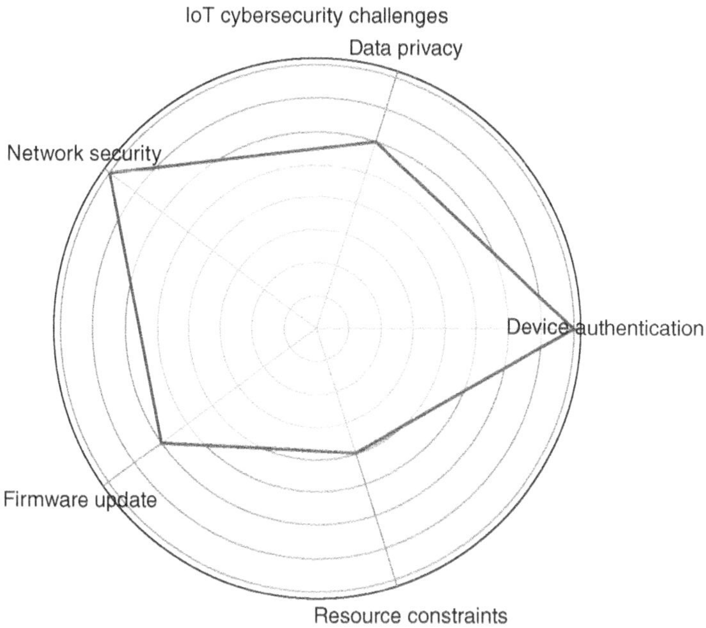

Figure 8.3 Common cybersecurity challenges in IoT. Source: Hewa Majeed Zangana.

As IoT devices are designed with networking capabilities and are deployed in large numbers, IoT device access control is more complex than traditional computing devices' access control. The following radar chart illustrates the big picture of difficulties concerning IoT cybersecurity (Figure 8.3).

- **Smart Cities**: Smart-city-related structures are more vulnerable to cyber threats because of the integration of different technologies. It uses deep learning techniques for securing smart cities and obtains promising models for anomaly detection and response [1, 13].
- **Financial Data Protection**: The field of finance employs case studies in the planning of secure systems for handling financial data. AI-based cybersecurity solutions in this sector are customized for the requirements of the financial industry, including streaming-based transaction surveillance [14].
- **Critical Infrastructure Protection**: The security of power grids and water supply, as well as other CI, has to be very high—the impact of cyberattacks on these systems is disastrous. Some of the prior research suggests that using reinforcement learning makes the cyber-physical system (CPS) resilient against cyberattacks [15, 16].

8.1.5 Integrating Artificial Intelligence and Machine Learning in Cybersecurity Applications

There is no doubt that the use of AI and ML is altering the way in which cybersecurity applications work. Due to the high data-processing efficiency of AI, the connections between cyber threats and the related patterns can be easily detected and analyzed as soon as possible [17, 18]. Explants on practical implementations of AI in cybersecurity reveal its versatility, especially in progressive authentication and behavioral pattern recognition which are critical in guarding information and structures [19].

8.1.6 Cybersecurity Education and Training through Case Studies

That being said, the practical implementation of cybersecurity principles has also been noticed in contexts of education. The use of case studies in training will also help educators bring real-world ideas to the students and help in giving them many opportunities to grasp more knowledge in cybersecurity [20, 21]. This management strategy gets future cybersecurity specialists acquainted with real-life problem-solving scenarios since the practical orientation of the method outperforms traditional methods with facilitated theoretical learning.

8.2 Case Study: Implementing Zero Trust Architecture in Enterprise Networks

The conventional style of implementing and managing networks has been focused on the centrally positioned network, with technology such as firewalls and intrusion detectors used to protect internal resources from external threats. However, the current increased sophistication of cyber threats and use of cloud solutions, remote work, and IoT devices make this approach ineffective. In response to the above challenges, Zero Trust Architecture (ZTA) has proved to be a strong and smart approach. By design, ZTA approaches assume that there are no default trusting relationships that should be placed with internal or external actors and constantly assess what is and is not allowed by formal security policies [20, 22]. Intrusion detection systems (IDS) are especially important in enabling the identification of an intrusion or an anomalous situation. The following flowchart shows the general design of an IDS and a general process of how the IDS detects and generates an alert (Figure 8.4).

8.2.1 Overview of Zero Trust Architecture

ZTA is a model where security controls are enforced for every connection, regardless of location. This framework prescribes the need to regularly check such accesses; it emphasizes identity-based

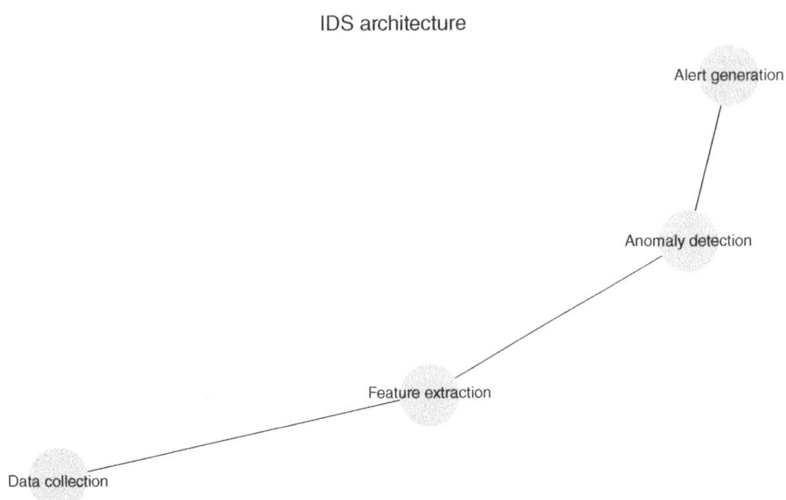

Figure 8.4 Intrusion detection system architecture. Source: Hewa Majeed Zangana.

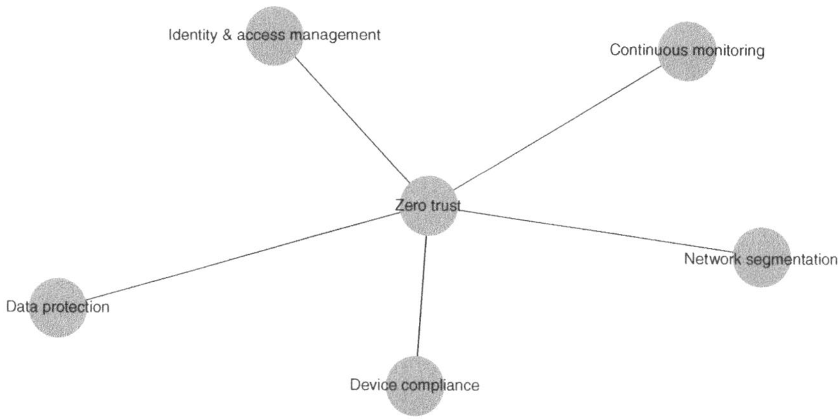

Figure 8.5 Zero trust architecture components. Source: Hewa Majeed Zangana.

access control as well as the principle of least privilege [16, 23]. Such a framework minimizes the chances of having an intruder, data leakage, or an attacker moving from one part of the network to another. That is why ZTA is relevant in a modern enterprise environment, where APTs and well-organized phishing attacks can successfully work through users even in the most protected perimeters [24]. We apply identity-based verification and a series of access control measures to enforce the principles of ZTA. The following diagram displays the main elements of ZTA, where identity and access management, network segmentation, and continuous monitoring are described (Figure 8.5).

8.2.2 Implementation Steps and Key Components

1) **Identity and Access Management**: Identity and access management (IAM) systems create the basis of ZTA since they enforce strict user and device authentication, limiting access to network resources. Multifactor authentication (MFA), single sign-on (SSO), and adaptive access policies (AAP) are used to enhance identity assurance [2, 25]. IAM needs to incorporate such tools in all applications and endpoints to enable organizations to enforce policy-based access and monitor access behaviors.
2) **Network Segmentation and Microsegmentation**: Microsegmentation plays a crucial role in the ZTA model as it involves segmentation of network resources into finer sections. This segregation reduces the attack surface so that an attacker who gains entry into a segment cannot move across the network owing to the separation [21]. Policies at the micro-level ensure that potential threats are contained within particular areas within an organization, helping protect data and systems.
3) **Continuous Monitoring and Analytics**: In yet another one, it is pointed out that ZTA requires constant scrutiny of the users or the devices, and traffic on the network that can be used to identify suspicious activities in real time [1, 7]. Sophisticated monitoring tools take advantage of ML as well as AI algorithms to notice peculiarities that may be as a result of a breach; hence, preventive measures can be taken. What Oduri [19] refers to as behavioral biometrics is used to set benchmarks and identify variations from normal user actions that may represent threats.
4) **Endpoint Security and Device Compliance**: Extension of the ZTA principles also applies to all devices to make sure that endpoint protection policies include, but are not limited to,

employee's devices, IoT, or any device connected to the network [3]. Organization's devices are compliance checked, an antivirus is installed, and updates are performed to check for compliance against organizational requirements as endpoint vulnerabilities persist to be targeted in organizations.

5) **Data Protection and Encryption**: Gartner noted that within the ZTA framework, encryption and tokenization are essential data-centric security controls to safeguard data both during transmission and in storage [15, 26]. Encryption saves information in the event of lost battle with attackers, hence reaffirming ZTA's principle emphasizing information security, irrespective of its position in the network.

8.2.3 Challenges in Zero Trust Architecture Implementation

Despite the fact that ZTA developed quite a promising security model, the practical realization of this model in an enterprise network is quite problematic and requires significant resources. One primary concern is the built-in connectivity of ZTA with traditional systems as such systems may not have the space to support present identity and access protocols or standards. The move to ZTA entails significant adoption of IAM solutions, AI-based monitoring tools, and network segmentation technologies that smaller organizations find hard to fund [14].

Additionally, ZTA depends on monitoring and analyzing, which might lead to privacy-related problems, especially, when it comes to observing user action [13]. Also, maintenance of compliance for devices in organizations where allowances are made for use of personally owned devices (bring your own device, BYOD) becomes difficult because the devices are not necessarily those that are provided by the organization or can in fact be controlled. Other issues can be found in the way access polices are set and implemented; most often, when the access level is set to the minimum, the users will find it difficult to work with the system or will become frustrated.

8.2.4 Case Study: An Enterprise Adopting Zero Trust Architecture

Detailed herewith is our hypothetical case study—a multinational corporation adopting ZTA to improve its cybersecurity status. More to this, the organization can testify to the fact that before embracing ZTA, it was operating under a perimeter model, which employed a firewall and VPN systems to ward off any intruders. Nonetheless, after experiencing several security cases with lateral movement, the company's IT moved toward the implementation of ZTA.

1) **Phase 1—Identity-Centric Security**: The company used IAM with MFA and established access conditions. The platform could then adapt authentication requirements to user conduct and risk factors due to risk-based authentication through AI [4].
2) **Phase 2—Network Microsegmentation**: It practiced intra-organization segmentation and utilized microsegmentation instruments to formalize specific areas within its network. This strategy minimized mobilization within the compound, therefore limiting the much-feared flanking maneuvers that can be executed by a personalized foe [6].
3) **Phase 3—Continuous Monitoring with AI Analytics**: By incorporating AI-based monitoring technologies, the threat could be analyzed in real time, so that the organization could recognize these regularities as threats and act promptly [5, 8].
4) **Outcome**: The ZTA model eliminated the possibility of access by unauthorized individuals to a large extent. Furthermore, the AI-based anomaly detection mechanism was able to detect and respond to threats of intrusion, thus reducing the chances of firm disruptions and the continuation of business [27].

8.2.5 Lessons Learned and Best Practices

1) **Early Stakeholder Engagement**: Due to the use of the ZTA by Microsoft, initial engagement with IT staff, compliance personnel, and end users is critical [28]. This allows for the creation of security policies that are relevant to an organizations' and user's goals and objectives.
2) **Continuous Improvement and Adaptation**: ZTA is not only an implementation process, but it also necessitates conducting recurring evaluations of security policies due to the appearance of new threats [10]. Policies such as IAM, monitoring, and updates to the compliance of devices need to be audited and updated more often to achieve the aim of ZTA.
3) **Emphasis on Training and Awareness**: Since it relies on user behavior and compliance, the education of the users on best practices in security is a necessity for ZTA [29]. Thorough training enables the users to appreciate why access has to be so strongly controlled and the importance of security.

As shown in this case study, ZTA has the potential to revolutionize enterprise cybersecurity and delivering definitive security in a constantly evolving threat environment. Nevertheless, implementations have to be slow and systematic, which, in turn, requires companies to spend more money on training and exactly—staying in compliance with changing demands.

8.3 Case Study: Cloud Security and Posture Management for Hybrid Environments

These innovations are modern concepts of business, and cloud computing has provided organizations with the tools they need to scale their resources on demand while maintaining value-added flexible hybrid environments. However, this shift brings a new set of security risks which are particularly complex in cases where data and applications are hosted both locally, and in the cloud, and across two or more clouds. This chapter discusses CSPM and its application to strengthen the cybersecurity of both traditional and emerging hybrid models based on real case use, technologies, and strategies to secure the hybrid cloud environment.

8.3.1 Understanding Cloud Security in Hybrid Environments

They combine an organization's private infrastructure with offsite public and/or private cloud and bring the benefits of flexibility, cost optimization, and scalability. Nonetheless, the security of such applications is challenging because each platform has disparate security needs, controls, regulations, and threats. According to Altulaihan et al. [2], the threats posed by both cloud and IoT are dynamic in nature, meaning that security measures have to be equally dynamic to meet the growing challenges of protecting data as well as the continuity of services. In such hybrid setups, pure traditional security measures tend to disappoint by denying new attack vectors associated with new complex architectures, and hence the need for CSPM.

8.3.2 Cloud Security Posture Management

Cloud Security Posture Management (CSPM) solutions help in the designed management of security policies and settings of cloud services. These include assisting in the detection of misconfigured settings, ensuring compliance, and minimizing risk by offering real-time monitoring of cloud resources and security postures. Such mistakes are one of the main reasons for data leakage, as

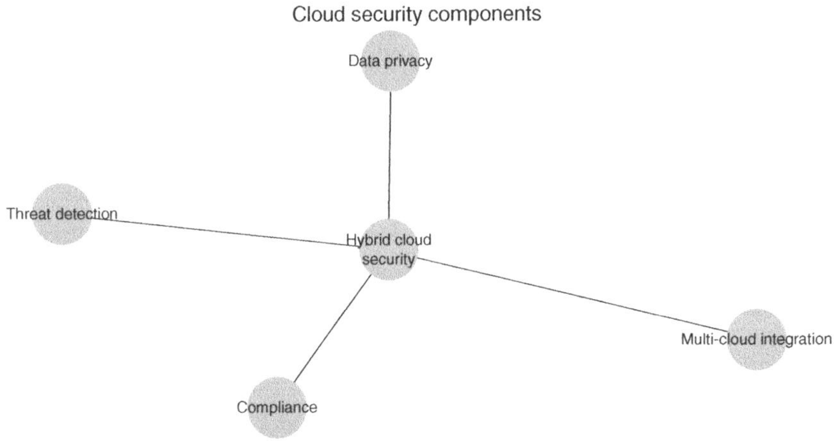

Figure 8.6 Cloud security challenges in hybrid environments. Source: Hewa Majeed Zangana.

explained by Fernández-Caramés and Fraga-Lamas [12], who noted that the incorrect setup of devices can grant unauthorized users access to sensitive data. With the help of CSPM, the task of identifying and correcting misconfigurations is carried out automatically, so there are no risks associated with human mistakes. Security management in such environments is unique in certain ways. These challenges have been presented in the following diagram: both internal and external threats, regulatory, and compliance (Figure 8.6).

8.3.3 Threat Detection and Risk Assessment

One of the principal purposes of CSPM is to recognize risks and opportunities that may be exploited in the future at the time of the potential threat not being realized. Integrating AI and ML technologies, CSPM can identify known vulnerabilities, evaluate potential harm, and rank remedial actions based on risk levels [5]. According to Chowdhury et al. [7], who predict in their forthcoming article that cybersecurity predictive analytics utilizing AI will help prevent threats, CSPM is crucial for hybrid cloud environments.

The integration of AI into CSPM enhances its ability to cope with complex environments. For instance, Gundaz and Das [30] discuss how conventional cyber threat detection in CI can leverage AI technologies, such as anomaly detection, to respond effectively to sophisticated attacks. This level of automated threat detection is essential in the hybrid models because monitoring threats through manual means may be tiresome and often time inconspicuous.

8.3.4 Case Study: Implementing Cloud Security Posture Management in a Hybrid Cloud Environment

Suppose a massive financial organization whose business just adopted a major approach to using the hybrid cloud in terms of cost and sovereignty of data. This gave the organization a hard time in monitoring security in its private data centers, as well as multiple cloud services. Through the use of the CSPM solution, this institution gained visibility in security compliance and real-time threats in their hybrid environment. As mentioned above, the CSPM tool highlighted many misconfigurations in cloud storage services that seemed to expose vast amounts of data. As Kafi and Akter [14] have pointed out, data protection for identified areas in financial services must maintain solemn security settings to prevent the occurrence of leakage. Using the prescriptive actions provided by the CSPM solution, the institution was able to avoid misconfigurations that could lead to data leaks and improve regulation compliance necessary to process finance-related information.

8.3.5 Cloud Security Posture Management's Role in Compliance and Governance

Regulations like General Data Protection Regulation (GDPR), Health Insurance Portability and Accountability Act (HIPAA), and Payment Card Industry Data Security Standard (PCI-DSS) become mandatory in the management of such a hybrid environment. With CSPM, the compliance process is made easy as the tool monitors and periodically records the security settings to determine the extent to which they meet legal requirements. According to Leszczyna [26], the act of compliance monitoring is crucial for the organization which crosses the border jurisdiction because in case of noncompliance, organizations may face huge fines and loss of reputation. As compliance status, when viewed from a CSPM solution, organizations can better handle compliance with regulatory frameworks. For instance, the aforementioned financial institution employed its CSPM solution that provided audit trails and ensured the organization's compliance with the financial laws more efficiently and effectively than ever before, rather than providing time-consuming and costly compliance reports.

8.3.6 Emerging Trends and Challenges in Cloud Security Posture Management for Hybrid Clouds

CSPM solutions must adapt as hybrid environments become more complicated as well as suffer from new dangers. Mishra et al. [31] propose that microservices and containerization, two of the leading emerging technologies, must be protected by much higher security levels as modern cyber threats become more diverse. Container security and DevOps integration are now embedded into CSPM solutions to bring security at design during development. Thus, while acquiring numerous benefits, CSPM is also subject to certain challenges, such as an increase in complexity in integrated hybrid environments, as well as an increased number of false positive alert generated. Paté-Cornell et al. [32] pointed out that although CSPM can decrease exposure, the strategy on how CSPM can work with other security tools like security information and event management (SIEM) and endpoint protection systems should be clear; otherwise, the huge number of alerts generated by CSPM can overwhelm the security team leading to hampering the purpose of generating these alerts.

8.3.7 Summary and Future Directions

CSPM is now a crucial part in protecting hybrid cloud solutions by constantly watching over the added layer, ensuring ongoing compliance, and better identification of threats. However, as technology grows, CSPM will have to build on its capacity to support security discretely across a broad and fractionated architecture. It can be postulated that with the evolution of AI and the advances in the utilization of ML, CSPM will become more effective in identifying potential threats and minimizing the role of manual intervention in supporting a consistent hybrid environment [6, 19]. In conclusion, CSPM can be seen as the core component of cloud security that allows organizations to reduce exposure to various risks, adhere to the required legal obligations, and safeguard their hybrid cloud resources. CSPM solutions are emerging technologies with significant potential for growth as ongoing innovations enhance both AI analytics and the integration of various systems within hybrid cloud environments to address contemporary cyber threats.

8.4 Application of Artificial Intelligence and Machine Learning in Cyber Threat Detection

The complexity of threats is rising and it means that advanced technologies like AI and ML are now necessary for cybersecurity solutions. The role that AI and ML play is that they help in the automation of the detection of cyber threats as well as in handling various types of threats faster than any human being can. Neural networks, decision trees, and clustering are used as ML methods for reading large volumes of data to identify threats that might not be recognized by other systems [7, 33].

8.4.1 Role of Machine Learning in Identifying Cyber Threats

The nature of ML to analyze large volumes of data has been very useful in detecting cyber threats. Due to the use of extensive datasets containing both normal traffic and attacker behavior, such systems can identify patterns characteristic of real attacks, including low-intensity or novel ones. For instance, ML algorithms can identify usually healthy network traffic and deviations from the norm to mark possible security threats [2, 6]. Supervised learning is useful in identifying familiar threats, but when novel risks are found, accuracy is more effectively achieved through the use of methods such as clustering or anomaly detection [10, 20].

8.4.2 Case Studies on Artificial-Intelligence-Driven Cybersecurity

AI has been applied in many actual situations to identify risks and address challenges in different industries. Chen et al. [13] made a literature review of deep learning models' applications to cybersecurity problems in smart cities for solving problems such as network intrusion and data leakage. The same observation was made by Chirra [1], who also discussed the ability to apply AI for safeguarding infrastructures of smart cities and suggested that threat detection should be less reactive in approach since new threats are continuously emerging and gaining significance. Further, in financial systems, AI-based systems have learnt to pick fraudulent transactions and ensure clients' data and important information's security. The use of the concept of ML to protect financial data is ubiquitous, as highlighted by the study of Kafi and Akter [14] to underscore the relevance of advancement in cybersecurity methods within fluid financial domains.

8.4.3 Predictive Analytics for Proactive Defense

Another sector where AI and ML are enhancing prediction models in the domain of cybersecurity is predictive analytics. Finally, anticipating data, predictive analytics can look at the forms of threats that are likely to happen and suggest protective measures that should be taken before an attack happens. For example, Chowdhury et al. [7] analyzes the use of big data and predictive analytics in comprehensively detecting new threats and risks instantly for improving the stability of the cybersecurity systems. Similarly, in Jimmy [4], the author underlines that risk estimation is useful, as it lets an organization direct resources where they are needed the most when carrying out predictive risk modeling.

8.4.4 Challenges and Future Directions

However, there are some issues that AI and ML are still weak solutions to cybersecurity, including data privacy, the requirement of large labeled datasets, and adversarial attacks. In addition, the use of AI models may pose a challenge of great resource requirement such as hulk up computational power; hence, it may not be an ideal solution for resource-constrained environments. In future works, efforts will be made to overcome these shortcomings through effective lightweight model designing and implementing privacy-preserving methods in the AI-based security models [5, 24]. AI and its branch—ML—are steadily taking their place in cybersecurity as they allow more efficient and proactive cyber threats' identification. This virtually means that the trend of using AI in cybersecurity is set to advance further with progressive improvements in algorithms' precision and speed identified as further paths to better defense against cyber threats across different sectors [34, 35].

8.5 Case Study: Deception Technology and Honeypots in Financial Sector Security

As a result, deception technology and honeypots have taken their positions in the spectrum of cybersecurity, especially in critical sectors where personal information is most valued such as in the financial industry. This chapter describes how these technologies are applied to the financial sector to increase protection, where impostors are used to deceive potential attackers, important installations, and the degree of possible breaches is reduced.

8.5.1 The Role of Deception Technology in Financial Sector Security

Deception technology gives organizations a way of going after the attackers with methods by presenting decoy environments. These deceptive targets, including bogus databases, credentials, and channels, resemble the genuine assets and draw the cyberattackers toward the decoy but away from the original systems [2]. In the financial sector, where customer data, transaction records, and business and financial strategies are exposed, the use of deception technology allows analysts to observe how attackers behave in a controlled environment. The insights developed can be used to enhance security measures in the organization [6]. When deploying deception technology, financial institutions can accomplish several essential objectives: (1) they become aware of internal threats; (2) they gain insight into more advanced attack types; and (3) they observe attack behavior without using real data. In the relatively enclosed spheres of such industries as banking and investments, even the least sophisticated attempts at hacking can result in major losses of both money and reputation; hence, the implementation of these technologies has now become invaluable [31].

8.5.2 Implementation of Honeypots in the Financial Sector

Within the spectrum of deception, honeypots are perhaps the most significant component since they are everything that looks like an irresistible target for cybercriminals. It is very usual to manipulate a honeypot in a way that will depict it as a valuable resource, like a secret database, an intranet connection, or a trading floor [8, 35]. When the attackers begin engaging with these honeypots, security teams are able to watch their activities in real time and collect data on the tactics employed by these attackers and the objective they seek to achieve [33]. For instance, a bank might undertake the development of a fake payment system to make it easy to catch the attackers who are interested in payment information. It also makes security experts study how the attackers manage to circumnavigate these measures, making the institution to fortify real payment systems. Thus exposed, honeypots become staging grounds for identifying possible threats and without risking real-world assets [22].

8.5.3 Advantages and Limitations of Deception Technology and Honeypots

In other words, deception technology and honeypots have great advantages, especially in threat identification and reconnaissance. These technologies efficiently identify zero-day attacks or threats that are not known to the cybersecurity world, because when interacting with the decoy systems, the attackers divulge their strategies [13]. These threats can be identified early enough with this information, enabling financial institutions to prevent threats before accessing critical systems [28]. Nevertheless, implementing deception technology also has some challenges. Realistically, steadily changeable and immune to show-off decoys of correspondingly high levels are hard to sustain and construct, what demands a lot of funds and, primarily, highly qualified personnel. However, attackers are now becoming wise to the whole idea of deception and might well devise ways of working around the decoys, and so honeypots can become useless if not regularly updated and monitored [20].

8.5.4 Real-World Examples of Deception Technology in Financial Institutions

In recent years, several financial institutions have integrated deception technology to deal with APTs that have been an extreme threat in the industry. For example, banks have utilized the network-based honeypots to safeguard the main systems against ransomware attacks. When attackers use ransomware, it runs in the honeypot where the bank's cybersecurity crew can study its content and devise how to counter it before it affects the real system [7]. In addition, honeypots are deployed to some investment firms for the purpose of facilitating observations of criminal behaviors, especially in cases of unauthorized trading. These decoy trading environments across landscape firms allow the identification and documentation of the outward behavior of attackers potentially useful for the further development of more accurate detection technologies [30].

8.5.5 Future of Deception Technology in Financial Security

While the concept of cyberspace threats is ever changing, so is the scope and capability of deception technology and honeypots in the financial environment. As for future work, the financial organizations are expected to apply AI and ML to maintain the self-governing honeypot approach, where honeypot parameters change depending on the activity of the attackers in real time [4]. Such advancements will help the financial institutions to move deeper into threat detection capability, leaving behind low response rates [14]. Also, new solutions in the sphere of prediction could allow institutions to forecast the next steps of an attacker and, thus, adapt their own defense strategy. For example, the following is a configuration of deception technology and behavioral biometrics: A combination of deception technology and behavioral biometrics, for instance, is likely to improve the financial sector's capability of identifying potential attackers using their engagements with the honeypots [24]. This approach further enhances the resiliency of the deception layer and extends the range of security solutions that target more complex threats.

8.5.6 Summary

Indeed, deceit technology and honeypots provide financial institutions with a competitive edge over the security of significant resources. Since they design systems minimizing the real systems, not only threats are siphoned, but rich information about existing attacker behavior is also collected. There are certain difficulties inherent in the implementation and use of these systems;

however, the gain arising from intelligence collection and preventive threat management makes these systems essential constituents of modern financial cybersecurity systems [26]. And as these technologies advance, it is and can be expected to be relied on more in protecting the financial sector from the threat that is future.

8.6 Real-World Implementation of Threat Intelligence Platforms

Threat intelligence platforms (TIPs) represent one of the most valuable tools of contemporary cybersecurity, as these help collect, process, and use knowledge about possible threats. These platforms are meant to optimize threat intelligence (TI) and support better and faster reactions to cybersecurity risks. Over time, TIPs do mature and therefore must be useful in addressing issues of cyber threats by strengthening an organization.

8.6.1 Overview and Functionality of Threat Intelligence Platforms

TIPs gather information from various sources that include inferior intelligence, commercial feeds, and self-generated data in order to make a consolidated threat perception. TIPs are especially useful since they minimize noise by collecting and organizing data inherent in TI and tailoring the information that organizations regard as crucial. Sherman et al. [20] opine that Threat Intelligence Platforms (TIPs) are particularly beneficial in CI sectors, as general equilibrium threat identification and response can prevent significant losses in operations and cash flow. TIPs' main tasks comprise threat data intake, threat data augmentation, comparison with historical data, and threat alert generation and automation [28]. When performed by TIPs, these processes enable the security teams to stay on the strategic levels and produce a much faster response [17]. Furthermore, TIPs also use a certain form of ML to predict and prioritize threats based on the pattern found in previous data to improve both the cycle time and the accuracy of threat identity [6].

8.6.2 Case Studies Highlighting Threat Intelligence Platform Effectiveness

Some examples concern the application of TIPs in various fields and illustrate the effectiveness of each case. For example, Fernández-Caramés and Fraga-Lamas [12] described how TIPs addressed the vulnerability issues in IoT-based contexts and how they could boost the security level of Industry 4.0. This study also stressed the fact that TIPs can be fine-tuned to meet the needs of smart cities and industrial applications of IoT, where a dynamic threat model and real-time countermeasure is critical. Further, Vrhovec et al. [9] observed that while using TIPs, there was potential to elaborate response and decision times in cyberspace, which are significant in cybersecurity environments where groups are faced with complex threats in real situations. Timeliness is a critical aspect of responding to cyber threats as this is a fast-growing problem that is only indicative of its infancy in organizations today. The following bar chart provides average response times, pre- and post-installation of the automated detection systems (Figure 8.7).

Another example is the use of CSPM for protecting CI against modern Advanced Persistent Threats (APTs). For instance, Ichino, along with Gundaz and Das [30], explored the application of TIPs in smart grid security. TIPs proved more effective in linking real-time data with TI feeds in a way that facilitates protective actions against plausible grid sabotage.

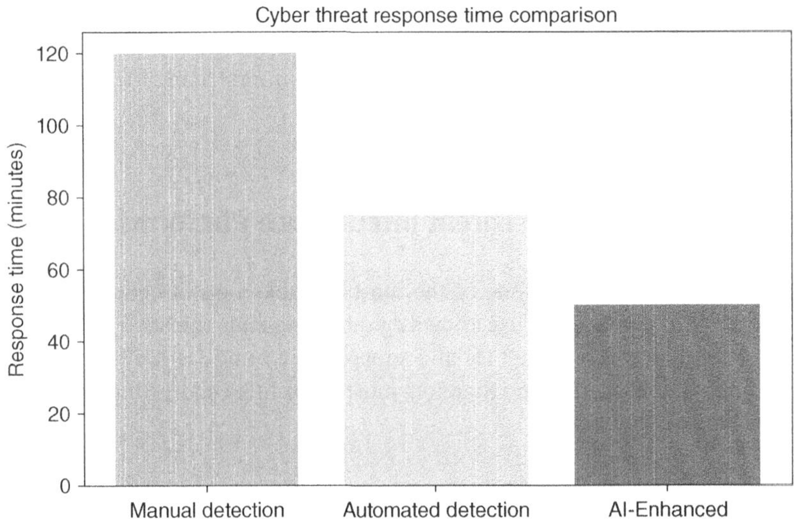

Figure 8.7 Comparison of cyber threat response times. Source: Hewa Majeed Zangana.

8.6.3 Challenges in Threat Intelligence Platform Implementation

However, TIPs also pose some implementation issues, as will be expounded below. First of all, the amount of threat information generated may literally be intimidating, no matter how sophisticated the automated means of sorting it out. According to Nassar and Kamal [5], data management and processing would need superior analysis tools and strong computing infrastructure. Furthermore, organizations have to make sure that TIPs are aligned with existing security solutions in order to achieve the best results [3]. Privacy and other regulatory issues present another issue, which is common in such sectors as the financial and healthcare industries. In any given TIP, there is normally a need to share sensitive data, which, if not well handled, can lead to data leak or other related malice or even infringe on the regulatory requirements set within the undertaking [14]. Thus, sustaining compliance with data protection laws is crucial in ensuring that the right information exchange is effected across networks through effective and strong data governance frameworks.

8.6.4 The Role of Artificial Intelligence and Machine Learning in Threat Intelligence Platforms

Advanced technologies such as AI and ML improve TIP functions by facilitating threat anticipation as well as behavior assessment. For instance, Chowdhury et al. [7] reveal that due to its predictive analytics capability, TIPs can predict the stamping of attack patterns from previous incidents, and this can be very useful in eradicating zero-day trends. This predictive functionality also fits in the general approach of AI cybersecurity, where the remedy is primarily proactive rather than reactive. Chirra [1] brought support to this by explaining how AI-enabled TIPs can effectively support smart city security due to the numerous IoT devices, which add to the security risks. In this case, by applying ML algorithms in TIPs, organizations are able to identify the outliers and anomalies in real time, even in a large dataset, thus having efficient use of optimization of the resources in the cybersecurity process as pointed out by Xenofontos et al. [23].

8.6.5 Future Directions and Emerging Trends in Threat Intelligence Platforms

With ascending cyber threats, TIPs are anticipated to build up automated processes, use the latest AI techniques, and boost end-user readability of threat information. According to Malasowe et al. [36], in the following years, TIPs will extend existing cybersecurity elements like behavioral biometrics and continuous authentication systems as the new settings are much more dynamic. In addition, TIPs will not only enhance the coverage of contexts, sources, and uses but also broaden the sources of data drawn from them and from nontraditional fields to create a rich TI environment [24]. Higher industrial cooperation and the exchange of information on threats and feasible measures will also be important in establishing TIPs as an indispensable building block of worldwide cybersecurity protection systems. Leszczyna [26], emphasized that the concept of CI is crucial in combating malicious targeted supply chain processes (MTSCP). If TIPs are going to address these challenges and take advantage of these new AI developments, TIPs can continue to grow to be the important tool that organizations require when the cybersecurity threat environment becomes much more difficult to manage in the future.

8.7 Endpoint Detection and Response for Remote Work Security

Endpoint detection and response (EDR) systems are critical for organizations in remote working environments because they offer endpoint protection, including real-time, continuous observances of threats on endpoint devices such as laptops, mobile phones, and IoTs, and respond to them autonomously. With an increasing number of people working from home due to the COVID-19 pandemic, the overall attack surface has increased dramatically; any endpoint that may touch an organization's network from a different location or with little-to-no security in place must be secured [1, 3]. It is used to identify malicious activities on the endpoints of an organization and allow the organization's EDR systems to respond and mitigate the attack. Different from conventional antivirus tools, EDR provides the following features: Intelligent, it detects threats based on the behaviors that do not conform to normal patterns; it can identify such behaviors and is capable of using the ML method to identify such behaviors. This type of monitoring is particularly beneficial to employees because it comes as a preventive measure following the shift to remote work, which introduces new cyber risks such as phishing scams, insecure Wi-Fi networks, devices with weak security provisions [6, 24].

8.7.1 Key Features of Endpoint Detection and Response Systems in Remote Work Security

1) **Real-Time Threat Detection**: EDR solutions are always examining the endpoints for any activities that look suspicious, and that involves logging into a system, transferring large files, or installing new applications. This capability is needed for detecting insider threats as well as APTs that could easily bypass traditional security mechanisms [8, 26].
2) **Automated Response and Remediation**: EDR systems often aid in the response to threats, including actions such as quarantining affected hardware, killing suspected threats, and sending notifications to security analysts. These actions are coordinated by EDR systems to lessen overall response times to threats, especially for distributed work environments where threats have to be mitigated quickly to lessen the level of compromise [11, 37].

3) **Enhanced Data Analysis**: EDR solutions are intended to analyze large datasets from endpoints with data analytics and ML algorithms to notice minimal indicators of compromise (IOCs). For example, using predictive analytics, it is easier to identify behaviors that deviate from historical records, enhancing the ways through which threats can be identified at an early stage [7, 13].
4) **Integration with Other Security Tools**: EDR solutions are currently developed to seamlessly fit into extended security solutions like SIEM systems, pulling from the network level info that is integrated together with the EDR data to give a more robust approach to threat detection across the organization [16, 28].

8.7.2 Challenges and Best Practices for Implementing Endpoint Detection and Response in Remote Work

Several are the challenges that accompany the idea of integrating EDR for remote work. First, sometimes, it becomes challenging to guarantee that all the endpoint devices are protected by an EDR software to be updated regularly; this is because some are using their personal devices at work (BYOD). This variability of devices also leads to software compatibility problems as well as a decrease in the monitoring efficiency [2]. Also, there are issues about privacy parity with security requirements because EDR systems might harvest data about the employees' activity, and if not dealt with properly, it will be a violation of privacy [17, 36].

Best practices for effective EDR implementation in remote work include:

- **Enforcing Strong Device Security Policies**: Building a great device security policy, for instance, requiring high-level secure and corporation-owned devices for any resource accessibility
- **Implementing Multifactor authentication**: Stacking up EDR with the multifactor authentication (MFA) which will further minimize the incidents of intrusion [20].
- **Conducting Regular Training**: Managing to provide updates on endpoint security measures to the remote workers to know their recommended practices and the threats that may be facing them [9, 22].
- **Continuous EDR and Endpoint Software Updates**: Regular EDR and endpoint software updates to mitigate threats from new emerging threats and adjust for the emerging security position [30].

EDR solutions can be considered as critical in terms of the protection of remote workers since they offer organizations multiple potent weapons to deal with potential endpoint threats. Since remote work is likely to remain widespread going forward and perhaps even more so after the pandemic subsides, these tools will be critical in supporting strong cyber protection measures and securing any business access to organizational assets [5, 18].

8.8 Case Study: Security Automation, Orchestration, and Response in Healthcare

With the focus on the protection of patient data, and guaranteeing continuity of essential services, security orchestration, automation, and response (SOAR) becomes increasingly relevant in healthcare. These are the following important applications of SOAR in the secure firmware hub controller (SFHC) environment: SOAR solutions are intended to solve multifaceted cybersecurity issues through automation of response processes, unification of various security systems, and coordinating the responses to threats in time. This case study will review experiences in a few sectors and will describe the applicability and implementation of SOAR systems in healthcare, especially how the inclusion of automation, orchestration, and AI enhances cybersecurity results.

8.8.1 Background and Importance of Security Orchestration, Automation, and Response in Healthcare

Because of the preservation of large amounts of sensitive data and because many healthcare facilities are interconnected within the IoT landscape, healthcare organizations are ideal for individuals attempting to conduct a cyberattack [2]. The use of medical IoT systems together with electronic health records (EHRs) and other computational assets has created additional vulnerabilities. Cyber threats to healthcare organizations include loss of medical and patient services, threatening the safety of patients, and causing huge financial and image losses [38]. In light of such stakes, the introduction of SOAR is considered to be preventive in the sphere of cyber threats and potential ways to boost the efficiency of the response.

8.8.2 Key Components of Security Orchestration, Automation, and Response Implementation

SOAR technology encompasses several core components that are integral to its success in healthcare environments:

1) **Automation of Threat Detection and Response**: SOAR platforms undertake mundane security operations such as threat input, notification, and responding processes. Prompted responses let healthcare institutions mitigate the rising volume of cyber threats without stressing the organizations' security workforce [13]. This is especially so since in present-day networks, threat detection can be very noisy, and many times, false positives are rife, especially under elevated situation awareness level of the threat detection systems [7].
2) **Orchestration Across Security Tools**: Healthcare organizations may employ various measures such as firewall IDS and endpoint protection software. All these tools are coordinated by SOAR and made to collaborate regarding threat responses. This enables coordination between systems and cuts down response time which can be important in patient care where delays very highly bring about patient harm [35].
3) **Integration of AI and Machine Learning for Enhanced Analytics**: AI and ML present in SOAR solutions enable facets of predictive analysis, containing anomaly detection and behavioral analysis. For example, AI-based analysis can detect security anomalies concerning the usage of medical equipment or EHRs to alert about a security threat before it gets worse [18, 37]. A larger degree of sophistication is especially useful for monitoring and analyzing large datasets for possible signs of malicious incidents [6].

The assessment of different defense mechanisms may be used to determine which method is the most useful. The following chart reveals success data derived from real-life research that has been conducted in the last couple of years for various kinds of security methods (Figure 8.8).

8.8.3 Challenges in Security Orchestration, Automation, and Response Deployment for Healthcare

All the same, the implementation of SOAR in the healthcare sector has several limitations. There are limitations, such as the compatibility of connecting with the usual systems in the healthcare

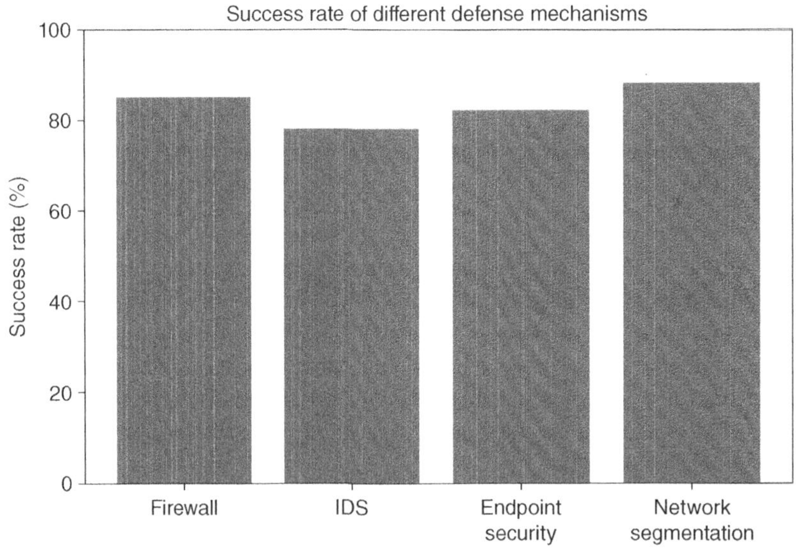

Figure 8.8 Success rate of defense mechanisms. Source: Hewa Majeed Zangana.

atmosphere because most traditional interfaces are not well suited to SOAR needs [30]. But when it comes to compliance issues, there exist new challenges today due to strict regulatory frameworks like HIPAA that enforce data privacy and has stiff penalty regime for its breach. It is notable that automated security actions may pose risks and violations to the privacy policies or make it difficult to access patient information, especially during emergency [19].

8.8.4 Case Example: Security Orchestration, Automation, and Response in a Large Hospital Network

A bright example of how the SOAR approach can be used in healthcare can be seen in practice at a large-scale hospital system that had constant ransomware threats. The network adopted the use of the SOAR platform in enhancing its cybersecurity. The solution provided the hospital with a system of only breaking off infected devices, informing management and other important people or groups, and also prevention of an ensuing infection without having to depend on human labor. Consequently, the response time dropped from hours to minutes, which helped the hospital to limit the effects of ransomware on patient services [28]. Moreover, concurrently, the SOAR platform was also carrying out predictive analytics using AI in order to alert on unusual user activity regarding areas with more secure information, such as EHRs. Using historical information about the incident, the platform was able to block unauthorized access and, therefore, potential data exfiltration attempts, proving the value of AI for SOAR [4].

8.8.5 Outcomes and Benefits

Several advantages have been realized from the application of SOAR in healthcare organizations. Some notable improvements include:

- **Enhanced Response Time**: Thanks to automation, threat activities have led to the emergence of prompt response procedures that have helped various healthcare facilities to bring their responses to incidents much earlier than the time cybercriminals would unleash much more devastating blows on their infrastructure [32].

- **Improved Incident Management**: In light of this, SOAR optimizes how security teams handle and respond to incidents by consolidating and organizing the received data [8].
- **Reduced Operational Costs**: Since operational routine chores are handled by automation, healthcare institutions can deploy resources more appropriately, and the costs of cybersecurity in the institutions are also lowered [36].

8.8.6 Future Directions

The future for security orchestration, automation, and response (SOAR) in healthcare aims to entail increased Advanced Cybersecurity Analytics and Predictive Threat (ACAPT) capabilities with sophisticated models of AI threat analysis and a better understanding of changes in risks. Recent trends point to the increase of continuous security monitoring and the use of learning models in SOAR software, which would afford healthcare facilities a flexible and proactive cybersecurity approach [9, 22]. Moreover, new technologies such as behavior biometrics and continuous authentication techniques have the potential to improve SOAR's capacity and dynamics, particularly in anticipating and mitigating risks that surface in mobile and wearable devices popular in patient care by the year 2024 as projected by [19]. Therefore, the use of security automation and orchestration in the case of SOAR in healthcare significantly demonstrates the ability to protect the patient's privacy and compliance with the standard. In the fast-evolving world of cybersecurity, by enhancing the response times, consolidating data on the incidents, and using AI-based solutions, SOAR platforms provide healthcare institutions with an innovative solution deserving attention. As the focus of healthcare organizations remains on maintaining SOAR technologies for future contingencies, with heightened focus on regulatory compliance and integration, it is going to be crucial for the ongoing endeavor to keep up with the ever-evolving technological and security landscape.

8.9 Using Blockchain for Data Integrity in Supply Chain Security

They have been introduced as the most effective means of improving the integrity of the supply chain data by solving problems of hacking, data manipulation, and fraud. Veracity of data becomes critical in the supply chain world since the information disclosed needs to be transparent, verifiable, and trustworthy to all those in the supply chain, right from the supplier to the distributor and finally the consumer.

Applying the blockchain also provides some benefits in the process of data protection in the supply chain. But one of the most important pros of using blockchains is the relative inviolability of the data put into the block, as it can't be changed without changing all the following blocks. This is why blockchain can be used to record or assure transactions or movements of products in the supply chain. For example, when there is production of a certain product, the natural sequence of flowing through the supply chain may be represented by blocks of information that have their cryptographic details that are unique and irreversible to previous records of the product starting from production up to the delivery point. In addition, blockchain technology ensures that no single entity controls the entire chain, as it is distributed. Supply chain participants have access to the same ledger, and all transactions are confirmed based on consensus. This structure reduces the opportunity for fraudsters to manipulate data. It builds confidence and credibility between the supply chain members, and the amounts of fraud, counterfeits, and unauthorized alteration of data are kept at a minimum. Some case studies and research papers have pointed to the usefulness of blockchain in protecting supply chain information. The work of Fernández-Caramés and Fraga-Lamas [12] reveals that blockchain makes supply chain transactions to be secure and transparent because every transaction in the chain is measurable. This effectiveness reduces risks of data manipulation and also helps to ensure data consistency throughout the chain of supply from the producer to the consumer, especially in industries such as manufacturing of drugs and food products, agriculture and the sales of luxury products, where maintaining origin of the product is very essential.

As Jang-Jaccard and Nepal [38] noted, blockchain technology can be used to secure essential supply chain data in smart cities. In the context of smart cities, where a large number of IoT devices are implemented for logistics, the importance of blockchain security for data protection in IoT systems becomes critical. Thus, using blockchain, connected IoT devices can send the information to a peer-to-peer network where the data cannot be changed by the sender or a third party. What makes the supply chain secure and also increases its efficiency is that third parties do not have to validate the transaction. Apart from being highly secure since its records cannot be altered, blockchain is combined with smart contracts due to its ability to optimize the security configuration management (SCMs). Smart contracts are digital contracts where the embedded terms of agreement are embedded into code that automatically executes them. These contracts can also compel compliance as certain actions are set to occur based on specific conditions, for instance, when a given product gets to a particular place or it has undergone a quality check. This functionality minimizes human factors and slow and fraudulent practices within the supply chain system and guarantees that all the participants stick to the set conditions. However, there are some issues related to adopting blockchain in a supply chain security environment. Tweneboah-Koduah [11] has rightly pointed out this limitation of blockchain-based systems; scalability becomes a challenge where the number of transactions and total number of participants are high, and this is a common feature in most supply chain applications. However, it is also noteworthy that there are matters associated with the assessment of excessive energy consumption and the impact on the environment of network maintenance of blockchains. However, due to the ability of blockchain in improving remote data accuracy in supply-chain situations, further research has been conducted in finding the best ways in which the scalability of blockchain and its energy consumption can be improved for effective functioning [13].

Enhancements to the conventional threat detection protocols are also supported by the integration of AI in the framework of blockchain. AI taken in conjunction with blockchain, as Balantrapu [6] points out, adds another layer of security for guarding against cyber threats by using analytical tools for detecting irregularities in the blockchain's records of transactions. The integration can result in even better and earlier means of protecting the supply chain information and data from unauthorized access or manipulation. The use of the blockchain in enhancing the security of a supply chain is relevant to the current global concern for more secure supply chain systems. Because blockchain is capable of delivering an efficient, safe, and tamper-proof means of recording and verifying exchanges, which can limit data manipulation and fraud, so blockchain has the potential as a revolutionary technological solution to create a higher level of transparency in supply chain processes [1, 25]. Therefore, the application of the blockchain platform is a valuable approach toward enhancing the data integrity within the supply chain. Due to its capabilities, it is immutable, depends on smart contacts, and has a decentralized type of storage, which guarantees that data is protected from manipulation and fraud. There are still some concerns like scalability and energy consumption, but now research is being done to solve all these problems. Blockchain integrated with AI for threat detection and predictive analysis makes the supply chain stronger against cyber threats, adding to supply chain security and quality [4, 25].

8.10 Insider Threat Detection and Prevention: A Case Study in the Government Sector

In the context of cybersecurity, the term insider threats comprises people within organizations including employees, contractors, or other trusted groups with malicious intent to harm the organization or otherwise erringly. These threats are more dangerous, especially in organizations, for instance, in government since they lead to major crises when data is compromised on security. This section aims to provide a case study in government domain concerning the identification and prevention of insider threats through the implementation of AI and ML, accompanied by case application and experience sharing to prevent new risks in the future.

8.10.1 Background: The Importance of Insider Threat Detection in the Government Sector

Government sector is the most struck by cyberattacks, and insiders are difficult to find for several reasons: privileged access to the information and infrastructure. Such threats can be as basic as data leakage, vandalism, or destructive acts on the systems on purpose to accidents due to ignorance or carelessness [10, 16]. Governments across the world are slowly awakening to the fact that these are real threats, and governments have started investing in cybersecurity and risk management of these threats, apart from applying ML and AI for detecting internal threats [13, 25].

8.10.2 Case Study: Government Agency's Approach to Insider Threat Detection

This case study involves a government agency that has only recently established a complex system for identifying and combating insider threats. Over the recent years, the agency has been involved in different data leakages even to external sources, and this was with both classified and sensitive information. The first issue was in defining activities that could be questionable and yet were coming from trusted sources, something that no other security systems were capable of capturing.

8.10.2.1 Phase 1: Identifying Risk Factors and Building the Detection Framework

The first activity in the initiative was to define the key causes of insider threat. These comprised access to materials not permitted, unusual transactions or processes, and alteration of users [7]. The agency engaged cybersecurity specialists to develop a highly sophisticated and self-driven detector using a ML algorithm that could study the employees and the logs, as well as monitor activities and dealings in real time [6]. A ML algorithm was trained using data from agency's systems, and traditional and recent attack data, as well as normal behavior patterns were included in the training data [5]. The model emphasized identifying the behavior patterns which are quite different from normal use. For instance, if an employee uses a lot of volume of data during the late hours or copies data to external devices not authorized, these were considered as anomalous.

8.10.2.2 Phase 2: Implementing AI and Predictive Analytics

The next step was to incorporate preventive measures where analytics was used to work out what the insider threats would do before they did it. Systems generated risk assessments for insider threats based on external events, for example, political circumstances and internal ones such as disgruntlement among workers or changes in their role [39]. This model also assisted in the identification of threats that required action to be taken against them, thereby decreasing false alarms while increasing the identification percentage [4]. For instance, decision-making frameworks that employ statistical and mathematical modeling methodologies were built to identify possible antecedents of insider threats by analyzing incident data to establish a connection, such as drastic alterations in the customary ways of how an employee would work or modification of their footprint on the network [19]. The agency also put into practice constant surveillance with the assistance of AI for employees' talking and sharing of emails, network interactions, and file usage which led to improved real-time and precise threat identification.

8.10.2.3 Phase 3: Response and Prevention

Having identified potential insider threats, the agency concentrated on a quick desired response. When an outlier was identified, notifications were instantly communicated to the cybersecurity team for further examination [14]. To avoid insider threats, therefore, the agency put measures including behavior-based login, continuous login through biometrics, and improved authorization procedures [27, 32]. Due to utilized ML algorithms, behavioral biometrics enabled the system to detect and verify users not only at the moment of the login but also during further activity. This also made it hard for an attacker to extort his/her way around the security measures that had been put in place [19]. Also, the agency put up an auto-response system that could quickly counter such actions by locking a user's account or flagging the particular document for review by management.

8.10.3 Results and Lessons Learned

The government agency had an advice reduction in successful insider threats after using this AI detection system. The system's sampling feature allows it to learn from data as well as incorporate new threats since it adapts to the changes that help in the sustenance of the security measures [10]. Furthermore, the predictive feature allowed managers to foresee possible threats before they became threats, and therefore, minimized the odds of data leak. One prime implication of this case study is the need to apply human interventions to ML in order to combat insider threats. While anomalies and risks can be automatically detected and predicted by AI, the decision-making and investigative processes should involve cybersecurity professionals who will decide whether a threat is new, modified existing, or a completely unrelated one [39]. Furthermore, it was necessary to incorporate regular awareness programs regarding cybersecurity to all the employees, especially since insider threats resulted from accidents [3].

8.10.4 Summary: Moving Forward with Proactive Insider Threat Prevention

This chapter shows the potent role of AI and ML for identifying and mitigating against insider threats, especially in sensitive organizations such as government institutions. These technologies give potent weapons for threat discovery, but their success hails on predictive analytics or monitoring, behavior biometrics and an organizational culture of proactivity and training of the employees. New trends in cyber threats call for a multilayer strategy that will incorporate both AI and ML as well as human supervision and direction. More studies should be conducted on the applicability of federated learning and other superior approaches to the detection of insider threats and data anonymization [2, 25]. Furthermore, expanding the application of these solutions to other fields, like healthcare or finance, can produce improved approaches to threat identification and enhance the analysis of insider threats at various domains. In today's world of advanced threats, it is crucial for businesses to adapt to cybersecurity threats that are developing every day. The following line graph shows an estimate of the growth of different cybersecurity areas within the next five years (Figure 8.9).

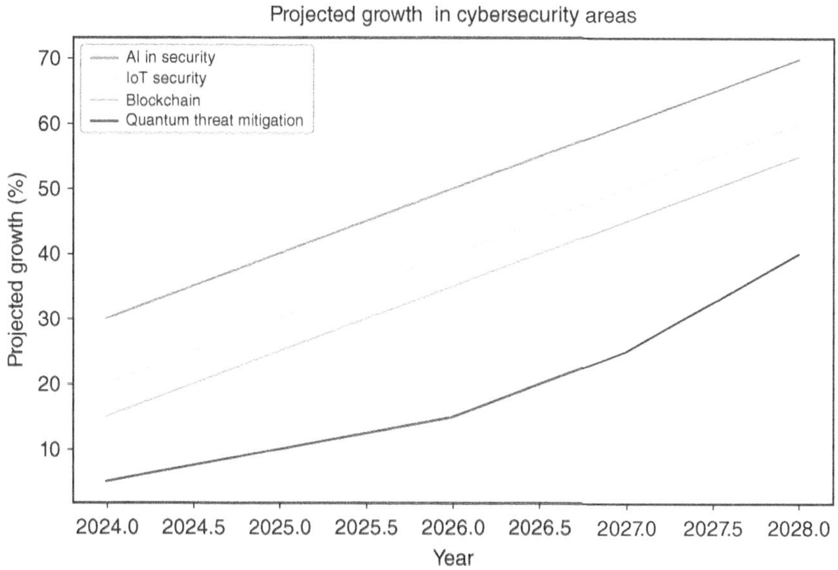

Figure 8.9 Future cybersecurity trends. Source: Hewa Majeed Zangana.

8.11 Cybersecurity in Critical Infrastructure: Protecting Energy and Utility Sectors

In this context, the defense of such vital infrastructure and primarily the energy and utility industries is in connection with the continuously progressing development of technologies—a problem that has become relevant in cybersecurity. These sectors are critically important in today's societies and economies AND are under growing cyber threat risk due to their dependency on digital systems and IoT growth. With the current advancement toward smart grids, automation, and the incorporation of AI in these industries, security threats have increased.

8.11.1 The Importance of Securing the Energy and Utility Sectors

Energy and utility sectors are critically important because they provide electricity and power to residences, commercial establishments, hospitals, and even the defense systems of our society. These sectors are adopting information technology in their operations to improve efficiency and productivity of the resources used. Nevertheless, these technologies also introduce new avenues for cyber threats including system halting, data leakage, and even monetary loss [16]. With the development of smarter features in CI, threats, for instance, unauthorized control mechanisms, or attacks to critical data, become crucial factors [16]. Hence, cybersecurity of these sectors is imperative to provide public security, economic resilience, and protect national security.

8.11.2 Common Cybersecurity Threats in Energy and Utility Sectors

Threats in the energy and utility industries are broad and can be directed at different levels of the system, ranging from IoT, communication channels, control, and even data storage level. Some of the most prominent threats include:

1) **Ransomware Attacks**: As evidenced in recent attacks on energy providers, ransomware is fast becoming a menace. Intruders gain access to systems, lock important data, and extort money for it to be unlocked [3].
2) **Advanced Persistent Threats**: Such advanced threats frequently entail unauthorized penetration into a network in order to mine information for long periods. Due to that, APTs can linger in the infrastructure of an organization, enabling the perpetrator to assail the operational data and manage systems without being sensed instantly [38].
3) **Denial of Service Attacks**: Denial of service (DoS) attacks affect the regular operation of systems through the deluge of traffic which resulting in unavailability of systems to intended users. In subcritical sectors, such as energy, this may cause significant service disruptions [11].
4) **IoT Vulnerabilities**: IoT integration in the systems of public utilities means that these systems can face a threat regarding unauthorized IoT device access or malicious data interception [2].

8.11.3 Mitigation Techniques and Best Practices

To address such emerging threats, the following remedial measures are being employed to protect energy and utility sectors. These solutions include:

1) **Artificial-Intelligence-Driven Threat Detection and Response**: Integrating AI and ML is significant in the improvement of security in the CI. Applying AI essentially allows organizations to enhance their chances of recognizing unusual and threatening activity in near-real time. Dedicating on the work of Balantrapu [6], it is recognized that predictive analysis, anomaly detection, and auto-response AI are getting critical to uphold strong security.
2) **AI-Enhanced Risk Management**: Some AI applications which are most useful for managing risks are those which are used to detect areas of weaknesses and deter potentially threatening cyber activities in real time. The constant monitoring of systems by these tools makes it possible to provide a forecast of attacks even before they happen [39].
3) **Behavioral Biometrics**: A relatively recent strategy for bolstering cybersecurity across such industries includes continuous authentication through behavioral biometrics. This technique assesses users' behavior patterns like typing and mouse movements in ways that would point out a figure that does not belong to the legal group of users [19].
4) **Data Encryption and Multifactor Authentication**: For securing important information, and avoiding intrusion into certain systems, strong encryption protocols and MFA should be implemented [14].

8.11.4 Case Studies and Real-World Applications

Some of the case studies presented illustrate the threats and the different ways through which the energy and utility sectors have developed measures to counter cyber threats. For example, in December 2015, one of the largest cyberattacks hit the Ukrainian energy sector and caused power blackouts across the country. This attack targeted country's electrical power system and, through the use of malware, overtook the systems and paralyzed operations. After this attack, attempts were made to further secure the grid from future threats, comprising of better intrusion detection technologies and better collaboration between the government and private sector's key participants [32].

One big example in the United States is the use of AI and ML in physically protecting the electric grid. By installing AI-based predictive maintenance systems, utilities are better placed to notice the earliest signs of system failure or even a cyberattack, minimizing the downtimes in the system and strengthening the grid [27].

8.11.5 The Role of Predictive Analytics and Machine Learning

Cybersecurity is being changed by predictive analytics, which means that the system can sense danger when it is still within its sphere. Network traffic information can be used by ML algorithms to determine a pattern and decide the probability of an attack happening. In the context of energy sector, predictive analytics is especially helpful in observing the grid behavior and detecting something unusual, which could point the finger at a cyberattack [7]. In addition, aligning advanced analytics with real-time monitoring applications can improve the capacity to contain cyber events and reduce the corresponding impact.

8.11.6 Summary

As CI continues to modernize, especially in terms of adopting newer technologies, especially in the areas of energy and utilities, cybersecurity is a constant consideration. The impact of these attacks is, however, enormous, and thus good protection needs to be put in place to defend the two sectors. It is important that next steps include great utilization of AI, ML, and predictive analytics to help prevent threats to these systems and improve their reliability and security. As more research about cybersecurity is being conducted and new strategies being applied, these sectors can protect themselves against new potential threats and provide the population with safe and reliable services.

8.12 Lessons Learned: Key Takeaways from Practical Applications

What immediately shows is cybersecurity is an ongoing process that has practical applicability to organizations' industries and security professionals. With everything from case study analysis to practical approaches in dealing with threats that have been documented in real life, here are some of the important things that may be learned from such experiences by companies, governments, and other organizations. In the following section, we discuss some of the important implications that emerged from real-life case studies in the context of cybersecurity.

8.12.1 Artificial Intelligence and Machine Learning as Essential Tools for Threat Detection

Traditional methods of detecting and combating cyber threats were completely overgrown by modern ML and AI. In practical solutions, these technologies have been found useful in improving the detection's speed and accuracy of threats. According to Balantrapu [6], AI-based systems can analyze large datasets in real time and thus respond to new threats faster. In the realm of cybersecurity, the use of ML models, mainly supervised and unsupervised learning methods, has helped the detection of anomalous shapes and the mitigation of modern assaults. Refs. [10, 31] have discussed about few more case studies to emphasize preventive AI for defensive measures across healthcare, financial domains, and IoT networking.

8.12.2 Challenges in Securing Smart Cities and Internet of Things Systems

Smart devices and complex structures of smart cities and IoT are new challenges for cybersecurity specialists. Examples of such implementations reveal that although these technologies create almost unassuming advantages, they create much risk. In their recent paper, Chen et al. [13] further note that smart cities need an adequate protection system for CPSs and big data. In the same context, Altulaihan [2] explains the frailty of IoT devices and the need for robust countermeasures. These domains indicate cases that having a wide range of and larger devices in their size leads to a significant challenge concerning attack surfaces, which require new types of predictive analytics and internet monitoring solutions.

8.12.3 The Importance of Cybersecurity Education and Training

One of the best practical experiences that we can learn is that education and training play a significant part in the improvement of cybersecurity. Therefore, practical activities like vulnerability assessments and modeling of cyberattacks are stressed as important challenges by Fernández-Caramés and Fraga-Lamas [21] for training the next generation of cybersecurity experts. In addition, the use of case as a teaching aid has been found efficient in practicing what is taught in the classroom. For example, Cai [8] points to the importance of applying real-life case studies when it comes to the process of learning at educational institutions, during which students manage to determine possible threats and countermeasures.

8.12.4 Risk Management and Predictive Analytics for Mitigation

Perhaps some of the most compelling findings of applied cybersecurity literature revolve around the need to adopt risk management approaches. Such a mentality is not efficient when it comes to threats found in modern days' threat environment. System security and cyber risks are now widely predicted using analytics and risk modeling applications. As Chirra [39] also puts it, risk management models based on AI algorithms can highlight risks and lesion how attacks could happen before they take place. Real-world examples within fintechs, as described by Kafi and Akter [14], reveal how these techniques may be applied by organizations for securing critical information and organizational functionality.

8.12.5 Emerging Threats and Evolving Attack Vectors

Cybersecurity is not a fixed entity and is still a constantly evolving space, and new threats are constantly being released. Real-life examples call for the need for organizations to be responsive when dealing with these new challenges. For example, the advancement of methods that are used in cyberattacks, particularly in matters concerning industrial control systems is explained by Kasaraneni [27]. As Gunduz and Das [30] have shown in their real-world case studies, in smart grid security, attackers take advantage of broken infrastructure. Further, Jang and Jaccard and Nepal [38] have sharper views that threats like ransomware, phishing, APTs are evolving and they need modern and creative approaches, integrating MLs with conventional methods of security.

8.12.6 Collaboration Between Disciplines for Enhanced Cybersecurity

Security is not just the province of IT managers any longer. This is why a data scientist, engineer, and cybersecurity specialist, collectively, can only make an effective team for combating contemporary threats. In the futuristic work by Hosen et al. [25], the authors explain how integrating cybersecurity with data science may enhance threat detection using vast amounts of big data analysis and utilizing monitoring instruments. Such an approach has been effective in various sectors to which healthcare also belongs as pointed out by Malasowe et al. [36].

8.12.7 The Growing Need for Advanced Defense Models

This means that as the volume of threats in the cyber world rises, defense models which are needed to protect against them also become more complex. However, it has become a new trend

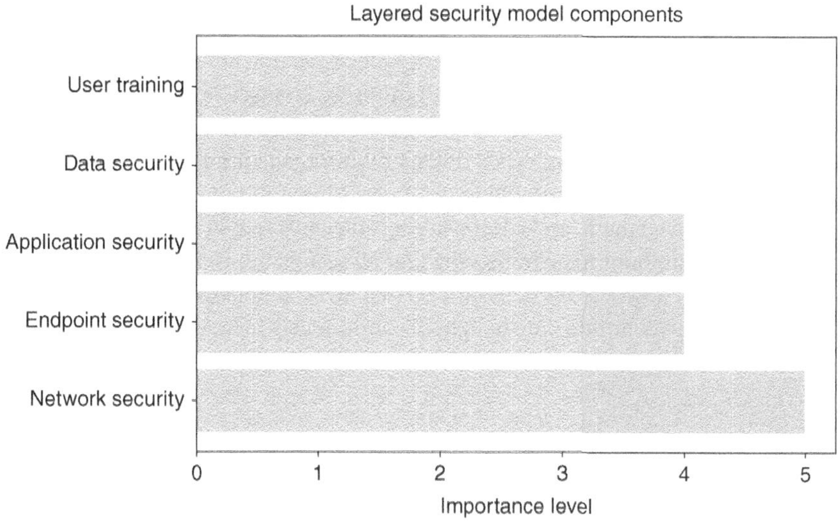

Figure 8.10 Overview of layered security model. Source: Hewa Majeed Zangana.

in many industries to incorporate the newest model that integrates old conventional methods with the newer-generation security solutions. According to Le et al. [35], modern defense systems that use AI, ML, cloud security, and blockchain technologies are more comprehensive in dealing with threats. Modern mass applications, for example, those used in financial and healthcare organizations, dictate the necessity of stack protection and the implementation of new technologies for further protection in the future. Multiple-layered protection paradigms constitute a framework of security solutions spread at different levels to offer full coverage. The following diagram shows a general layered security architecture, and important components at each layer are shown (Figure 8.10).

8.12.8 The Role of Continuous Monitoring and Authentication

Another important factor which became clear in actualizations of practical cybersecurity is the ongoing and dynamic nature of the process in terms of authentication. As cyberspace threats advance in complexity, the use of only static security precautions is clearly inadequate. Oduri et al. [19] posit that there should be perpetual authentication processes, with the use of behavioral biometrics for guarding systems, especially in sensitive sectors such as banking and, of course, government. The use of such technologies enables the systems to independently check the identity of users and observe for suspicious activities in real time particularly the internal and external threats.

8.12.9 Vulnerability Management and Rapid Incident Response

A key point derived from the authors' discussion of practical application of cybersecurity strategies is the need for vulnerability management and an effective incident response plan developed by organizations. Paté-Cornell et al. [32] show through examples that industries associated with CI, like energy, need sound processes in place for risk detection and rapid reaction if an event happens. In the same way, Tuma et al. [28] highlight the fact that the response time in terms of the detection, analysis, and response to attacks directly impacts the reduction of the consequences of cyberattacks.

8.12.10 Summary

The realistic cases give important insights into cybersecurity processes that are crucial for organizations to learn to prevent cyber threats as they evolve. Continuous changes in the cybersecurity landscape, coupled with the support of advanced technologies including, AI and ML, predictive analytics, and other methods, and combating cyber threats in an organization requires a group effort. Furthermore, one cannot overemphasize the issue of performing monitoring as a continuous process and vulnerability, management, and administering efficiency risk strategies. Over time, continued innovation will be paramount to guaranteeing that all sectors are viable and safe when running their operations online. These lessons demonstrate that all stakeholders need to continue to be knowledgeable, adaptive, and communicate in light of continuously increasing cybersecurity threats.

8.13 Conclusion

Concisely, the adoption of AI and ML into cybersecurity architectures has triggered a revolution in the way threats are identified, prevented, and responded to. Modern security challenges related to cyberspace indicate that the use of complex approaches different from classical models is necessary. Real-time data analysis as well as an overview of big data are possible due to AI solutions that allow understanding and preventing threats as soon as possible. Transferring from negative or reactive approaches to positive or preemptive modes of cybersecurity improves both the solidity and capability of security systems.

In every case cited as well as the practical applications made in this chapter, it is clear that systems accredited under AI have enhanced the detection of threats, estimation of risks, and handling of incidents. These technologies have been applied in various organizations comprising the healthcare system, financial organizations, manufacturing industries, and smart city organizations, among others, and have proven to work well. Nonetheless, some of the issues that are associated with the use of this approach include the following ethical issues, the need for specialists in handling the system, and the fact that adapting to current threats can, at times, be a tedious task. In future, challenges in deploying AI to enhance cybersecurity will also grow parallel with the development in deep learning, natural language processing, and predictive analytics. With the help of these technologies, one can create a better protected, more intelligent, and more resistant system. However, constant development and cooperation should be considered to work through the deficits and enhance the usage of AI in cybersecurity. Last, cybersecurity merged with AI's fast-evolving capabilities promises a future that has brought forth a proactive means of countering threats inherent to the digital environment and securing computing systems. The continuation of the sophistication of security systems through the utilization of AI technologies will not only help secure important infrastructures but also ease the creation of new and improved, smart, safe, and secure internet environments in every business around the globe.

References

1 Chirra, D.R. (2021). AI-enabled cybersecurity solutions for protecting smart cities against emerging threats. *International Journal of Advanced Engineering Technologies and Innovations* 1: 237–254.

2 Altulaihan, E., Almaiah, M.A., and Aljughaiman, A. (2022). Cybersecurity threats, countermeasures and mitigation techniques on the IoT: future research directions. *Electronics (Basel)* 11 (20): 3330.
3 Humayun, M., Niazi, M., Jhanjhi, N.Z. et al. (2020). Cyber security threats and vulnerabilities: a systematic mapping study. *Arabian Journal for Science and Engineering* 45: 3171–3189.
4 Jimmy, F. (2021). Emerging threats: The latest cybersecurity risks and the role of artificial intelligence in enhancing cybersecurity defenses. *Valley International Journal Digital Library* 564–574.
5 Nassar, A. and Kamal, M. (2021). Machine learning and big data analytics for cybersecurity threat detection: a holistic review of techniques and case studies. *Journal of Artificial Intelligence and Machine Learning in Management* 5 (1): 51–63.
6 Balantrapu, S.S. (2024). A comprehensive review of AI applications in cybersecurity. *International Machine Learning Journal and Computer Engineering* 7 (7).
7 Chowdhury, R.H., Prince, N.U., Abdullah, S.M., and Mim, L.A. (2024). The role of predictive analytics in cybersecurity: detecting and preventing threats. *World Journal of Advanced Research and Reviews* 23 (2): 1615–1623.
8 Cai, Y. (2018). Using case studies to teach cybersecurity courses. *Journal of Cybersecurity Education, Research and Practice* 2018 (2): 3.
9 Vrhovec, S., Fujs, D., Jelovcan, L., and Mihelic, A. (2020). Evaluating case study and action research reports: real-world research in cybersecurity. *Journal of Universal Computer Science* 26 (7): 827–853.
10 Banik, S. (2022). Case studies of machine learning in cyber threat detection. *Unique Endeavor in Business & Social Sciences* 1 (1): 192–204.
11 Tweneboah-Koduah, S., Skouby, K.E., and Tadayoni, R. (2017). Cyber security threats to IoT applications and service domains. *Wireless Personal Communications* 95: 169–185.
12 Fernández-Caramés, T.M. and Fraga-Lamas, P. (2020). Use case based blended teaching of IIoT cybersecurity in the industry 4.0 era. *Applied Sciences* 10 (16): 5607.
13 Chen, D., Wawrzynski, P., and Lv, Z. (2021). Cyber security in smart cities: a review of deep learning-based applications and case studies. *Sustainable Cities and Society* 66: 102655.
14 Kafi, M.A. and Akter, N. (2023). Securing financial information in the digital realm: case studies in cybersecurity for accounting data protection. *American Journal of Trade and Policy* 10 (1): 15–26.
15 Li, C. and Qiu, M. (2019). *Reinforcement Learning for Cyber-physical Systems: with Cybersecurity Case Studies*. Chapman and Hall/CRC.
16 Zografopoulos, I., Ospina, J., Liu, X., and Konstantinou, C. (2021). Cyber-physical energy systems security: threat modeling, risk assessment, resources, metrics, and case studies. *IEEE Access* 9: 29775–29818.
17 Pattyam, S.P. (2021). Artificial intelligence in cybersecurity: advanced methods for threat detection, risk assessment, and incident response. *Journal of AI in Healthcare and Medicine* 1 (2): 83–108.
18 Khan, M. (2023). *Exploring the Dynamic Landscape: Applications of AI in Cybersecurity*. EasyChair.
19 Oduri, S. (2024). Continuous authentication and behavioral biometrics: enhancing cybersecurity in the digital era. *International Journal of Innovative Research in Science, Engineering and Technology* 13: 13632–13640.
20 Sherman, A.T., DeLatte, D., Neary, M. et al. (2018). Cybersecurity: exploring core concepts through six scenarios. *Cryptologia* 42 (4): 337–377.

21 Fernández-Caramés, T.M. and Fraga-Lamas, P. (2020). Teaching and learning IoT cybersecurity and vulnerability assessment with Shodan through practical use cases. *Sensors* 20 (11): 3048.

22 Thakur, K., Qiu, M., Gai, K., and Ali, M. L. (2015). An investigation on cyber security threats and security models. *2015 IEEE 2nd International Conference on Cyber Security and Cloud Computing*. IEEE. 307–311.

23 Xenofontos, C., Zografopoulos, I., Konstantinou, C. et al. (2021). Consumer, commercial, and industrial IoT (in) security: attack taxonomy and case studies. *IEEE Internet of Things Journal* 9 (1): 199–221.

24 Obi, O.C., Akagha, O.V., Dawodu, S.O. et al. (2024). Comprehensive review on cybersecurity: modern threats and advanced defense strategies. *Computer Science & IT Research Journal* 5 (2): 293–310.

25 Hosen, M.S., Al Mamun, M.A., Khandakar, S. et al. (2024). Cybersecurity meets data science: a fusion of disciplines for enhanced threat protection. *Nanotechnology Perceptions* 236–256.

26 Leszczyna, R. (2021). Review of cybersecurity assessment methods: applicability perspective. *Computers & Security* 108: 102376.

27 Kasaraneni, R.K. (2019). AI-enhanced cybersecurity in smart manufacturing: protecting industrial control systems from cyber threats. *Distributed Learning and Broad Applications in Scientific Research* 5: 747–784.

28 Tuma, K., Sandberg, C., Thorsson, U. et al. (2021). Finding security threats that matter: two industrial case studies. *Journal of Systems and Software* 179: 111003.

29 Reuvid, J. (2018). *Managing cybersecurity risk: cases studies and solutions*. Legend Press Ltd.

30 Gunduz, M.Z. and Das, R. (2020). Cyber-security on smart grid: threats and potential solutions. *Computer Networks* 169: 107094.

31 Mishra, A., Ghosh, S., and Mishra, B.K. (2019). Cybersecurity: a practical strategy against cyber threats, risks with real world usages. In: *Cyber Security in Parallel and Distributed Computing: Concepts, Techniques, Applications and Case Studies* (ed. D.-N. Le and R. Kumar), 207–220. Wiley.

32 Paté-Cornell, M., Kuypers, M., Smith, M., and Keller, P. (2018). Cyber risk management for critical infrastructure: a risk analysis model and three case studies. *Risk Analysis* 38 (2): 226–241.

33 Rosado, D.G., Santos-Olmo, A., Sánchez, L.E. et al. (2022). Managing cybersecurity risks of cyber-physical systems: The MARISMA-CPS pattern. *Computers in Industry* 142: 103715.

34 Sharma, P. and Gupta, H. (2024). Emerging cyber security threats and security applications in digital era. *2024 11th International Conference on Reliability, Infocom Technologies and Optimization (Trends and Future Directions)(ICRITO)*. IEEE. 1–6.

35 Le, D., Kumar, R., Mishra, B.K. et al. *Cyber Security in Parallel and Distributed Computing*. Wiley.

36 Malasowe, B.O., Aghware, F.O., Okpor, M.D. et al. (2024). Techniques and best practices for handling cybersecurity risks in educational technology environment (EdTech). *NIPES-Journal of Science and Technology Research* 6 (2).

37 Mavani, C., Mistry, H.K., Patel, R., and Goswami, A. (2024). The role of cybersecurity in protecting intellectual property. *International Journal on Recent and Innovation Trends in Computing and Communication* 12 (2): 529–538.

38 Jang-Jaccard, J. and Nepal, S. (2014). A survey of emerging threats in cybersecurity. *Journal of Computer and System Sciences* 80 (5): 973–993.

39 Chirra, D.R. (2022). AI-driven risk management in cybersecurity: a predictive analytics approach to threat mitigation. *International Journal of Machine Learning Research in Cybersecurity and Artificial Intelligence* 13: 505–527.

9

Future Directions in Cybersecurity

Luay Albtosh[1] and Sia Gholami[2]

[1] *Capitol Technology University, Laurel, MD, USA*
[2] *The Institute of Electrical and Electronics Engineers, San Francisco, CA, USA*

9.1 Introduction

In cyberspace, rapid technological changes are an opportunity for progress and growth, as well as a threat to security. The escalating complexity of essential systems such as the IoT and new generations of information technology (IT) facilities and harmful actors have led to broader attack vectors [1, 2]. Businesses cannot defend against corporations by using conventional methods that have failed in protecting against advanced cyber threats and malwares; new techniques that have come to the market need to be adopted to favorable end by creating new threats.

Machine learning (ML) and artificial intelligence (AI) present some possible ways of improving cybersecurity, as all these methods allow detecting, predicting, and countering threats in real time [3, 4]. For instance, federated learning creates a decentralized platform that enhances data privacy but still addresses threat detection, which is crucial where data security is a concern [5]. The application of deep learning (DL) models also has the possibility to detect the anomalies and produce distinct patterns attached to cyber intrusions, especially in Internet of Things (IoT) and Industrial Internet of Things (IIoT) systems, where there is no effective centralized control [6, 7]. Another important domain in the future cybersecurity evolution is the cybersecurity mainstay in digital change processes in different fields. While industries adopt the use of innovations such as digital twins and Industry 4.0, new risks come into existence that need to be addressed concerning the secure execution of these integrated systems [8, 9]. Responsive to modern problems, cybersecurity measures that take account of the specifics of certain domains like low-carbon transportation and electric vehicles are becoming more relevant because of the extended nature of the challenges they are bound to pose for public policy and privacy [10, 11]. However, over time, big data analytics has been useful in the cybersecurity space to parse through big data for insights about networks and threats. Big data in cybersecurity enables the organization to start envisioning the risks that are taking shape, and this is quite crucial in sensitive areas such as supply chain and healthcare [12–14].

As the following bar chart shows, the existing cybersecurity threat is characterized by various threats' frequencies categorized below; this kind of visualization will assist in comprehending the nature of risk exposure to particular cyber threats, enhancing strategic focus in risk management of cyber threats in higher learning institutions.

Defense in Depth: Modern Cybersecurity Strategies and Evolving Threats, First Edition. Edited by Hewa Majeed Zangana.

In the following sections of this chapter, these and other promising directions for cybersecurity will be discussed. We will explore what AI and ML are, why there is a challenge that existing cybersecurity solutions are not generalizable across domain-specific industries and why cyber-resilience strategies are necessary for future digital economy platforms. Moreover, this chapter will discuss the role that current regulations and awareness campaigns will play in these advancing technologies in building a comprehensive cybersecurity environment.

9.2 Artificial Intelligence and Machine Learning for Predictive Security

AI and ML are two of the most progressive technologies in the world today that have reshaped the cybersecurity space through transformed possibilities of predictive security. Given a continuously growing level of sophisticated cyber threats, using AI and ML to design protection methods is crucial. The large data amount analysis in real time can prevent possible threats before they occur and strengthens the security measures [3, 13]. The following flowchart shows how an AI-driven predictive security system works with a ML algorithm to recognize patterns, anomalies, and other threats from real-time data inputs that have been collected from the previous time. This visual also gives insight into how using predictive models readjusts cybersecurity from a reactive model to a proactive model.

9.2.1 Artificial Intelligence-Driven Predictive Models

By utilizing AI, models help security teams move from security that is reactive to security that is proactive. These models apply ML algorithms to systematize past data to identify suspicious and new threats [15, 16]. Besides assisting in the recognition of near threats, predictive models are not static, and they improve threat recognition with time as they collect new data [17, 18]. For example, it is pointed out that unsupervised ML strategies could be effective at anomaly detection, which often results in the identification of either unknown or previously unrecognized threats to networks [19].

9.2.2 Machine Learning Techniques for Cyber Threat Detection

ML techniques are increasingly utilized for cyber threat detection due to their ability to analyze vast amounts of data quickly and accurately. In particular, these techniques can process network traffic, user behavior, and system logs to identify patterns indicative of potential threats. They are fast, efficient, and have been implemented in numerous applications; see Figures 9.1 and 9.2 for a depiction of ML.

This chapter shall focus on two ML techniques in cyber threat detection; they are among the most popular: supervised ML algorithms and unsupervised ML algorithms, along with reinforcement learning. Supervised learning is most effective for known attack types; basic methods include clustering of anomalies, which can help detect new and unforeseen threats that are not identifiable through supervised learning [6, 12]. Another solution has been federated learning, which enables threat intelligence sharing while aiming to protect data privacy—a crucial factor in today's world of increasing regulatory enforcement [5].

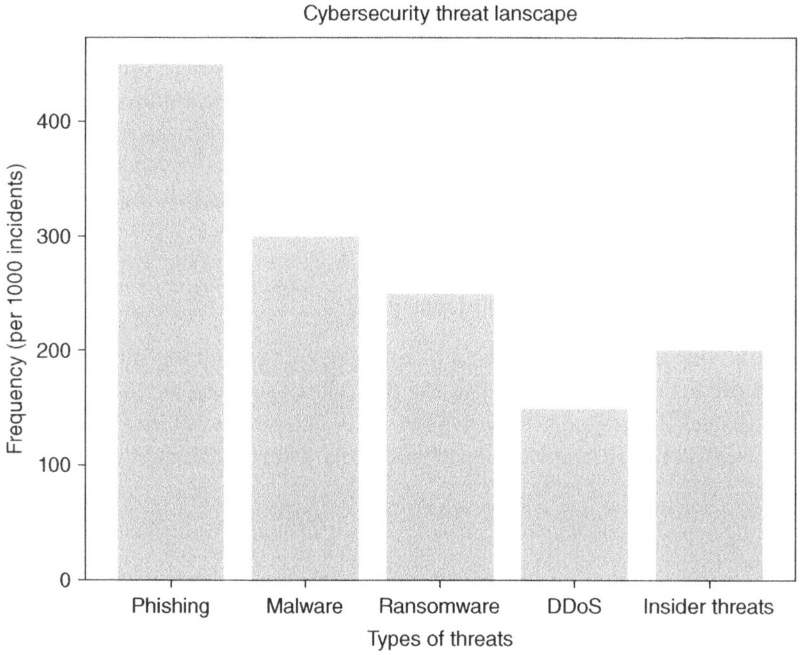

Figure 9.1 Cybersecurity threat landscape. Source: Hewa Majeed Zangana.

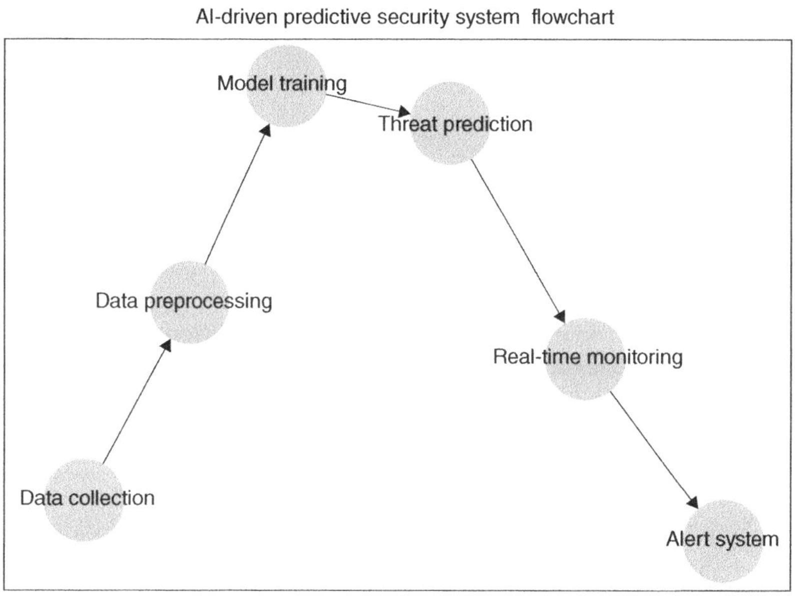

Figure 9.2 AI-driven predictive security system. Source: Hewa Majeed Zangana.

9.2.3 Enhancing Industrial and Internet of Things Security

AI and ML are being applied to secure the IIoT and Industry 4.0 systems, where cyber threats could cause various disruptive effects to operations [20]. Subsequently, the integration of AI with the cybersecurity of IIoT can help to enhance the processes of protection against risks and prevent attempts to control critical infrastructure [21]. This has become even more notable, especially with the increasing use of smart devices where the use of ML is effective in continuously analyzing for any irregularities in IoT devices in real time [1, 11].

9.2.4 Application in Critical Infrastructures and Industry 4.0

AI has helped cybersecurity among key areas such as healthcare, energy, and logistics become much stronger due to its predictive features [10, 14]. As the role of security in these sectors increases, AI delivers consistent and reliable requirements to counter risks before they occur [9, 22]; predictive security is important in supply chain cybersecurity, given that disruptions herein impact multiple sectors.

9.2.5 Future Directions

The application of AI and ML in the cybersecurity domain will increase as these technologies change, with an emphasis placed on improving the precision of the existing algorithms and decreasing the number of false positives. There is a growing development of research focusing on the issues of concern relating to AI within cybersecurity, including data protection and ethical issues [8, 23]. Further on, the focus would be made on working together with other institutions in order to improve the predictive security for the global goals by using new AI techniques in cybersecurity [4]. AI and ML are poised to remain a crucial component of cybersecurity and contribute to new approaches to threat detection and prevention and to the even more robust basis for digital transformation and Industry 4.0 [7, 24].

9.3 Quantum Computing and its Impact on Cryptography

Current developments in the context of quantum computing (QC) have become a marvel in terms of cryptography—and with that comes advantage as well as disruptive threats. The original types of defensive approaches are based on mathematical puzzles including factorization of huge numbers or discrete logarithms, which classical computers cannot solve within several millennia. But, with the help of principles like superposition and entanglement used in quantum computers, these problems can get solved exponentially faster; they are a threat to many of the current cryptographic solutions [15].

As a matter of fact, one of the dominating algorithms in quantum computing, Shor's algorithm, is capable of factoring large integers—thus undermining cryptographic methods such as Rivest–Shamir–Adleman (RSA). If QC reaches the level of qubits and error correction that makes it useful at a large scale, it will compromise these cryptographic protocols that underpin the security of communications over the internet. This means that a transition to contemporary cryptography that would be, commonly referred to as post-quantum cryptography [12], is required. These methods are based on mathematical problems that are considered to be resistant to quantum attacks for the current algorithms, such as lattice, hash, and multivariate polynomial [5]. Currently, the cybersecurity industry actively discusses post-quantum cryptography to create algorithms immune to quantum threats; however, there are several issues for application. First, there is also the problem of reducing the efficiency of the system, where many of these algorithms need more resources than their classical counterparts [11]. Second, migration from contemporary cryptology to quantum-safe algorithms will be a process of learning new protocols and tested ones, taking time to develop secure protocols, conduct tests, and shape standards for new compatible, integrated, and efficient systems (Ibid). Another stellar class of systems is quantum key distribution (QKD) that facilitates secure communication by the principles of quantum mechanics. QKD is also theoretically resistant to further development of interception in contrast to classical key exchange protocols, as any interception leads to detectable deviations [1]. This technology is yet in its infancy and is expensive. Both parties require sophisticated equipment and cell radio is conceivable only within a limited area due to present-day constraints [25].

These new paradigms are presently being newly investigated within the cybersecurity field, although it is [18] specified that the organization of quantum-resistant algorithms with current systems, structures, and frameworks may pose complicated technical, financial, and practical concerns. Furthermore, also with regard to cryptographic problems, it is underlined that due to the increasing prospects of using quantum computers, in this field, the world community has to focus on the development of post-quantum cryptographic standards and their subsequent transition to the application of quantum computers when they will have more extensive practical use [26, 27]. In this chart, the author outlines ways in which quantum cryptography differs from other cryptographic methods that exist. It indicates that the principles of quantum mechanics, such as entanglement, has an inherent bonus compared to classical strategy in terms of secured gambling (Figure 9.3).

Strengthening the resilience of solutions is now a matter of stepping up efforts in the cybersecurity domain, thanks to the further development of quantum computing. Given this realization, people are persistently striving toward the creation, assessment, and standardization of post-quantum cryptography as a preventive measure, given that the chances of the growth of quantum computers capable of genuinely threatening cryptographic security are inevitable [28, 29].

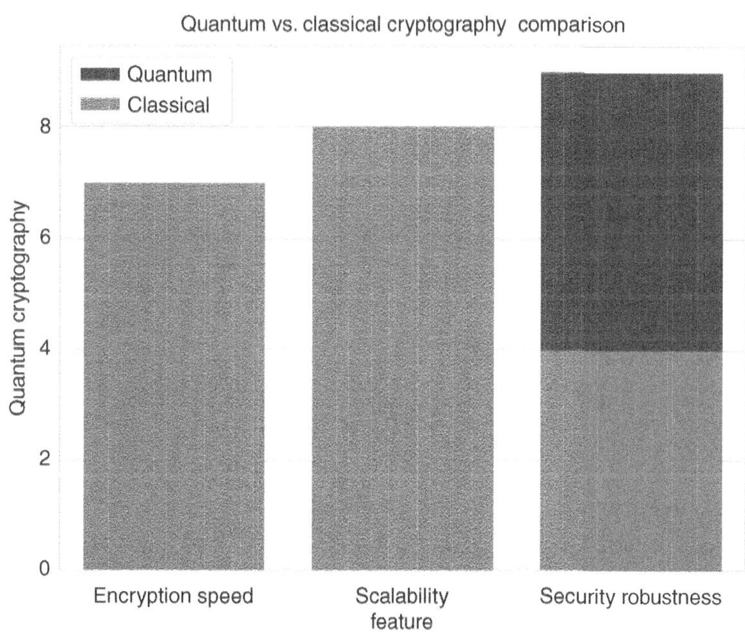

Figure 9.3 Quantum cryptography vs. classical cryptography comparison. Source: Hewa Majeed Zangana.

9.4 Cybersecurity for the Internet of Things and Cyber-Physical Systems

Integration of IoT and cyber-physical systems (CPS) is already a global trend in organizations and industries across many sectors, including smart city, healthcare, and industrial applications that require IoT and CPS; cybersecurity issues have become increasingly apparent. IoT and CPS will have multiple interconnected units that collect, send, and analyze data, which makes them have large risks that could be exploited by attackers. Securing these systems needs solutions to the problems presented by such systems like the presence of diverse devices, low processing power, and high scalability needs.

The second premising factor in IoT and CPS security is a diverse set of connected devices and protocols that prevent the unification of security solutions. As stated by Admass et al. [15], the presence of such diversity raises the probability of more attack surfaces and makes security more challenging to manage. Furthermore, low-energy and memory-constrained IoT devices cannot effectively perform traditional encryption algorithms, hence the need for lightweight cryptographic algorithms [1, 7]. Scholars like others [5] suggest federated learning and other decentralized models as likely ways for improvement of the security while not overwhelming the devices. This showcases that federated learning improves IoT security because it allows for distributed threat intelligence with the protection of end users' data. The following is the workflow diagram of federated learning, depicting how model training is done on the edge, threat data collected, and aggregated over the network (Figure 9.4).

Another significant problem that has to be solved to provide IoT and CPS security is the real-time processing of the data that is frequently necessary for many applications. Alani [12] noted that for data types and use cases like healthcare and autonomous cars, the data cannot be delayed which is a downside of complex security concepts. Cao et al. [10] also state that security solutions should be compliant with low-latency trends where it is needed most, such as low-carbon transportation. To this end, solutions like the use of intrusion detection systems tailored for low latency are being considered [26]. There are significant indications that AI and ML can improve IoT and CPS security in recent years. For example, Roshanaei et al. [3] share how ML models can parse data that IoT devices produce to identify suspicious patterns and anticipated invasions. Similarly, Pinto et al. [19]

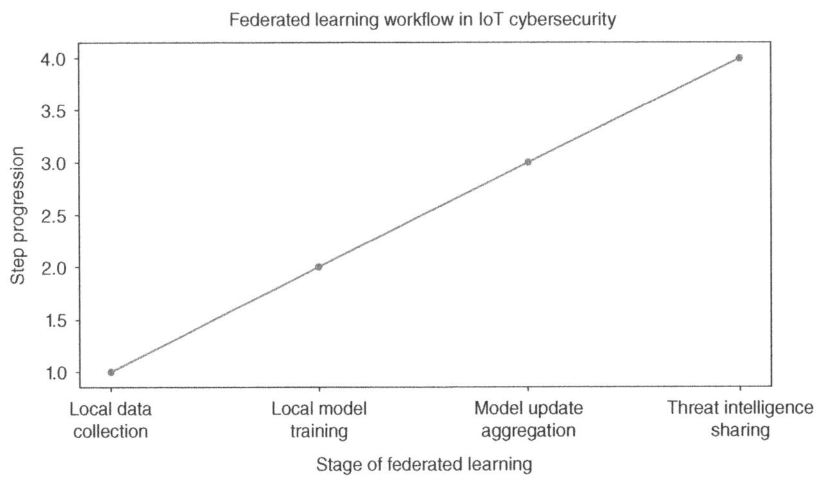

Figure 9.4 Federated learning workflow for cybersecurity in IoT. Source: Hewa Majeed Zangana.

state that using unsupervised learning techniques is capable of making security measures highly flexible in CPS environments due to unstructured data flow from CPS systems.

Such novel domains as applying digital twins in industrial processes make IoT security even more problematic. The proxy refers to a virtual copy of physical structures that enables real-time monitoring and management of performance. Nevertheless, Alshammari et al. [8] observe that digital twins improve the number of data points and communication channels that may be threated. Therefore, protecting digital twins from cyberattacks is not only an issue of the traditional protective elements but also other safety elements characteristic of the digital environment and new ways of interacting within this context between the physical and digital world. In general, IoT and CPS security require cooperation between institutions belonging to both the government and private industries. Chennamaneni et al. [23] specify by enhancing cybersecurity consciousness and develop perceived security learning instruments like AI-based games. However, the policies/restrictions also have a vital role in contributing to safe IoT practices. Khan et al. [30] emphasized the problem of compliance with the regulation of connected and automated vehicles, pointing to the infeasibility of a collection of rules that would be too varied to be effective. The chart below illustrates the variations in correct classifications and the number of false positives across several AI approaches used for anomaly detection in CPS. This data highlights the performance of these models in alerting individuals to any unusual activities in real time (Figure 9.5).

Possible areas of future studies are further enhancement of the proposed security models, more suitable for selected IoT use cases based on desired attributes such as security by design for IoT use cases of healthcare and manufacturing industries [20]. Other recommendations include improving the ML algorithms that ML systems apply to increase or detection accuracy and decrease of the number of false positives as these systems become popularized in IoT spaces [4]. Additional recommendations include enhancing the ML algorithms used in these systems to improve detection accuracy and reduce the number of false positives, especially as these systems gain popularity in IoT environments [4].

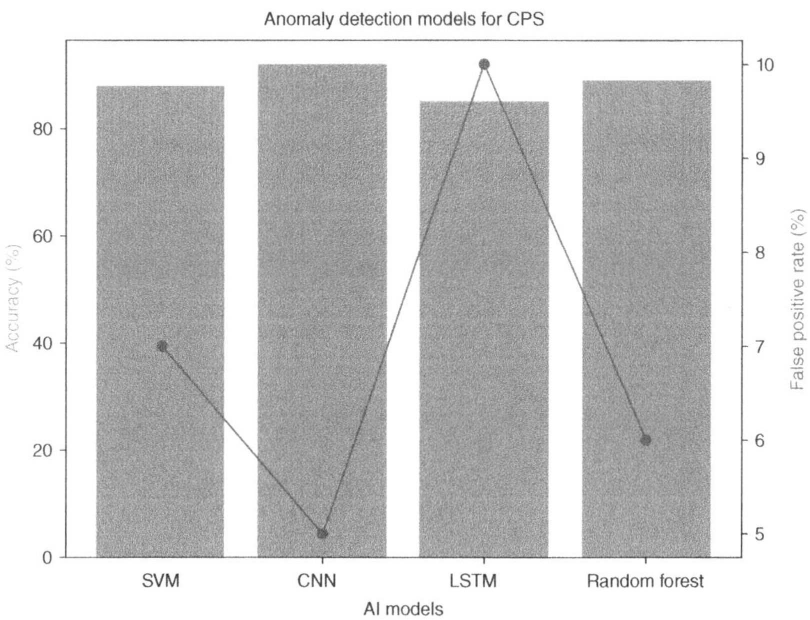

Figure 9.5 AI-driven anomaly detection in cyber-physical systems. Source: Hewa Majeed Zangana.

9.5 Blockchain and Decentralized Security Models

Security systems in different industries have been shifted from traditional approaches as blockchain offers decentralized methods of information security. The overall proposition of blockchain application in cybersecurity is based on distributed ledger technology (DLT) that guarantees data records are strictly checked and recorded in blocks. It is found that by decentralizing the data, blockchain improves transparency and eradicates the problems of data breaches, as it adopts a decentralized model [10, 12]. The old broad traditional security models are critical as they only focus on one aspect of security and do not distribute it throughout the network; one breach can make a whole network succumb to different dangers of cyberspace [18]. Blockchain, on the other hand, works on the known peer-to-peer network where many nodes must approve the transactions, and this dramatically reduces the chances of an outsider breaching the network [2]. For example, in supply chain management, the decentralized security models with the help of blockchain technology can provide real-time tracking of the product origin and can reduce the efforts of fraud [22, 29]. The other important use of the blockchain in security is in the creation of safe identity management solutions. Blockchain has a decentralized approach, which benefits the sides as users are free to control and verify their digital identity on their side. This independence not only protects from identity theft but also increases the protection of data by reducing the input of personal details [16, 19]. Assuming health records are sensitive in nature; this makes the adoption of the blockchain-based identity management models particularly relevant, especially in the medical record management where privacy and data correctness are critical success factors [14].

Still, there are often issues concerning the scalability of blockchain-based security, as well as, for instance, the energy concerns with approaches as proof of work (PoW). Concerns arise mainly when transactions are more since a decentralized ledger may need a lot of computational power to support more transactions, and this will result in environmental impact and costs. Other consensus types like proof of stake (PoS) and others are being developed to help overcome these drawbacks, while previously planning a more appropriate integration of blockchain in cybersecurity purposes [3, 5]. Similar to the case with blockchain, integrating AI with cybersecurity also presents future

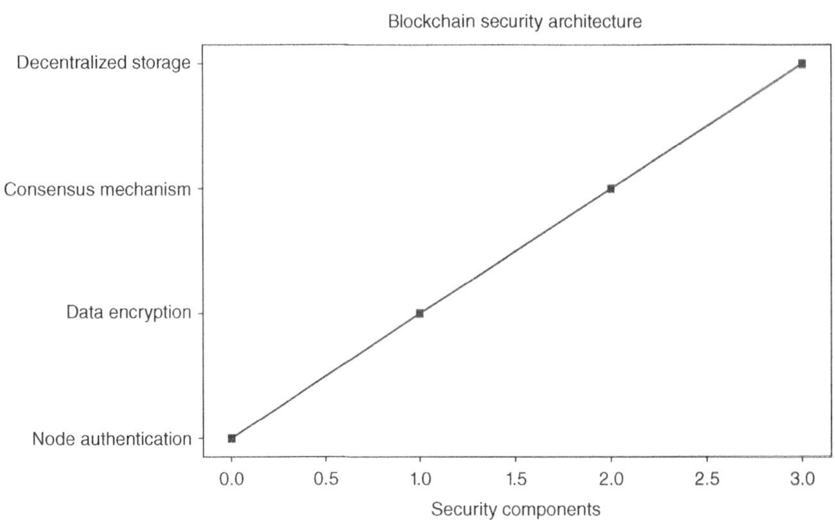

Figure 9.6 Blockchain security architecture. Source: Hewa Majeed Zangana.

innovations in protection. AI can complement blockchain by performing real-time monitoring for potential threats and associated predictive analytics to assess the security risks and to mitigate them as early as possible [4, 21]. For example, the combination of AI models with blockchain technology can develop safe and tenant-like systems for IoT and industrial automation areas where threat identification and counteraction are best done quickly [1, 20]. The following diagram provides an overview of the essentially decentralized security model of blockchain by focusing on some constituent pieces including peer-to-peer verifications, distributed ledgers, and the blocks that are encrypted. By breaking up the architecture in this way, you reduce the points of failure and increase openness (Figure 9.6).

In other words, because blockchain is inherently distributed and immutable, it is well suited for improving the security of various domains. This chapter has looked at how the integration of blockchain with other emerging technologies of the future will probably set the foundation of the future security models as the industries tighten their usage of the digital transformation techniques that require stronger data protection [15, 17].

9.6 Enhanced Privacy Techniques: Homomorphic Encryption and Secure Multiparty Computation

Homomorphic encryption (HE) and secure multiparty computation (SMPC) are two modern solutions that can provide outstanding opportunities in the sphere of cybersecurity. Importantly, as the threat landscape expands particularly across IoT, Industry 4.0, and automation, these approaches afford a clear manner for processing information within defined systems while ensuring that sensitive information is not exposed to malicious actors.

9.6.1 Homomorphic Encryption

HE enables data processing on the encrypted data, and without decrypting the data, ensuring that its security is maintained throughout the processing period. This type of technique is helpful when privacy of the data is an issue, but the data has to be processed in some other location in cloud computing or in multiparty communication systems. For example, in horizontally distributed secure data sharing in transportation networks or medical records in healthcare, HE imposes no exposure on data but allows computational processing in real time. PAGE 4: According to Alani [12], Big Data and Cloud environments, despite their significant advantages, present substantial vulnerabilities. However, HE provides an important layer of protection.

The computation support available from HE to make computations encrypted makes it appropriate for IoT and connected devices to need high-level security and low processing power. The privacy aspect in the IoT frontier and how HE removes limitations by allowing computations on data across the distributed devices has been exposed by Ahmed and Yunus [1].

9.6.2 Secure Multiparty Computation

Secure multi-party computation (SMPC) is also one of the complicated methods among all the parallel and distributed computing techniques because it enables multiple parties to compute a function on their inputs without revealing their inputs. This approach is applicable where two or more parties involved in a joint analysis do not require the other party to view their data. For instance, in the context of supply chain cybersecurity, as demonstrated by Layode et al. [2], SMPC is beneficial because it allows multiple members to assess potential security threats without exposing sensitive data.

SMPC has been deployed in contexts where there is a need to foster cooperation for protection, for example, in Industry 4.0 through the use of twin digital technology. Alshammari et al. [8] stress in their paper from 2021 on the cybersecurity for digital twins and the manner in which SMPC can provide improved privacy toward interrelated systems by securely evaluating sensitive data for realistic settings among several digital twins.

9.6.3 Challenges and Future Directions

Nonetheless, both HE and SMPC come with the problems associated with increasing computational cost and scalability. As we have seen, while HE can be applied effectively, it usually requires a high amount of computational power—an aspect that remains prohibitive for resource-constrained IoT devices [31]. While using SMPC is relatively easy in the abstract mathematical sense, it may be hard to compute in actual use cases given real-world limitations such as network latency and overall message passing. These techniques are crucial for improving effectiveness and availability. ML and AI are essential for enhancing efficiency. Roshanaei et al. [3] indicate that AI should be incorporated into cybersecurity for resilience. Consequently, it is evident that HE and SMPC are two robust privacy-preserving tools available in the cybersecurity domain. While both have special benefits and drawbacks, these fundamental aspects have to be explored in future research to pave the way for proper application of the presented methods in a number of different sectors, starting with IoT and continuing with Industry 4.0.

9.7 Human-Centric Cybersecurity and Behavioral Defense Mechanisms

Certified cybersecurity technician (CCT) in recent years was not just a technical approach to protection, but an approach centered on human characteristics and decision-making. This shift acknowledges the fact that many activities performed by human beings are the first line of defense and at the same time are infamous for being the vulnerable points in any system, for instance, falling for phishing scams or forgetting to change their passwords. It is crucial to improve the focus on human factors in the approaches to cybersecurity since the counteraction has to consider the ways people may influence the system.

User-centric cybersecurity is the approach that embraces education, behavioral changes, as well as devices that are friendly to the user in a bid to avoid weak points from the users. In their study, Admass et al. [15] found out that by training the user to assess the risks related to a cyber threat, the probability of being a victim of a social engineering attack would be significantly minimized. On the same note, Alani [12] asserts that risks can be detected from user interactions in big data analytics due to the increased volumes. Therefore, the problem does not only involve utilizing a proper understanding of human behavior but also formulating cybersecurity policies to match people's strengths and weaknesses [8]. The above notion has suggested that there are explanations and behavioral defense mechanisms like gamification and security training for enhancing users' security awareness [23]. Creating cybersecurity training in an effective and more engaging way can help avoid the issue of training boredom and enhance the participants' consistent effectiveness in terms of security principles applied during training. That is more relevant in high-risk settings because when the threat surfaces, but it is not constant, frequent and stimulating training can assist staff in maintaining their guard up for an extended period [16]. The use of AI in human-centric security also has begun receiving significant interest. ML, on the other hand, can use pattern recognition of users to identify signs of threats from the traffic [3]. These systems can incorporate or compute from previous performance and also generate warning alarms to allow for immediate security action. Al-Hawawreh et al. [25] provide examples of how ChatGPT and similar models help create contextual training materials that may apply cybersecurity education exactly to the extent and in a manner that would correspond to each user's behavior.

Also, such behavioral defense mechanisms are being introduced to adapt to certain industries and uses. For instance, in the supply chain management, recognizing the behavioral factors of vendors and partners has become critical to ensuring security in the supply chain [22]. In healthcare, behavioral defenses are specifically designed to guard information about patients, as Shah and colleagues describe when it comes to radiology AI systems since data leaks can have adverse impacts on patients' rights and lives. For further incorporation of the human-centric principle, future research has to investigate further how these behavioral defenses fit into other approaches of cybersecurity, like federated learning [5] and IoT technologies [1]. Further, Rauf [18] has proposed that bio-inspired approaches which can integrate and develop as per human behavioral models should have to be implemented in cybersecurity. This is because as organizations adopt these strategies, the convergence of technology with people-oriented solutions will be key in addressing and evolving the cybersecurity space.

9.8 5G and 6G Network Security

5G technology has provided a means through which global communications have evolved through higher speed, low latency, and an immense number of devices. This advancement though has brought about new challenges to cybersecurity because of the dependence and integration of network functions on software. In subsequent steps toward 6G, these issues are set to worsen as the technologies will involve AI-controlled network management, distributed edge computing, and next-gen IoT systems, all of which demand fresh notions of security [1, 30].

In 5G, the security threats are as a result of the multiple network layers with security threats that affect the decentralized core network as well as the distributed edge network. Less significant points comprise risks of intrusion in software-defined networking (SDN) and network functions virtualization (NFV) that the SDN virtualization of resources enlarges with the NFV virtualization. These concerns are further exacerbated in 6G because the increased implementation of AI and ML in the network control planes raises more questions in terms of the capabilities of adversaries to tamper with these systems as well as issues with model poisoning and data privacy concerns [5, 11]. As a result, federated learning has come out as a promising solution to secure novel 5G and 6G systems since it prevents data leakage and enhances privacy by processing data locally. Federated learning enables several devices to coordinate to train ML models without the transfer of raw data, thus aiding in protecting distributed network components. However, federated learning also comes with other issues that need to be addressed including the privacy and security of the learning process and how to prevent what is known as a model poisoning attack, where malicious data, can actually contaminate the model shared among all the different devices [3, 6]. Another area of interest he mentioned is the security of the IoT environments facilitated by 5G and 6G. As billions of IoT devices integrate into these networks, the vulnerability of such networks to attacks and data losses is high. Risk can be managed through the proper implementation of strong authentication methods, robust encryption techniques, and the incorporation of AI-based detection systems, as well as ML-based detection methods. However, IoT also needs to be secure and protected within 5G and 6G networks with solutions that are also increasing to deal with device trust and often detecting these compromised devices in real time [2, 7].

6G will also lead to new applications in sensitive areas such as health, transportation, or smart manufacturing that imply a high risk from a cyber perspective. To solve the aforementioned dilemmas, it is imperative to proceed beyond mere work on specific technological ideas; regulatory and policy upgrades are indispensable to guarantee stable safety that will shield user data as well as the integrated services' unassailable solidity. For example, the provision of policy on data localization and the flow of data across borders will have to adapt in order to accommodate the extremely dynamic process of internationalization of network structures [15, 29]. In summary, there is an escalating need for network security to be enhanced as we shift from 5G to 6G. There will be a need to create and enact broad, continually changing security strategies incorporating software and law to protect these new generation networks from various emerging security threats.

9.9 Cybersecurity in Cloud Computing and Edge Environments

As organizations turned toward cloud and edge computing for storing and analyzing data, several new fields of cybersecurity were developed. Regarding benefits, cloud computing offers expandable and rather polymorphic resources, while it brings issues of data protection, multi-tenancy threats, and virtualized environment's weaknesses to mind. Just like edge computing, which means that data processing takes place closer to the source, it also minimizes latency but has its share of security issues that are brought about by the decentralized nature of the networks.

As a result, cloud computing security could be a weakness and be different than the common practices of physical termination and constant monitoring. A centralized model could provide an inadequate approach to addressing the issues of flexibility and extensibility inherently tied to cloud offerings. Admas et al. [15] also addressed the increase in complexity of cybersecurity frameworks and the need to develop strategies that will provide a dynamic or real-time protection for cloud environments. According to Alazab et al. [5], the concept of federated learning can improve the security of the cloud space since data and model learning are distributed, and thus, the risks of a centralized attack are moderated. Nevertheless, this approach seeks to address privacy problems versus the proper management of data and information. In edge computing, decentralized resources increase cybersecurity threats such as device tampering and data integrity issues. Collectively, edge devices can be found in physically insecure environments, making them vulnerable to physical attacks that might be inconceivable to supervising centralized systems. Ahmed and Yunus [1] argue that IoT has endpoint security issues, and this is connected to edge computing systems. Since edge environment operates under less supervision and with immediacy to end consumers, establishing secure communication and reliable encryption is crucial to avoid adversaries' compromise and unauthorized access to resources [20]. Similarly, Roshanaei et al. [3] have also clearly pointed out that the use of AI for the recognition of anomalous situations in edge networks is possible; while it indicates some interesting future works to be carried out in this regard, it is quite a demanding approach in terms of available resources. Belkhamza [32] notes that it is becoming critical to have an elastic security framework that can flexibly adapt constantly to the challenges arising from a partially centralized but partially distributed cloud-edge context. The process of initiating such frameworks includes the use of AI and ML to create algorithm which may prevent future cyber threats from escalating. However, to realize this goal, there are some barriers that have to do with data openness, data portability, and compliance, as highlighted by Alani [12].

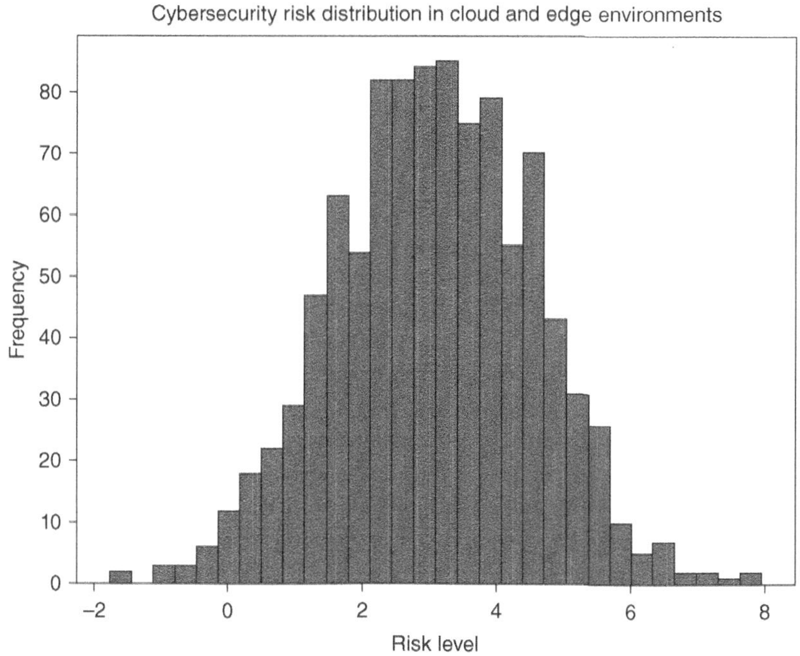

Figure 9.7 Cybersecurity risk distribution in cloud and edge environments. Source: Hewa Majeed Zangana.

Thus, the future trends of cybersecurity in cloud and edge computing will be associated with the development of an immunity that would entail self-repairing designs and automatic answering mechanisms. In their article, Yu et al. [21] suggest making resilience ML-driven and provide solutions that are dynamic over the environment and the ever-changing cyber threat. Such improvements are expected to bring not only more security but also efficient resource management between cloud and edge systems. This histogram shows the risks accrual in the cloud and edge computing domains, with the emphasis on heightened security threats. The examination of these distributions can help in creating specific risk management measures (Figure 9.7).

Due to the integration of cloud and edge systems, it becomes crucial to get layer cross-cutting security which secures data through every stage such as storing in the cloud and processing in the edges.

9.10 Zero Trust Architecture and Adaptive Security Models

Cyber threats are progressively becoming more and more complex, and therefore, any security models employed by organizations have to offer security at every layer of the organization's framework. One of today's most widely used methodologies for protecting modern networks is called zero trust architecture (ZTA). The zero trust (ZT) model works on the basis that there is no perimeter where trust can be assumed, whether users are internal or external. Any time somebody tries to access a system, this is viewed as a potential threat and thus has to be checked out before being allowed. In a ZTA identity, device health and behavior are continuously verified; hence, the mechanism checks on the activities of users even after granting them access to the system.

ZTA solves several major shortcomings in conventional approaches to security. One of the skills that it brings is protection from insider threats which have emerged as a crucial issue in the context of remote working and cloud infrastructures. Due to its operation on the concept of least privilege, the users of ZTA are given only the basic privilege needed for them, thus denying the attackers more grounds on which they could launch an attack. Additionally, it is the case that ZT policies are beneficial in preventing breaches from spreading throughout the network. Other than ZT, adaptive security models have become almost synonymous with the current security environment. Adaptive security models are supposed to work according to the data accumulation and risk assessment. They are not like the traditional models that have standard measures or rules that are used in the execution of the model. This flexibility helps an organization to prevent various risks while at the same time ensures that system integrity is maintained. Most of the adaptive security models propose incorporation of the ML and AI algorithms to foresee or detect any irregularity in users' activities or network traffic that might correspond to instances of violation. These models are most beneficial in more heavy-duty applications like IoT structures that can accommodate vast numbers of devices and information than earlier; conventional security measures are also not adequate within these structures. For example, ML-based solutions are already integrated into many adaptive security architectures because they can adjust and hone their threat-detection algorithms by studying increasing amounts of data. Furthermore, the application of ML together with the ZT Security architecture has proven to be an effective approach as the combination of the validation undergone by ZT models and approaches with the flexibility and predictive characteristics of AI was explored by Roshanaei et al. [3].

However, the introduction of such comprehensive models has several problems, such as increasing the quality of the training sample and preserving the stability of AI models against adversarial ones [5]. Adaptive security models are critical in the IoT application area because of the diverse nature of IoT networks and threats that are likely to prevail. Since IoT devices are inherently difficult to secure due to their small computational capabilities and communication protocols, the use of adaptive models is even more important [1]. When integrated with adaptive security, the ZT approach forms a security framework to protect IoT systems against new-age threats since it verifies the security state of every connected device at runtime. Additionally, federated learning is getting attention as a promising approach for improving adaptive security in the distributed setting. In federated learning, data does not need to travel far; only the model updates travel to other devices, reducing the exposure of sensitive information to threats, thus the importance of federated learning in securing systems that run in the cloud or across multiple edge devices [5]. This method not only enhances the privacy of data but will also enable designing a stable framework of ML models that can easily identify any fraudulent action in real time. As highlighted in the case of both ZT and the adaptive security model, changes needed must be underpinned by right investments. To be more precise, Refs. [11, 15] listed various studies that substantiate the fact that future cybersecurity systems will employ all four models to develop a sound and highly resistant defense structure. Threats are a fluid concept that needs an ongoing and evolving solution that not only incorporates the elements of security while also is able to learn and respond to changes in threats.

This flowchart shows an example of how ZT security model works in a way which examines each access request. ZT was designed to apply to modern digital landscapes as it assumes each user and device to be compromised (Figure 9.8).

Therefore, the application of ZTA and adaptive security models reflect a change in the perception of how organizations address cyber threats. These models provide the required agility, fault tolerance, and more importantly, microscale adjustability to counter highly evolved and continually evolving threats from the cyber domain. By incorporating the use of AI as well as ML in such frameworks, the capability in identifying, detecting, as well as counteracting threats is also advanced, resulting in a stronger and safer network.

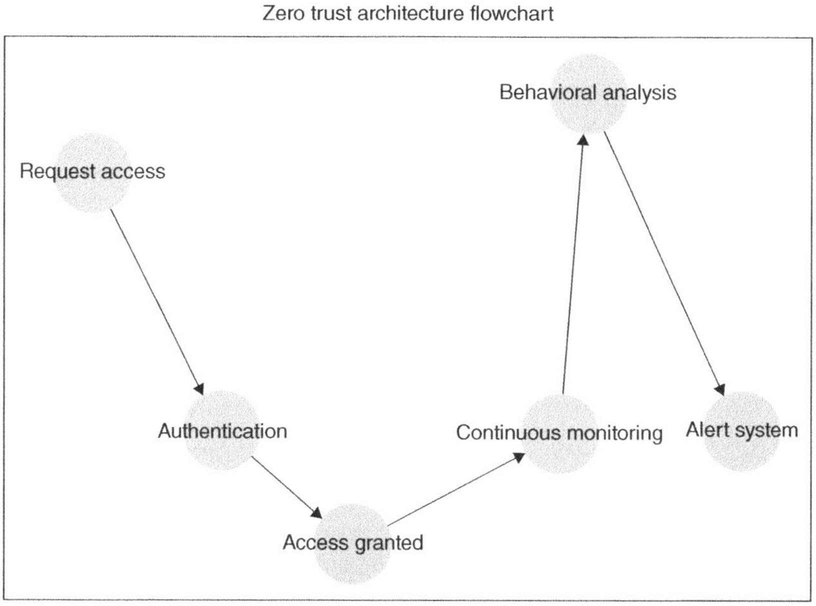

Figure 9.8 Zero trust architecture. Source: Hewa Majeed Zangana.

9.11 Biometric Security and Next-Gen Authentication Mechanisms

Biometric security has evolved to act as a critical technology in addressing the stability and effectiveness issues of current authentication technologies across portable gadgets to restricted zones. It is realized out of identified inherent characteristics inherent within biometric features, for instance, fingerprints, iris, face, and voice, which are not easy to imitate compared to the password approach. With the advancement in cyber threats and with more and more information streams and a huge volume of data being stored and transferred over networks, the importance of biometric systems in controlling access to these resources is becoming vital. The innovative growth of ML and AI has made advancements for biometric technology, thus supporting it as the newest generation of the authentication solutions that offer higher levels of security, extensibility, as well as comfort.

9.11.1 Evolution of Biometric Authentication

Passwords and personal identification numbers (PINS) have long been known to be unsafe; user information is exposed to threats from brute force, phishing, and social engineering. These have resulted in the increase in usage of the biometric systems as a better option than the former. Another well-known modality by now inherent to mobile devices is fingerprint scanning, recently augmented by facial scans, iris and voice recognition, and even behavioral fingerprints, the patterns of which encompass keystrokes and gait [4]. The ever-increasing demand for better systems that are secure, faster, and also easy to use has prompted the improvement of both hardware and software of biometric systems.

9.11.2 Machine Learning and Artificial Intelligence in Biometric Systems

ML has come a long way in helping improve the kind of biometric systems, especially in image processing and pattern recognition. By improving the recognition effectiveness and the speed of

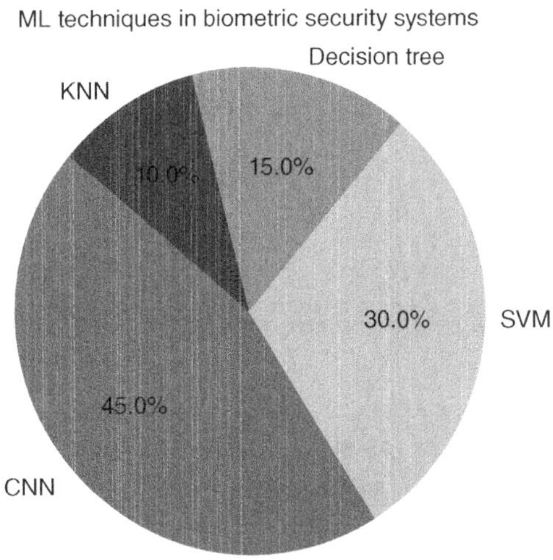

Figure 9.9 Machine learning techniques in biometric security systems. Source: Hewa Majeed Zangana.

biometric data processing, ML models are able to differentiate between similarities that might be very narrow. Convolutional neural networks (CNN)-ML-accompanied systems or DL models, for instance, CNNs are used for improving the quality of biometric capture, reducing errors, and identifying attempt frauds. For instance, AI can enhance facial recognition so that the current methods do not get overshadowed in the future due to variant in light, angles, and aging. The pie chart below displays the survey regarding the application of ML analyses in biometric security systems. Other methods like CNNs and support vector machines (SVMs) are used broadly for cancer diagnosis or fingerprint and facial recognition (Figure 9.9).

Another very rich and prospective area of biometric security is federated learning. This decentralized approach to ML means that biometric data can be processed on local devices, which also ensures the users' privacy because raw data never has to be sent to central servers [5]. In doing so, federated learning is useful to obtain general knowledge in the company without the disclosure of users' identities—an issue of major importance in systems of biometric identification.

9.11.3 Multi-Factor Authentication and Biometrics

Substituting biometrics along with passwords or using tokens as the dominant security technologies in multifactor authentication (MFA) frameworks. Underpinning security enhancement, MFA enhances multiple layers of verification, thus minimizing the vulnerability of the system to unauthorized access. For instance, a user might require to use his fingerprint in addition to a one-time password which will be sent to user's phone. However, when it comes to tackling new cybersecurity threats, MFA systems integrated with biometrics and relying on behavioral and contextual data become more popular. Such systems can capture a number of biometric properties, device characteristics, position, and other context hints to verify the identity of an access request [19].

9.11.4 Challenges in Biometric Security

However, there are several challenges that are associated with biometric authentication systems. One of the concerns is so-called spoofing when an attacker uses a fake fingerprint or a model of the face to get into the restricted area where facial recognition is used. As a remedy, several researchers are developing means of countering spoofing based on DL algorithms to distinguish real biometric input [12]. Furthermore, the matter of privacy and data protection should be also considered, because biometric data is normally classified as sensitive and non-changeable. Laws like General Data Protection Regulation (GDPR) set within the Europe Union and California Consumer Privacy Act (CCPA) in California have brought into focus the requirement to have sound and good data privacy governance in biometric authentication [25].

Another issue is the issue of diversity and integration of biometric systems. Not all people have biometric features that could be easily distinguished (for example, people with missing fingers or indistinct faces). To counter this, multitudes are designing better systems, for instance, by voice recognition or even behavioral biometrics that can accommodate many users [15]. In addition, the issue related to capacity is persistent, as large-scale biometric systems, for instance, at the level of national security or public health, should be able to work through the significant amount of data without compromising effectiveness.

9.11.5 Future Directions in Biometric Authentication

In future, knowing the tendency in the development of cybersecurity, it can be suggested that the usage of biometric authentication mechanisms will be refined. For the future, the biometric security system will use one or more modalities (for example, multimodal biometrics that will ensure more secure authentication). Immersing AI for amplification of decision-making in conjunction with real-time anomaly detection in biometric systems can give another dimension of protection and the capacity to detect unusual access patterns or a probable violation. Furthermore, the advancement in these quantum computations could result in better encrypted methods for biometric data, making the data more secure against attacks. In the near future, the increasing popularity of the usage of biometric-based security, and authentication in particular, will necessitate the development of open standards and frameworks. Future work in shared learning and privacy-augmented ML procedures will be vital in tracking privacy concerns needed in these systems [27].

9.11.6 Summary

Biometric security is revolutionizing the concept of authentication systems and has provided innovators with solutions that are both secure and easily utilized. More advanced AI and ML incorporation continues to evolve the next generation authentication mechanisms that can greatly improve the biometric systems' accuracy and robustness. Biometric applications in the future will embrace more development of multimodal biometric systems, secure integration with other authentication methods, and an emergence of new privacy-preserving technologies to deal with arising difficulties in the field (C1). Last, many scholars agree that biometric security will be of utmost importance in protecting the digital environment that is continuously under the onslaught of enhanced levels of cyber threats.

9.12 Ethics and Responsible AI in Cybersecurity

Total Quality Management (TQM), Corporate Governance, and IT Management: The ethical use of AI in cybersecurity has brought both potential solutions and new ethic issues as well. As the use of AI solutions progresses, one has to think about privacy, security, accountability, and fairness of AI solutions. Ethical considerations in AI for cybersecurity are important on two fronts—to make cybersecurity systems safe and secure on one hand and to minimize negative externalities, which include exacerbating bias or trampling on people's rights on the other.

9.12.1 Privacy and Data Protection

An issue already tied to the application of AI in the functioning of organizations is data management and especially the protection of personal information. Large-scale data handling for various tasks such as anomaly detection, threat analysis, and intrusion detection is common in AI systems. However, this data may contain writing, personal, or/and confidential data, which leads to data privacy and protection issues. These threats could be addressed by some of the privacy-preserving technologies like federated learning, where the data does not have to travel to the cloud to be processed, as discussed by Alazab et al. [5].

9.12.2 Bias and Fairness

This is another important ethic resulting from the implementation of AI systems: the ability to make distinctions. Any AI models, especially those used in intrusion detection or threat classification, will be bias with that of the input data fed to the model in the learning process. For instance, an AI system may be trained with data from specific geographic areas or network conditions; it may fail or even antagonize users or other equipment outside those regions. This issue has been looked into especially in the applications of cybersecurity, especially in ML [3]. To overcome such challenges, scholars have demanded larger and diverse data and openness in algorithm and model decision-making [17].

9.12.3 Accountability and Transparency

The decision-making processes of AI systems in cybersecurity are often ambiguous, that is, it is very hard to know how a particular security decision is arrived at. It is all the more worrisome given that the operation of AI remains opaque, especially when the systems are being decisive, for example, determining whether particular networks should be blocked or if a person poses a threat. However, to increase the level of confidence in AI cybersecurity systems, there is a necessity to explain their decision-making process. Authors have stressed the need for developing Explainable AI (XAI) models that will assist security practitioners in comprehending the decision-making logic of AI [4].

9.12.4 Security Risks and Adversarial Attacks

Alas, AI is not free from threats, and it can enhance the possibility of detecting cyber threats as well. The major form of threat is adversarial attacks, whereby adversarial players deceive AI models to breach security systems. This is a clear indication that the AI model deployed in cybersecurity needs to be very cautious and able to handle such attacks. Thus, the methods, including adversarial training to train an AI system with the perturbed data to provide robustness, are becoming prevalent to address this matter [7].

9.12.5 Ethical Artificial Intelligence for Cybersecurity in the Internet of Things

Internet of Things or IoT is a growing area of concern for cybercrime, if not for the complexity that IoT creates if not for the increased entry points for criminals. AI is effective in improving the security of IoT systems with the constraint that it should be implemented and follow the correct ethical benchmarks. For instance, AI systems should understand that IoT possesses several characteristics including low processing power and restricted resources, without jeopardizing on protection of devices and networks [1, 8].

9.12.6 Regulatory Compliance and Ethical Standards

Given continued technological developments regarding AI, and cybersecurity, this requires the formulation of clear regulations on how AI should be used and developed. It is imperative that governments and organizations work together to first establish rules and regulations in this field that will see international standards implemented throughout the world in AI applications for cybersecurity, while at the same time observing individual rights. There are emerging and dynamic trends with cybersecurity regulations, which are both opportunities and risks and will be discussed later; dealing with those risks will be the collective responsibility of all actors [16, 28]. Overall, AI within the framework of cybersecurity presents innovative possibilities while also raising ethical questions. To effectively address the contemporary trends in AI application, it is essential to consider key aspects related to them. Striking a balance between innovation and ethical implications is one of the most critical challenges in the application of AI. We are thus proposing to develop AI systems that have privacy protection, fairness, accountability, and regulatory compliance as their cornerstones to fight cyber threats, while at the same time passing the ethical test in the new digital world.

9.13 Cybersecurity for Autonomous Systems and Artificial Intelligence Agents

Advancements in autonomous systems (AS) and AI agents stabilize numerous industries, but they also present substantial security challenges. Many AS are now being integrated into critical infrastructure and everyday applications, making it essential to ensure their security. These systems, which operate using ML, DL, and data-driven models, are vulnerable to adversarial attacks, data poisoning, and denial of service (DoS) attacks, all of which could significantly compromise their performance and accuracy [15].

9.13.1 Threat Landscape for Autonomous Systems and Artificial Intelligence Agents

Transport systems, healthcare, and industrial operations require independent systems, which makes them more vulnerable to cyber threats. These risks include the potential manipulation of decision-making processes and the possibility of unauthorized access to control systems. For example, in relation to vehicular ad hoc networks, the attackers can take advantage of the vehicle-to-vehicle (V2V) communication links and cause an accident or interfere with the basic operation of the vehicular system [11, 30]. In addition, the AI agents can fall prey to adversarial attacks whereby even minor modifications of the input data can lead to misclassification or inaccurate predictions [5]. They can jeopardize the dependability and security of AI systems, as these technologies can be easily manipulated. A significant issue is that the methods used to train AI agents are often complex and opaque, making the challenge of ensuring protection much more difficult. Deep learning (DL) models, while powerful tools for classification, are notorious for being opaque or 'black boxes.' This means it is challenging to explain why a particular classification was produced and to identify any underlying flaws [6]. Such as in healthcare or self-driving cars, this lacuna of clarity starts to look very worrisome for any society if blame for mishaps is going to be cast [14].

9.13.2 Approaches to Cybersecurity in Autonomous Systems

In view of the emerging cybersecurity risks in AS, scholars are investigating several emerging high-level approaches. An example of a novel technique, federated learning, presents an effective solution to boost the security and privacy of ML learning models deployed in automated systems [5]. This approach is actually a form of distributed learning where many localized devices collectively train one model, but no identifiable data is passed among them, and this makes a system more secure against data leakage as well as more reliable. Another branch is aimed at the combination of AI- based security protocols with the autonomous system. For example, it is possible to use AI agents for the purpose of observing system activities, identifying suspicious activities, and responding to threats in real time [3]. Such capability of self-healing can greatly improve the robustness of the AS because these can bounce back from cyberattack without the need for direct human intervention. Additionally, new models for intrusion detection are being built based on AI to detect dangerous activities in real time and thus prevent them from occurring [26].

9.13.3 Regulatory and Ethical Considerations

The application of AI for AS also requires evaluation of legal provisions and policies regarding the utilization of AI. With the AI systems being deployed in the most crucial applications, it means that the existing laws need enhancement to be able to deal with these systems. This includes defining AI safety, privacy, and explainability requirements and guaranteeing that AI agents can be made to answer for their actions [32]. Moreover, the ethical issues associated with applying AS, especially in the military and healthcare domains, should have enhanced risk analysis in order to avoid misuse or cause any bad consequences [23]. Given the fact that AI systems are gradually more and more independent, urgent and suitable policies regulating the liberty of ideas and technological and information superiority, and, at the same time, ensuring security and ethical non-tolerance should be developed. Both governments and industries must develop and set prospective regulations that will adequately navigate the challenges AI brings while promoting innovation and confidence in cybersecurity.

9.13.4 Future Directions

In the future, several areas will focus on enhancing the cybersecurity of autonomous systems (AS) and AI agents. Firstly, the advancement of explainable AI (XAI) technology is crucial for improving the interpretability of security risk decisions made by AI, thereby enabling better risk minimization [4]. Moreover, AI integration with blockchain technology could address privacy and decentralization problems with data handling and the verification of the authenticity of safety descriptions of AS [21]. Further, the progression of further optimization of ML methods such as reinforcement learning and adversarial training can go a long way in developing robust AI systems that are not easily vulnerable to cyber threats [17, 18]. The present and future of protecting AS from cybersecurity threats is self-adaptive and intelligent methods, continuously adapting and learning about new threats as they appear so that the self-governed systems remain secure, dependable, and trustworthy.

9.13.5 Summary

Where the AS and AI agents are to be deployed in a critical application, their vulnerability to cyberattacks will further increase. To achieve this, the following approaches will be applied which are the

AI- based defense techniques, federated learning, and ethical standards. Through the mitigation of these hiccups, the future of autonomy can be significantly protected, especially as it introduces secure forms of AI into different industries.

9.14 Cybersecurity Workforce Development and Skills of the Future

Technological change, particularly regarding the use of AI, ML, and the IoT, also requires an ongoing growth in the production of a strong cybersecurity workforce. As the number and complexity of cyber-related threats continue to rise and evolve, it has become important that organizations must have an appropriately trained cybersecurity workforce and adequate security systems to address those challenges.

The following line graph provides an expected trend of various chief skills required for cybersecurity for the next decade in considering present trends coupled with developments in technology. This visualization raises more awareness about the need to develop updated AI, data analytics, and IoT security skill sets for future cybersecurity experts (Figure 9.10).

9.14.1 The Growing Need for Cybersecurity Professionals

Cybersecurity specialists are highly valued when it comes to the defense of both virtual and real resources against a wide array of cyber threats. As Admass et al. [15] have pointed out, today's threats are much more sophisticated than just hacking into a company's network, and the best defense against these threats is finding professionals who have technical knowledge but can also analyze new types of attacks. With the emergence of various cyber threats such as ransomware,

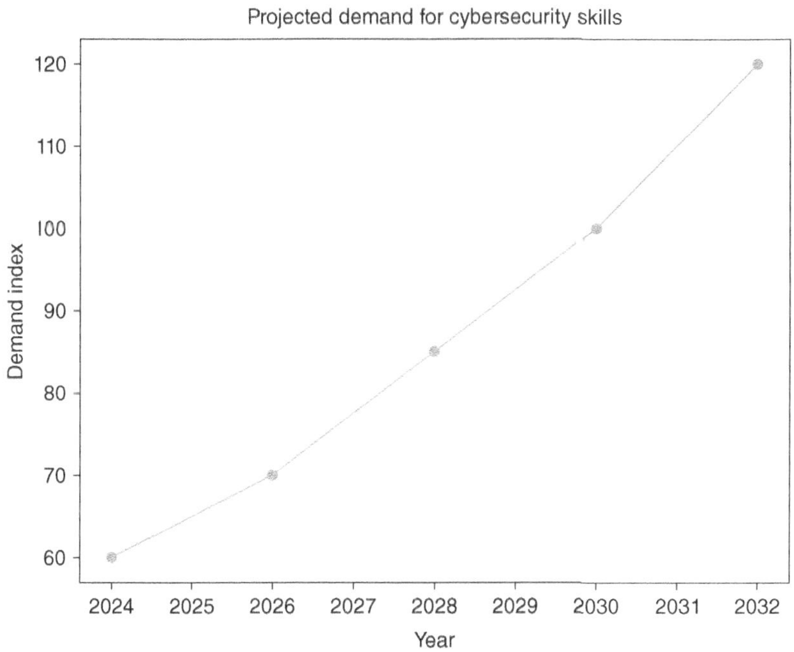

Figure 9.10 Future cybersecurity skill demand forecast. Source: Hewa Majeed Zangana.

phishing scams, and an increasing number of attacks on critical infrastructure, the need for ready and able IT support that can identify, prevent, and mitigate the threat has never been higher. Moreover, the advancement of new technologies clearly defines the future of cybersecurity as well. For instance, recent IoT advancement means that there is a need for specialists who understand security issues concerning the complex integration of devices [1]. A need for more intensive training in emerging areas, including IIoT and smart distribution, is required in industries as varied as manufacturing to energy [19, 20].

9.14.2 Key Skills for the Future Workforce

In its fourth year, International Information System Security Certification Consortium (ISC2) proudly presents its most dynamic conference yet, as advancing cyber threats challenge the skill of today's security personnel. Several core competencies will be essential for the workforce of the future:

1) **Technical Expertise in Artificial Intelligence and Machine Learning**: AI, along with ML, has emerged as the latest trends which are prominent in reshaping the cybersecurity threat detection and response [3]. Cybersecurity personnel will have to be conversant with programming languages and coding to design and build models of ML that will independently recognize unusual behaviors, forecast threats, and act correspondingly in situations where decisions are made instantly. This knowledge will prove useful in areas such as intrusion detection [26] and self-driving security of the new-age technology such as self-driven vehicles [30].
2) **Cybersecurity for Industrial Systems**: When companies shift toward digitalization, cybersecurity talent will be required to safeguard major structures. Industrial specialists will have to grasp various sophisticated aspects of protecting industrial systems including manufacturing facilities and power grids that are becoming IoT and other smart-integrated entities [22, 28].
3) **Data Analytics and Big Data Security**: Due to the concentration of data across several industries, big data management and analysis, alongside the security aspects of the same, will be a crucial factor that cybersecurity specialists will need to learn and master. Alani [12] observes that cybersecurity professionals must be able to address challenges confronting big data and leverage big data analytics systems in order to forecast and mitigate security threats.
4) **Cybersecurity for Autonomous and Electric Vehicles**: With the advent of electric and especially, autonomous vehicles, there is a rising demand for people to protect the communication systems in these vehicles [11]. The union of AI, ML, and the 5G link in vehicle systems raises new security concerns that will manifest specialized difficulties.
5) **Ethical Hacking and Red Teaming**: With the increase in organizations' implementation of advanced defensive solutions, we are likely to require more experts in offensive technologies such as Ethical Hacking/Red Teaming. They imitate some actions to see the weak points of an organized structure before such lapses can be profited by the wrongdoers [33].
6) **Cybersecurity in Digital Twins and Simulations**: When digital twins are useful in many industries, from construction to healthcare, these professionals would have to protect these real-world counterparts. Simulations in cybersecurity and the usage of both AI and game-based awareness programs present opportunities for educating the workforce about cybersecurity, as well as preparing them for real-life situations [23, 27].

9.14.3 Training and Education in Cybersecurity

In response to these demands, cybersecurity education and training programs must change. Current employees will have to learn and adapt to new skills, and upgrades, and new employees will have to learn about state-of-the-art technologies. According to Nasir [16], cybersecurity concepts should best be learned through practical sessions and with an element of realism that is driven through simulations of real life. The examples are initiatives originating from cooperative relations between academies, companies, and the government to design training strategies that will meet the current and future demands. Interdisciplinary skills will also be another characteristic that will form a focus while looking at programs. Due to the connections among different realms of cybersecurity with other domains like data analysis and AI, supply chain management, among other fields, individuals working in these fields equally require the attribute of interdisciplinary understanding and practice in order to come up with complex security solutions [2, 29].

9.14.4 The Role of Cybersecurity Research

They do this by focusing on telling research stories which is so vital when defining the future of cybersecurity. As indicated by Al-Hawawreh et al. [25], AI solutions like ChatGPT and other similar applications may help to organize cybersecurity basic jobs, in addition to presenting several emerging concerns that must be tackled through research, the case of federated learning in enhancing cybersecurity [5] remains a promising opportunity to secure decentralized networks while protecting data.

It is also important for the researchers to attend not only to the technical aspect of problems that arise but the aspect that concerns people and organizations involved in cybersecurity. With increasing extensity of threats, the user aspect—training people, dealing with behavioral risks, and promoting cybersecurity mentality—will remain one of the most significant fields to investigate [14].

9.14.5 Summary

The emerging need of the cybersecurity workforce will necessitate a combination of technical skill set, flexibility, and convergence of fields. With the advancement of technologies such as AI, IoT, and digital twins, cybersecurity professionals need to be trained in how to deal with diverse systems and technology. By educating and by continued research and training, particularly with a focus on collaborations, the cybersecurity workforce will indeed be ready for future task.

9.15 Anticipating Future Threats: Threat Landscape and Emerging Attack Vectors

The last decades have seen the growth of digital space, which has brought changes and diversification to the forms and levels of cyber threats. The presence of IoT, AI, Industry 4.0 has made new threats possible and introduced new methods of attacking. In order to counter these new types of threats, it is important to keep themselves updated with the dynamic nature of cyber threats as well as future ones. Several key drivers that are hence influencing the cybersecurity threat outlook consist of emerging technologies, digital transformation applications, and the convergence of systems and devices.

9.15.1 Evolving Threat Landscape

Increased integration of complex structures, which include IoT and smart structures, means that the threat landscape is larger now. The risk that resides when devices become part of core industries such as transportation, healthcare, and energy increases. For instance, the issue of cybersecurity in electric and flying vehicles is arguably an important area of concern because the technological invention is now a reality and, at the same time, represents a cyber asset that can be exploited with highly advanced technological attacks [11]. Furthermore, Industry 4.0 technologies like AS, digital twin tools, IIoT and more have added new dimensions to cybersecurity attacks especially with regard to its core message of making the security of machine-to-machine communications reliable. Just as those technologies evolve, so does the danger they face, or, in other words, the depth of threats increases. Unfortunately, cybercriminals are now all too good at finding those holes within these means, which may include vulnerable connected devices, outdated software, and poorly protected networks. Furthermore, due to the development of new methods based on AI in cybersecurity, new opportunities appear for the use of these technologies as tools for attacking [3]. This makes the analysis of defense structures a very fluid and almost inexhaustible one because new threats are evolving at the same rate as defense mechanisms.

9.15.2 Emerging Attack Vectors

Consequently, parallel to the evolution of technologies, new attack vectors are coming out. AI/ML are being incorporated in performing multiple attacks such as neural network (NN)-based ML to generate more effective, contextualized, and focused phishing messages [21]. Likewise, DL models are being applied to create even better and sophisticated malware which tends to evade usual security solutions [6]. These attacks apply pressure on IT departments to seek powerful mechanisms capable of identifying and eradicating these rising risks in real time.

Digital twin protection is also an evolving area of cybersecurity. With the increasing use of digital copies of physical systems, particularly in manufacturing and construction, there is a heightened susceptibility to cyber threats [8]. Sacrificing the physical twin can lead to undesirable outcomes, such as the destruction of infrastructure, leakage of an organization's secrets, or a loss of trust from the public. Moreover, the frequency of supply chain attacks grows steadily and constitutes one of the most popular types of attacks. Because organizations rely on a complex network of suppliers and vendors, the security of this supply chain must be considered in terms of associated risks. Hackers are now focusing on supply chain vulnerabilities; some of the links might be small suppliers who cannot provide adequate security measures like large companies [29]. Such incidents are usually subtle, and the impacts can expand as an awful lot of the framework is affected.

9.15.3 Future Cybersecurity Directions

In responding to these emerging challenges, cybersecurity personnel and scholars are thus pinning their attention on several future trends. This suggests that one area of development is federated learning for cybersecurity that enables training of a model, across multiple decentralized devices, with local data and information remaining private and secure. This approach has the potential of enhancing the security of IoT devices and other distributed systems [5]. Besides, it was noticed that the use of AI in cybersecurity applications can significantly account for the prevention of threats. AI and ML can easily and quickly detect patterns and anomalies as compared to a manual process for timely threat identification [4].

That is why such areas that require enhancing the security of cybersecurity systems in relation to new threats have gained the greatest attention. Innovators are trying to improve the resilience of the anti-cybersecurity methods toward adversarial interference or so-called zero-day exploits. It involves creating new and enhanced protocols to enhance the device-to-device communication security and boost the encryption algorithms to enhance security for the information in transit [18]. There is also a push for better cyber awareness measures, especially for end users who are as a result of attacks originating from non-IT expert users and therefore represent a major cause of cybersecurity breaches [16]. Another one critical emerging technologies that needs closer attention is cybersecurity of autonomous and connected vehicles. As these vehicles become incorporated into public transit and trucking fleets, the attractiveness of those targets as potentials for cyberattacks rises. It is expected that for these sorts of vehicles, specifically tailored security architectures for their communication systems, as well as the software that will be onboard these vehicles, will be designed to combat various external invasions [30]. In conclusion, future cybersecurity threats should be properly addressed at the present stage by studying new threats and implementing new ideas in the sphere of protection. The increased coupling of systems in different sectors and growing system complexity requires ongoing research and the use of powerful tools such as AI, ML, and federated learning. With threats advancing the way they are, and new ones arising, it becomes paramount for industries and governments to join together in protecting against ever-advancing cybercriminals and keep the digital foundations of the world today safe.

9.16 Conclusion: Preparing for the Future of Cybersecurity

Being a rapidly growing field due to the constant emergence of new technologies and methods of cyber threat creation, further development of cybersecurity requires active searching for threats and attempts to counter them. The increased sophistication of the current computing environment and the future growth of both IoT connectivity and the adoption of AI and ML all serve to underscore the need for robust and timeless cybersecurity paradigms. Building security into these systems is a constant process of developing new security solutions and learning more about the new threats to security that are appearing all over the world. The advent of innovative frameworks like federated learning, ML-based intrusion detection systems, and AI-aided threat modeling presents an effective direction for strengthening defenses in different sectors [5, 26]. Furthermore, it will be crucial for interaction between the private sector, the government, and academia to determine the future of cybersecurity. The cases in the critical infrastructure, electric and flying vehicles, and logistics systems, and the security issues experienced in the digital transformation present a need for multiple disciplinary solutions that are both secure and that can be scaled [25, 30]. In addition, the emerging sectors such as connected vehicles and Industry 4.0 sectors will lead to constant updates to regulations governing them due to keeping pace with the fast growth of technologies [2, 9].

With more development of new technologies like the blockchain, AI, and DL, their importance in enhancing cybersecurity can't be underestimated. The use of AI for threat detection and prevention can accumulate benefits of swifter response times while presenting enhanced accuracy in identifying possible threats [3, 4]. In a similar vein, while ML is being employed extensively in using algorithms for the detection of anomalies, the utilization of AI-based games for cyberspace awareness [23] shows how variants of approaches to address cybersecurity are being considered in the current world. To move toward that future, we need to break away from the traditional notion of cybersecurity. With digital transformation happening at a fast pace, it is only a matter of time before new risks occur for which organizations have to be ready. Such preparation includes investing in research, increasing the role of security awareness, developing a perspective capable of identifying possible risks connected with the new technologies, and, at the same time, creating a basis for using them as a new form of security. Thus, the role of strategic and collaborative coordination at the widespread cross-sectoral level will be the key to building a future cybersecurity system oriented to immediate response to new threats and challenges [15, 17]. Finally, it will not be a fixed kill piece that will determine the future of cybersecurity, but will be a constant process of implementation and improvement of what is new in the market, and good cybersecurity processes fit for developing and implementing standardized frameworks to act against cyber threats. In that aspect, we can ensure that the future of cybersecurity is safeguarded, defended, and ready for risks and opportunities that are in store for the future.

References

1 Ahmed, M.A.M. and Yunus, N.A.M. (2024). Securing the IoT frontier: exploring the limitation and future directions in cybersecurity. *International Journal of Internet, Broadcasting and Communication* 16 (2): 1–9.

2 Layode, O., Naiho, H.N.N., Labake, T.T. et al. (2024). Addressing cybersecurity challenges in sustainable supply chain management: a review of current practices and future directions. *International Journal of Management & Entrepreneurship Research* 6 (6): 1954–1981.

3 Roshanaei, M., Khan, M.R., and Sylvester, N.N. (2024). Enhancing cybersecurity through AI and ML: strategies, challenges, and future directions. *Journal of Information Security* 15 (3): 320–339.

4 Kaur, R., Gabrijelčič, D., and Klobučar, T. (2023). Artificial intelligence for cybersecurity: literature review and future research directions. *Information Fusion* 97: 101804.

5 Alazab, M., Priya, R.M.S., Parimala, M. et al. (2021). Federated learning for cybersecurity: concepts, challenges, and future directions. *IEEE Transactions on Industrial Informatics* 18 (5): 3501–3509.

6 Macas, M., Wu, C., and Fuertes, W. (2022). A survey on deep learning for cybersecurity: progress, challenges, and opportunities. *Computer Networks* 212: 109032.

7 Tariq, U., Ahmed, I., Bashir, A.K., and Shaukat, K. (2023). A critical cybersecurity analysis and future research directions for the internet of things: a comprehensive review. *Sensors* 23 (8): 4117.

8 Alshammari, K., Beach, T., and Rezgui, Y. (2021). Cybersecurity for digital twins in the built environment: current research and future directions. *Journal of Information Technology in Construction* 26: 159–173.

9 Khalid, H., Hashim, S.J., Ahmad, S. et al. (2020). *Cybersecurity in Industry 4.0 context: background, issues, and future directions. The nine pillars of technologies for industry* 4: 263–307.

10 Cao, Y., Li, S., Lv, C. et al. (2023). Towards cyber security for low-carbon transportation: overview, challenges and future directions. *Renewable and Sustainable Energy Reviews* 183: 113401.

11 Alqahtani H, Kumar G. Cybersecurity in electric and flying vehicles: threats, challenges, AI solutions & future directions. ACM Computing Surveys. 57 ; 1-34 2024;

12 Alani, M.M. (2021). Big data in cybersecurity: a survey of applications and future trends. *Journal of Reliable Intelligent Environments* 7 (2): 85–114.

13 Walton, S., Wheeler, P.R., Zhang, Y., and Zhao, X. (2021). An integrative review and analysis of cybersecurity research: current state and future directions. *Journal of Information Systems* 35 (1): 155–186.

14 Shah, C., Nachand, D., Wald, C., and Chen, P.H. (2023). Keeping patient data secure in the age of radiology artificial intelligence: cybersecurity considerations and future directions. *Journal of the American College of Radiology* 20 (9): 828–835.

15 Admass, W.S., Munaye, Y.Y., and Diro, A.A. (2024). Cyber security: state of the art, challenges and future directions. *Cyber Security and Applications* 2: 100031.

16 Nasir, S. (2023). Exploring the effectiveness of cybersecurity training programs: factors, best practices, and future directions. *Proceedings of the Cyber Secure Nigeria Conference.*

17 Banik, S. (2023). Future directions for ML in cybersecurity. *Revista de Inteligencia Artificial en Medicina* 14 (1): 401–430.

18 Rauf, U. (2018). A taxonomy of bio-inspired cyber security approaches: existing techniques and future directions. *Arabian Journal for Science and Engineering* 43 (12): 6693–6708.

19 Pinto, S.J., Siano, P., and Parente, M. (2023). Review of cybersecurity analysis in smart distribution systems and future directions for using unsupervised learning methods for cyber detection. *Energies (Basel)* 16 (4): 1651.

20 Mekala, S.H., Baig, Z., Anwar, A., and Zeadally, S. (2023). Cybersecurity for industrial IoT (IIoT): threats, countermeasures, challenges and future directions. *Computer Communications* 208: 298–320.

21 Yu, J., Shvetsov, A.V., and Alsamhi, S.H. (2024). Leveraging machine learning for cybersecurity resilience in industry 4.0: challenges and future directions. *IEEE Access* .

22 Cheung, K.F., Bell, M.G.H., and Bhattacharjya, J. (2021). Cybersecurity in logistics and supply chain management: an overview and future research directions. *Transportation Research Part E: Logistics and Transportation Review* 146: 102217.

23 Chennamaneni, S., Pradhan, P., Chebolu, V. et al. (2023). Designing cybersecurity AI based awareness games for citizens: best practices and future directions. *2023 International Conference on Sustainable Computing and Data Communication Systems (ICSCDS).* IEEE. 407–412.

24 Yusuf Enoch, S., Ge, M., Hong, J.B., and Kim, D.S. (2021). Model-based cybersecurity analysis: past work and future directions. arXiv e-prints. arXiv-2105.

25 Al-Hawawreh, M., Aljuhani, A., and Jararweh, Y. (2023). Chatgpt for cybersecurity: practical applications, challenges, and future directions. *Cluster Computing* 26 (6): 3421–3436.

26 Ferrag, M.A., Shu, L., Friha, O., and Yang, X. (2021). Cyber security intrusion detection for agriculture 4.0: machine learning-based solutions, datasets, and future directions. *IEEE/CAA Journal of Automatica Sinica* 9 (3): 407–436.

27 Kavak, H., Padilla, J.J., Vernon-Bido, D. et al. (2021). Simulation for cybersecurity: state of the art and future directions. *Journal of Cybersecurity* 7 (1): tyab005.

28 Jamil, N., Qassim, Q.S., Bohani, F.A. et al. (2021). Cybersecurity of microgrid: state-of-the-art review and possible directions of future research. *Applied Sciences* 11 (21): 9812.

29 Sobb, T., Turnbull, B., and Moustafa, N. (2020). Supply chain 4.0: a survey of cyber security challenges, solutions and future directions. *Electronics (Basel)* 9 (11): 1864.

30 Khan, S.K., Shiwakoti, N., Stasinopoulos, P., and Warren, M. (2023). Cybersecurity regulatory challenges for connected and automated vehicles–state-of-the-art and future directions. *Transport Policy (Oxf)* 143: 58–71.

31 Altulaihan, E., Almaiah, M.A., and Aljughaiman, A. (2022). Cybersecurity threats, countermeasures and mitigation techniques on the IoT: future research directions. *Electronics (Basel)* 11 (20): 3330.

32 Belkhamza, Z. (2023). Cybersecurity in digital transformation applications: analysis of past research and future directions. *ICCWS 2023 18th International Conference on Cyber Warfare and Security Academic Conferences and publishing limited.*

33 Pelluru, K. (2019). Enhancing cyber security: strategies, challenges, and future directions. *Journal of Engineering and Technology* 1 (2): 1–11.

10

Conclusion: Building a Resilient Cyber Defense Framework

Hewa Majeed Zangana

IT Department, Duhok Technical College, Duhok Polytechnic University, Duhok, Iraq

10.1 Introduction

In the world where businesses are connected through the internet and are running in the digital space, cyber resilience has become an imperative for organizations that target on safeguarding their valuables from diverse and emerging sophisticated cyber threats. In cybersecurity, "resilience", loosely translated, means the ability of a system to prevent an attack and then continue to work while and after an attack. In this chapter, Akinsanya et al. [1] correctly observe that the developmental direction of cyber resilience strategies entails frameworks that focus on operational continuity even if the systems are contaminated. Cybersecurity is not a "Fort Knox" approach, which focuses only on preventing an attack; it has to be more proactive and robust in nature, starting from prevention, early detection of attack, methods to counter the attack, and finally how to deal with post-attack scenario. By cultivating such a complex strategy, organizations establish what is called "Defense in Depth," which is a concept [2]. Conklin and Shoemaker [3] also note that one of the main ideas to support this concept is that the architecture of cyber-resilient systems needs to be built with changes and recovery solutions as the key ideas in their conceptual framework.

Cyber resilience is also critical regarding business continuity (BC) in an organization. AL-Hawamleh [4] posits that cyber resilience frameworks are the foundation upon which organizational stability against cyber threats is built. Turning to the work of Kannan et al. [5], their study on cyber resilience in business security indicates that such frameworks help organizations continue functioning as threats escalate, thereby protecting critical data and resources. In addition, current technologies with regard to cyber defense include the basic necessity of including the integration of artificial intelligence (AI) and machine learning (ML) as part of a robust cyber defense plan, as they help in automating processes of threat detection and mitigation [6]. These proposals, along with classical guard mechanisms, provide a reliable protection against both expected and new potential threats. According to Ahmed et al. [7], the concept of cyber resilience suggests that organizations should extend their architectures away from cybersecurity and to cyber defense as well as to foster resilience at scale. They are also to adopt adaptively and proactively organizational resilient strategies in compliance with international norms on cybersecurity. This integrative approach is important, bearing in mind that Efthimiopoulos [8] established the use of "Smart defense" strategies by North Atlantic Treaty Organization (NATO) in relation to its cyber reformist agenda. This way, organizations enhance their strategies against cyber threats apart from being aligned with international benchmarks [9]. The range and frequency of these threats have

Defense in Depth: Modern Cybersecurity Strategies and Evolving Threats, First Edition. Edited by Hewa Majeed Zangana.

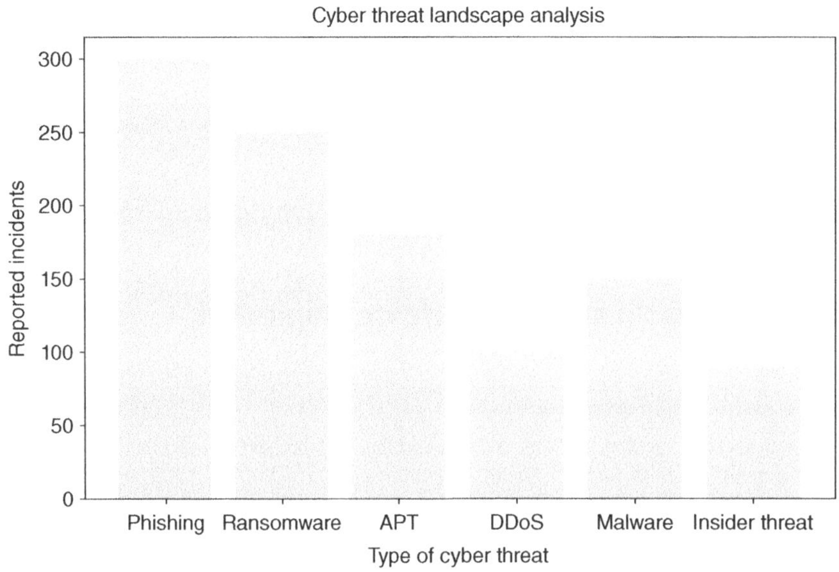

Figure 10.1 Cyber threat landscape analysis. Source: Hewa Majeed Zangana.

to be clear for the development of a sound defense strategy. The attached chart is a classification of cyber threats that will assist in the determination of what to focus on due to high prevalence and or patterns (Figure 10.1).

In this chapter, the author investigates the complexity of cyber resilience, as a methodology to address and develop protective measures for systemic threats in the cyber domain. It tries to offer a conceptual framework, based on existing knowledge, including that presented by Refs. [10, 11], to help organizations strengthen their cybersecurity arrangements. When implementing resilience into systems, the path is set for a future that not only protects against attacks but also fosters a society capable of coping with the persistent cyber threat while adapting to new challenges and evolving security landscapes.

10.2 Core Components of a Resilient Cyber Defense Framework

Cyber preparedness involves developing a robust foundation for an organizations' cybersecurity that enables it to occupy a defensive position which may be used in case of a cyberattack. Establishing an effective framework of strategic elements for constructing resilient and continuous organizational structure in the face of current cyber threats requires the following. These are discussed in this section using recent frameworks and models of the core components.

1) **Risk Management and Vulnerability Assessment**: Risk management from cyber threats lies as the bedrock of any stability and solid defense in cybersecurity. It involves screening the likelihood of hazard in the organizational framework, its risks, and the likelihood of incurring a risk score [12]. A risk management approach allows resource allocation to focus on high risks, hence minimizing vulnerability. Hence, using both vulnerability assessments, accompanied by continuous checks, offers a recurring process for reinforcing walls gradually [13].
2) **Defense-in-Depth Strategy**: Defense in depth (DiD) is a security model to safeguard an organization's resources by the use of multiple layers of defense. This process guarantees that

even if one layer has been penetrated, there are other layers that will still provide protection. Pureti [14] explains that DiD is applicable when it comes to defense against Advanced Persistent Threats (APT) and other complicated cyber threats. The use of single security tools and technology like firewall intrusion detection systems (IDS), and antivirus solutions enhances the security structure [9].

The application of the DiD model involves the use of layers for the security of digital assets, as illustrated below. All layers provide protection against specific forms of attack, and even if a layer has been breached, the system continues to run (Figure 10.2).

3) **Cyber Incident Response and Recovery**: Computer misuse countermeasure plans allow organizations to effectively address the consequences of cyber incidents. Conklin et al. [15] describe that an incident response is a process which outlines methods for identifying, evaluating, and escalating cyber threats. For instance, a recovery strategy, on the other hand, helps in the restoration of services and the sustaining of operations disrupted by a disaster [16]. To avoid incidents affecting the organization for a long term, some organizations create a way, whereby they can quickly resume normal operation. An effective structured incident response lifecycle therefore helps an organization manage incidents. The lifecycle above explains in detail each of the phases of preparation, implementation, maintenance, and recovery (Figure 10.3).
4) **Continuous Monitoring and Real-Time Analytics**: What is more, monitoring and analyzing security threats in real time are necessary to prevent and counter threats as they appear. Through big data analytics, AI, and ML, an organization can find anomalies, which might signify an attacker is nearby [6]. Such an approach to monitoring also fosters a robust defense by reducing the time it takes to respond and by increasing detection capacities [2]. AI should be used for real-time monitoring, which enables preventive action. The following graph shows the various forms of marks which AI algorithms have been able to identify over time (Figure 10.4).
5) **Cyber Resilience Engineering**: Cyber resilience engineering particularly concerns itself with the ability to develop structures that can sustain disruptions and recover easily. According to Ross et al. [17], resilience engineering incorporates protection strategies directly into the setup and design of systems, thereby preventing cybercriminals from exploiting those vulnerabilities.

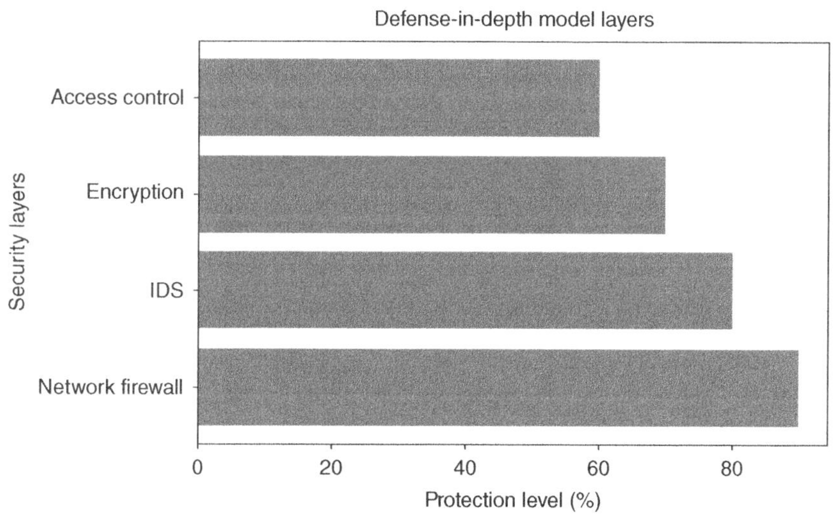

Figure 10.2 Defense-in-depth model layers. Source: Hewa Majeed Zangana.

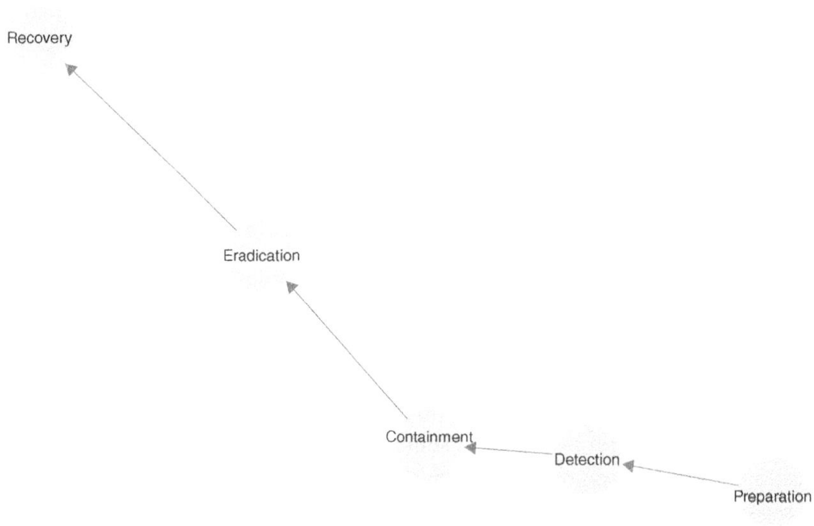

Figure 10.3 Incident response lifecycle. Source: Hewa Majeed Zangana.

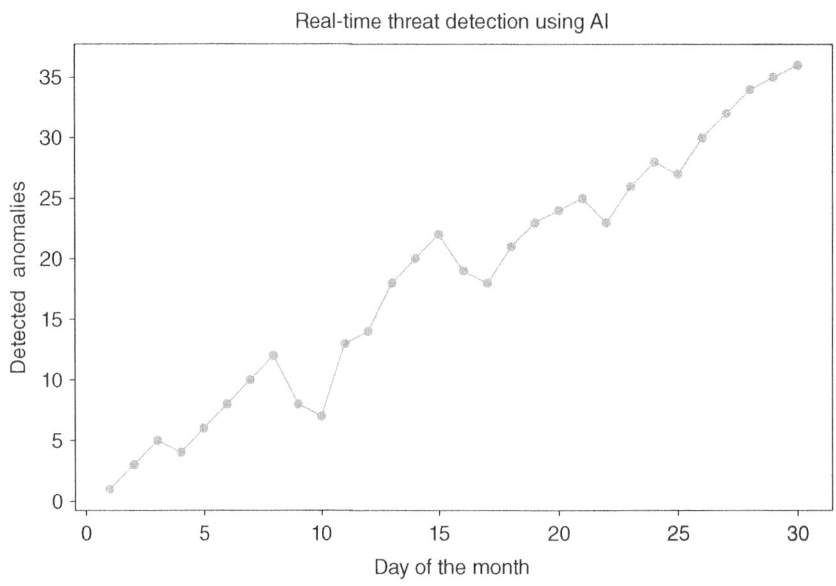

Figure 10.4 Real-time threat detection using AI. Source: Hewa Majeed Zangana.

This approach, also highlighted by Bolish et al. [18], emphasizes the design of systems that are intrinsically capable of continued operation should a cyber event occur.

6) **Training and Awareness Programs**: This book showed that cyber resilience depends on much more than technology; it requires the workforce to be informed and ready. Ongoing employee functions on cybersecurity awareness empower workers with adequate understanding of case and handling mechanisms of cyber risks [19]. Through creating security awareness in organizations, organizations manage to reduce risks that arise from human factors which are among the leading causes of security risks [10]. There is no doubt that people are vulnerable to

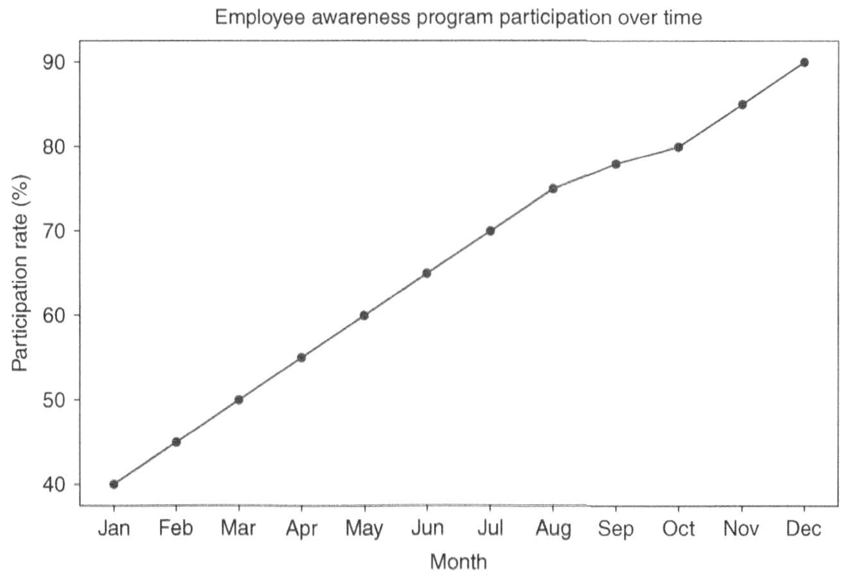

Figure 10.5 Employee awareness program participation over time. Source: Hewa Majeed Zangana.

cyber threats and have a big impact on large organizations' cybersecurity risk profile. Through such routines, the number of security incidents that are related to the human factor can be lower, which is seen in the following participation trend (Figure 10.5).

7) **Collaboration and Information Sharing**: It also directs cooperation with other organizations, and membership with information-sharing networks improves an entity's capacity to adapt to changing threats. National Institute of Standards and Technology (NIST) and NATO provide the real-time intelligence and coordinated centers and practice sources to the organizations for enhancing the cyber defense [20]. This kind of cooperation makes it easier to predict and counter threats, helping in the establishment of a more coherent defense system. Collaborative work involves pooling of a number of insights from various entities. The following diagram represents an information-sharing network among various entities (Figure 10.6).
8) **Adaptive Frameworks and Policy Development**: Last but not least, parameters of cyber defense frameworks must be dynamic to fit into the ever-evolving cyber ecosystem. Kanann et al. [5] further note that organizations should implement flexible policies and frameworks that fit new emerging technologies and new types of threats. Policies that make sure that updates are frequent, and the firm complies with cybersecurity standards and flexible defense plans help the firm develop a proactive defense system that can overcome future problems [21].

Therefore, the cybersecurity framework must have a strategic, technological, and human capability for the defense system to be effective. The integration of risk management, multilayered protection, monitoring, and shared industry initiatives makes organizations more prepared for cyber risks, thus sustaining their operational capabilities. The above components therefore combined in a comprehensive strategy that could be embraced by any organization to effectively enable it to counter cyber adversities and achieve cyber resilience. An adaptive cyber resilience framework means that there is BC and the company can go on performing important functions even if it is under attack. The following chart illustrates the key elements in resilience for business sustainability (Figure 10.7):

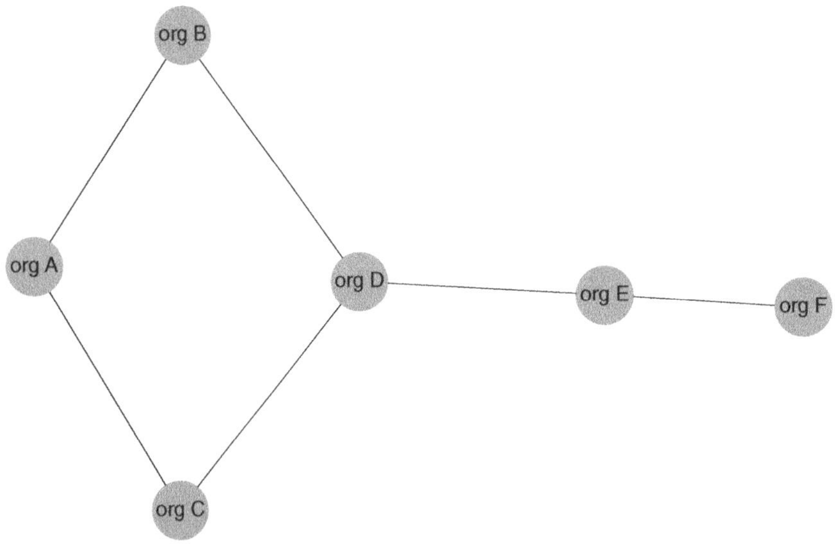

Figure 10.6 Collaborative defense information-sharing network. Source: Hewa Majeed Zangana.

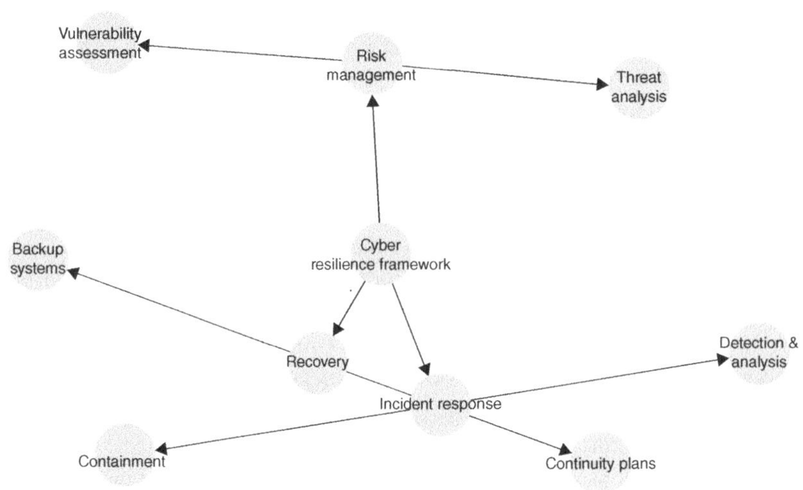

Figure 10.7 Cyber resilience framework for business continuity. Source: Hewa Majeed Zangana.

10.3 Proactive Threat Management and Anticipatory Defense

By realizing that cyber threats are ever changing, organizations will have to make changes from having measures put in place that are only defensive in nature. This approach plans for the cyber threats, which allows organizations to put up a line of defense that prevents cyber risks from emerging and controls them when they occur. The concept of prevention includes early identification and effective counteraction measures, including predictive analysis, behavioral surveillance, and threat information exchange to improve protection levels for system reliability and retain business activity [1, 7]. Signs show that threat management requires speed in terms

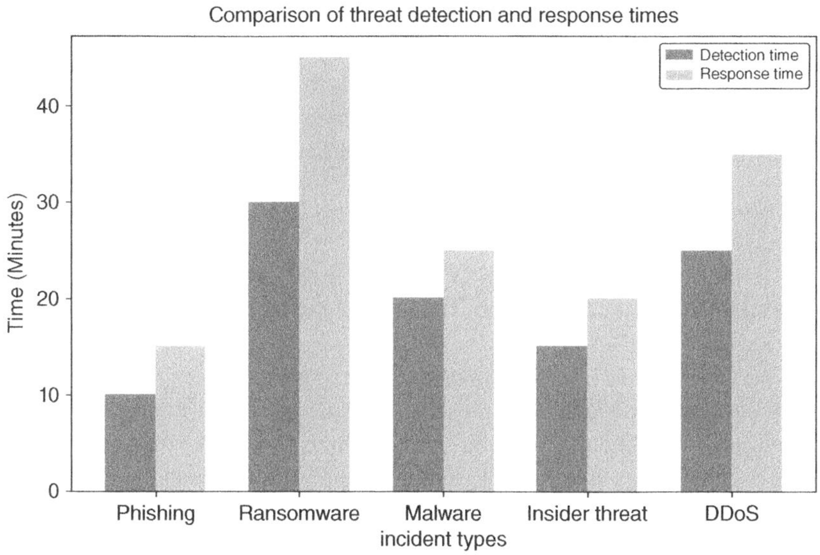

Figure 10.8 Comparison of threat detection and response times. Source: Hewa Majeed Zangana.

of identification and action. This chart shows response time analysis for several sets of cyber incidents and points out potential improvement (Figure 10.8).

10.3.1 Anticipatory Defense Strategies

It refers to practices intended at predicting and countering security threats, with newer methods such as using ML and anomaly detection included. Such techniques help to prevent possible threats which can be observed in the behavior of the tested party, as well as in the statistical data. For instance, CYDRES—cyber defense and resilient systems that concern the security of grid-interactive buildings demonstrate that preventative methods can defend essential structures [22, 23]. The deployment of layered defense, zero-trust (ZT) models and strong access management frameworks additionally strengthen the security environment through a range of hurdles for the adversary [24].

10.3.2 Collaboration and Information Sharing

Strengthening of cybersecurity measures also needs cooperation because many times, threats are present beyond the organizational level. Information sharing on new threats is possible with the help of complex strategies as NATO's Smart Defense and national strategies [8, 25], thus establishing extensive, predictive defense against highly developed massive attacks. Besides, when using frameworks for cyber resilience, organizations can guarantee that they continue functioning in case of constant cyber threats [3, 5].

10.3.3 Continuous Monitoring and Adaptive Resilience

Inferring consistent audit mechanisms helps in minimizing threats and ensures that defense grows with the threat. Thus, measures such as behavioral monitoring and coping, into-action adaptive ML models allow real-time changes to cybersecurity policies based on what threats are seen, which reflects in the developmental process of cyber resilience management frameworks and vulnerability management frameworks aimed at supporting such coping strategies [1, 12]. This approach is specifically useful for dealing with APTs and guarantees that the organization is able to counter new trends in the attacks [9, 17]. In totality, implementation of proactive, anticipatory, and layered defense enables organizations to transition from mere fight and retardation to integrated DiD strategies.

10.4 Building Resilience Through Zero Trust and Adaptive Security

How enterprises can utilize and combine both ZT and adaptive security is the focus of this chapter because both models are essential to adequately serve as lines of defense against today's threats. ZT, which implies a security concept centered on the idea that one should not trust and must instead check and confirm everything asking a user, device, or application demanding access to any resources, is employed [13, 24]. Relocating from perimeter security methods to a model which does not rely heavily on implicit trust fits the trend toward the need for higher security in the environments facing more sophisticated cyber threats [12, 14].

Adaptive security, on the other hand, is a system that lets the security of systems change its security profiles depending on the threat profiles and context of the systems [18]. As the system is constantly identifying possible threats and changing its reaction to threats without human intervention, adaptive security is an addition to the ZT model. According to Meng et al. [26], adaptive systems can integrate intelligent threat detection which detects threats and prevents them, useful for grid-interactive efficient buildings [23]. This adaptive capability feeds into a comprehensive architecture of cyber resilience that helps to apply quite preventive as well as reactively the best defense line continuities [7, 22]. When implemented in parallel with adaptive security the idea of ZT serves as a protection against a wide range of threats including the most sophisticated ones as APTs and ransomware. This combined approach can also be viewed in conjunction with cybersecurity management frameworks that propose a combination of risk mitigation and response approaches to achieve BC following a cyberattack [3, 5]. According to Orme [9], it is important because these frameworks help protect against the Internet of Things (IoT) threats because they are a more effective approach that is largely suitable in these complex systems as threats are constantly changing. Integrating ZT and adaptive security into a cyber-resilience framework strengthens security and also promotes a secure environment of constant evaluation and alteration. From adaptive security with AI & ML to advanced threats that traditional perimeter security do not address, organizations can add adaptive security models, with the objective of improving their detection and response to compromises [6, 16]. Moreover, based on the ideas provided by the NIST—an engineering approach to one's cybersecurity—the integration of ZT and autonomous system (AS) fulfills all the required standards [17].

The ZT architecture is designed on the premise that it would "never trust, always-check". Figure 10.9 illustrates the components of the ZT framework that protect the organization's digital perimeters.

Combination of ZT and adaptive security models is the foundation for constructing a strong and sustainable strategic solution for cybersecurity threats (CT). As organizations have increasingly encountered multilayered security threats, integrating these models not only provides adequate security but also enables them to transition smoothly as needed which has become important due to recent scholarly developments in cybersecurity resilience literature [1, 8].

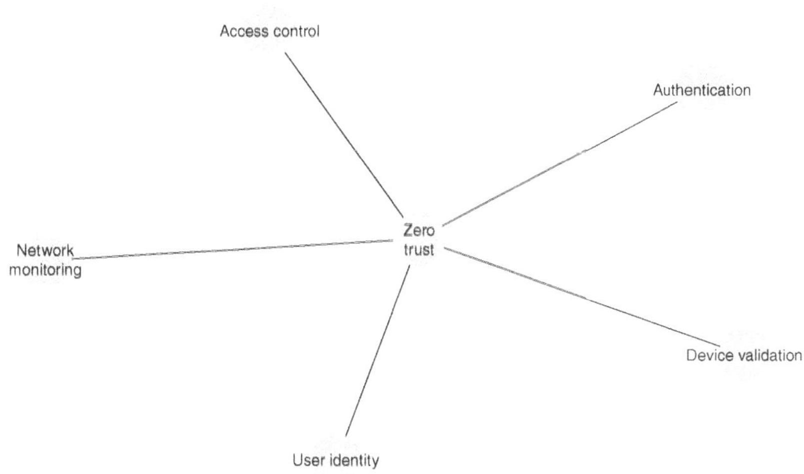

Figure 10.9 Zero trust architecture components. Source: Hewa Majeed Zangana.

10.5 Incident Response and Recovery Planning

Incident response and recovery planning are critical in attaining cyber resilience and confirm that an organization is capable of promptly identifying, handling or mitigating, and recovering from cyber incidents. Effective planning helps organizations reduce risks from cyber threats, quickly return to normal operation, and strengthen protection.

A robust incident response plan typically involves four critical phases: subprocesses include preparation, identification and assessment, isolation and elimination, and cleanup [7]. These phases allow organizations to pre-cooperate for an attack and give a mechanical manner to manage dangers and comeback to ordinary following an attack. Conklin and Shoemaker [3] observed that the more effectively an organization has planned and prepared how it will respond to incipient threats, the more resilient that organization will be and the better it will do at containing and controlling threats before the threats manifest in the network extensively. In the preparation phase, specifying responsibilities and tasks and categorizing incidents and staff's training on incident management are determined [1]. It is also the most important phase in order to build efficient measures for fast response and shortening the loss of system availability. It is advised that organizations hold frequent training, simulations, and or table-top exercises to create a flexible respond force [27].

The detection and analysis phase mainly ensures that the likelihood of an incident is detected via systems and evaluated indicators of compromise [4]. It is possible to improve the detection capabilities for organizations by applying big data and ML, given the fact that cyber adversaries increasingly use techniques that allow them to avoid detection by traditional methods [6, 22]. In addition, information organizations might use extensive frameworks that employ both cybersecurity and cyberspace defense to decrease event response time and false alarms [16]. Controlling and eliminating phase involves quarantining affected computer systems, deleting malicious software and addressing known weaknesses. As Bolish et al. [18] explained that containment addresses the parameters to reduce an attack's transmission, whereas comprehensive eradication aims to remove any evidence of the threat. This step is important to reduce the likelihood of getting infected again and, therefore, maintain organizational and decrease the possibility of protracted disruption to its workings. Finally, in the recovery phase, one reorganizes, checks on the system to ensure it is running in an optimal manner, and learns from any encountered problems [9]. This stage is also beneficial for organizations because it provides an opportunity to enhance the existing key strategies aimed at safeguarding organizations against cyber threats and make necessary changes [23]. It also involves strengthening the scaffolding of organizational continuity policies and disaster-ready systems to address future situations in a better manner [12]. However, these works also highlight several other phases related to the business model framework (BMF) that are worth discussing: post-incident review and continuous improvement if the need arises [17]. Adaptive crisis assessment (ACA) improves response plans, enabling an organization to address new threats and adopt new technological environments in the long run, specifically enhancing organizational resilience [13].

10.6 The Role of Automation in Enhancing Resilience

Robotic integration is one of the significant factors that increases the defense of today's complex cybersecurity systems because it speeds up processes, erases human errors, and optimizes threat identification and eradication processes. In networks, there are tools that can start analyzing networks as soon as they are connected to help in the detection of abnormal situations, meaning that an attack is underway and also start counterreactions automatically. It also helps organizations to address threats faster, hence reducing risk impacts and the ability to continue operations [7, 27]. Automated security solutions involve the use of AI and ML to develop methods that work proactively and are critical for building an effective system. Such technologies can adapt from patterns within datasets to identify new, previously unseen threats and defend in a different manner. Such flexibility is crucial for addressing APT and sustaining the systems' resiliency in the face of persistent cyber threats [1, 13]. Automation also enhances the ZT security design, in which users are constantly authenticated and checked at all levels and layers in the network, so there is more protection. That approach allows for the identification of infected parts and the containment of loss, while critical processes continue within the organization. Thus, we find that automation extends to defense mechanisms and contributes to the overall BC process which forms a core of cyber resilience [5, 24].

Furthermore, another area that is best approached through the use of automated systems is vulnerability management, which forms an important foundation toward the achievement of the organization's resilience objectives. They can scan, patch, and rectify vulnerabilities, at times making a system less vulnerable to attacks. Thus, the automation of such processes helps organizations not constantly draw their cybersecurity experts' attention to these tasks and spend their time on more important work [12, 14]. Automated systems, therefore, offer the flexibility and strength required to counter new threats, thus placing them at the center of the construction of excellent cybersecurity structures [3, 17].

10.7 Human Factors and Building a Security-Aware Culture

Developing a security-aware culture across an organization is crucial in order to make an organization cyber resilient. The other factor that relates greatly to Center for Internet Security (CIS) is the human factor since workers' behaviors, perceptions, and level of cybersecurity knowledge and resultant actions also determine the level of exposure of an organization to cyber threats.

This section is a consideration of the core components of security mindset development in an organization and specifically the human element and training.

10.7.1 The Role of Awareness and Training

Workforce is the key to the implementation of security-conscious culture, and the key to this implementation is sufficient education and training of the workforce. Educational initiatives important to develop special prevention exercises with reference to more often observed cyber threats, rules to protect "inside" information, and necessary measures in information protection are useful for an employee to better assess potential risks [8]. Ideally, such programs are explicitly cyclical and reflect changes in the landscape of cyber risks and contain information on new strategies employed by the attackers and information regarding newly identified vulnerabilities. Multiple investigations have indicated that employee training increases security awareness concerning phishing and other social engineering techniques, which are the commonest attack types [9, 24].

Another aspect of the creation of resilience through awareness training is also table-top sessions that portray the actual world cyber-secure breach with numerous procedural explanations of approaches on how to address such emergencies and the ways how employees should react to them in critical conditions [17]. This generates responsibility and preparedness from the employees, which, in turn, helps in immediate containment of the incidents which is important for the growth and development of the company being in Li [28].

10.7.2 Leadership and Culture

It was found out that the commitment of leadership plays a crucial role in the success of the security frame check sequence (FCS). CEOs and managers must embrace and support cybersecurity programs and become role models on the subject within an organization [25]. To foster a cyber-resilient culture, leaders must actively involve themselves, whereby they can occasionally talk about cybersecurity, support costly secure technological solutions, and align cybersecurity with organizational goals [20]. Such a systems approach guarantees that the top management sets cybersecurity policies and practices to prompt all organizational tiers for security ownership [1].

10.7.3 Behavioral Changes and Security Practices

Among the main sources of security threats is people make mistakes, for example, share data or reuse the same passwords for different accounts. Culture management aims at making people in an organization adopt certain behaviors that will enhance cybersecurity. For example, adoption of good passwords, adoption of two-factor authentication, and avoiding dangerous behaviors such as opening links from unidentified sources are some of the good practices that should be encouraged and reminded through organizational practices [3]. In this viewpoint, it is possible to regularly refresh concepts of individuals on first principles and transform security into the habitual approach observable in day-to-day operations.

10.7.4 Security Policies and Empowerment

There is no doubt that as a result of this importance, sound and easily understandable security policies are crucial to enable the employees to know the level of responsibility they have in the organization's security. Shareholders must be effectively informed in order to engage them in confidence for a common aim, avoiding any feeling of insecurity (Estay et al., 2020). The independence to report unusual behaviors without termination increases vigilance in detecting possible threats and strengthens employees' involvement in the organization's protection realm [18].

10.7.5 The Impact of Psychological Factors

Cyber resilience strategies, therefore, need to take into account psychosocial factors that may influence the responses from the employees regarding security measures. Stress, working pressure, and attitude toward the job and organizational commitment disrupt the rules of security. It can result in negligence or business transactions that involve high risk, for example, compromising physical security because of ease [13]. Corporations that invest in employees' health, in general, as a part of the cybersecurity management strategy, will realize that employees will be more responsive to security strategies and be more cautious.

10.7.6 Summary

Therefore, developing a security-aware culture is not a mere technology enforcement process but is a concept that requires addressing people, management, behavioral and psychological approaches. Employees are crucial individuals within an organization if they are informed, empowered, and motivated to be proactively involved. Implementing these field-based human-centric approaches alongside other resilience models enhances organizational preparedness and response to cyber situations greatly [5, 10]. By ensuring that awareness creation is escalated, the leaders' support integrated in the organizations' policies, and right behaviors practiced consistently, organizations can achieve an automatic cybersecurity perception among all the employees, enhancing their security [2].

10.8 Compliance, Regulation, and Governance as Resilience Enablers

As criminals adapt to the digital age and new threats surface, companies and their networks are most times lacking adequate nontechnical layers of defense. It is therefore valuable in the creation of tiers of structure, policies, and regulations aimed at allowing resilience, protecting digital assets, and strengthening business contingency and responses to incidents. Regularity with the inaptly identified market standards is the framework that supports organizational resilience when it comes to cybersecurity once it aligns efforts toward the industry-benchmarked governance frameworks like NIST or International Organization for Standardization (ISO) [1, 17, 18]. Monitoring compliance needs to be constant because compliance laws and threats are ever changing. This flowchart depicts a compliance-monitoring framework which can be implemented with the aim of continuous change (Figure 10.10).

10.8.1 Regulatory Compliance and Cyber Resilience

Regulations are vital to building basic standards of cyber defense since they allow organizations to preserve and enforce security rules compatible with legal requirements and corresponding industries. For example, architectures like GDPR in the European region not only charge penalties for noncompliance but also compel entities to develop data protection and response measures

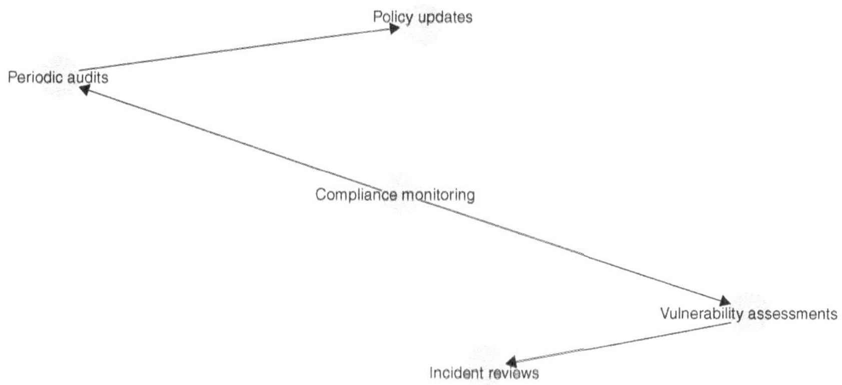

Figure 10.10 Framework for continuous compliance monitoring. Source: Hewa Majeed Zangana.

that improve organizational robustness [7]. However, the regulations are more prescriptive about the processes, where the organizational members have to continuously scan and update the environment to create resilience by being ahead rather than behind risk events [3, 11]. In the same way, regulatory authorities want the compliance programs to include the response plans in case of an incident, which makes governance as crucial in resilience [8, 29].

10.8.2 Governance as a Resilience Enabler

By establishing roles and responsibilities of governance frameworks, it is achieved that extend across the organization, and these frameworks enhance resilience. Good corporate governance also entails the formulation of policies that connect cybersecurity plans with corporation's goals to minimize the occurrence of cyber threats and to respond and recover quickly in the event of an occurrence. The implementation of governance can also support cybersecurity and operational continuity as frequent risk assessment and continuous improvement mechanisms are proposed [2, 20]. Governance also empowers an organization to develop organizational culture of resiliency, as well as ensure that all levels of organizational structure are involved in enhancing cyber awareness [9, 28]. An effective governance structure makes the organization more flexible, which allows it to operate effectively in responding to change in regulation or new threats.

10.8.3 Bridging Cybersecurity, Defense, and Resilience through Compliance and Governance

Compliance and governance are complementary to cyber defense when integrated and form the foundation of lasting protection strategies. A number of scholars call for the usage of defensive and resilient approaches so that organizations are able to contain, mitigate, and strive for operational normalcy in attacks [13, 24]. Frameworks like NIST's Cybersecurity Framework puts resilience as a core element, integrating compliance and governance into every process in cybersecurity in an effort to address potential threats before they become a big issue [15]. This makes it conform with new tendencies of resilience that bring understanding into an initialized assessment, adaptive policies, and compliance, which allow for the development of a more flexible defense system [19, 30].

10.8.4 Resilience through Continuous Compliance and Monitoring

It has been seen that a continuous process of compliance checks and updates for security policies is the need for the hour to stay secure in the face of ever-emergent threats. Continuous compliance makes organizations ready for meeting new regulatory standards and upcoming cyber risks by the means of periodic audits, vulnerability investigation, and compliance checks. Such practices allow identifying potential exposures and noncompliance issues, ensuring that besides meeting the requirements, organizations also build a protective shield against possible cyber threats [5, 26]. Fostering culture for improvement also helps organizations to quickly respond to new changes in laws, technologies, as well as threats intelligence which in turn enhances resilience [4, 27].

10.8.5 Building a Culture of Resilience

Last but not least, the need for growing organizational culture to embrace organizational resilience as the logical element of the compliance and governance framework cannot be overestimated. Boss engaging the employees of an organization at every level in learning about and participating actively in resilience initiatives makes resilience work as an organizational imperative [25]. For instance, integrating wide security awareness programs enables the employees to identify and prevent possible threats; it thus minimizes many possibilities of human error, which remains a weakness of cybersecurity [10, 16]. Developing this type of culture also fosters more anticipatory mentality, where governance and compliance are done not as tick checklist boxes, but are at the core of an organizational mission [6, 21]. Consequently, if organizations develop sound compliance, regulation, and governance systems, then they can bolster their cyber defenses but also transform their organizations in ways that prepare them for tackling new forms of adversarial play in cyberspace.

10.9 Collaborative Defense: Strengthening Resilience Through Partnerships

When entities are interacting in the contemporary interconnected world, it is imperative to synchronize in order to increase cybersecurity standards. Through partnerships, organizations, industries, and even nations can create a unified front to combat cyber threats. Sharing information, experiences, and lessons learned—or borrowed—can enhance defenses against cyber crises [7, 10]. This is not just about the exchange of information, but about building a community where people collaborate to mitigate risks and exposures, prevent and handle incidents, and enhance security practices.

10.9.1 Benefits of Collaborative Defense

Among the main benefits of collaborative defense is the efficiency in sharing threat intelligence to ensure that threats are as likely to be contained before emerging into full-fledged threats. Aksinsanya [1] found that the visibility of information about threats, risks, and prevention measures increases organizations' readiness and response times, therefore decreasing the consequences of cyber threats. It also means that through partnerships with governmental agencies, cybersecurity firms, and industry consortia, organizations can benefit from the best detection and response techniques revealed by leaders in the field, for instance, five key technologies for enabling a cyber-resilience framework [2]. Also, cooperation with national defense and intelligence authorities, for instance, NATO, and partners in the Smart Defense project, represents the importance of the idea of the collaborative approach in cyberspace protection [8]. Such partnerships mainly include the exchange of information on APTs, threats, and incidents targeting critical infrastructures (Cis) and new threats and risks influencing numerous industries and geographic locations. Programs like NATO's framework help governments and industries to be prepared against massive cyberattacks and cut down risk by working collaboratively [20].

10.9.2 Developing Trust and Standards in Collaborative Defense

One of the main critical success factors that characterizes collaborative defense activities is the level of trust among the members because participants have to discuss numerous vulnerabilities and incidents and share related information that expose them to further threats. Safitra et al. [29] opine that in spite of the extensive sophistication across the globe, there is a need to develop common understanding and reference points of cybersecurity. These frameworks ensure that company presents coherent concept on security measures and requires participants to have better understanding of each other's roles and tasks in implementation of security measures. An overview of such frameworks is exemplified by the DiD model, which aims to provide an organization with multitiered baseline protections. Collaboration: According to Orme [9], DiD frameworks can be strengthened through cooperative efforts. Each layer of protection integrates knowledge, incident response tactics, and threat modeling. It is understood that the integration of DiD practices in a multi-organizational environment is a way to enhance organizations' protective shroud on multiple levels, therefore increasing their immunity.

10.9.3 Technology and Knowledge Transfer

They also encourage collaboration in technology transfer where organizations that have developed enhanced cyberspace solutions can learn from superior organizations. For instance, such frameworks as CYDRES for protecting the CI illustrate the idea of how collaboration with stakeholders can yield the implementation of new defense mechanisms developed to counter more or less advanced cyber threats [22]. This technology diffusion empowers the organization that may not be large or may not have the resources to fight cyber threats to improve their security posture, particularly in critical industries that experience a shortage of cybersecurity assets. Furthermore, collaborative defense also fosters the use of ML and AI that is applied in the formulation of analysis based on electronic data in cybersecurity. According to Haider [6], the AI solutions are used more frequently in the collaborative defense where AI analyses data in the incident networks and automates the response processes in real time. This mutual integration of AI accelerates a preventive stance toward cyberspace threats since the time for their identification and counteraction shortens.

10.9.4 Challenges and Considerations in Collaborative Defense

Despite the mentioned advantages, the collaborative defense model requires solving certain problems, including legal and regulatory compliance issues which can differ greatly depending on the geographic locations and branches of the industries. Conklin et al. [15] argue that managing these differences involves creating regulatory compliance for the two entities to account for their various jurisdictions of operation but in a way that can foster increased cooperation. Additionally, multiple cybersecurity measures and solutions often lead decision-making within the organization to be more complicated and time-consuming, thus necessitating continuous training, funding, and collaboration [19]. Another challenge that has been identified is the one bearing to do with the third-party dependency, which seems to present organizations with supply chain threats. Sharma et al. [12] call for the incorporation of a vulnerability management framework that will be fully adopted in the collaborative defense strategies concerning the weaknesses likely to be observed due to the partnerships. This approach implies frequent risk evaluation and revision so that partners maintain high security measures, thus reducing probabilities of weakness throughout the ecosystem.

10.9.5 The Future of Collaborative Defense

This is because, in future, more emphasis will be placed on collaborative defense as threats advance in sophistication. The plans may therefore involve the creation of international cooperation in terms of national boundaries in order to come up with common cybersecurity norms and procedures. As such, by establishing collaboration at this level, governments and organizations need to improve the probability of addressing vulnerabilities in the CI and protect the shared digital environment [4]. Also, the emergence of blockchain as a way of sharing data in collaboration networks and the concept of ZT could mean that data sharing across these networks will be more secure and more trustworthy than at any other time in the past, thus reducing the possibility of a data breach [24]. In conclusion, there is an opportunity to enhance the involvement of collaborative defense in strengthening resilience with the use of partnerships. CSPs can support a new generation of online security enhancement by virtually exchanging goods, experience, and strategies with other organizations from the ecosystem. Nevertheless, for collaborative defense to reach its greatest potential, challenges relating to trust, legal compliance, and operational complexity should not be viewed as threats and instead be managed and overcome so that more beneficial alterations can be made, and defensive measures can be improved to fit changing CTs.

10.10 Evolving with Emerging Technologies and Threats

These and other, newer kinds of threats perpetrate an ever-evolving and increasingly complex threat environment within which organizations operating in the digital age attempt to protect themselves and their valuable resources. But as organizations rely more and more on linked technologies, the old ways of thinking about security are not enough. In particular, new and emerging risks combined with the disclosed growth rates of sophisticated technologies make organizations rethink their security paradigms. It has now become the norm to develop protective systems that can act proactively, tolerate such threats, and be able to restore such systems quickly.

10.10.1 Emerging Cybersecurity Threats

New generation threats such as complex cyber threats, ransomware, and APTs attack the ill prepared and old and new systems alike. It was established that these attacks can bring financial, operational, and reputational losses to organizations. Advanced and frequent cyberattacks have been witnessed, especially within healthcare, financial, and government organizations. Bots and their handlers are becoming more sophisticated daily, applying every trick they can use to avoid being caught and ensuring they deliver maximum havoc. The evolving threats are therefore pushing organizations more and more from conventional defensive mechanisms to more proactive and dynamic security models. With the creation of the IoT, AI, cloud computing, new breaches arose in businesses. For example, devices of IoT are considered to be less secure as such they leave openings for attackers. Just like that, modernizations such as AI and ML have augmented cybersecurity measures used by defenders as well as weaponized by cyberattackers. These technologies for defense and offense are blurring in the continuum of cyberspace threat.

10.10.2 Advancing Cyber Resilience

As a result of these threats, there has been the emergence of the concept of cyber resilience, whereby business aims at minimizing cyber threats not only for themselves but also for their clients, maintaining business processes, and recovering from any such attacks. According to Akinsanya et al. [1], frameworks need to be developed to combat the emerging entities of cyber threats in a connected world. Cybersecurity and BC frameworks are linked to support the identification and management of threats and their impact using flexible and contingent safeguards that help organizations minimize disruptions and conquer the attack surface. Some research stress that only an integrated approach should be used toward the problem of cyber resilience. For example, AL-Hawamleh et al. [21] noted that adequate designing a sound cyber resilience plan is a crucial approach toward increasing the cyber defenses and organizational continuity amid increasing cyber threats. Cyber defense should be aligned with the concept of resilience because it enables organization's systems to continue functioning even after a breach; while minimizing the time an organization and its systems are unavailable because of a cyberattack [7]. Enduring protective strategies have become imperative at the organizational level owing to dynamic threat environment. This encompasses the process of using multiple layers of security as well as constant surveillance and its solution-finding processes. Cyber resilience, based on explanations of Conklin and Shoemaker [3], is almost as much about recovery since the potential attack's prevention.

10.10.3 Leveraging Emerging Technologies for Cyber Resilience

New technologies, therefore, have an important role to play in improving cyber resiliency. Examples of CT technologies include the use of AI and ML in proactive threat identification and incident management. These technologies help organizations process big data in real time and also facilitates identification of irregular patterns/behaviors and respond accordingly to threats. Since AI is applied for the purpose of automated response and decision-making, an organization can shorten the time required to identify the attacks and contain them.

However, those technologies also raise several problems. Despite the fact that with the help of AI, security can be improved, cybercriminals can also use this tool to increase the level of attacks. Thus, there is a necessity for the use of AI for defense and the regulation of possible risks related to its application in the course of the organization [12]. Further, there are efforts to incorporate blockchain technology as a way of strengthening security and data credibility in decentralized structures and supply chains [22]. However, the emissions generated by quantum computing are favorable in a way and also pose threats. While quantum computing could change professions like cryptography, it is unsafe for modern cryptography techniques that use algorithms which could be decrypted with the use of quantum computers. Scientists are further looking for quantum-shielded encryption in order to prepare the security processes for the arrival of that technology [25].

10.10.4 Adapting Cyber Defense Frameworks

The best practices have to be updated regularly because the threats are ever evolving. Despite that, Dickson and Goodwin [2] have noted that in order to achieve cyber resilience, organizations must create systems from scratch, reflecting cyber resilience principles, so the entire system is ready to counteract breaches. The DiD tactic is still integral, relying on several stages that make it barely possible for the attacker to penetrate the systems. In addition, frameworks should apply updates and evaluations frequently to address newly developed risks. Based on the same author, it is vital that the above proposal is an ongoing and dynamic process since the threats are continuously emerging, and there are continuous changes in technology.

10.10.5 The Role of Collaboration and Policy

It is also important to note that new threats need to be met and the resilience to be developed cannot be created in isolation, but needs coordination among various organizations, government, and industries. Computer security has become an important issue that requires international cooperation as well as investments by the government with the help of private enterprises to share threat intelligence and come up with collective strategies for addressing new threats in the field. Standardization of frameworks of cyber resilience such as that developed by Ross et al. [17] offers direction on how organizations can improve on the state of cyber resilience. It will be seen that governments have the immense responsibility of setting cyber resilience policies that require as well as direct the organizations of a country toward safeguarding networks as well as information. These policies should encourage best practices, enhance information exchange, and offer ways of rewarding resilience structures [11]. In the same way, regular training and development must be provided for the employees in order to create the cybersecurity culture across the organization level and guarantee that each worker knows his/her contribution to the enhancement of organizational security.

10.10.6 Summary

By the time new media technologies introduce new trends in the online platform, the threat increases in equal measure. Cyber resilience models that rely on an organization's defense ability and BC plan are critical in the modern world for any organization to bounce back and grow after a cyberattack. Using new technologies and flexibly applying methods used in defending against cyber threats, organizations can prepare to counteract unexpected threats in the future without halting their activity. Such works as Refs. [1, 21] promote the need for the development of dynamic frameworks that would address emergent technologically enabled issues as well as the more recurrent cyber threats. When approaching the question of cybersecurity, the goal should not be limited exclusively to shielding a system and its contents, but to maintaining functionality in spite of the attack.

10.11 Case Study: Resilient Frameworks in Action

The cyber resilience frameworks are finding high acceptance as organizations and governments look to enhance their protection against the constant threats posed in the cyber environment. These frameworks are designed to achieve holocaust as well as the post-holocaust restoration of systems and data with minimum business disruption. This chapter also discusses several real-life cases of the cyber resilience framework in practice with emphasis on lessons learnt across sectors.

10.11.1 Cyber Resilience in Business Continuity: The Case of AL-Hawamleh's Framework

While assessing the level of cyber resilience in organizations, AL-Hawamleh [4] underlined the significance of developing a strong framework for cyber resilience to ensure organizational sustainability and operational continuity in terms of increasing cyber threats. In this context, the author presented a broad approach which included risk management, threat countermeasures, and recovery procedures. It also emphasizes the issue of identifying organization's key assets and the potential of cyber threats to disrupt business processes. This approach can guide organizations on the right strategies to ensure they strengthen their protection from potential assailants while allowing the recovery of business processes. All the details disclosed above show that the framework was successfully implemented in several medium-sized enterprises, where it allowed to quickly restore the operations after the targeted cyberattack. Thus, the framework incorporated both reactive and proactive models to guarantee that businesses could implement continuity management even in the aftermath of highly sophisticated threats. This case illustrates the ability to incorporate elements of resilience into the strategic planning for cybersecurity at an early stage.

10.11.2 Cyber Resilience for Government Systems: The Role of Kanaan et al.

The article by Kanaan et al. [5] extended a study a cyber resilience framework to the government organization and the need for better cybersecurity in the light of increasing cyber warfare. What other two authors have noted in their work is the requirement to have a layered security approach where one uses the technology to supplement other organizational structures at the national level to protect critical data in structures such as the power grid. As they have suggested integrating resilience planning into the very heart of the government's cyber defense strategy, they have offered a model which does not only respond to the current cyber threat but also protects from potential breaches. The described framework was taken into practice in a national cybersecurity center; it has shown remarkable results and reduced response time during large-scale attacks. Interestingly, the use of intelligent systems such as AI and ML enabled the system to only forecast possible exposures to exploits and avert attacks before they turned into something worse. The case described by Kanaan et al. shows that the phenomenon of cybersecurity can be associated with the issue of timely prevention of threats to governmental and infrastructural facilities.

10.11.3 Building Cyber Resilience from Day One: A Corporate Perspective

In the corporate context, Bolish et al. [18] did the proactive work of initiating construction of cyber resilience from scratch. They insisted that resilience measures should be integrated during the early design of each system such that the security aspects of an organization's IT assets form the backbone of the infrastructure. This kind of approach has been incorporated into an operational model known as "Cyber-Resilience-by-Design" by the leading corporations in the fields of finances and care, where the data is especially vulnerable. The successful use of this framework was as shown by a financial institution that received frequent cyberattacks, but the organization barely felt a disruption in services as most of them continued to function online. Organizational resilience was identified to have been driven by poor implementation of resilient systems like incident detection automation, back up, and BC frameworks. This example goes a long way toward illustrating the usefulness of considering resilience as an integrated starting point rather than an add-on process.

10.11.4 A Holistic Approach to Cyber Resilience in Critical Infrastructure: Li et al.

Li et al. [22] examined the use of a cyber resilience framework in protecting grid-interactive efficient buildings (GEBs) to support today's grid-interactive efficient buildings. The CYDRES framework was developed to respond to the challenges of cyber threats on these smart buildings and keep their performance efficient. Combining cybersecurity and system design gave the framework a real-time approach that enabled the shielding against evolving threats. In the case of a simulated cyberattack on a GEB, the proposed framework did detect potential risks and quarantine infected devices while minimizing interruptions to building functions. This chapter details an example of how frameworks for cyber resilience can be applied to highly interconnected systems, such as smart grids, and the potential of utilizing similar approaches within other sectors of CI.

10.11.5 Cyber Resilience in Military Systems: Efthymiopoulos' NATO Approach

In his article, Efthymiopoulos [20] explored the use of a cyber resilience framework in the context of NATO defense and security agenda, with more emphasis to the resilience or lack of it of NATO to cyber threats capable of disrupting military operations. The NATO cyber resilience solution provides a layered defense of its systems where it uses preventive measures and real-time threat identification and then has a quick fix principle. This approach is thought to be multifaceted and work to ensure that even if a cyberattack gets past the outer layers of security, NATO forces are still able to carry out their roles effectively and quickly bounce back. This model has been applied and proven during different warfare activities, let alone the fact that it has shown operational continuity during very critical situations. This chapter has highlighted the key lessons that have emerged from NATO's approach and how they have shaped resilience concepts across the military and defense domains globally but with a rising focus on resilience in both the operational and strategic levels.

10.11.6 Frameworks for Cyber Resilience in the Internet of Things

These problems are added by the development of IoT technology in the modern world of interconnected devices. In this regard, Aksinsanya et al. [1] analyzed how the resilience of structural frameworks can mitigate various risks in IoT networks. Their research also put forth an analytical framework of IoT security that incorporates generic security best practices with specific IoT security resilience techniques. It assists in the achievement of the safety of IoT environments and in making a solution to guarantee the services offered by IoT gadgets to proceed even if some parts of the network are attacked. Of all the cases that Orme [9] have discussed in their work, one of them is the utilization of this framework in a smart city framework where the IoT items ruled all the menu progressing from the red lights to the transports. Thanks to the resilience framework, the city was able to continue working, even though hackers tried to attack the IoT system several times. The effectiveness of the framework in this sense also shows that it is indeed appropriate in today's complex interconnected world.

10.11.7 Summary

Thus, a variety of the cases described in this paper demonstrates the increasing role of cyber resilience frameworks in businesses. Both private enterprises and governmental organizations, as well as CI providers and militaries worldwide, are turning to such frameworks to mitigate cyber risks and maintain operations during inevitable cyber threats. Since threats are constantly developing and tend to become increasingly complex, the role of cybersecurity systems that can be easily adapted to them will remain highly important. These real-life accounts can help other organizations learn from what has gone before and how cyber resilience can be built into each organization's strategic plan for the next generation of cybersecurity threats.

10.12 Key Takeaways and Best Practices for a Resilient Cyber Defense Framework

Thence, a strategic and multidimensional model for cyber defense has been created by entailing robust cyber defense strategies with effective operational continuity. It is recommended to make objectives relevant to adaptations, risks, and constant enhancements of defenses as this approach would cover all aspects of managing new threats in a timely manner. Here, some brief overviews and recommendations for strategies of developing and applying cyber resilience are introduced.

10.12.1 Understanding Cyber Resilience: Bridging the Gap Between Security and Continuity

Cyber readiness is thus greater than merely a continuation of cybersecurity; it embraces the practice of security processes and procedures within the processes of continuity management of businesses from the time of attack and through the recovery period. In line with Ahmed et al. [7], it is imperative for cybersecurity and cyber defense to come closer, adopt common understanding, and initiate resilience. Cyber resilience frameworks should focus on incident prevention, as well as the reduction of the aftermath and time to remediation. This means making sure that the organizations lay down defense mechanisms that are aimed at caution, as well as the recovery process after an attack has occurred.

10.12.2 Adopting a Holistic and Layered Defense Approach

A layered defense strategy amalgamates several layers to guard against various types of threats in cyberspace. In accordance with Bolish et al. [18], the building process of the strong defense strategy should start with the assessment of threats and then proceed with the establishment of strong security systems that include network, application, and data levels of defense. This should integrate physical controls along the perimeter with IDS, and security information and event management (SIEM), behavior analytics, and continuous monitoring for foreseen threats. Following that, Akinsanya et al. [1] also emphasize the need to conduct a conceptual analysis of emergent resilience frameworks. They come up with the argument that research often reveals the need to establish dynamic systems to adapt to new threats and technologies in order to maintain the security of any organizational network.

10.12.3 Prioritizing Continuous Monitoring and Incident Response

Monitoring and managing incidents are the two key aspects of cyber resilience. It has been stressed that timely detection of an attack coupled with fast reaction to it significantly reduces the loss. As suggested by Conklin and Shoemaker [3], organizations need to implement a changing strategy to address the incidents, given the diverse threats in the cyber world. Risk appraisal and drills serve as effective means of determining weaknesses in the defense strategy or acquiring suggestions for revamp of the response mechanism.

10.12.4 Integrating Business Continuity and Disaster Recovery Plans

Since an effective cyber defense structure is a continuous and not event-specific process, it should be very much tied to the BC and disaster recovery strategy of the organization. According to [21], these plans should be practiced and synchronized with cybersecurity measures in order to have efficient disruption recovery in the event of a cyberattack. Both cybersecurity and business processes should be covered by resilience frameworks so that customers, data, etc., must be recoverable as soon as possible with less impact on business operations and consequent costs.

10.12.5 Training and Capacity Building for Staff

People are often cited to be the weakest line of defense in organizations' cybersecurity posture. One of the best practices when it comes to enhancing a facility and organization's cybersecurity is conducting regular cybersecurity training for everyone. [19] affirm that one key strategy in establishing a cyber-resilient force is through building capacity through education. They should regularly organize training and awareness in electronic security threats among members of staff and how to guard against them, for example, the mechanisms used in the execution of phishing scams.

10.12.6 Leveraging Advanced Technologies for Proactive Defense

AI, ML, and automation when incorporated into strategies drives improvement to the Cyber Defense framework. Another technology that can be expected to assist in threat detection and incidents response include artificial intelligent technology that can help minimize time taken to respond to threats and increase on accuracy of threats detection. In the article by [24], the authors describe how AI and ML contribute to improving the efficiency of cybersecurity systems, as the algorithms analyze the patterns emerging and improve the strategy for countering cyber threats. In the same line, [6] discusses on future possibility for AI and ML to identify intricate pattern of attack, helping with timely prevention.

10.12.7 Establishing Strong Governance and Compliance Structures

To ensure a sustainable cyber resilience strategy, two critical components must be established. First, Cyber Governance Management is essential. It provides direction and ensures that every part of the organization understands its individual and collective responsibilities regarding cybersecurity.

Second, Cyber Resilience Leadership is crucial. This component fosters effective leadership in resilience efforts across the organization. Together, these elements form the foundation needed to maintain and enhance cyber resilience over time.

It is critical to mature cyber governance to ensure that different organizations have a clear line of sight on their individual and combined responsibilities when it comes to cybersecurity resilience cyber governance. This is in formation of interdepartmental groups whose role is conducting risk analysis, sharing intelligence data, and the formulating continuity plans. [4] points out that there is a need for good governance and compliance to guarantee that different cybersecurity initiatives form part of the organization's agenda and are consistent with the law.

10.12.8 Emphasizing a Risk-Driven Security Strategy

A permissive approach to security is oriented on determining what risks can be tolerated and providing protection for the assets most at risk. Risk assessment and management perspective are employed in the conceptual development of a cyber-resilient architecture as espoused by [15]. The security risk should therefore be assessed over time and modified depending on the type of risk that an organization faces. There should be swift, tough choices on the best use of available resources, and this planning should factor in quantitative and qualitative risk analyses.

10.12.9 Creating a Cyber Resilience Culture

Building a culture of resiliency is needed to guarantee almost everybody in the firm appreciates the need for cybersecurity and or has the ability to contribute toward the firm's cybersecurity program. According to [11], there is a need to foster organizational culture that empowers resilience at different tiers. It should consist of a set of norms as to openness, cooperation, and learning on parts of both security and serving of continuities.

10.12.10 Aligning Cyber Defense Strategies with Business Objectives

Last but not least, a good cyber resilience strategy has to be consistent with the business goals of the organization. [5] also believe that BC and security are not just two opposing entities but are, in fact, two very closely related business pillars that are further eligible for a perfect integration that will allow the achievement of both goals. This demonstrates that the cybersecurity framework should be devised in a way that always enables business growth, by guaranteeing that critical services must always be up and running even in the event of cyberattacks. It is therefore proposed that organizations should adopt the concept of resilience as a strategic plan which should form part of the strategic plan formulation process.

10.12.11 Summary

The existing threats and variants continue to demonstrate the need for a robust cyber defense framework where possible risks can be addressed and business disruptions minimized. Depending on enacted defense mechanisms, using modern technologies, and the culture of cybersecurity readiness, it is possible to improve the current state for defending an organization from cyber threats and for faster emergency response. Referring to the guidelines presented in this section, organizations can develop an effective concept of a defensive and a reactive approach that effectively addresses and mitigates cyber threats.

10.13 Conclusion: Future-Proofing Cyber Defense for Long-Term Resilience

Thanks to the digital transformation, the need for reliable, flexible, and sustainable cybersecurity measures has become more important than ever. Cyber threats are approaching faster and are not static, but dynamic and adaptive and take advantage of the cracks in both the hardware and the software. Hence, to secure the future of cyber defense for businesses and organizations, one must go beyond threatening and challenge the organizations to be ready to respond to the next form of risks that may come. Proactive sustainability and adaptability strategies are another essential aspect of developing sustainable cybersecurity imperatives for the future. Cyber resilience shifts the cybersecurity focus from protecting against breaches to learning how to continue business operations after attacks. The approach that focuses on ensuring the sustainable nature of the cyberspace protection strategy is always based on the key components of an organization's IT system's foundation, the integration of innovative technologies, and the constant process of improvement and awareness.

10.13.1 Evolving Cyber Resilience Frameworks

The concept of cyber resilience has evolved from simply encouraging defense against cyber threats to encouraging the promotion of security, recovery, and continuity [1]. Another key finding of the research is that a dynamic and scalable system, like a cyber resilience framework that [15] mentioned in their paper, is crucial when the threats worsen. These frameworks of risk management should then be adaptable on a case-by-case basis and updated now and then to capture the dynamic risks involved and should be ready in terms of automation, real-time monitoring skills, and predictive risk modeling analysis.

New and more sophisticated threats require intelligent, multifaceted security model that relies on DiD and threat intelligence Cougar and Defense, as well as the utilization of ML, AI, and blockchain to improve the ¬flexibility of security mechanisms. The implication is that, similar to any other facet of life or business, future-proofing cyber defense must incorporate frameworks that provide for the creation of defensive layers on the network as well as organizational defense depth at the cultural level. It has been noted that [18] identified the importance of creating cyber resilience from day one as a lasting defense strategy, wherein cybersecurity principles are integrated into the very fabric of the organization's systems.

10.13.2 Leveraging Advanced Technologies for Future Resilience

So it is crucial for organizations to deploy solutions which incorporate up-to-date techniques that may help combat changing threats. As [6] notes, cybersecurity AI and ML help in identifying and preventing threats before they can cause a lot of damage. Intelligence threat identification, protection solutions, and AI programs all can analyze greater quantities of data than previously possible and notify organizations of discrepancies and opportunities for invasion. Further, the use of blockchain will enhance integrity and transparency in data, whereby it will be difficult for data to be tampered with or be under attack. The fact that blockchain offers a means of tracking execution that is impervious to alteration puts it at the heart of protecting both business and major infrastructure, like those mentioned in the study by [22]. Integration with the decentralized system such as blockchain strengthened a barrier not only to conventional cyber threats, but also to the quantum-computing-based risks.

Besides these technologies, the continuous development of systems such as the CYDRES to protect the smart grid [23] shows that resilience in complex systems is a critical area of future study. With the advancement of IoT and connected devices across various industries, there is the corresponding increase in vulnerability that hackers take advantage of that requires DiD that is proactive and heavily dependent on automated response mechanisms.

10.13.3 Building a Culture of Cyber Resilience

As much as one would expect highly innovative tools and systems, human contribution is still a major investment toward adapting cybersecurity. The final recommendation for strengthening cybersecurity is to implement practices that become an institution's permanent feature. Consumer protection requires organizations to develop a cybersecurity-conscious employee group capable of addressing cybersecurity imprints that are both technical and social. According to [27], incorporating profound cyber resilience training, organized awareness, and leadership engagement would help create a security culture. It is also convenient to note that the power in any organizational setting possesses the need for constantly updating the workforce skills and knowledge about threats in modern society. This includes continuous development of budgets to continually fund cybersecurity education, certification, and knowledge retention techniques. Cybersecurity culture, therefore, means that any exposures, threats, and risks are promptly recognized by employees, and professionals; in turn, the organization can support the overall resilience of the ecosystem.

10.13.4 Collaborative Approach to Cyber Defense

Cyber defense's future also relies heavily on partnership. Cyber threats are global in nature and are most likely unmanageable when faced by a single organization. Analyzing the works of [20, 29], it is important for organizations and companies to start collaboration with one another and with the government and state institutions, as well as across borders, for collective perceptions of threats and respective solutions. Cyber defense has become the public–private partnership since threats can be reduced through joint efforts, awareness can be enhanced, and timely responses can be made.

Further, frameworks as described by [17] acknowledge the idea of providing an institutionalized framework of resilience subject to collaboration between IT, security, and operations teams. Many tactics, such as cooperative ventures' sharing of intelligence, help organizations to counter adversaries and contain attacks more effectively.

10.13.5 Strategic Planning for Long-Term Resilience

Last, the identification and planning give the critical input toward attaining the long-term cyber resilience. Despite this, organizations must create elaborate strategies that are meant to address risk management, disaster recovery, and BC. According to the theoretical framework developed by [5], strengthening organizational cyber defense entails understanding risks and opportunities of an organization, possible cyber threats, and prevention and mitigation measures. Such plans should have guidelines such as communication models and roles, depths and frequencies of exercises, etc. Furthermore, new types of resilience strategies should be designed taking into account new technological applications, business goals, and new types of threats. This includes being able to analyze systems that are prone to threats, challenges of vulnerabilities, and check the potency of developed stress checks that can tell of the ability of a system to resist superior attacks and the ability to recover in the case of break-ins.

10.13.6 Conclusion

Finally, it is for this reason that organizations must design a cyber defense framework for the future that entails the application of advanced technologies; the right organizational culture; and long-term planning. Cyber resilience is not just about being ready to repel attacks that come from experience, but ready to face the unexpected, ready to change in real time, and ready to keep on business as usual in the worst of times. Through robust solutions, proper implementation of such technologies as AI and blockchain as well as advancing the information security community globally, organizations will effectively defend themselves from existing risks as well as prepare for future threats in an uncertain future. The next great frontier in cybersecurity is emerging today: strengthening the ability of these systems to inevitably fail and yet remain functional and deliver critical services.

References

1 Akinsanya, M.O., Ekechi, C.C., and Okeke, C.D. (2024). The evolution of cyber resilience frameworks in network security: a conceptual analysis. *Computer Science & IT Research Journal* 5 (4): 926–949.

2 Dickson, F. and Goodwin, P. (2019). Five key technologies for enabling a cyber-resilience framework. US45455119, IBM.

3 Conklin, W.A. and Shoemaker, D. (2017). Cyber-resilience: seven steps for institutional survival. *EDPACS* 55 (2): 14–22.

4 AL-Hawamleh, A. (2024). Cyber resilience framework: strengthening defenses and enhancing continuity in business security. *International Journal of Computing and Digital Systems* 15 (1): 1315–1331.

5 Kanaan, A., AL-Hawamleh, A., Aloun, M. et al. (2024). Fortifying organizational cyber resilience: an integrated framework for business continuity and growth amidst escalating threat landscapes. *International Journal of Computing and Digital Systems* 16 (1): 1–13.

6 Usman Haider, A.Z. (2024). Building resilient cyber defense architectures: AI and machine learning in cloud and network security.

7 Ahmed, M.F., Molla, A.H., Uddin, M.R., and Chowdhury, T.R. (2023). Advancing cyber resilience: bridging the divide between cyber security and cyber defense. *International Journal for Multidisciplinary Research (IJFMR)* 5 (6): https://doi.org/10.36948/ijfmr.2023.v05i06.10726.

8 Efthymiopoulos, M.P. (2016). NATO smart defense and cyber resilience. Tufts University May.

9 Orme S. (2019). Addressing issues with defense-in-depth, APTs, and IoT with active cyber defense cycle and cyber resilience. Utica College.

10 Hubbard, G.A. (2023). State-level cyber resilience: a conceptual framework. *Applied Cybersecurity & Internet Governance* 2 (1): 1–14.

11 Galinec, D. (2023). Cyber security and cyber defense: challenges and building of cyber resilience conceptual model. *International Journal of Applied Science and Development* 1: 83–88.

12 Sharma, N.A., Kumar, K., Khorshed, T. et al. (2024). Evading cyber-attacks on Hadoop ecosystem: a novel machine learning-based security-centric approach towards big data cloud. *Information* 15 (9): 558.

13 Siegel, C.A. and Sweeney, M. (2020). *Cyber Strategy: Risk-driven Security and Resiliency.* Auerbach Publications.

14 Pureti, N. (2022). Building a robust cyber defense strategy for your business. *Revista de Inteligencia Artificial en Medicina* 13 (1): 35–51.

15 Conklin, W.A., Shoemaker, D., and Kohnke, A. (2017). Cyber resilience: Rethinking cybersecurity strategy to build a cyber resilient architecture. *ICMLG2017 5th International Conference on Management Leadership and Governance.* 105.

16 DAS, E., Sahay, R., Barfod, M.B., and Jensen, C.D. (2020). A systematic review of cyber-resilience assessment frameworks. *Computers & Security* 97: 101996.

17 Ross, R., Pillitteri, V., Graubart, R. et al. (2019). *Developing Cyber Resilient Systems: A Systems Security Engineering Approach.* National Institute of Standards and Technology.

18 Bolish, S., Dodge, M., Mitalo, E., and Westing, R. (2024). Building Cyber Resilient Systems from Day 1. *2024 IEEE Aerospace Conference.* IEEE. 1–8.

19 Moore E. (2020). Building cyber defense training capacity.

20 Efthymiopoulos, M.P. (2019). A cyber-security framework for development, defense and innovation at NATO. *Journal of Innovation and Entrepreneurship* 8 (1): 12.

21 AL-Hawamleh, A.M. (2024). Securing the future: framework fundamentals for cyber resilience in advancing organizations. *Journal of System and Management Sciences* 14 (10): 130–150.

22 Li, G., O'Neill, Z., Wen, J. et al. (2023). CYDRES: CYber Defense and REsilient System for securing grid-interactive efficient buildings. *Proceedings of the 10th ACM International Conference on Systems for Energy-Efficient Buildings, Cities, and Transportation*. 307–309.

23 O'Neill, Z., Wen, J., Wu, T. et al. (2024). Securing grid-interactive efficient buildings (GEB) through cyber defense and resilient system (CYDRES). Texas A & M Univ., College Station, TX (United States). Texas A & M

24 Muhammad, T., Munir, M.T., Munir, M.Z., and Zafar, M.W. (2022). Integrative cybersecurity: merging zero trust, layered defense, and global standards for a resilient digital future. *International Journal of Computer Science and Technology* 6 (4): 99–135.

25 Ridout, T. (2016). Building a comprehensive strategy of cyber defense, deterrence, and resilience. *The Fletcher Forum of World Affairs. JSTOR* 63–83.

26 Meng, B., Larraz, D., Siu, K. et al. (2021). Verdict: a language and framework for engineering cyber resilient and safe system. *Systems* 9 (1): 18.

27 Annarelli, A., Nonino, F., and Palombi, G. (2020). Understanding the management of cyber resilient systems. *Computers & Industrial Engineering* 149: 106829.

28 Li, I. (2024). Cyber resilience frameworks: exploring cyber resilience frameworks and strategies for organizations to recover from cyber attacks and maintain operational continuity. *Cybersecurity and Network Defense Research* 4 (1): 1–15.

29 Safitra, M.F., Lubis, M., and Fakhrurroja, H. (2023). Counterattacking cyber threats: a framework for the future of cybersecurity. *Sustainability* 15 (18): 13369.

30 Savold, R., Dagher, N., Frazier, P., and McCallam, D. (2017). Architecting cyber defense: a survey of the leading cyber reference architectures and frameworks. *2017 IEEE 4th International Conference on Cyber Security and Cloud Computing (CSCloud)*. IEEE. 127–138.

Index